CONSTRUCT.
IN THE LATE ROMAN COUNTRYSIDE

This book is the first comprehensive treatment of the "small politics" of rural communities in the Late Roman world. It places the diverse fates of those communities within a generalized model for exploring rural social systems. Fundamentally, social interactions in rural contexts in the period revolved around the desire of individual households to insure themselves against catastrophic subsistence failure, and the need of the communities in which they lived to manage the attendant social tensions, inequalities, and conflicts. A focus upon the politics of reputation in those communities provides a striking contrast to the picture painted by the legislation and the writings of Rome's literate elite: when viewed from the point of view of the peasantry, issues such as the Christianization of the countryside, the emergence of new types of patronage relations, and the effects of the new system of taxation upon rural social structures take on a different aspect.

CAM GREY is Assistant Professor in the Department of Classical Studies at the University of Pennsylvania, where his research covers the social and economic history of the later Roman Empire. He is also a co-director of the Roman Peasant Project, an archaeological project located in southern Tuscany that amounts to the first systematic, interdisciplinary attempt to analyze the houses, farms, and lived experiences of the Roman peasantry.

CONSTRUCTING COMMUNITIES IN THE LATE ROMAN COUNTRYSIDE

CAM GREY

CAMBRIDGE
UNIVERSITY PRESS

CAMBRIDGE
UNIVERSITY PRESS

University Printing House, Cambridge CB2 8BS, United Kingdom

Cambridge University Press is part of the University of Cambridge.

It furthers the University's mission by disseminating knowledge in the pursuit of education, learning and research at the highest international levels of excellence.

www.cambridge.org
Information on this title: www.cambridge.org/9781107500013

First published 2011
First paperback edition 2015

A catalogue record for this publication is available from the British Library

Library of Congress Cataloguing in Publication data
Grey, Cam, 1972–
Constructing communities in the late Roman countryside / Cam Grey.
p.   cm.
ISBN 978-1-107-01162-5
1. Rome – Rural conditions.   2. Country life – Rome – History.   I. Title.
HN9.G74   2011
307.720937–dc22
2011010569

ISBN 978-1-107-01162-5 Hardback
ISBN 978-1-107-50001-3 Paperback

Contents

Preface

Intuitively, we feel we know what a community is, even if we often find it hard to identify the precise characteristics that define it. The term evokes notions of common interest and regular interaction, shared identity and interdependence. Romantically, we might conjure up visions of picket fences and carefully swept streets, block parties and cookouts. More prosaically, we may think of neighborhoods and church committees, university campuses and online gaming forums. In each case, the fundamental ideas are the same: A community is simultaneously a sustaining social milieu for the individuals who belong to it, and a complex collection of obligations and expectations that those individuals must continue to meet in order to remain members. Membership confers the privilege of scrutinizing the claims of others to belong, but also opens one up to the same process of scrutiny. These complementary, potentially contradictory considerations underpin our experience of community on an everyday basis today, and we should expect them to have underpinned the everyday lives of the inhabitants of the ancient world as well.

Communities in the late Roman world are not hard to find. We observe (to take merely a few examples) communities of aristocrats, sometimes spread over considerable distances, sustained by the exchange of letters, literary trifles, and the produce of their estates; communities of barbarian *foederati*, settled in a variety of ways and on a multiplicity of terms within the boundaries of the empire; civic communities, experiencing transformations in their physical and ideological composition as they come to reflect Christian, rather than pagan, values and sensibilities; religious communities, which might come to blows with one another over matters of doctrine or interpretation of Scripture; and monastic communities from the deserts of Egypt to the mountains of eastern Gaul. It does not seem a stretch to assume that there were communities of agriculturalists in the countrysides of the Mediterranean world in the period as well, but the quotidian rhythms of those communities, the principles, expectations, and practices that sustained them across the breadth of that world, have not to date been the subject of a stand-alone study.

This book is aimed at filling that gap. In the process, it seeks to reconnect the agrarian history of the ancient Mediterranean world with agrarian histories of other periods and other regions. I do this on the assumption that all parties might have useful insights to offer each other on questions of common interest, and with the intention of exploring certain problems that have become politically or philosophically fraught in contemporary contexts. Many of these problems congregate around the emergence of a globalized economy, resting principally upon the economic principles of capitalism, and largely dominated by the most politically and economically powerful nations. But, at base, they rest upon realities that are little different from phenomena that we can observe in the late Roman world.

The late Roman empire was, fundamentally, a diverse collection of culturally, politically, and socio-economically unique communities linked together by bonds of interdependence that were sustained in large part by a collective fiction of unity and common purpose. That collective fiction was subjected to a congeries of pressures over the course of the fourth and fifth centuries: military reversals and political turmoil, religious and philosophical transformations, economic downturns and fiscal crises. The world that emerged from those pressures was both unmistakably different from what had gone before, and characterized by deep and enduring continuities with the past. This coincidence of fundamental changes and equally fundamental continuities has been the subject of much scholarly debate in recent years, and those debates do not need to be rehearsed here. But it is worth making explicit the coincidences between the concerns of contemporary scholarship on the transformation of the ancient Mediterranean world, and contemporary concerns with the transformation of our own world. I do so not in order to trumpet the relevance or timeliness of the present work, but merely to acknowledge the extent to which it reflects its social, cultural, and intellectual context.

The "small worlds" of the agriculturalists who are the focus of this book encompassed complex, complementary collections of communities, which orbited around satisfying the subsistence and social needs of their households and families. In the writing of this book, I have found myself in a similar situation, and I wish to acknowledge each of my communities in turn. The University of Pennsylvania has provided financial and institutional support over the course of this project, and in addition I have been fortunate to receive grants and fellowships from the Loeb Classical Library Foundation; the Herbert D. Katz Center for Advanced Judaic Studies; and the Penn Humanities Forum. The students in my undergraduate course on marginal populations in the Roman world provided a particularly fertile forum for exploring ideas at a crucial time in the creation of the manuscript. I am grateful also to the participants in a seminar on the management of risk at the American Philological Association's Annual Meeting in Philadelphia in 2009.

These communities of scholars have collectively commented upon, criticized, and helped refine the arguments and propositions presented here, although they should not be held responsible for any inconsistencies or infelicities that remain. Chris Wickham and the late Dick Whittaker submitted the doctoral dissertation that bears only passing resemblance to the present document to a searching examination, and I am grateful to them for their generosity in doing so. In addition, I thank the anonymous readers for Cambridge University Press, whose comments and responses have led to revisions that, I hope, have improved the manuscript in fundamental ways. Michael Sharp, my editor at the Press, has displayed patience and friendship over the long period of time that has elapsed between the promise and the completion of this project.

The members of the academic community of the University of Pennsylvania have served as a constant reminder of the ways that different communities can intermingle: my colleagues in the Department of Classical Studies and elsewhere at Penn are not only a challenging and stimulating community of scholars, but also a collection of friends and quasi-kin. The "village" that they represent has enriched me in countless ways, both intellectually and personally. I thank also the friends who have given of their time, expertise, and knowledge to read and discuss the manuscript in its various forms: Kim Bowes, Ari Bryen, Nate Roberts, and Steve Rowe. They know that, by acknowledging my debt to them here I anticipate future opportunities to repay that debt, although I know that the balance will always remain unequal.

Peter Garnsey, who supervised the doctoral dissertation at the University of Cambridge out of which this book has grown, has been a source of wit and affection, wisdom and intellectual rigor in equal measure over more than a decade. I acknowledge with pleasure and gratitude his friendship and guidance. I also remember with the most profound respect and fondness John Crook, who guided me through both the intricacies of Roman law and Cambridge's better eateries. I am grateful for the home-away-from-home that I have in Fort Smith, Arkansas, together with all the members of that household. While my own parents and brothers have long been geograph-ically far removed, they have remained a constant, constantly supportive presence throughout the completion of this project. Finally, and most importantly, it is my family that sits at the center of my social network, just as it did for the peasants and *rustici* of the late Roman world. And so, I offer this book to Ann, and to Isabel. They are not merely my small world. They are my whole world.

List of abbreviations

Papyrological sources are abbreviated in accordance with:

Oates, J. F., Bagnall, R. S., Willis, W. H. and Worp, K. A. (1992), *Checklist of Editions of Greek and Latin Papyri, Ostraca and Tablets*, 4th edn., Bulletin of the American Society of Papyrologists, Supplement 7.

Epigraphical sources are abbreviated in accordance with:

Bérard, F., Feissel, D., Petitmengin, P. and Sère, M. (2000), *Guide de l'épigraphiste: bibliographie choisie des épigraphies antiques et médiévales*, 3rd edn., Paris.

Full references to *corpora* of papyri and inscriptions may be found in these editions.

Journal titles are abbreviated following *L'Année philologique*.

Rabbinic sources have been abbreviated in accordance with:

Strack, H. L. and Stemberger, G. (1996), *Introduction to the Talmud and Midrash*, 2nd edn., ed. and trans. M. Bockmuehl, Minneapolis, 374–5.

Citation of other collections and texts follows or is modeled upon:

Jones, A. H. M. (1964), *The Later Roman Empire*, Oxford vol. II, 1464–76.

Where other citations are abbreviated, currently accepted standard practices have been observed. Where no standard practice exists, abbreviations and citation practices are signaled in the citation of the text in the Bibliography. Where multiple editions exist, the text used here is specified.

In addition, the following abbreviations have been adopted:

CoptEncyc = Atiya, A. S., ed. (1991), *The Coptic Encyclopedia*, 8 vols., New York.

PLRE I = Jones, A. H. M., Martindale, J. R. and Morris, J. (1971), *The Prosopography of the Later Roman Empire, Volume I AD 260–395*, Cambridge.

PLRE II = Martindale, J. R. (1980), *The Prosopography of the Later Roman Empire, Volume II AD 395–527*, Cambridge.

PO = *Patrologia Orientalis*, Paris. References to works in this series will be by author, text, then page number of the relevant volume.

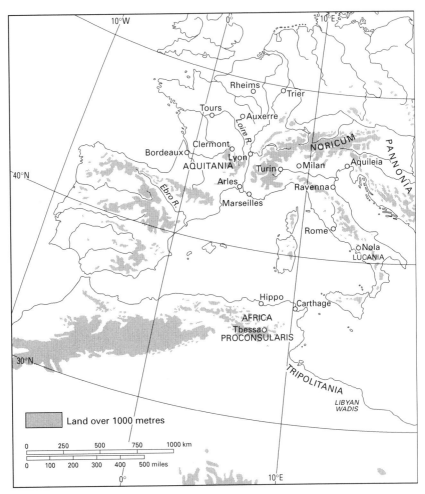

Map: The late Roman world (sites and regions discussed in the text).

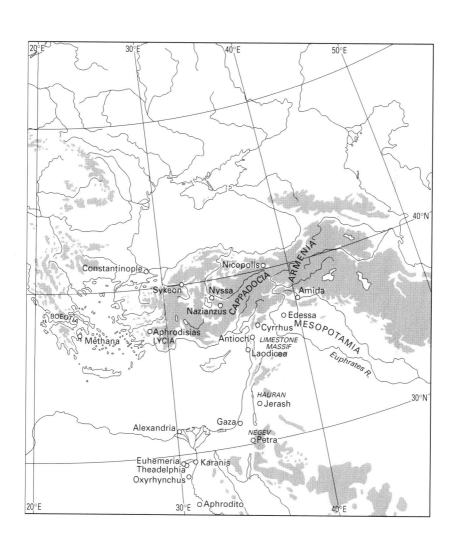

Introduction: Studying rural communities in the late Roman world

What did rural communities look like in the late Roman world? How did they work? What socio-economic mechanisms were available to peasants of the period for managing subsistence and social risk? The questions are disarmingly simple. But the project of answering them is dogged by the same evidentiary and methodological problems that have long trammeled attempts to answer similar questions for earlier periods. The late Roman world boasts a greater body of written sources relevant to the subject than in earlier centuries, but detailed accounts of the day-to-day workings of rural communities – such as have underpinned comparable studies in medieval, early modern and contemporary contexts – are still almost entirely absent. In the main, the sources that we do possess reflect aristocratic concerns and perspectives more than those of peasants. That is, they focus principally upon problems of organization and control of labor, transmission of rents and taxes, and the nature and form of power and dependence, rather than upon the maintenance of a subsistence livelihood or the negotiation of the "small politics" of rural communities. When the inhabitants of rural communities do appear in these writings, they are characteristically treated as an undifferentiated mass, their social, economic, and political motivations misunderstood, their networks of mutual support and reciprocity beyond occasional mentions of interactions with our aristocratic authors largely opaque.

In this book, I seek to recapture these networks of mutual support and reciprocity, using the written sources in conjunction with archaeological material and theoretical models drawn from comparative contexts and disciplines. I engage in particular with debates in those disciplines concerning the internal workings of rural communities, the nature of relations between the members of those communities and outsiders, and the impact of externally generated changes upon those structures of interaction. I suggest that, in spite of the limitations of our evidence, the countrysides of late antiquity provide an ideal context for contributing to these debates.

In championing the late Roman world as a particularly fruitful field for exploring questions current in agrarian studies more broadly, I emphasize the opportunities provided by two factors. On the one hand, the rural landscapes of the late Roman world were almost infinitely diverse in terms of physical topography, economic structures, and social systems. On the other hand, peasant communities exhibit certain behaviors that are broadly congruent and comparable across time and space. Consequently, we must construct a schema for studying the interplay of the generalized and the unique within and between those communities.

In the following chapters, this tension between the general and the specific is never very far from the surface. Such an approach amounts to an attempt to carve out an analytical middle ground between the grand survey, where the pattern is privileged over the particular; and the micro-study, where the presentation of the particular is an end in itself. I deliberately overstate this distinction in the interests of making explicit an analytical problem that tends to be recognized only implicitly. I argue here that it is crucial that we entertain both of these positions simultaneously and seek to mediate between them, in order to avoid a string of over-schematic, broad-brush generalizations about rural life in late antiquity, on the one hand; and a collection of discrete, balkanized micro-regional studies of individual communities that eschews larger analytical categories and questions, on the other. In what follows, therefore, I seek to accommodate complexity, diversity, and uniqueness within a structured schema.

The second factor marking the late Roman world as an ideal context for this study is the presence of an identifiable and identifiably different system of tax assessment and, to a lesser degree, collection. To a certain extent, this new tax system dictates the chronological boundaries of this study, for I take it to represent a recognizable, comparatively unified set of pressures which may be observed interacting with existing socio-economic structures in different physical contexts in a variety of ways.[1] Therefore, I limit this study to the period between the introduction of this new system of taxation in the late third century and the dissolution of effective centralized control over it, at least in the western provinces of the empire, in the late fifth century.[2] Equally importantly, this tax system provides a relatively detailed and coherent body of documentation upon which we can draw.

---

[1] Fuller discussion in Grey (2007b), 368–70. Cf. Ando's cautions about the extent to which the system can be attributed solely to Diocletian and his colleagues in the Tetrarchy: Ando (2008), 45.
[2] Note Ando's critique of the fetishization of dates and periodization in late antique studies more generally: Ando (2008), 32.

Consequently, we are able to evaluate the evidence that survives for the responses of the inhabitants of rural communities to the tax system of the late Roman world in the light of strategies that we can observe or imagine them employing in other contexts, and in response to other pressures.

The coincidence of heterogeneity and similarity in the rural communities of the period, coupled with the existence of an identifiable, relatively widespread motor of change, allow us to escape from the tyranny of the particular that has assailed many micro-studies of peasant communities in other fields.[3] Throughout this book, I emphasize the immense diversity in the evidence for peasant communities in the late Roman world. I propose that this diversity takes as its context a set of generalized, generalizable constraints, which, in broadly comparable ways, shaped and impacted upon the strategies employed by rural communities in managing subsistence and social risk. I argue throughout this book that it was the impulse to manage these two kinds of risk, and not the desire to evade or resist the fiscal demands of the state, which lay at the heart of decision-making in the rural communities of the late Roman world.[4] Further, by focusing attention upon these imperatives we are able to create an account of socio-economic relations in the countrysides of late antiquity which acknowledges the perspective of the peasants and other rural denizens who constituted the bulk of the population. Such a project produces a picture that usefully complements and partially corrects existing accounts, which have tended to embrace the perspective of the aristocratic authors of our surviving sources, and as a consequence have privileged the needs and objectives of the late Roman state and its agents.

To this end, I begin with an exploration of the peasantry, the nature and composition of their families, households, and communities. Next, I outline strategies for managing and negotiating the fundamental tension between cooperation and conflict within rural communities, before placing alongside those strategies an account of the various ways in which the members of those communities interacted with powerful outsiders in the period. I then use these networks of interaction as a framework for examining the changes wrought by the new tax system introduced by Diocletian and his colleagues in the Tetrarchy. I place particular emphasis upon the ways in which *rustici* were able to exploit the vocabulary and personnel of

---

[3] Cf. the brief comments of Anderson (1997), 504; Hahamovitch and Halpern (2004), 4–5. For a comparable account of rural change, exploiting a similar dynamic of similarity and difference, cf. Cronin (2005).

[4] Below, 169–72, for a succinct statement.

that tax system to achieve their own, locally focused objectives. In the remainder of this chapter, I situate this project within two complementary scholarly contexts. First, I survey the current state of scholarship on rural communities in the late Roman world, outlining briefly the debates that inform those studies. I then place alongside those debates a complementary set of problems, which are informed by current studies of rural communities in other historical and anthropological literature. I begin, however, with a brief account of the types of evidence that we possess for our study.

SOURCES FOR THE STUDY OF RURAL COMMUNITIES IN LATE ANTIQUITY

Peasants constituted the bulk of the population of the Mediterranean world and Europe throughout antiquity. MacMullen, rhetorically perhaps, suggests that the deprived masses constituted 99 percent of the population, but even a more cautious estimate would put the proportion of agriculturalists in the Roman world at something over 80 percent.[5] However, the inhabitants of the rural communities of the late Roman world have left few traces of themselves. Their dwellings and settlements are difficult to identify in the archaeological record, and have in any case received relatively little attention in contemporary scholarship. Moreover, the project of enlisting archaeological evidence to answer questions of demography and social structure is a difficult one at best.[6] When we turn to the written sources, first-hand accounts of the internal dynamics of rural communities in the period are perilously few. Some inscriptions have survived, for example, commemorating a community's collective action or acknowledging the noteworthy exploits of an individual, but it is difficult to determine the typicality or exceptionality of these incidents, and in any event the epigraphical evidence is relatively thinly spread.

Arguably our richest evidence for the views and perspectives of small agriculturalists may be found in the petitions and other legal documents that have survived in the papyrological sources from Egypt. However, significant doubts have been raised in recent scholarship over the validity of assuming that these documents represent anything more than the views and interests of the wealthiest inhabitants of the villages and towns of the

[5] MacMullen (1974) 122; Garnsey and Woolf (1989), 154; Scheidel (2007), 80–1.
[6] Cf. Zadora-Rio (1995), 148–9; van Ossel and Ouzoulias (2001), 154; Sodini (2003), 26–7; 46–7; Chavarría and Lewit (2004), 4–7.

Egyptian countryside.[7] These cautions about the representativeness of the papyrological evidence are valid, but they can in part be mitigated by two considerations. First, we should expect the fortunes of individual house-holds within rural communities to have fluctuated from year to year and generation to generation according to the composition of the household, its capacity to manage its economic resources and social networks, and the share of luck it has enjoyed in avoiding a significant subsistence crisis or other destabilizing factor.[8] Second, and as a consequence, we may imagine that even if the less well-off members of rural communities lacked the means of their wealthier neighbors, they shared much the same set of concerns, and would have been motivated to satisfy or meet those concerns in similar ways. It seems reasonable, then, to regard the papyrological sources as reflecting a set of common expectations and assumptions, even if the evidence they provide is skewed to the wealthier residents of the Egyptian countryside.

These eyewitness accounts of the internal functioning of rural commun-ities must be supplemented by sources which, at best, illuminate only indirectly the phenomena that are the principal focus of our inquiry. Broadly speaking, we may array those sources around three analytically distinct poles: imperial legislation, largely surviving in a somewhat trun-cated and disaggregated form in the two massive legal codifications under-taken under Theodosius II in the mid-fifth century and Justinian around a century later; rhetorical, historiographical, literary, and epistolary sources written by the aristocrats who dominated the municipalities of the Roman world and served also as members of the Imperial bureaucracy; and Christian literature, including moralizing and theological tracts, as well as heroic portraits of holy figures purportedly interacting directly with the members of rural communities in the period. In reality, of course, the analytical boundaries between these different types of texts were somewhat fluid, but we may for the sake of convenience discuss the sources for rural communities under these three broad headings.

We should expect both consonances and dissonances in the perspectives taken by authors writing within these three genera, and this can be illus-trated most clearly with reference to a series of texts that were long taken as evidence for the emergence of a new type of patronage, labeled Patrocinium, in the countrysides of the late Roman world. Those sources are, first, a collection of laws grouped under the rubric *De Patrociniis Vicorum* in the Theodosian Code, together with a later law on the same subject preserved in

---

[7] Bagnall (1993a), 5–6. Cf. Keenan (2007), 227.   [8] Cf. below, 34–5.

the Justinianic Code; an oration delivered by Libanius of Antioch to the emperor Theodosius I in around 390 detailing the abuses perpetrated by and under the auspices of military figures who offered protection from local tax collectors to villagers in the Antioch Valley; and an account of the desperate ends to which small landowners were driven in mid-fifth-century Gaul by Salvian, presbyter of the church of Marseilles.[9] It was long argued that these texts attested to the emergence of a single, new type of patronage relationship aimed simultaneously at defrauding the state of tax revenues and dispossessing the peasantry of their belongings and freedom until they occupied a position of dependence that was little short of slavery. In the most recent scholarship, this notion has been rejected in favor of a more nuanced and complex picture, and I return briefly to this debate below. Here, I use the texts most commonly employed in that debate as a convenient schema for exploring the ways in which the perspectives offered by these three types of evidence may be approached and employed in our account of social relations in the countrysides of the late Roman world.

Seven laws together constitute the legislation which was collectively taken in the earliest scholarship to illustrate the phenomenon of Patrocinium. These laws span just over 100 years, and are addressed to a range of imperial officials in the eastern provinces of the empire more generally, and Egypt in particular. The principal aim of this legislation appears to have been to ensure that revenues taken from small agriculturalists were transferred to the Imperial coffers.[10] The phenomenon identified as particularly detrimental to that process was protection offered to these individuals by a range of powerful figures. If the laws are to be taken completely at face value, those figures included local *curiales*, members of the court of the *Comes Aegypti*, and present and former imperial officials up to the rank of Augustal Prefect, *vicarius* and *magister militum*.[11] The laws envisage these individuals either explicitly offering protection to small agriculturalists from tax officials, or being approached by agriculturalists seeking that protection. They prescribe a range of punishments and penalties for those found to be transacting such arrangements, including fines of increasing severity and confiscation of the property in question.[12]

We should be wary of overestimating the pervasiveness of the phenomena identified in these laws, and cautious about the impression of coherence

---

[9] *CTh* XI.24 (360–415); *CJ* XI.54.1 (468); Libanius, *Or.* XLVII, with Norman in his introduction to the Loeb text of this oration for dating, 498–9; Salvian, *De Gubernatione Dei* V.8.38.
[10] De Zulueta (1909), 5; Krause (1987), 73–4; Jaillette (2005), 206.
[11] *CTh* XI.24.3 (395); 4 (399). Below, 207–8.   [12] *CTh* XI.24.2 (360); 4 (399).

that has been imposed by the process of codification. It seems unlikely that the fourth and fifth centuries witnessed the emergence for the first time of systematic, widespread evasion of taxes, effected by means of illegal protection.[13] We may imagine, rather, that protection from or mediation with tax officials was part of relationships contracted by some small agriculturalists, at least, with their wealthier, more powerful neighbors throughout the Roman world. Consequently, it is not the emergence of the phenomenon of patrons protecting their clients from the demands of tax officials that requires explanation so much as it is the importance attached to this phenomenon in legislation of the late Roman Empire. Such an approach focuses attention upon the role and aims of legislation in the period. In what follows, I argue that the perspective of the state was relatively limited and its objectives were somewhat circumscribed. I emphasize also the prescriptive and normative vision that the legislation offers of the ways in which socio-economic interactions should function in the countrysides of the late Roman world. I illustrate these propositions with reference to laws concerning the registration of *coloni* in the tax rolls of the period, a phenomenon which has likewise enjoyed a prominent place in accounts of the socio-economic trajectories of the period, and undergone a similar process of reevaluation in recent decades.[14]

The legislation of the late Roman world was largely reactive in character and relatively limited in its scope and application.[15] That is, laws tended to be issued in response to a petition, request, or inquiry, and were characteristically addressed to a particular official whose geographical and administrative area of competence was, to a greater or lesser extent, limited and defined. Laws concerning the registration of *coloni* on the tax rolls occasionally acknowledge these limitations explicitly, and the surviving evidence for the practice is geographically dispersed and heterogeneous in nature. Fundamentally, then, these laws were not motivated by the desire to bind *coloni* to the land upon which they were registered and place limitations upon their economic freedom, but, rather were a consequence of more general impulses in the fiscal policy of the period.[16] Here, as elsewhere in the legal *corpora*, the principal objective of the legislation was to ensure the smooth transition of tax revenues to the imperial coffers. That process was

---

[13] Contra, e.g., Giliberti (1992), 203–14. Cf. the measured comments of Wickham (2005b), 528–9.
[14] Carrié (1982); Carrié (1983); Giliberti (1999); Scheidel (2001); Rosafio (2002); Grey (2007a); Sirks (2008).
[15] Cf. Connolly (2010), 9–10; Grey (2007a), 160. Also Harries (1999).
[16] Limited scope: e.g. *CJ* xi.52.1 (393, Thrace); *CTh* xi.1.26 (399, Gaul). Broader fiscal concerns: cf. Grey (2007a), 171.

to be effected through the establishment of clear hierarchies of responsibility for the tax burden assessed on a particular area of land. In the case of registered *coloni*, those hierarchies could, ideally, be traced from the tenant through his or her landlord to the curial tax collector, his colleagues in the municipal tax machinery and the governor of the province, before those taxes were then transmitted via imperial officials to the state's treasuries.[17] It is here that we observe a fundamental contradiction in the legislation of the period, for in the eyes of the promulgators of that legislation, the interposition of a powerful figure from outside that chain of fiscal responsibility was likely to affect the flow of revenue. Equally, though, it was precisely those individuals who were granted or accorded responsibility for ensuring that flow, both through the establishment of complex, overlapping hierarchies of assessment, collection, and supervision, and through the attribution of responsibility for collection of taxes to landlords and patrons in the period.[18]

We should not imagine the legislation collected together in the two great codifications of the period to provide a unified, univocal picture of the socio-economic landscapes of the late Roman world, any more than we should expect the landscapes themselves to have been the same over time and space. Nevertheless, the laws do, to a certain extent, present a coherent account of the forms that those landscapes were expected or imagined to take and the manner in which they were expected or imagined to function.[19] These texts present an idealized, normative vision of socio-economic relationships and practices, one which privileges the need of the state for a steady flow of revenue by focusing upon the control of labor and the allocation of hierarchies of responsibility. Powerful rural landowners and patrons were expected to cooperate and collaborate with the state in the collection and transmission of revenues. Purchasers of land were expected to petition the municipal tax officials to ensure that their names were registered in the tax rolls as responsible for the fiscal obligations of the land, and small agriculturalists were expected to refrain from leaving the fields for which they had been assigned fiscal responsibility by the process of registration.[20] In reality, each of these expectations was out of step with established practices,

---

[17] Grey (2007a), 165–9. Below, 192–3.

[18] Cf. Grey and Parkin (2003), 295–6; Grey (2007a), 166. Fuller discussion below, 200–1.

[19] The issue of coherence in late antique legislation and governance is a thorny one. See the brief comments, with further references, of Ando (2008), 45 with note 62. Cf. Scott (1998), 22 for a comparative perspective on the problematic relationship between legislation and the realities it purports to describe or delimit.

[20] Cooperation of landowners: *CTh* XI.7.2 (319, Britain); *CTh* XI.1.14 = *CJ* XI.48.4 (371S, East). Registration of names: *FV* 35.3–4; 249.5–8; *CTh* XI.3.5 (391, East). Refrain from movement: *Brev.* V.11.1 = *CTh* V.19.1 (365, East); *CTh* IV.23.1 = *CJ* XI.48.14 (400, Gaul).

although those practices were not necessarily aimed explicitly at resisting or defying the state. Rather, they were motivated by more fundamental concerns: for aristocratic landowners, the effective exploitation of their land and labor resources; for small-scale agriculturalists, the effective management of subsistence risk.[21] Consequently, in pursuit of the realities of late Roman rural socio-economic landscapes, we must be wary both of uncritically adopting the rhetorical vocabulary employed by the state and of assuming that the portraits painted in the legislation were exact mirror images of those realities, for the precise relationship between the two is likely to have been considerably more complex in reality.

An equally complex relationship exists between the evidence of the legislation and the testimony of our other sources. Libanius' oration "On Protection Systems" (*Peri tôn Prostasiôn*) provides a case in point. Libanius' oration purports to be a detailed disquisition upon the difficulties faced by members of the curial class of Antioch when attempting to collect the taxes owed by the inhabitants of the villages in Antioch's hinterland. Libanius suggests that some, at least, of those villages have come under the protection of members of the military, and have thereby become emboldened not only to resist the demands of the tax collectors, but also to despoil and prey upon their neighbors. Recourse to the courts is to no avail, for the judge is either corrupt or fearful of reprisals. In Libanius' account, these factors together constitute a threat to the state, for tax revenues are thereby put at risk. We should not take Libanius' claims completely at face value, for it has long been recognized that in drawing this connection he reveals his awareness of what was important to the state rather than necessarily identifying the root of the problem he is describing.[22] For one thing, the attention he lavishes upon his own legal problems with certain of his tenants allows for the suspicion that his concern is more personal, and revolves as much around his own status and reputation as it does around the fiscal harm suffered by the state.[23] Indeed, in other orations, Libanius crafts himself carefully as a rhetorician, civic benefactor, and champion of the city of Antioch in the mold of the orators and litterateurs of the Second Sophistic.[24]

This preoccupation with personal status and issues of self-representation is evident elsewhere in the sources emanating from aristocratic authors. The letter collections of men such as Symmachus and Sidonius Apollinaris, for example, betray signs of a careful process of image construction, comparable to those identified in the collection of Pliny the Younger, which served as

---

[21] Cf. Grey (2007b), 365–7.   [22] Petit (1955), 189 at note 4; Krause (1987), 84.
[23] Libanius, *Or.* XLVII.13–16. Below, 147.   [24] Cf. Liebeschuetz (1972), 192–208.

something of a model for later writers. These collections contain a small number of letters written for or at the request of tenants, rural laborers, and farm managers, and we may conclude, with caution, that such letters constitute a subtle shift in the nature of the apparatus of self-representation employed by these aristocratic writers.[25] However, just as in the case of Libanius, the focus of these letters is not the bearers or petitioners themselves, but rather the performance by the author of the behavior befitting a patron, and the confirmation of his ongoing relationships of reciprocal exchange with the recipients of those letters. It is not surprising that these texts betray their authors' preoccupation with questions of power, status, and reputation, for such concerns were central to the world and world-view of the aristocracies of the late Roman world. But the corollary of this is that the picture they provide of the motivations and objectives of the inhabitants of the countrysides of the late Roman world is at best partial and imperfect.

Authors writing in explicitly Christian genres provide similarly incomplete and refracted views of the socio-economic strategies available to small agriculturalists in the period. In the account of Salvian of Marseilles, for example, these small landowners found themselves ruined by the insatiable demands of the tax collector, and turned in desperation to larger landowners who, they hoped, would protect them. Ultimately, according to Salvian, the price they paid for this protection was their land and the economic independence of their children. They were, in addition forced to accept responsibility for the taxes on that land, even though they no longer owned it.[26] Salvian enlists this brutal portrait of antagonism between the powerful and the relatively powerless in the Gallic countryside as part of his project to emphasize the fact that Roman aristocrats were directly responsible, through their immorality and sin, for the desperate straits in which Roman society found itself.[27] This moralizing project subsumes and consumes Salvian's portrait of the fate of the rural poor. As a consequence, we should be wary of placing too great a weight upon the composite picture that he constructs of small landowners mortgaging their property and their future in response to the depredations of the tax collector, and transacting arrangements with their rich neighbors that lead to their loss of the basic rights of Roman citizenship. The suspicion remains, too, that the *pauperes* and *coloni* who populate his text should probably be equated more with lesser members of municipal aristocracies and independent small

---

[25] Image construction: e.g. Zelzer (1995); Sogno (2006), chapter 3. Cf. Garnsey (2010), 46–9. Subtle shift in focus: cf. Grey (2004), 36–7; Grey (2008), 301–2. Further discussion below, 137–9.
[26] Salvian, *De Gubernatione Dei* v.   [27] O'Donnell (1983) 26; Grey (2006), 166–7.

landowners than with the *rustici* who resided in the countrysides of the late Roman world.[28]

We observe this tendency for the focus of attention to slip upwards from *rustici* to the lowest echelons of our aristocratic authors' own social stratum elsewhere in the sources.[29] In this regard, our Christian authors are not so very different from their pagan fellows, who tended to limit their interest in "the poor" to individuals who had fallen from a state of relative comfort into temporary misfortune.[30] It is true that the Christian sources do betray a more explicit concern for the care of those less fortunate than themselves. Salvian's focus upon the fundamental importance of harmonious relations of reciprocity and mutual obligation between the wealthy and powerful on the one hand and their less fortunate fellows on the other is echoed in sermons and other Christian tracts of the fourth and fifth centuries. Characteristically, this interest in aiding the less fortunate is expressed using the familiar vocabulary of beneficence and reciprocity that together constituted expectations and practices of patronage in the Roman world. Bishops, for example, employed this vocabulary in describing their own actions vis-à-vis members of their congregations, and extended its ambit to encompass the intercession and protection offered by saints to their devotees on earth.[31] They embraced also the rhetoric of care for the poor, expressing that duty in terms which emphasized the reciprocal relationship that it constructed and nourished between the giver and God. This understanding of the role of the poor in mediating the reciprocal relationship between Christians and God became a fundamental component in rhetorics of giving in the period.[32]

Nevertheless, we should be cautious about assuming that our Christian texts represent a qualitatively different vision of the nature and importance of relations between the powerful and the relatively powerless in Roman society, for two reasons. First, the sources of the fourth and fifth centuries reveal that the rhetoric of care for the poor was only imperfectly matched in

---

[28] Grey (2006), 171–2; Jones (2009), 132; 158. Cf., for more general comments on the terminological vagueness in our ancient sources, Parkin (2006), 77–8.

[29] See the detailed exposition of Humfress (2006). Also Wickham (2005b), 386–7.

[30] Grey and Parkin (2003), 289–93. Cf. the nuances of Finn (2006), 32–3.

[31] Beneficence and reciprocity between bishops and their congregations: Ennodius, *Ep.* VIII.8. Intercession by saints: Ambrose, *De Paenitentia* II.10.91; Hilary of Arles, *V. Honor.* XXXI.8; XXXV.21; Prudentius, *Peristephanon* X.835; Gregory of Tours, *Gloria Martyrorum* LXXXII; Gregory the Great, *Dial.* II.38.2.

[32] See, for example, Gregory of Nyssa, *De pauperibus amandis; de beneficentia* col. 460. Cf. the detailed account of Finn (2006), 116–75. Note, however, that the giving continued to be focused principally upon the giver rather than the receiver: MacMullen (1990), 265.

practice. Insofar as Christian aid to the disadvantaged was systematized and organized in the period, the bulk of the church's resources and attention were devoted to aiding individuals who had fallen from a position of relative comfort into temporary misfortune. That is, while our Christian authors employed the vocabulary of abject poverty and evoked images of the destitute and hungry in order to excite sympathy, guilt, and generosity in an audience, they tended to direct the fruits of that generosity towards recipients who were not quite so abject.[33]

A sermon delivered by Gregory of Nyssa, purportedly on behalf of the poor, in the third quarter of the fourth century, may serve as a useful example of the tendency for discussions of the poor to slip between these two different categorizations.[34] Gregory offers a harrowing portrait of the plight of the poor in the city of Nyssa. He portrays these individuals sheltering where they can, completely at the mercy of passers-by for their subsistence, bereft of even the most basic possessions. However, before we embrace Gregory's presentation as evoking the realities of life for the most disadvantaged in the cities of late antique Asia Minor, it is worth reflecting upon the frame he places around his description. Gregory both opens and closes this passage with some more specific comments, in which he identifies these destitute figures as victims of war, strangers, and exiles. That is, they are individuals laid low by their immediate circumstances rather than permanently subjected to a state of poverty and wretchedness.

This tension between rhetorics and practices of Christian charity may be attributed, at least in part, to fundamental limitations upon the resources available to aid the disadvantaged, and a corresponding impulse to direct and delimit the distribution of those resources along clearly known and carefully defined paths.[35] Broadly speaking, Christian authors of the period spoke of the destitute, but they gave to the genteel poor. The individuals who are the principal focus of this inquiry fell into the cracks between these two extremes, for they were neither abject enough nor deemed deserving enough of aid to receive anything more than fleeting and cursory attention. Consequently, while the hagiographical texts, sermons, and theological treatises of the period represent a significant quantitative increase in the

---

[33] Cf. Finn (2006), 67–76; 88–9 for prioritization of recipients of charity.

[34] Gregory of Nyssa, *De pauperibus amandis* col. 457. Cf. Holman (2001), 145; 147 for dating, context, and purpose of this sermon.

[35] Cf. Ambrose, *De Officiis* ii.76–7; Gregory of Nazianzus, *Oratio.* iv.iii. Such a strategy also offered some safeguards against fakers and charlatans: cf. Socrates, *Hist. Eccl.* vii.17. For comparable attitudes and practices among pagans and Jews, see, for example, Ammianus Marcellinus, *Res Gestae* 27.3.6; *bBava Mesi'a* 71a; *pPeah* 8.9.

volume of materials that can be brought to bear on our subject, Christian authors present the *rustici* that populate their texts using much the same collection of tropes and topoi as their pagan forebears and fellows.

A second caution follows from this observation, for in exploiting the same literary devices as pagan authors, Christian writers reveal that, regardless of their expressed, explicit statements of social conscience and the greater presence in their texts of the less fortunate, rural inhabitants of the late Roman world, they remained fundamentally embroiled in the same sets of concerns that occupied their pagan peers: power and authority, status and reputation. Thus, for example, the impulse to assert the superior authority of God's representatives on earth over the emperor and his officials is central to Christian discourse in the period, in a variety of contexts. It finds spectacular and personal expression in the confrontation between Ambrose of Milan and the emperor Theodosius over the latter's handling of the destruction of a synagogue in Thessalonica, when the bishop remonstrated in public with the emperor and forced him to back down on the issue.[36] Surely there can be no clearer example of conflict between secular and religious power structures in the period, and no more explicit statement of the emergence of an ecclesiastical career path as a viable means for Roman aristocrats to pursue positions of power and authority in the communities of the late Roman world.

The same impulse can be found elsewhere in Christian sources of the period. Peter Brown has persuasively argued, for example, that the emergence of a rhetoric of care for the poor among Christian writers of the fourth century may be attributed, at least in part, to a political discourse over the obligations of the Christian church and its bishops to acknowledge the duty of care for these individuals, in return for tax exemptions and a position of privilege and status in the social hierarchy of the late Roman state.[37] We observe a similar interest in asserting claims to power and status in hagiographical texts of the period, which characteristically emphasize the ways in which the saints whose lives are celebrated transcended secular power structures, or were the recipients of veneration and respect even from participants in those power structures. Thus, for example, members of the imperial bureaucracy turn aside to visit the saint, or appeal to him for intercession or healing. For this reason, too, the emperor and his family

---

[36] Ambrose, *Epp.* 40–1.
[37] Brown (1992), 75–103; Brown (2002), 33–4. Also Horden (2005), 362–3; Finn (2006), 33–4. Corbo (2006), 108–9, 133–4 overreaches slightly in arguing that these claims were met with imperial legislation ceding responsibility for the poor to the clergy in the period.

seek his counsel, or compete to win his favor.[38] The centrality of the power and authority of the saint in these narratives once again casts the rural populations with whom he or she came into contact in the role of supporting actors, performing bit parts with minimal character development and fleeting time on stage.

On the other hand, it is the hagiographical literature that provides some of our most detailed evidence for conflicts within rural communities, and interactions between members of those communities and the powerful figures who lived alongside them, and placed various demands upon them. Characteristically, the authors of these texts focus upon the holy figures who are the heroes of their stories and their conflicts with other claimants to positions of influence or dominance over rural communities. In those conflicts, they emphasize in particular the prescience, holiness, or power of the saint, and as a consequence they often situate interactions between their heroes and *rustici* within the context of conflict with and victory over supernatural or demonic forces. Scholars have therefore tended to be wary of this literature, choosing either to question or reject these accounts of saintly intervention in the affairs of *rustici* as mere tropes of the genre, or to seek rational explanations for the miraculous events with which they are littered. In what follows, I pursue a different strategy. I neither reject nor assume the absolute truth of the miracles, exorcisms, healings, and judgments performed by saints, bishops, and holy figures in the late Roman world. Instead, I aim to explicate these vignettes within their cultural and psychological contexts. I therefore focus particular attention upon the unexpected, the inconsistent, and the seemingly unexplainable, for in these elements we catch glimpses of realities that were far messier, far less coherent, and far less straightforward than the comforting narratives constructed by our authors of saints exercising their power over willing, resigned, or cowed *rustici*.[39]

In sum, *rustici* appear only briefly in our surviving sources, and it is likely also that their motivations and objectives are often consciously or unconsciously misunderstood by the authors of those sources. However, this need not deter us from our project. Throughout this book, I will argue that we can observe the inhabitants of rural communities in the period doing more than merely suffering or experiencing the socio-economic dominance and demands for taxation of the state and its aristocratic agents. Indeed, they

---

[38] Cf., for example, *V. Sim. Styl. (S)* 79; 91; Sulpicius Severus, *V. Mart.* 17; Constantius, *V. Germani* 7; 23–4; 35.

[39] For further on reading the hagiographical texts, see Grey (2005), 56–8.

emerge from our sources as conscious actors, both individually and collectively, whose decisions and behavior could impact upon the more powerful individuals with whom they came into regular contact. In explicating these decisions and the agency that they represent, I employ three interconnected strategies. First, I adopt an explicitly comparative and interdisciplinary analysis, in order to generate theoretical models against which to measure and compare the evidence available to us. Second, I spread my evidentiary net as widely as possible, and construct a spectrum of plausible responses, structures, and strategies in rural contexts throughout the Mediterranean world. Third, I advocate close reading of our few more detailed accounts, both with and against the grain of those texts, so that we may capture what is not said – and is therefore either assumed or ignored – as much as what is said. The resulting picture allows us to escape existing analytical frameworks of the peasantry in the late Roman world, which have tended to be dominated by the somewhat limited, and limiting, perspective of the fiscal system. The result is a fuller, more complex account of the multitudinous forms that social networks and structures of interaction took in the period.

AGRARIAN HISTORIES OF LATE ANTIQUITY

There is a relative dearth of studies explicitly focused upon the social and economic structures and strategies of rural communities in the late Roman period.[40] Peasants and the peasantry are often evoked in the literature, but characteristically it is in much the same ways, and on much the same terms, as the ancient sources: as a relatively undifferentiated mass, whose social and economic decision-making is either glossed over or elided with those of the aristocrats who served as their neighbors, landlords, patrons, and tax collectors. In scholarship on the subject, the focus upon socio-economic mechanisms within and between rural communities and outsiders tends to

---

[40] Cf. Schachner (2006) for a relatively comprehensive bibliography of recent scholarship. Also the collection of articles in Lefort, Morrisson and Sodini (2005). The present study is chronologically bracketed by the studies of MacMullen (1974) and Kaplan (1992), which continue to be the standard synthetic historical works on the subject. Archaeologists have focused a certain amount of attention upon the problem, although the phenomena they have addressed are largely complementary to those of the present work, and characteristically the temporal horizons of those studies encompass the medieval and Byzantine worlds more than the period under discussion here: cf. Lewit (1991/2004); Faure-Boucharlat (2001); Lo Cascio (2001); Gauthiez, Zadora-Rio and Galinié (2003); Barceló and Sigaut (2004); Bowden, Lavan and Machado (2004); Christie (2004); Decker (2009); See also the important survey articles of van Ossel and Ouzoulias (2000); Chavarría and Lewit (2004); Bowes and Gutteridge (2005); For slightly fuller discussion, Grey (forthcoming); below, 46–52.

slip, in two ways. On the one hand, it goes upwards in a manner analogous to our authors, towards the interests of aristocrats and the state to control labor for purposes of taxation and to establish normative categories of alliance between the powerful and the relatively powerless.[41] On the other hand, it slips sideways to concentrate upon analytically complementary structures, such as tenancy, wage labor, and slavery, which have long been implicated in debates over the transition from Roman to post-Roman or medieval patterns of labor organization, and exploitation and management of land.[42]

In the most recent accounts of the agrarian history of the period, attention has focused with increasing intensity upon three phenomena: the differential trajectories of large-scale agricultural exploitation in the eastern and western halves of the late Roman and post-Roman world; the effects of these trajectories upon labor relations; and the corresponding contrast between the fates of the peasantries in the two regions.[43] These debates have largely been transacted within an analytical framework that privileges problems of production, labor exploitation, and extraction of surpluses. As a result, the rich social and cultural palettes of rural communities have been rendered slightly monochromatic. Rural artisanal production and pastoralism have been analytically detached from the peasant economy, and placed in separate categories of economic behavior.[44] Within the peasantry itself, attention has focused upon the extent to which they were landowners in their own right, or merely landless laborers, tied in relationships of dependence to their landlords. These distinctions in economic behaviors and constraints have been taken as meaningful proxies for the social networks available to peasants. Such an approach has a certain heuristic value, as well as a long intellectual heritage. But it occludes the socio-economic vitality of individual peasant households, which engaged in a variety of economic behaviors at different times in their lifecycles.[45] It also minimizes the fundamental importance of a multiplicity of kinship, friendship, and other reciprocal relationships that individual households

---

[41] See, for example, the collection of essays in *Journal of Agrarian Change* 9.1 (2009).

[42] Cf. the comments of Shaw (2008), 110. See now the nuanced analysis of different leasing and land management arrangements in the eastern provinces by Decker (2009), 73–7.

[43] Most explicitly Wickham (2005b), chapters 8–9. Note the important critiques and responses of Sarris (2006a); Sarris (2009); Banaji (2009). Also, with specific reference to the diocese of Oriens, Decker (2009).

[44] Although cf. Keenan's more subtle account of relations between agriculturalists and pastoralists in Egypt: Keenan (1985).

[45] Cf. Gallant (1991), 14; Bagnall and Frier (1994), 64. Note, however, Verdon's cautions about the utility of the lifecycle as an analytical construct: Verdon (1998), 41–2. Further discussion below, 27–32.

maintained with rural inhabitants who were more or less coeval with them, but whose principal economic role was not agriculture.

The absence of these kinds of relationships from much of the existing scholarly literature is somewhat surprising given the relative richness of the available materials, but it can be explained, at least in part, by the dominance of two phenomena in the scholarship of the socio-economic history of the late Roman world. The first is the project of defining the nature of the late Roman state, explicating its trajectory of decline, dissipation, or disappearance, and assessing the impact of that trajectory upon the aristocracies and, to a lesser extent, peasantries of the period. This debate has most recently been revitalized by Chris Wickham in his magisterial account of the period between *c.* 400 and *c.* 800, which has stimulated fundamental reevaluations of the collection of continuities and changes that accompanied the political transformations of the fifth to the eighth centuries in Europe, the Mediterranean, and the Near East.[46] The second is the task of explicating the nexus of taxation and dependence, as traced principally through the legal sources, which has been taken as a proxy for the entirety of rural socio-economic relations in the late Roman world. While scholars now acknowledge that these sources provide only a partial account of the socio-economic matrices of late Roman country-sides, nevertheless, the historiographical institutions of Patrocinium and the "colonate of the late Roman empire" continue to exert a disproportional influence on studies of the period.[47] In what follows, I offer brief comments upon how the current project fits with and complements each of these debates.

There can be no doubt that, however we choose to characterize the processes whereby the late Roman state gave way to the successor kingdoms of the early medieval West in the fifth century and fell in the seventh century to the forces of Islam in the East, they entailed massive changes for the aristocracies of the Mediterranean world. There were also trickle-down effects for the agriculturalists who both farmed the large estates of the

---

[46] Wickham (2005b). While Wickham's book is not the only recent contribution to the field, and it stands in a long line of grand, synthetic accounts, nevertheless it has exercised an extraordinary, if entirely justified, influence over the scholarship since its publication: see in particular the analytical and critical comments of Shaw (2008).

[47] Note, in particular, Wickham's attempts to reformulate these debates within the context of a quite different set of analytical problems: Wickham (2005b), 523–9. This has been critiqued by Banaji (2009), 72–3 as among the weakest sections of the book, although one could equally suggest that the issues might profitably be put aside entirely. A state's attempt to quantify its resources for purposes of taxation is accompanied by a fundamental simplification and constriction of the reality: Scott (1998), 11–12; 22–3.

wealthy and exploited their own smallholdings.[48] But to limit our analysis merely to the effects of the former upon the latter is to tell only part of the story. We must also countenance the influence that the "small politics" of rural communities could have on interactions between the members of those communities and both the state and its aristocracies. That is, alongside analyses of the impact of changes in the large-scale economic networks that revolved around the needs of the state and the demands of its aristocracies upon rural social structures must be placed two complementary projects. The first focuses upon the smaller-scale economic concerns of peasants and other rural inhabitants and the ways in which those concerns might operate independently of or in unexpected relations with the economies of the empire and its aristocracies. In recent scholarship these smaller-scale concerns have received a certain amount of attention, and they will weave in and out of the analysis of the following chapters.[49]

The second, which underpins the approach taken in this book, regards social structures and strategies not as epiphenomena of economic processes, but as carefully constructed and maintained networks in their own right. In this project, I draw on a small but growing body of more intensely focused monographs, which offer rich, thick descriptions of the socio-economic matrices of regions as geographically dispersed as Egypt and Gaul, North Africa, Italy and Syria.[50] As already noted above, this book functions as something of a bridge between these intensely focused micro-studies and the broad synthetic accounts that have dominated the field of late antique socio-economic history in recent years, for it aims both to illuminate broad structures of interaction which were characteristic of rural communities in antiquity as in other periods, and to elucidate the specific forms that those structures might take in particular contexts.

In modern scholarship, as in the written sources, taxation and dependence have long loomed large as a pair of explanatory principles. In the earliest studies of the period, scholars tended to concentrate upon two interlinked phenomena, which were taken to be emblematic of the character of late Roman rural social relations. First, the new tax system of the period was directly implicated in discussions of the "colonate of the late Roman empire." This institution, it was long argued, was a type of registered tenancy that highlighted the deleterious effects of fiscal policy

[48] Wickham (2005b), 56; 434; Sarris (2006a), 402–7; Whittow (2007), 699–700; Banaji (2009), 60–2.
[49] Cf. Grey (2007b), 364–7; Grey (forthcoming). Also Decker (2009), 86–97; Erdkamp (1999), 556–7.
[50] Trombley (2004); Zuckerman (2004); Ruffini (2008); Arcuri (2009); Dossey (2010). Cf. Jones (2009) for urban contexts in late antique Gaul.

upon the socio-economic independence of small agriculturalists in the period.[51] Second, scholars focused upon a new type of patronage, labeled Patrocinium, which was taken to have disadvantaged both the state and peasants, as powerful landowners shielded the latter from the fiscal demands of the former, but at the price of their economic independence and even their property.[52]

In the most recent scholarship, the significance accorded to both of these phenomena in socio-economic histories of the period has been subjected to a collection of challenges that are cumulatively irresistible. Scholars no longer consider them to be homogeneous institutions, but stress instead regional variation in the forms that both took, and point towards processes of development, which have been somewhat obscured by the legal codifications that constitute the bulk of our evidence. Most significantly, it is now generally agreed that both were inextricably enmeshed with the fiscal process, and amounted essentially to legal problems, rather than social or socio-economic phenomena.[53] Nevertheless, the vestiges of the impulse to concentrate upon the two to the exclusion of other considerations remain, with the result that the study of the countrysides of the late Roman world has tended to be largely isolated from scholarship on the same subject in other periods and regions. In what follows, I briefly survey current trends in the comparative literature, and note points of intersection that might profitably be explored further.

STUDYING RURAL COMMUNITIES IN THE LATE ROMAN WORLD

The study of peasants, the communities in which they live, and the nature of their interactions with other members of their societies has long been a preoccupation of scholars in the social sciences.[54] In recent decades, the intellectual concerns of this endeavor have undergone a series of transformations, as scholars focus increasingly upon social relations and the dynamics of agrarian production, property, and power in peasant

---

[51] For the earliest scholarship, cf. Clausing (1925). More recent surveys in Giliberti (1999); Scheidel (2001); Grey (2007a).

[52] The most detailed account of both the historiographical phenomenon and the historical evidence remains Krause (1987). Cf. also now Jaillette (2005).

[53] For detailed discussion of the current state of these questions, cf. Jaillette (2005), 199–205; Grey (2007a), 158–60.

[54] For a succinct overview, see Bernstein and Byres (2001).

communities in a variety of contemporary and historical settings.[55] For the purposes of our current project, four broad problems in the literature are pertinent. First, there is enduring disagreement over the utility of identifying a distinct peasant economy with its own unique rationality and logic, and over the implications of such an identification. Second, a lively debate continues to surround how best to characterize the makeup of the peasant community, and how to evaluate the extent and nature of its internal cohesion. Third, while scholars generally agree that peasants are characteristically enmeshed in relationships of dependence with wealthier, more powerful figures, the precise characteristics of those relationships and the extent to which peasants might retain autonomy are hotly debated. Finally, scholars disagree about the role of the peasantry in driving or responding to change, whether economic, demographic, technological, or political. The boundaries between these areas are, of course, fluid, but they provide a useful structuring device for the current project, and function as a broad set of questions and problems around which to organize the chapters that follow. Here, I offer some brief remarks which serve to frame the discussions that will make up the bulk of this book.

Any study of rural populations will inevitably confront problems of definition. It is tempting to limit such discussions to agriculturalists with families who lived together in households, and formed communities. But at each point, questions arise. How strictly can agricultural production be separated from other economic roles in rural contexts, such as pastoralism, artisanal production, or hunting? What, for that matter, of specialists such as reapers and foresters, coopers and blacksmiths? And how useful in any event is it to separate these roles, if our interest is in determining the structure and functioning of communities? It would seem that in such circumstances a definition of the peasantry that focuses upon economic factors alone is insufficient, but scholars remain divided over how best to tackle the question, and the problem is compounded by comparable controversy over the nature and composition of peasant families and households.[56] In the next chapter I address these issues by proposing an approach that focuses upon both these analytical units and the relationships between them. This approach underpins the arguments put forth in the chapters that follow about the internal dynamics of rural communities, their relations with outsiders, and their interactions with the state's fiscal demands and agents.

---

[55] Note the remarks of the new editors of the *Journal of Agrarian Change*: Johnston, Kay, Lerche, and Oya (2008).
[56] The problem is summarized by Bernstein and Byres (2001), 4–8. Fuller discussion below, 34–46.

However, adopting a relational approach to our subject, and stressing the fluidity of boundaries between analytical categories should not amount to the outright rejection of the label "peasant," for to do so is to throw out the heuristic baby with the terminological bathwater. Throughout this book, I choose deliberately to employ this term when talking about the residents of the countrysides of the late Roman world. I do so in full awareness of the debate and controversy that surround the concept, and with the explicit aim of provoking further debate on the subject. There are also pragmatic reasons for embracing the terms "peasant" and "peasantry." For all the attendant intellectual baggage, they function as convenient shorthands for a complex, fluid set of concepts and identities. They also serve to situate the arguments and propositions advanced in this book within the broader context of agrarian studies, and allow for communication of those ideas across disciplinary and temporal boundaries.[57] In embracing this terminology, I therefore privilege broader issues such as ease of communication and the fertility of discourse over the narrower strictures imposed by a concern for terminological precision and definitional exactness.

In recent studies, scholars have moved away from regarding the peasant community as a cohesive, homogeneous collectivity. Analyses of communities in a variety of contexts have emphasized the existence of conflict alongside cohesion, and stressed the impact of competing interest groups upon the dynamics of those communities.[58] Any analysis of the rural communities of the late Roman world must acknowledge that these communities were in reality collections of individual households that chose, found it advantageous, or were constrained to live in close proximity to one another and to cooperate in certain social, political, and economic endeavors. The interests of those households could, and frequently did, conflict with the interests of other households and with the interests of the community more generally. In such circumstances, conflict was likely. Our task is to determine the form that that conflict took, the effectiveness of mechanisms for its mediation and management, and its impact upon the integrity and dynamics of the collectivity. This task constitutes the subject-matter of the second and third chapters, and in identifying the maintenance of subsistence and social risk as the fundamental concerns of those communities I offer a clear and consistent set of principles

---

[57] Cf. Shanin (1982), 424; below, 27–32.
[58] Cf. the brief comments in Bernstein and Byres (2001), 23–6. Also Pohl (2003), 6, for this phenomenon and its implications for the study of early medieval barbarian communities. More broadly, Ortner (1995), 179. Further discussion below, 63–74.

for the analysis of relations with outsiders contained in the remainder of the book.

In managing their internal dynamics, these communities also characteristically interacted with a series of powerful figures on the margins of their world, and participated in a variety of relationships of power and domination with them. In chapter 4, I identify these figures of power, explore their claims to power and authority, and examine the terms in which their interactions with each other and with peasants were transacted. Scholars have long debated the degree to which these interactions should be characterized as antagonistic, and the extent to which resistance was possible. In the late Roman world, as in other periods, relations between unequals were characteristically described in terms that evoked the notion of patronage, an ongoing arrangement of reciprocity between individuals of unequal wealth, power, and status. Recent theoretical literature on this subject acknowledges that vocabularies of patronage or dominance function as normative statements, which contribute to an ongoing process of construction and reconstruction of the relationships they describe.[59] As a consequence, a significant proportion of interactions between would-be patrons and putative clients involve a complex series of negotiations over the terms and foundations of the authority exercised by the former. However, we should not forget that both antagonistic and negotiated relations between the powerful and the relatively powerless were played out against a backdrop of mutual ignorance and indifference. In the fifth chapter I argue that each of these three analytical axes of interaction is fundamental to an appreciation of the full range of asymmetrical relations in the late Roman world. While our sources attest a series of relatively sharply drawn and carefully constructed interactions between potentates and *rustici*, the vocabularies and structures of power expressed in those sources were in reality relatively sparsely distributed across the social and economic landscapes of the late Roman world.

This incomplete dispersal of networks of power has implications for our analysis of the impact of the tax system of the period, and this analysis constitutes the sixth and seventh chapters. These chapters take as their context recent scholarship upon processes of agrarian change.[60] Change in this sense is often linked to the introduction of new technologies and

---

[59] Most explicitly, Braddick and Walter (2001). Fuller discussion below, 158–67

[60] The impulse is most clearly expressed in the recent name change of the *Journal of Peasant Studies* to the *Journal of Agrarian Change*: Bernstein and Byres (2001), *passim*, particularly 1–3, 36–7 explore the scholarly trajectories and rationale behind this name change. Cf. also, more recently, Wegren (2004), 555; Cronin (2005), 13–4 and *passim*; Grischow (2008), 65.

patterns of agricultural exploitation, which, in contemporary accounts, at least, is one element in a nation's embrace of the economics of capitalism and a global economy. Such processes tend to be somewhat fraught for participants, particularly the agriculturalists who have long relied upon a demand for labor, and who might be squeezed out by newer and more efficient agricultural tools and practices. But these new tools and practices may also open up space for exploitation and negotiation, and be accompanied by consequences that were entirely unforeseen by their instigators. This complementarity of threat and opportunity pervades accounts of change in the scholarly literature, and has produced a rich body of theoretical literature.[61] In the present context, I concentrate on two agents of change in the countrysides of the late Roman world.[62] The first, Christianity, I deal with implicitly throughout the book. I note instances of individuals exploiting Christian vocabularies and institutions, as well as examples of conflict and resistance arising from the novel claims of the new religion and its proponents. The second, the new tax system of the late Roman world, I explore in detail. I acknowledge the new and very real pressures that the fiscal system placed upon the integrity and vitality of rural communities in the period. But I emphasize also the ways in which its vocabulary and structures could be accessed, exploited, and manipulated by *rustici* in pursuit of their own socio-economic objectives in their own communities. That is, while rural social structures and strategies were impacted in fundamental ways by new practices and bureaucracies of tax assessment in the period, they should not be regarded merely as epiphenomena of the fiscal system. Rather, fiscal structures took as their model existing networks and patterns of social interaction, which retained their richness and diversity in the period.

Acknowledging and seeking to capture the rich textures of rural life in the late Roman world amounts to both a narrowing and a broadening of focus: narrowing because it is the household and the community that sit at the center of this study; broadening because peasant households and communities are analyzed as part of much larger contexts that encompass not only links with urban-dwelling aristocratic landlords and local potentates, but also connections with fellow-peasants and more marginal figures. These figures are less visible in our sources but nonetheless fundamental to our

---

[61] Threat: Scott (1985); Scott (1986); Cronin (2005). Opportunity: Axelby (2007); Wegren (2004), 555–6.

[62] For the enduring relevance and utility of these phenomena as factors in the transformations of the period, cf. Ando (2008), 32–3.

understanding of the functioning of rural communities in the period. Further, we must acknowledge that peasants actively and self-consciously establish and maintain networks of relationships, motivated by factors that are rational, but not purely economic. Therefore, in exploring those motivations, I place alongside the ascribed motivations of our sources a series of alternatives, imputed to our agents on the basis of comparative literature and an analysis of the social matrices in which they found themselves. The resulting "constellation of the possible" provides a series of plausible and suggestive alternatives to existing analyses of the peasantry, and allows us to move beyond the scant evidence for the mechanics of decision-making, socio-economic differentiation, and interpersonal relations within rural communities in the late Roman world.

Further, this "constellation of the possible" leads us to suppose that, as in all periods, peasants in late antiquity were perpetually involved in complex, ongoing processes of negotiation with their fellows over their relative standing within their communities, and their corresponding capacity to call upon others for aid in the event of subsistence crisis. They participated in a multiplicity of overlapping, intersecting relations with the powerful figures who lived on the edges of their communities, which alternately served to bind the community more closely together and threatened to tear it apart. And they were, at least in some circumstances, able both to adapt their networks of risk management in response to the new demands of the tax system, and to take advantage of the opportunities presented by that tax system. While we should not expect the *rustici* of the late Roman world to have been universally successful as individuals and communities, we must acknowledge that they were not merely a voiceless, powerless mass. In this book I seek to recover the sound and volume of their voices and to explore the extent and limits of their power.

CHAPTER I

Constituting communities: peasants, families, households

Scholarship on the peasantry of the late Roman world has tended to view them as if down the barrel of a telescope, analyzing socio-economic relationships and strategies from the point of view of the demands and pressures that the state and its aristocracies placed upon them. This chapter constitutes a first step towards inverting that telescope, and looking back up it to see how the concerns, politics, and constraints of individual peasants and their communities might simultaneously have impacted upon their interactions with each other, with more powerful figures, and with the state.[1] I do this by focusing attention upon explicating and defining the components of rural communities, and sketching the relationships between them. I suggest that, while the evidence for the composition of rural communities in the period is anecdotal and patchy, it is possible to construct a plausible picture of the individuals and groups that might have constituted those communities. As our analysis moves progressively from the individual, through the family and household to the community, the balance between theoretically informed supposition and empirically derived proposition will gradually shift. That is, while we are somewhat limited in the concrete conclusions we can draw about intra- and inter-household relations, we can with a certain degree of confidence offer some hypotheses about the structure and makeup of a variety of rural communities in the period.

I begin with a discussion of terminology, exploring both the boundaries around specific entities and the fundamental importance of focusing upon connections between those entities. This project presents considerable challenges. To what extent is it reasonable to speak of the peasantry as a concrete, discrete class? How are we to determine the composition of the "typical" peasant household, and is the exercise analytically useful? What is a

---

[1] Cf. Blanton and Fargher (2008), 10 for calls to "study up" from the base of society.

community? In what follows, I propose a twofold approach to these questions. First, I suggest that we must identify and define these entities, but that those definitions must be flexible enough to encompass the immense diversity of economic niches, social systems, and physical environments that constituted the rural contexts of the late Roman world. In pursuit of this project, I connect existing debates in the social sciences with the evidence that survives from the period. Here, and in the following chapters, I argue for the general applicability of analytical categories and concepts drawn from comparative literature, while emphasizing the uniqueness of each particular community.

Second, I argue that integral to the project of definition is the elucidation of the relationships between these individuals, households, and communities. Such a project has three implications. In the first instance, it entails adopting a multiscalar analysis of social structures and networks, which explores simultaneously individual peasants; the families and households of which those individuals were a part; and the communities which were composed of collections of individuals, families, and households.[2] At each analytical level, we should expect a series of overlapping, often contradictory relationships, which create a congeries of mutual responsibilities that cannot all be satisfied simultaneously. In the second instance, focusing attention upon relationships amounts to a conscious acknowledgment of the manner in which the protagonists of this account were both constrained by the social, economic, and cultural structures which constituted their lived experience and able to affect, manipulate, and shape those structures to their own advantage. In broad analytical terms, then, I suggest that agents and structures are inextricably intertwined in a series of mutually implicated relationships. This relational perspective provides the conceptual framework that underpins the remainder of the book.[3]

PEASANTS AND *RUSTICI*

What is a peasant? Modern scholars are divided, between those with a preference for making generalized (and generalizable) propositions about

---

[2] See the classic demonstration of the desirability of an eclectic approach to the peasantry in Wolf (1966), and further comments in Bernstein and Byres (2001), 4. Cf. Whittlesey (1989), 227; Spencer-Wood (1989), 113 for slightly more elaborate typologies. Also Harris (1982), 147; Chaytor (1980), 39; Freter (2004), 93–4; Bowdon (2004), 407; Schofield (2003), 5–6. For Byzantine Egypt, see now Ruffini (2008). Cf., however, Verdon (1998), who observes a fundamental tension between individual and social levels of analysis.

[3] Intertwining of agents and structures: cf. below, 98–105. Utility and value of relational perspectives in the social sciences: cf. Yeganehlayegh (1981); Wellman, Frank, Espinoza, Lundquist, and Wilson (1991); Emirbayer (1997).

the peasantry, and those committed to particularism in exploring a specific community existing in a unique context. In recent scholarship on the question, particular attention has focused upon the usefulness of the terms "peasant" and "peasantry" as analytical tools, and the uniqueness of the peasantry as an economic or social category.[4] On the one hand, it has been argued that the economic rationality of the peasantry can be clearly identified and separated from the economic behavior of other sections of society. In this construction, the uniqueness of peasant economic decision-making is emphasized, although it is also recognized that, in specific circumstances, peasants will adapt to the constraints of their environments in diverse and variable ways. On the other hand, it has been observed that peasants are inextricably enmeshed in complex economic and social relationships with outsiders, and that the particular characteristics and distribution of these sets of relationships are likely to have a significant impact upon the economic strategies available to peasants, as well as familial and social structures within their households.[5]

The terms in which this debate has been conducted provoke extreme positions, some of which have become needlessly entrenched. Certainly, one does not need to regard the peasantry as calculating, capitalist entrepreneurs to acknowledge that the satisfaction of subsistence needs can be reconciled with the pursuit of profit. I return to this proposition briefly in the following chapter, where I suggest that the management of risk underpins decision-making among agriculturalists, but that we must understand risk as a multidimensional phenomenon, encompassing social and cultural as well as economic elements.[6] It suffices to note here that strategies of risk management are characteristically complex, and often involve acts which may at first blush appear to be at odds with the interests of an individual peasant or his household. Consequently, to approach peasant decision-making solely as a question of economic rationality is to apply an unnecessarily limiting lens of interpretation to our evidence.

Further, by using definitions derived from economic practices, we make artificial distinctions between the strategies that might be pursued by an individual, household, or community. Ownership of land, tenancy, and wage labor, for example, should not be treated as distinct types of economic

---

[4] Shanin (1982), 411 argues in favor of the heuristic value of the terminology. So, too, does Hanawalt (1986), 5, drawing upon Hilton's classic definition of the peasantry (Hilton (1975), chapter 1). Note, however, the doubts of Akram-Lodhi (2007), 560–1. For a historical context on the question, with specific reference to the ancient Mediterranean, cf. Halstead (1987).

[5] The debate is succinctly summarized by Bernstein and Byres (2001), 4–8, with further references.

[6] Entrepreneurs: cf. the provocative and stimulating comments of Stone (2005), 6–14. Risk: below, 60–3.

activity, for all might be employed concurrently or sequentially by the same household. Likewise, rural artisanal production and the small- or medium-scale maintenance of sheep or goats, cattle or pigs can only with difficulty be detached from the economic activities of a "peasant" household.[7] Moreover, to focus attention solely upon peasants practicing agriculture or agro-pastoralism results in a monochromatic rendering of the rich social and cultural palettes of rural communities. Consequently, any project seeking to engage in a discourse across temporal, geographical, and disciplinary boundaries must both assume general categories of analysis and recognize the uniqueness of particular sets of circumstances.

We must therefore entertain two complementary analytical positions. On the one hand, it seems reasonable to assume that the rural landscapes of the late Roman world were populated primarily by peasants, who shared certain common economic and social goals, and were subjected to comparable limitations and constraints upon their capacity to meet those goals. Equally, however, we must acknowledge that agricultural communities in the late Roman world were immensely diverse in their settlement patterns, economic behaviors, and networks of socio-economic exchange.[8] The internal dynamics, sense of unity, and cohesion of any group of agriculturalists will have varied according to an array of factors: the spatial organization and size of their settlement; the nature of relationships both between individual households and between the community and any powerful outsiders with links to or claims upon the members of that community; the type of agricultural activity and the socio-economic constraints that that activity placed upon individual households and communities.[9] Consequently, any attempt to define peasants, their households, and communities must tread a perilous path between creating definitions that are so tight as to be prescriptive and exclusive on the one hand; and working with general ideas that are so vague and ephemeral that they carry little or no analytical weight on the other.

It has been proposed that, in broad terms, rural populations continued largely unchanged into the fourth and fifth centuries and beyond in terms of their makeup, economic practices, social exchanges, and much of their

---

[7] Ownership and tenancy: Palladius, *Op. Ag.* 1.6.6. Subsistence and the market: *CTh* XIII.1.3 (361). Cf. Erdkamp (1999), 556; Wickham (2005b), 386–7, although note a change of emphasis at 544. Cf. Schofield (2003), 80.

[8] For a brief survey, see below, 46–52. Also Grey (forthcoming). Note Kaplan's more detailed account of variability of agricultural regimes in the Byzantine period: Kaplan (1992), 25–88. Cf. Akram-Lodhi's description of "trajectories of variation": Akram-Lodhi (2007), 561.

[9] Wickham (2005b), 436–7 provides a complementary list of factors. Cf. also Mukhopadhyay (2000), 160–1 and passim.

ritual behavior.[10] The economic orientation of the majority of these individuals towards agriculture, and their customary involvement in relations
of political dominance that entailed claims upon their produce prompts
us to label them peasants. However, we should be careful not to force
these individuals to conform too rigidly to the terms of our definitions. The
nature of our sources renders it difficult to recover the considerable socio-
economic differentiation that no doubt existed between and within these
populations.[11] Further, it is likely that boundaries between the poorest
members of the elites resident in or near a rural community or in the nearby
municipalities and the wealthiest members of rural communities themselves
were permeable. It was possible, though probably exceptional, for certain
peasants to attain a position of considerable wealth and status, not only
within their own communities but also in the political hierarchy of the
empire.[12] Consequently, the populations that are the subject of this study
constitute a somewhat elastic category, and we should avoid imposing a
definition upon them that is overly limiting or exclusive.

Further, to limit our study to peasants *tout court* – that is, settled
cultivators, whose agricultural exploitation was essentially for subsistence,
who performed agricultural tasks personally and controlled their own labor
and land[13] – is to miss much of the rich human tableaux of the countrysides
of the late Roman world. In many cases, it is difficult to distinguish
production for subsistence from production for the market, and agriculturalists can certainly be observed selling produce at market on a relatively
small scale.[14] A law of Julian seeks to distinguish this type of market activity
from the behavior of merchants, who were liable for payment of the *collatio
lustralis*, when it acknowledges that the residents of the rural estates of
senators are entitled to sell their produce either on the estate itself or at
nearby markets.[15] Peasants may also be observed traveling further afield in
order to engage in market activity. We may surmise, for example, that two
members of the village of Kefr Haya in Syria, whose death in a tavern in
Laodicea is commemorated by their friends and family, had traveled to that
town for commercial purposes.[16] Such activities raise questions about the
utility of focusing too narrowly upon agriculturalists cultivating solely or

---

[10] Wickham (2005b), 12.
[11] Cf. MacMullen (1990), 257; Wickham (2005b), 558–9.
[12] Note the striking case of a former reaper who rose to membership of the local council of the town of
       Mactar in North Africa: *CIL* VIII.11824 (fifth century, Mactar).
[13] Thus Wickham (2005b), 386, who expands upon this minimalist definition in ensuing paragraphs.
[14] Erdkamp (1999), 556–7; 563. Cf. Bernstein and Byres (2001), 22.   [15] *CTh* XIII.1.3 (361).
[16] *SEG* 20, 372 (342, Kefr Haya).

even principally for subsistence, and the problem is complicated further by instances of entrepreneurial behavior such as the speculation in the land market that emerges occasionally from the papyrological sources of Egypt, or the complex exchanges of rental rights documented by a collection of wooden tablets from late fifth-century Tbessa in North Africa.[17]

We must also take into account a series of figures who lived alongside peasants, or at the margins of their world, and who appear only fleetingly in our sources. They include woodchoppers and huntsmen, witches and magicians, peddlers and reapers. It is likely that in many cases they participated in regular, if by no means unproblematic, interactions with peasants, and probable that some peasants, at least, had close and enduring links with these individuals, through kinship, friendship, and other reciprocal relationships. Shepherds might run their sheep between or through fields owned and tended by villagers. As a consequence, they may, for example, be observed in disputes with villagers in Egypt over access to and use of pasture.[18] The customary nature of connections between pastoralists and the sedentary inhabitants of both rural and urban contexts is attested by legislation attempting to prevent urban dwellers from sending their children to the countryside to be raised by them. These vignettes reveal that relations between shepherds and local agriculturalists will have been complex, and it is likely also that some shepherds, at least, counted peasants among their kin.[19] However, while kinship was useful in mediating between nomadic pastoralists and sedentary agriculturalists, it was not a necessary component of relations between the two. In a letter to Augustine, a certain Publicola observes that nomadic tribesmen might be employed to guard the crops of the local peasants, and to accompany and guard baggage trains.[20] Publicola is concerned that these *barbari*, through their oaths to pagan deities, will pollute the Christian crops which they have undertaken to protect. In passing, however, he reveals that these agreements were of long standing and customary for both parties. It seems reasonable to suggest, therefore,

---

[17] Speculation: *P. Vindob.* G 25871 (373, Arsinoite/Heracleopolite), published by Hoogendijk (1995). Cf. Bowman (1985), 138; Rowlandson (1996), 176. Exchange of rental rights: Albertini Tablets, published by Courtois et al. (*TA*). Mattingly (1989), 403 note 2; 404 note 5 collects the extensive literature on the subject of Mancian tenure.

[18] Sapin (1998), 113; 115; *P. Cair. Isid.* 79 (early fourth century, Karanis); *P. Cair. Masp.* 1.67087 (sixth century, Aphrodito); cf. the republication and discussion of this text in Keenan (1985). More detailed discussion of shepherds by Neri (1998), 143–51. Also, more briefly, Kaplan (1992), 277–8.

[19] Conflicts between shepherds and agriculturalists: Keenan (1985). Prohibition on having children raised by shepherds: *CTh* IX.31.1 (409, Italy). Complex relations: Theodoret, *Hist. Rel.* XXVI.2; XXX.3; *V. Sim. Styl. (S)* 1; Besa, *V. Shen.* 3–4. Cf. Le Roy Ladurie (1978), 69; 72–3. Also Erdkamp (1999) for permeable boundaries between peasant economies and other economies.

[20] Augustine, *Ep.* 46.1. Cf. Whittaker (1978), 347; 357.

that arrangements between pastoralists and the inhabitants of nearby villages, estates, and towns could emerge over a long period of time, bring with them a collection of mutual benefits, and involve a complex collection of obligations and relationships.[21]

Laborers, artisans, and experts of various sorts also inhabited rural communities, or lived on their fringes. Palladius notes the presence of professional reapers and other rural-based specialists, and a fifth-century inscription from Mactar in North Africa signals the social prestige that such an individual might attain.[22] We catch glimpses of woodcutters and foresters in legislation directing that *saltuenses* not be recruited into the military, and the rural poor may also be observed waiting for work at markets, cult sites, and around the estates of wealthy landowners.[23] Itinerant merchants, traveling carpenters and tinkers may also occasionally be glimpsed moving from village to village, and between town and countryside.[24] Finally, practitioners of magic, witches, and shamanic figures are attested in the hagiographical literature as well as the sermons of certain bishops, where they are characteristically portrayed as charlatans. In the hagiographical texts, at least, their claims to minister to the ill or demonically possessed are exposed as false by the holy figure. It is difficult to determine the extent to which these individuals were fully embraced as members of a community, although we should not automatically assume that they engendered quite the suspicion and distrust that they receive in our sources.[25]

Peasants cannot easily be detached, either analytically or in reality, from these other inhabitants of the countrysides of late antiquity. In what follows, therefore, I largely eschew narrow, economic, or political definitions of "peasant" and "peasantry," in favor of a more pragmatic approach to the denizens of these worlds. I emphasize the heterogeneity of rural communities, the households and families of which they were constituted. I also deliberately maintain a sense of vagueness and imprecision about the economic activities, social and political status of the individuals under

---

[21] Cf. Axelby (2007), 46–7.

[22] Palladius, *Op. Ag.* VI.4.I; VII.2.I; *CIL* VIII.11824 (fifth century, Mactar). Cf. Sozomen, *Hist. Eccl.* VI.28; *V. Genovefae* 49.

[23] Woodcutters and foresters: *CJ* XII.33.3 (Arcadius and Honorius to Pulcher, *mag. mil.*); Gregory of Tours *Glor. Conf.* 30. Cf. Montanari (2003). Rural poor seeking labor: Optatus, *Contra Don.* 3.4, with Shaw (1981), 70–1. Augustine, *Contra Gaudentium* 1.32; *Enarr. in Psalm.* 132.3. For fuller discussion of the wide range of rural activity, see Barker (1989), 63. Also Garnsey (1980), 34–5, and the treatment of MacMullen (1967), esp. chapter 6.

[24] *Ed. Diocl.* 17; Theodoret, *Hist. Rel.* VII.2–3; *Nov. Val.* XXIV.I.I (447); Kaplan (1992).

[25] Faith healers, magicians, holy figures: e.g. Theodoret, *Hist. Rel.* VII.2–3; Mark the Deacon, *V. Porph.* 28–31; Caesarius of Arles, *Serm.* L.I; LII.I; 5; Gregory of Tours, *Virt. Mart.* 1.26. Cf. Horden (1993); Mathisen (1996); Jones (2009), chapter 8.

discussion.[26] As a consequence, when I speak of peasants or agriculturalists, *rustici* or the inhabitants of rural communities, these labels should not be regarded as analytically concrete terms, but rather as more loosely focused collective nouns which encompass the heterogeneity of rural residents outlined above.

Ancient authors were not as troubled by problems of definition as are contemporary scholars, and in any event they paid relatively little attention to the inhabitants of the countrysides of the late Roman world.[27] When not impelled to interact directly with these individuals, our authors characteristically regard them with indifference, ignoring their motivations or aspirations, and obscuring or denying their capacity to act on their own behalf. We may attribute this indifference in part to ignorance, although the regularity and frequency of contact between aristocrats and agriculturalists in the period is difficult to determine.[28] For our current purposes, it suffices to observe that the impression we gain from our sources is that these individuals were so ubiquitous as to elicit little or no special comment. They formed a largely homogeneous backdrop to the actions of our authors and their subjects, or, occasionally, provided a convenient screen behind which a more prominent or recognizable figure could hide. In the hagiographical literature, for example, the guise of a rural laborer proved useful if one needed to escape notice. A monk undertaking a journey across Egypt to visit the ascetic father Pachomius did so dressed as a husbandman.[29] Similarly, when forced to flee into exile, Athanasius, patriarch of Alexandria, disguised himself as a hired laborer, and the holy man Hilarion also adopted the tactic when hiding in Sicily from his admirers.[30]

This combination of ubiquity and homogeneity in the written sources renders the residents of the countrysides of the late Roman world almost completely anonymous to us as individuals. When they do emerge from the texts singly or in small groups, they appear in a limited number of roles, and participate in a restricted collection of relationships. They are tenants and laborers on the estates of wealthy landowners, and in that role they receive a certain amount of attention in the legal sources of the period, which reveal a concern to define the terms of the agreements between the two more closely, and to intervene in the resulting or concomitant social and economic relationships.[31] Occasionally we witness

---

[26] Erdkamp (1999), 570–1. Cf. Schofield (2003), 6.   [27] Cf. above, 5–15.
[28] Further discussion below, 172–6.   [29] *Paradise* 1.120.
[30] *History of the Patriarchs of the Coptic Church of Alexandria*: PO 1.403–4; Jerome, *V. Hil.* 37.
[31] This is the legislation concerning the so-called "colonate of the late Roman Empire." For fuller discussion of the literature, issues, and sources, see now Grey (2007a).

them taking the initiative in their relations with a landowner or patron, and requesting intercession or aid. Such requests characteristically revolved around legal disputes and conflicts within their own communities, but occasionally they involved intercession with another figure of power, or an agent of the state. Just as occasionally, we observe them speaking for themselves, raising an inscription to commemorate the construction of a church or public building, or representing their interests to a local magistrate in a legal dispute. In such circumstances we catch glimpses of expressions of collective identity that centered upon the locality where they dwelled, or the profession that they practiced. But these are fleeting moments at best, and while we may assume that the rural populations of the late Roman world possessed a relatively keen awareness of the distinctions that separated them from each other, those distinctions are largely opaque to us.[32]

We should not be discouraged by these considerations and limitations upon our capacity to recover the lived experience and self-perception of the peasant in the late Roman world. But they do to a certain extent determine the form that our inquiry can take. In the following chapters, I embrace the vignettes and snippets of information about agriculturalists and *rustici* in the late Roman countryside, in pursuit of two complementary projects. On the one hand, I extract these vignettes from the texts in which they are embedded, and employ them in the construction of a series of theoretical models for the forms that socio-economic interactions might take. Those models amount to a collection of options, which together constitute the "constellation of the possible" with which we ended the previous chapter. On the other, I seek to contextualize each moment within its particular physical, socio-economic, and political matrix. I argue that, alongside differences in the physical form of rural communities across the late Roman world, we observe differences in the makeup and distribution of their networks of reciprocity and risk management, as well as in the character that their exploitation of those networks took, both individually and collectively. Those differences are, once again, only hinted at in our sources, but, in combination, these hints may allow us to distinguish the form, nature, and composition of the various types of rural communities in the period with more subtlety and precision than has hitherto been possible.

---

[32] Comembership and coresidence: *IL Tun* 1568 (235, Tunisia); *AE* 1995.553 (late third to early fourth centuries, Italy). Internal self-differentiation: MacMullen (1990), 257.

FAMILIES AND HOUSEHOLDS

In most cases, it is likely that the individuals who appear so fleetingly in our ancient sources were members of families who lived together in households. When we attempt to analyze these families and households, however, we are again confronted by seemingly intractable problems of evidence. In what follows, I briefly discuss some key definitional and methodological issues, and explore the somewhat limited written and material evidence for peasant households and families in the period. I suggest that, in accord with the position taken above regarding attempts to define the peasantry, we should be cautious of imposing too narrow or strict a set of constraints upon the evidence. We should also resist the urge merely to insert evidence from better-documented periods into the gaps in our ancient sources. As a consequence, we are caught in a methodological conundrum: on the one hand, we must acknowledge immense differences between peasant households across time and space, as well as over the course of an individual household's somewhat erratic lifecycle; on the other hand, for purposes of analysis, we must also assume certain similarities and congruences both between the constraints placed upon peasant households and in the strategies that they employed in responding to and managing those constraints.[33]

The task of studying the family and the household in antiquity is hampered by fundamental problems of definition and approach. What is a household? What is a family? How are the two connected, and upon which unit of analysis should we focus our attention? Recent scholarship on the subject treats both as socially constructed phenomena, which are in a constant process of change and transformation.[34] We must imagine these processes both to have played out over the course of an individual household's lifecycle and to have been a regular, seasonal occurrence. A single household is likely to change both its composition and its nutritional or caloric needs many times as children are born, grow, marry, or leave, adult members take work elsewhere, or the household takes in a boarder or

---

[33] Variation: Bagnall and Frier (1994), 64, using the Egyptian census documents of the High Empire. Cf. Harris (1982), 144; Mukhopadhyay (2000), 149. Similarities: Wickham (2005b), 558, but note Verdon's critique of the notion of the life-cycle as a normative concept: Verdon (1998), 41–2.

[34] Socially constructed: Rapp, Ross, and Bridenthal (1979), 175; Harris (1982), 150. Note in particular the detailed critique of the collectivist assumptions of much scholarship on the family and household in Verdon (1998), 24–34. Constant change: Bagnall and Frier (1994) on Egypt under the High Empire. Cf. Bowdon (2004), 408. More generally, Emirbayer (1997), 305 with note 38, suggests that change is the constant in social relations, not continuity or sameness.

purchases a slave.[35] Additionally, it will also expand and contract with the seasons, as different times in the calendar year bring with them different economic demands and opportunities.[36] Our task is further complicated by the fact that a single household might conceivably contain several families, while, equally, a single family could be spread over a number of households.[37] Consequently, while normative categories such as the nuclear family or the "typical" peasant household provide a vocabulary for describing static points in a constantly changing process, the categories are imperfect and the moments when they pertain are fleeting.[38] Further, the available sources serve to obscure those moments as often as they reveal them. A census declaration from early fourth-century CE Egypt illustrates the point eloquently: in addition to Aurelius Sakaon, the individual making the declaration, the document lists his son, two brothers, a nephew, and four other men described simply as relatives or their sons.[39] The resulting household of nine taxable individuals reflects a collection of processes and decisions within and between members of an extended family group that are impossible to reconstruct. It suffices to observe that it can only with great difficulty be shoehorned into any normative expectations of what constituted a typical family or household.

Nevertheless, it is worth dwelling briefly upon the task of defining the family and the household, for these units form the basis of the communities that are the principal subject of our study. In both ancient sources and modern debates, the two enjoy a close semantic connection.[40] In antiquity, the term *familia* denoted the collection of individuals legally subject to the *potestas* of a *paterfamilias*, but the domestic unit was most commonly described as a *domus, oikos,* or *oikia*.[41] These latter terms privilege the real, physical structure of the house and the act of residence over legalistic notions of descent or obligations. A comparable distinction is visible in contemporary scholarship, too, where the family is often interpreted in terms that stress its affective and moral attributes, while the household is treated as a collection of individuals who reside together under the same

---

[35] Slaves in peasant households: *Testamentum S. Remigii* 83; 88; *Querolus* 68–9. Children leaving: Sidonius, *Ep.* v.19; Cassiodorus, *Variae* VIII.33.4. Cf. Harris (1982), 149; Verdon (1998), 45.

[36] Seasonal variation: Erdkamp (1999), 557–8.

[37] Cf. Schofield (2003), 86. Also Freter (2004), 93–4, using slightly different terminology.

[38] Cf. Latreille and Verdon (2007), 70. Also Harris (1982), 144; Schofield (2003), 81; Bernstein and Byres (2001), 23, with further references.

[39] *P. Sakaon* 1 (310, Egypt).

[40] Cooper (2007a), 132–4. Cf. Harris (1982), 145, citing Rapp, Ross, and Bridenthal (1979).

[41] See the discussion of Harper (forthcoming). Also Bagnall and Frier (1994), 57.

roof.[42] In reality, however, descriptions and analyses tend to slip relatively freely between the notions of family and household, according to the taste of the reporter and the object of his or her attention.[43] This slippage should be regarded as fundamental to any definitions of the phenomena rather than a somewhat frustrating analytical fault, for it reveals the essential complementarity of the concepts and the fuzziness and incompleteness of boundaries between the two, both in antiquity and in contemporary scholarship.

The family does not admit of easy definitions. Scholars now largely agree that it is not a naturally constituted phenomenon, but, rather, a unit constructed in response to particular social and economic pressures in a specific context. They also acknowledge its central importance as the locus around which a raft of relationships and connections congregate.[44] But they remain divided over how best to analyze the family as an institution. It appears in the scholarly literature in a variety of guises. At its most restrictive, analysis of the family could, for example, focus solely upon the group collectively responsible for raising the socially acknowledged progeny of a woman.[45] We might alternatively choose to regard the family as entailing a set of moral expectations and practices that are collectively acknowledged and reproduced, or construct it in terms of its marriage practices, demographic regime, and the networks of kinship within which it was enmeshed.[46] Each of these approaches stresses the ideological, moral dimension of the family as an institution. Collective membership of a family carries with it a set of mutual obligations that, while ill-defined and somewhat elastic, are morally binding. As we shall see, an individual's failure to fulfill those obligations might lead to certain tensions and conflicts between family members.

There is no shortage of scholarship on the family in antiquity. For the most part, however, that scholarship is focused upon relatively wealthy urban-based families.[47] This is principally a product of the surviving sources. These consist of inscriptional, legal, and philosophical texts which

---

[42] The literature is vast. Laslett (1972), 25, provides the classic definition, which has been the subject of considerable controversy and criticism: Harris (1982), 144–5; Chaytor (1980), 39. More nuanced approaches to defining the household in Rapp, Ross, and Bridenthal (1979), 176; Spencer-Wood (1989), 113.

[43] Harris (1982), 150; Mukhopadhyay (2000), 150.

[44] Verdon (1998), 24–46 provides detailed references and discussion. Also Schofield (2003), 81; Hanawalt (1986), 3.

[45] Biological definition: Verdon (1998), 40.

[46] Rapp, Ross, and Bridenthal (1979), 174–5. For the late Roman context, see now Cooper (2007b). Also Nathan (2000), 11–12 and *passim*, who collects and discusses further references.

[47] A point made by Harper (forthcoming), who surveys the relevant literature. Cf. Krause (1991) for a detailed study of families and households in late antique Gaul.

derive largely from a narrow segment of the population, and reveal a set of normative expectations that were shared by a small proportion of Roman society. It is difficult to determine the extent to which these expectations were met, mirrored, or even acknowledged by the bulk of the rural-dwelling population, for it is likely that their family forms and structures were at least in part a product of their local economic environments and the unique social systems within which they were enmeshed. As a consequence, the peasant family is elusive as a unit of analysis, for it is difficult to pin down the precise nature of the collection of expectations, pressures, and practices that together constituted a particular family's collective identity.

We catch glimpses of peasant families, usually in situations where mutual expectations have not been met, or there is disagreement over the nature of those expectations. A case in point is a petition from Aurelia Artemis, daughter-in-law of a recently deceased man, accusing her sister-in-law, Annous, of reneging upon her responsibility for paying the taxes due on an estate which had been bequeathed collectively to her and her siblings.[48] The document derives from a small collection of papyri that detail the fiscal, economic, and legal affairs of a certain Aurelius Sakaon and his family, who lived in the village of Theadelphia in Egypt during the fourth century. We are unable to determine the origins of this dispute, or judge who is in the right, for we possess only one side of the conflict. But the text allows us to glean, indirectly, some snippets of information about the form that this family took. We may surmise, for example, that the two protagonists did not live together, and so we may tentatively conclude that this family, at least, comprised a number of distinct households.

More revealing, however, are the terms in which the dispute is presented to the prefect and *stratêgos*, for Artemis depicts the conflict as the direct result of Annous' transgression of codes of behavior that one might expect of family members. She portrays herself as a model mother, acting in order to protect the interests of her children, who are minors. Annous, on the other hand, has violated the expectation that an aunt act in the interests of her kin and preserve the integrity of the family. Annous appears elsewhere in the archive as a rapacious figure, involved in a series of ongoing, multifaceted disputes with her kin. In another petition to the *praeses* lodged by Sakaon on behalf of her great-nephew, Aithiopias, she is accused of taking advantage of the economic naivety of minors, shirking her fiscal obligations, and placing financial gain above her moral duty to her family.[49] But this same Annous was able to enlist the aid of Sakaon and other members of the family when,

---

[48] *P. Sakaon* 37 (284).   [49] *P. Sakaon* 40 (318–20).

upon the death of her daughter Nonna's husband, Zoilos, she wished to remove her forcibly from Zoilos' household.[50] We witness here the complexity of relations between the members of a single family.

This petition from Artemis against Annous reveals a dispute that is private in its origin and nature which has spilled beyond the boundaries of the family. Particularly striking is her decision to associate moral transgressions and fiscal evasion, perhaps in order to ensure the interest of the state or its representatives in proceedings.[51] While we have no way of knowing whether conflicts of this kind were typical of peasant families in Egypt, let alone the rest of the Mediterranean world, we can at least conclude that the behaviors described here were transgressive, and plot the points of transgression as a means of establishing accepted norms of interaction within these families. We observe, for example, the assumption that altruism might exist within and between the members of a family, even if we may suspect that, in matters of money and property at least, the reality could be quite different.[52] We catch glimpses also of the pressures that the expectations of the tax system might place upon the internal cohesion of a family unit, particularly if that unit was already prone to fission or conflict, as seems the case in this instance.

Conflict between family members is visible in other circumstances, too. Our sources suggest that certain patterns of Christian behavior provoked discord within families in the period.[53] The explicit claims of the Christian community to provide a new type of family for its members had the potential to create tension with existing familial structures, and the phenomenon is particularly clear in the case of martyrdom in Christianity's early history.[54] But this tension did not disappear with the legitimation of Christianity as a religion. It may be traced in the experience of some ascetics and would-be ascetics, who endured the disapproval of their parents and other family members over their decision to pursue the mortification of their bodies in pursuit of salvation.[55] It is possible that this conflict can be attributed in part to the pressure that the demands of Christianity placed upon the internal harmony of a family or household. We may imagine, for example, that the spectacular examples preserved in the hagiographical

---

[50] *P. Sakaon* 48 (343), with further discussion below, 66–7.   [51] Cf. below, 216–24.

[52] Cf., for example, *P. Abinn.* 56 (n.d.), a conflict between a brother and sister over an inheritance.

[53] The precise nature of this discord remains controversial: compare the positions of Goody (1983) and Verdon (1988). Goody's position is further critiqued by Saller and Kertzer (1991), 10.

[54] The most eloquent and detailed account is probably the early third-century account of the Martyrdom of Perpetua. General discussion in Bradley (2003), who provides further examples.

[55] Cooper (2007a), 138 for asceticism as an attack on the family as well as the body. Note also Harper (forthcoming), suggesting that asceticism was an apt response to the demographic regime of antiquity.

literature of individuals divesting themselves of their property when they embraced a life of asceticism would not have been met with the approval of all members of that individual's family. It is likely that conflicts of this sort played out even within relatively humble households, such as that of Simeon the Stylite, who, we are told, grew up in the village of Sis in the Nicopolis region of Syria, and exhibited the first traces of his Christian calling while tending his family's flock of goats and sheep as a child.[56]

We observe conflict of a different kind in connection with the practice of *oblatio*, the giving over of a child to a monastery for raising. We should expect that this practice could be inspired by a number of motivations, both acknowledged and unacknowledged, and carrying different weights in different circumstances. Christian piety might intersect with the need to maintain the equilibrium of the household and the desire to have a child educated in a particular manner, as well as economic considerations and perhaps even an appreciation of the effect that a connection with a nearby monastic establishment might have upon the standing of the family in the community.[57] This last consideration reveals that the practice need not be anonymous, nor did it necessarily entail the severing of all ties between the oblate and the family itself.[58] While it is impossible to obtain any clear indication of the frequency with which *oblatio* was practiced by peasant families, the early sixth-century Rule of Benedict recognizes the existence of families who could not afford to pay a donative to the monastery when they gave over their child, and instructs them simply to draw up a document vowing their solemn intention to offer their child up, and to do so in the presence of witnesses.[59]

The sources preserve hints that these ongoing connections between family and oblate might prove problematic for both the family and the

---

[56] *V. Sim. Styl. (S)* 1–3.

[57] Note Boswell (1988), 228–9, who regards the practice as primarily a form of abandonment, though "not inherently incompatible" with spiritual or religious considerations. By contrast, de Jong (1996), 5–7, begins from the assumption that "it was precisely what sources claimed: a gift to God" and is consequently reluctant to countenance what she regards as the imposition of "contemporary sensibilities" to provide "rational" explanations. This debate has recently been revisited, for early Byzantine Egypt at least, by Papaconstantinou, who draws on a unique archive of child-donation documents from the Theban Monastery of Saint Phoibammon dating from the sixth through eighth centuries. Papaconstantinou explores the question with particular reference to the economic impact that donation of a child might have upon both the donating family and the monastery, and the ways in which the latter might exploit the cult of Phoibammon to insure itself against economic risk: Papaconstantinou (2002a); (2002b). The oblation of children in order to ensure a greater financial inheritance for their siblings is criticized by Basil of Caesarea, *Ep.* II.199; Jerome, *Ep.* III.130; Salvian, *Ep. Tim. ad eccl.* III.4. Cf. de Jong (1996), 21.

[58] Boswell (1988), 231 at note 9; 235–236; Rousseau (1999), 151–2. Cf. Clark (1994), 26–7.

[59] *Reg. Ben.* 59.

monastery. Daniel the Stylite's hagiographer offers a relatively full account of his parents' attempts to offer him to a monastery over a period of several years. Eventually the abbot relents and accepts the young man, but cautions his parents against visiting him too regularly.[60] In the provisions of Basil of Caesarea concerning the handover of children, it is stipulated that such handovers must be made in the presence of witnesses, so that later misunderstandings or scandals could be avoided.[61] Likewise, in the Rule of Benedict, wealthy parents are instructed to offer a solemn vow that they have disinherited their child, and thus removed any temptations to return to the secular world.[62] We may imagine that this stipulation also served to remove the possibility of regret or a change in the circumstances of the family that offered up an oblate leading to an attempt to retrieve the child from the monastery.

It is difficult to generalize about the characteristics or decision-making processes of the ideal peasant family or families from these isolated examples, and it would be incautious to do so. Their typicality is doubtful at best, and any utility they possess as normative statements is limited. However, this is not cause for pessimism. Rather, we should embrace these examples precisely because they are exceptional, and use their exceptionality as a tool for illuminating the normal.[63] These depictions of moments where the norms and expectations of family life are violated or subjected to pressure have been carefully constructed by their authors. By choosing to emphasize fission within the family group as a consequence of an individual's Christian piety, or focus upon the mutual incompatibility of the biological family and the family of Christ, Christian authors delivered a powerful message about the all-encompassing, uncompromising nature of their religion.[64] The papyrological sources offer glimpses of the potential for misunderstanding or disagreement over the roles of kin relations. It is likely that these misunderstandings and disagreements created a situation where the vocabulary of kinship and family relations could be used both to emphasize sharing and mutual obligation, and to perpetuate existing relationships of power and dominance.[65]

The nature and realities of these power relationships within rural families are almost completely invisible to us. But we may, perhaps, glean some

---

[60] *V. Dan. Styl.* 3–5.
[61] Basil of Caesarea, *Regula a Rufino Latine versa*, c. 7, p. 39, with de Jong (1996), 18.
[62] *Reg. Ben.* 59, with de Jong (1996), 26–7.
[63] Harris (1982), 144; Bowdon (2004), 409–10. For a more general theoretical statement of the principle, see Olsen (2009), 373.
[64] Cf. *Acta Pauli et Theclae* 7–13. Also Clark (1994), 1–2.
[65] Harris (1982), 149–50. Further discussion of the papyrological materials in Bagnall (1993a), 188–99.

further hints about them from the evidence that survives for slaves in rural contexts, as well as discussions of the practice of selling children into slavery – or, more properly, selling their labor to another for a fixed or indeterminate period of time.[66] These relations are, of course, exceptional in many ways, but they also clearly demonstrate the intermeshing of power and affection, dominance and interdependence that we may imagine to have existed within all families in the period. In an anonymous fifth-century comedy from Gaul commonly referred to as the *Querolus*, we observe interactions between the title character and his slave, Pantomalus. Those interactions are, at least in part, conditioned by the conventions of Latin comedy, and the characterization of Pantomalus is largely a collection of stock tropes about the immorality, laziness, and sexual promiscuity of slaves.[67] But we catch hints of shared economic activities, reliance upon each other and even a small amount of mutual respect in their relationship: Pantomalus is explicit about his preference for Querolus as a master, for all their quarrels, over Querolus' neighbor Arbiter, whose exercise of power over his slaves is not mitigated by any concessions to affection or mutual understanding.[68]

Power and affection are also inextricably enmeshed in the phenomenon of parents selling the labor of their children to another. The legal intricacies of this phenomenon are not our principal concern here, but it is clear that the practice occupied something of a grey area in Latin legal literature. The children in question were not considered legally slaves, but their position was regarded as in some sense analogous to slavery; but nor were they completely free, for the legislation emphasizes repeatedly their right to regain their rightful status as free persons.[69] For our current purposes, what is at issue is the contours of power and affection that might attend this phenomenon. We may imagine, for example, circumstances comparable to those we witnessed in the case of *oblatio*, where the child's parents seek or expect to maintain some kind of contact with their child. We may imagine, further, that this might create a certain tension or conflict with the expectations and even the rights of the individual possessing control over the child's labor. Augustine appears to be troubled by questions not so very far removed from these when he questions a correspondent named

---

[66] Slaves in rural contexts: cf. Samson (1989), 102–7; Vera (1992–3); Bagnall (1993b), 227–32; Koptev (1995); Grey (2011b), 497–8; 500–2. Sale of children: Humbert (1983); Vuolanto (2003).

[67] Cf. *Querolus* 64; 68–9.

[68] *Querolus* 73. For shared activities, cf. *P. Cair. Isid.* 141 (n.d.), a fragmentary text which identifies a female slave of one of Isidorus' neighbors participating in a nocturnal raid.

[69] For fuller discussion, Grey (2011b), 491.

Eustochius about the relative rights of a *colonus*, his landlord and the individual to whom the *colonus* has sold his son over the body and labor of the child.[70] Of course, we should not necessarily expect legal definitions to have mirrored or even resembled social systems as they operated in reality, but the coincidence of complementary and potentially contradictory relations of power, and the likely interpenetration of those relations with considerations of emotion and affection offers some food for thought.

At any rate, while the realities of the peasant family in the late Roman period are largely impossible to recover, we may at least affirm the enduring force of the family as an ideal and idealized unit, characterized by a sense of mutual obligation and collective responsibility. We are on only slightly firmer ground when we turn to recovering the realities of peasant households in the period. Generally speaking, the household tends to be regarded in the theoretical literature as an economically cooperative unit based primarily on co-residence and characteristically involving kin who are co-mensal.[71] In reality, each of these criteria is open to question. Scholars have challenged the utility of coresidence as a marker of households, either arguing that living together is relatively meaningless as a determinant of economic behavior or suggesting that coresidence is an activity that has been consciously undertaken rather than being merely an epiphenomenon of membership of a household.[72]

Likewise, kinship functions only imperfectly as a marker for membership of a household, for in addition to a relatively broad range of kinfolk, a household might also contain slaves and other domestics, as well as boarders, both voluntarily and compulsorily lodged there.[73] The fifth-century agronomist Palladius assumes a certain degree of economic cooperation within the household when he remarks upon division of labor, observing that women and children are particularly suited to the collection and storage of acorns, and noting the skills of women in the raising of hens, "insofar as it

---

[70] Augustine, *Ep.* 24*. Cf. Lepelley (1983a); Humbert (1983); Grieser (1997), 95–6.
[71] Latreille and Verdon (2007), 70–1 provide the classical census definition of the household. Cf. Whittlesey (1989), 228; Gallant (1991), 12–13.
[72] Meaningless: Kertzer, Hogan, and Karweit (1992), 103–4; Erdkamp (1999), 559; Bowdon (2004), 408; Freter (2004), 93–4. Activity: Verdon (1998), 35–7.
[73] Macfarlane, Harrison, and Jardine (1977), 175–9; Harris (1982), 145, notes Laslett's own uneasiness with this concept. Also Verdon (1998), 39 on vagueness of the concept of the "kinship group." Slaves in the household: *Testamentum S. Remigii* 83; 88; *Querolus* 68–9; Sidonius, *Ep.* III.9. Cf. Hezser (2003) for the impact of household slaves on the integrity of the Jewish family in Roman Palestine. For compulsory lodging in the late Roman period, note the billeting of soldiers and the phenomenon of *hospitalitas*, although it is most likely that these were imposed only upon relatively wealthy landowners: see, for example, Paulinus of Pella, *Euch.* 282–5; 573–5; *V. Sim. Styl. (S)* 7, and the recent discussion of Maas (forthcoming), who cites the relevant literature.

seems work."[74] Caution is needed, however, for while economic cooperation is often a feature of the household, it is by no means universal or unproblematic.[75] Certainly, it is not always the case that economic units and residential units are coterminous, or that economic behavior within the household is fundamentally different from interactions between members of the household and outsiders.[76]

In reality, the constitution of the household was in a state of constant flux. The sixth-century testament of the bishop Remigius of Rheims in northern Gaul provides a case in point.[77] Among a series of provisions and stipulations, Remigius bequeaths a number of estates to a variety of heirs. Characteristically, those estates are transferred together with the sitting tenants, who are identified by name. In some circumstances Remigius seeks to confirm existing arrangements between himself and these tenants or proposes changes to those arrangements. Thus, for example, he orders that a slave of his who had been in the possession of a certain Mellovicus be left to one of his heirs. It is likely that this Mellovicus is the *porcarius* mentioned with his wife earlier in the will, and we may therefore surmise that this provides evidence for a household specializing in the grazing of pigs. However, pigs require relatively little care, so it is worth speculating further on the circumstances in which extra labor would be required in this particular context.[78]

While we are none the wiser as to the arrangement between Mellovicus and Remigius concerning this slave, the language used to describe the relationship between Mellovicus and the slave, together with the fact that he was transferred to one of Remigius' heirs (rather than Mellovicus himself, perhaps) suggest that he was not a part of Mellovicus' household at the time of Remigius' death. It is therefore possible that he fulfilled a part of the labor requirements of the household for a specific time in the family's lifecycle. His absence from Mellovicus' household at this juncture may indicate that the family had reached a point in its lifecycle where it was able to maintain its equilibrium from within, perhaps as a result of the maturity of Mellovicus' son Vernivianus. Alternatively, he may have been loaned to Mellovicus in an ongoing, year-to-year arrangement for a limited, but

---

[74] Acorns: *Op. Ag.* XII.14. Chickens: *Op. Ag.* 1.27.1.

[75] Harris (1982), 145; Erdkamp (1999), 559–60. Note the dissonance between economic units and family groups in *P. Sakaon* 37 (284); 40 (318–20); 49 (314).

[76] E.g. *P. Oxy.* 903 (fourth century). Cf. Harris (1982), 146, criticizing Laslett's threefold definition of the household. Also Schofield (2003), 80.

[77] For a discussion of this source, including an affirmation of its authenticity, in spite of the reputation of the ninth-century author of the *Vita Remigii*, see Jones, Grierson, and Crook (1957).

[78] *Testamentum S. Remigii* 57–63. Wickham (1983/1994), 131.

regular time period. It is possible, for example, that he was required to assist in driving the pigs to a nearby market center for slaughter. In this interpretation we may imagine that Remigius is making arrangements for the agreement between himself and Mellovicus to continue under his heir. While these suggestions are, ultimately, tentative and impossible to prove, they offer hints of a household characterized by complex labor arrangements and a fluid membership set.

In addition to both seasonal variation and change over the lifecycle, it is likely that peasant family forms and household structures differed both from region to region and according to the economic activities undertaken.[79] Once again, the limited nature of our sources renders it difficult to move very far beyond this rather trite generalization, but some tentative comments are possible. On the basis of Egyptian census returns from the first three centuries CE, it has been suggested that rural households there were characteristically more complex and slightly larger than urban ones, which tended to be nuclear in form.[80] Although we should expect other economic niches to have been represented among the members of these households, they are likely to have derived their livelihoods principally from some form of mixed agro-pastoral activities. The will of Remigius offers a contrasting picture. The sample is small, and no doubt shaped by Remigius' personal connections with these individuals. Nevertheless, the peasant families that emerge from his will appear smaller, characteristically a married couple and their offspring. We encounter, for example, Enias, a *vinitor* whose family appears to comprise himself, his wife Muta, their daughter Nifastes and at least one son, Monulfus. The family of Mellaricus, who worked a vineyard in Lugdunum, his wife Placidia and their son Medaridus may be similar. It is tempting to ascribe the differences between these households to a combination of local practices, mores, and structures and the differential economic constraints of agro-pastoralism and vine cultivation, but such conclusions must remain tentative at this point.[81]

Given the limited nature of our sources, it may be more fruitful to regard the household as a locus of shared activities, and the family as a group of individuals whose mutual obligations to one another form the basis of their commitment to a collection of shared activities.[82] Those shared activities

---

[79] Wickham (2005b), 551, overgeneralizes the predominance of the nuclear family in this period. Cf. Mukhopadhyay (2000), 159 for variation in contemporary India.

[80] Bagnall and Frier (1994), 66–8, followed by Harper (forthcoming).

[81] *Testamentum S. Remigii* 55–7; 80–2. Cf. the woodsman and his wife in Gregory of Tours, *Glor. Conf.* 30.

[82] Rapp, Ross, and Bridenthal (1979), 176–7.

will vary from context to context, for they are embedded in the unique collection of socio-economic relations that together constitute an individual community. We may imagine, for example, that women filled different socio-economic niches in different contexts, and their status within the household and the community is likely to have varied as a consequence, but our sources are, again, frustratingly opaque.[83] In his account of the life of St. Severinus of Noricum, Eugippius remarks upon the miraculous healing of a woman, who was able to return to working in the fields "with her own hands as was the local custom."[84] By contrast, Salvian of Marseilles offers hints that women were understood to hold a position of particular influence in the households of Aquitaine. However, the reference is oblique and little of a substantive nature can be gleaned from it, for it takes as its context a general attack upon the morality of these women's husbands, and the futility of maintaining virtue within the household if its head behaves without virtue.[85]

Nevertheless, Salvian's comments about the impact of inappropriate behavior by the *paterfamilias* upon the integrity of the household and the moral health of the community are illuminating. Those connections are part of a deep, undergirding set of assumptions about the relationships between individuals, their households or families, and the communities of which they were a part. The same sorts of assumptions occur elsewhere in the ancient literature. In a curious account of demonic possession and communal conflict in the sixth-century village of Buzaea, for example, the actions of a few individuals threaten to overturn the moral compass of the entire community. It is only after the holy man, Theodore of Sykeon, steps in that communal equilibrium is restored.[86] Comparable instances of the actions of an individual or individuals having a disruptive or deleterious impact upon the integrity of a community may be found in other hagiographical texts.[87] We may imagine, then, that in addition to maintaining a balance between its requirements and its resources, the collective activities which a household performs can be envisaged, ideally, as replicating and perpetuating existing relations and structures between its members, and

---

[83] Scheidel (1995), 204. Also Wickham (2005b), 551–8. Cf. Barker (1995), 38, figs. 18; 19 for women hoeing and plowing in the Biferno Valley in Italy.

[84] Eugippius, *V. Sev.* 14.3. Cf. Scheidel (1996), 7.

[85] Salvian, *De Gubernatione Dei* VII.4.17. The linked opposites here are typical of Salvian's style and his rhetorical purpose: cf. Grey (2006), 165–7.

[86] *V. Theod. Syc.* 43. Fuller discussion below, 163–4.

[87] E.g., Eugippius, *V. Sev.* 12, with fuller discussion below, 113; *V. Sim. Styl. (S)* 64, with comments below, 134–5.

with other individuals, families and households.[88] Collectively, those structures constitute the foundation upon which communal relations rest, and it is the explication of those relations that forms the bulk of the following chapters. First, however, I sketch the physical and demographic boundaries within which that study will take place.

COMMUNITY AND COMMUNITIES

It is arguably at the level of the community that peasants and their fellows are most visible in the textual and archaeological record of the late Roman world. The powerful figures whose actions in defrauding the imperial treasury are so heavily criticized in the legal sources tend to interact with groups of *rustici*, and the pattern is repeated by Libanius and, to a lesser extent, Salvian.[89] Hagiographical literature of the period attests saints and holy figures encountering, converting and living alongside communities of agriculturalists throughout the empire. Those communities are most commonly envisaged living in settlements such as the populous and fractious villages of Egypt, or those whose physical remains dominate the Syrian Limestone Massif.[90] Caution is necessary, however, for two reasons. First, while the village is the most visible rural settlement type, the most characteristic in the eastern provinces of the empire, and the most intuitive for contemporary scholars, it was by no means the only option available to rural dwellers in the period. The countrysides of the late Roman world contained hamlets, farmsteads, and villa estates as well as villages. It is likely also that some agriculturalists resided in towns or cities and traveled backwards and forwards between their dwellings and their fields. These patterns of regular movement over relatively short distances were part of a broader phenomenon of mobility among the rural communities of the Mediterranean, encompassing seasonal relocation, regular movement around a relatively circumscribed region, and longer-term, longer-distance travel.[91]

---

[88] Rapp, Ross, and Bridenthal (1979), 176; Bowdon (2004), 418. For Salvian's vision of the ideal community, Grey (2006), 167–71.

[89] Discussed above, 9–11; below, 160–1.

[90] Limestone Massif: Tchalenko (1953); Tate (1992); (1995); (1997); (1998). Note the recent synthesis of their contrasting views concerning the economic foundations of these settlements in Wickham (2005b), 443–8. Cf. Kaplan's detailed typology and analysis of the various types of village in the Byzantine period: Kaplan (1992), 89–134. Also Decker (2009), 33–44.

[91] Cf. Horden and Purcell (2000), 377–83; McCormick (2001), 237–67; Grey (2004), 26–7; Grey (forthcoming).

Second, we should be wary of automatically assuming that the village community, or indeed any community resting primarily upon collocation of residence, was the only or even the most typical type of community in the period.[92] Some kinship groups, at least, are likely to have been relatively widely dispersed across the landscape, and inscriptional and written evidence attest the existence of cult sites that functioned as the focal points for religious communities encompassing similarly widespread regions. In what follows I begin with a discussion of the multiplicity of rural settlement types in the late Roman world, followed by a treatment of the other types of communities that are visible in the countrysides of the period, before exploring the implications of this variety for our understanding of the concept of the "rural community." In the following chapters, I build on these observations, outlining first the internal structures of rural communities, then the interactions between those communities and powerful outsiders, and finally the ways in which these networks of relationships adapted to the pressures and opportunities that accompanied the new fiscal system of the period.

While our focus is principally on rural contexts, it would be unwise to ignore urban centers completely, or to assume that the fate of the two can easily be detached in the period. In some circumstances, it is true, towns and their hinterlands did indeed experience quite different fates. In North Africa, for example, rural market sites emerged as alternative foci to urban centers, while in Italy, archaeological evidence suggests that towns were economically marginalized in the Albegna, Gubbio, and Biferno Valleys.[93] Further, we should expect regionally specific phenomena such as the relocation of army units, the settlement of barbarian *foederati*, or natural disasters to have impacted in unique ways upon local economic networks and to have altered local settlement patterns and distributions in the short and medium term. For the most part, however, the two continued to coexist in symbiotic relations, and the fate of the one was intertwined with the fate of the other over the longer term. Certainly it is not difficult to find

---

[92] Zadora-Rio (1995), 150. Macfarlane, Harrison, and Jardine (1977), 1–2; 9–14. Colleyn (1983) offers detailed comments about the theoretical and conceptual issues. Note also Besnier and Hopital (1983); Bonneau (1983); Capogrossi Colognesi (1983) for rural communities in Roman contexts. Cf., for medieval England, DeWindt (1987), 163–5; Schofield (2003), 5. For more detailed arguments and comparative perspectives, Breman (1982); Boomgaard (1991). Further references in Bernstein and Byres (2001), 36.

[93] North Africa: Optatus, *Contra Don.* 3.4; Shaw (1981), 69; Potter (1995), 66–73; 79. Italy: Brown (1981), 43; Ward-Perkins (1988), 16–8; Potter (1995), 90; Cambi and Fentress (1989), 81–2; Whitehead (1994), 191; Lloyd, in Barker (1995), 238; Patterson (1987), 136. Cf. for Spain: Keay (1991), 84–5. Gaul: Loseby (2000), 89–90. Egypt: Haas (2001), 54–5. Also Christie (2000), 55; Bender (2001), 188–9.

examples of relatively regular and easy movement between city and country, and to surmise on this basis that socio-economic links between the two were close.[94] It is clear, for example, that cities continued to function as a refuge for peasants in times of food shortage, physical danger and environmental upheaval.[95]

These were not the only circumstances in which *rustici* could be found in urban environments. In Gaul, for example, an early fifth-century law attempts to solve problems putatively caused when registered tenants were discovered serving in municipal *curiae* and urban guilds.[96] We must assume that these individuals were relatively well off, and as a consequence we may contrast their reasons for moving to the local urban center with the experience of the children whom the sixth-century bureaucrat and litterateur Cassiodorus observes being sold in a market in Lucania, so that they might have the opportunity for a better life in the city.[97] These two examples may be taken to represent the extremes in a broad spectrum of motivations and circumstances that might lead agriculturalists to move to the city on a temporary, semi-permanent, or permanent basis. They may be placed alongside evidence which reveals that, in some circumstances, agriculturalists could customarily reside in urban centers, and issue forth on a daily basis to work their fields.[98]

The written sources also attest individuals whose normal or expected abode was the city relocating on a temporary or permanent basis to the countryside. A counterpoint to Cassiodorus' observation is provided by a law of Honorius, which forbids the inhabitants of towns from allowing their children to be raised by shepherds, but acknowledges that the customary practice of handing over children to other *rusticani* may continue.[99] The context of the law seems to be a concern for security, manifested in distrust for the mobility of pastoralists which renders them difficult to keep track of, and therefore to control. We may surmise, further, that in some circumstances aristocrats whose principal residence was in the city might indeed choose to send their children to their rural estates for rearing by *nutrices*, or wet-nurses, and we catch indirect glimpses of this practice in the

---

[94] Libanius *Or.* L.23 notes regular movement by peasants between country and town. Also, for North Africa Riggs (2001), 288; Lepelley (1979), 47–8. More generally, de Ligt (1993), 129; Horden and Purcell (2000), 385–6. Cf. Garnsey (1979), 4.

[95] Peasants flee to cities: Herodian, *History*, VIII.2; *Chronicle of Pseudo-Joshua the Stylite* 38, with Garnsey (1988), 3. Marriage between rural and urban dwellers: *CTh* V.18.1.4 = *CJ* XI.48.16 *mut.* (419, Italy). Note also the banishment of *peregrini* from cities in times of crisis: Ambrose, *De Officiis* III.45–52; Ammianus Marcellinus, *Res Gestae* XIV.6.19.

[96] *CTh* XII.19.2 (400, Gaul), with Grey (2007a), 163.   [97] Cassiodorus, *Variae* VIII.33.4.

[98] Cf. Eugippius, *V. Sev.* 10.1.   [99] *CTh* IX.31.1 (409, Italy).

correspondence of the late fifth-century Gallo-Roman aristocrat Sidonius Apollinaris.[100] Legislation concerned with the fulfillment of urban liturgies hints at more permanent movement by members of municipal councils, urban craftsmen, and members of urban guilds. While these laws are underpinned by the assumption that those individuals are motivated by a desire to evade their duties in the cities, the reality need not be quite so explicitly antagonistic, for rural populations of the Mediterranean world were highly mobile, and we may imagine that these populations moved backwards and forwards between urban and rural contexts on a relatively regular basis.[101]

This context of regular intra- and inter-regional mobility encourages an analysis that distinguishes between the village or agricultural community on the one hand, which was circumscribed by the boundaries of a relatively clearly defined physical settlement, and the rural community on the other, which was principally a demographic and regional phenomenon, and therefore more diverse, inclusive, and dynamic in its membership.[102] In this book, our attention will move regularly backwards and forwards between these two types of community. Therefore, it is worth surveying briefly the settlement history of the late Roman countryside. The most recent scholarship has tended to eke out a middle ground between expecting universal, inevitable decline in all regions on the one hand, and assuming widespread rural prosperity, on the other. The picture that emerges from the archaeological evidence is one of diversity and change throughout late antiquity and into the early medieval period. However, we may, with caution, posit some constants and draw some broad distinctions between the eastern and western provinces of the empire. These physical differences may, again with caution, be placed alongside certain structural, relational, and behavioral differences that will emerge over the course of the following chapters.

In the western provinces of the empire, we witness a gradual process of transformation in the distribution of settlements during the fourth, fifth, and sixth centuries.[103] With some notable exceptions, such as the Danube

---

[100] Sidonius, *Epp.* II.2.10; V.19, with Koptev (2004), 298; Grey (2008), 289–90.

[101] *CTh* XII.18.1 (367, Egypt); XII.18.2 = *CJ* X.38.1 (396, Illyricum); *CTh* XII.19.1 (400, Gaul), with Grey (2007a), 163. Also *Apa Mena: Further Miracles*, 75, 151. For the tendency of the Imperial legislation to ascribe fiscal motivations to acts that may be interpreted more prosaically, see below, 206–13.

[102] Zadora-Rio (1995), 147. Cf. DeWindt (1987), 164–5; Schofield (2003), 3. The village community is the focus of Kaplan's account, and of Wickham's: Kaplan (1992), 195–202; Wickham (2005b), chapter 8. Cf. also Giliberti (1992), 177, who defines a community in Egypt in the period as "un gruppo di liberi contadini – non importa se fittavoli o proprietari – stabiliti nel medesimo centro abitato, e legati d'obblighi collettivi di carattere pubblicistico."

[103] General surveys in Ripoll and Arce (2000); Chavarría and Lewit (2004); Cheyette (2008).

and Balkans regions, cities and towns continue to be attested in these landscapes, and it is possible that in some regions those urban agglomerations became loci around which rural settlements clustered more closely than in previous centuries.[104] There is a certain amount of evidence for the construction of urban walls in the period, and it is possible also that in some circumstances the inhabitants of the surrounding countrysides abandoned their dwellings for the safety of the nearby town. It is therefore tempting to conclude on the basis of these processes that some regions experienced a greater need or desire for security. Equally, however, we should expect that, in some cases, urban fortification was driven more by civic pride and prosperity than by uncertainty and fear.[105] At any rate, we may posit some degree of physical relocation of rural populations, particularly in the *limes* regions of Germany and northern Gaul. Further, it is occasionally possible to connect that relocation to the gradual expansion of certain sites in the countryside or the abandonment of others. The net result of these shifts in population distribution may be summed up as the beginnings of villages in western Europe, although the precise details of the process are unclear.[106]

However, in the period that is the principal focus of this study, there can be no doubt that small, dispersed hamlets, villas, and farmsteads also continued to be features of the landscape, even if they gradually reduced in number and increased in relative size.[107] In archaeological terms, the most recognizable site in the period was the Roman-style villa. The various fates of these sites in the period may be taken as emblematic of the variety of possible settlement patterns in the late- and post-Roman world. Some appear to have been fortified over the course of the fifth century, and there is evidence for the survival of a good number of these villas into the sixth century and later. As in the case of urban fortifications, we should expect that the reasons for fortification of these sites were many and varied. Security concerns are likely to have been responsible in some circumstances, although the fulsome praise that Sidonius Apollinaris lavishes upon his friend Pontius Leontius' massive, fortified villa of Burgus offers hints that

---

[104] Danube: Poulter (2004). Balkans: Dunn (1994); Brandes and Haldon (2000). Cf., for Gaul, Fixot (2000); Heijmans (2006). Hispania: Díaz (2000).

[105] Uncertainty: Brühl (1988), 43. Bender (2001), 191. Town walls as an identifying feature of a late Roman town: Christie (2000), 57–8.

[106] Cf. Périn (2004); Arthur (2004); Durand and Leveau (2004); Wickham (2005a); Cheyette (2008).

[107] Hamlets, villas and farmsteads in Gaul and northern Europe: van Ossel (1983), 165; van Ossel (1992), 87; 171; van Ossel and Ouzoulias (2000), 139. Cf. Mancassola and Saggioro (2001), who fix the period for the disappearance of villas in the lower Verona basin to the fifth century. In Africa: Ørsted with Ladjimi Sebaï (1992), 95; Mattingly and Hayes (1992), 414–5; Jones, Keay, Nolla, and Tarrús (1982), 258. Wickham (2005b), 465–6.

some local aristocrats might have been motivated by the desire to enhance their social prestige among their peers and dependents.[108] Equally, and by contrast, we observe the reuse and repurposing of some villa sites in the period, as churches or monasteries, an artisanal installation or pottery kiln, a periodic or temporary habitation.[109] It is possible also that some villas enjoyed an afterlife as, first, proto-villages, and then later fully fledged villages and towns.[110]

At any rate, throughout the western provinces in the period, the most fundamental continuity was of diversity. The proposition may be most succinctly illustrated with reference to North Africa, where extensive survey work has revealed a multiplicity of small, medium, and large rural settlements between the third and seventh centuries. In some regions the number of sites appears to have dropped in the period, while in others it increased. Relative densities are difficult to determine, and as a consequence it is unclear whether the evidence reveals a straightforward case of settlement redistribution. At most, we may conclude that long-established practices of large-scale agricultural exploitation in the province came to an end, and this is likely to have had trickle-down effects for smaller-scale agriculturalists as well.[111]

While the eastern provinces experienced comparable diversity in the period, they do not appear to have been characterized by quite the same degree of population redistribution. We may attribute this difference, at least in part, to the preexistence of a strong tradition of village settlement in regions such as Egypt, Syria, and Palestine. There is some evidence to suggest an increase in the number of small sites in some regions the period, although the implications of this remain unclear.[112] Villages certainly continued to flourish throughout the eastern provinces, and in some regions rural settlement appears to have experienced a boom. This impression is

---

[108] Sidonius, *Carm.* XXII.121–5. Cf. van Ossel and Ouzoulias (2000), 147. Also, the general discussion of Scott (2004).

[109] Paulinus of Nola, *Ep.* 31–2; Sidonius, *Ep.* IV.24.3–4, with Percival (1997), 1–2; Stern (1992), 490. Note the catalog of van Ossel and Ouzoulias (2000), 147; and cf. Wickham (2005b), 473–81.

[110] Afterlives of villas: van Ossel (1983), 162; 164; 167–8; van Ossel (1992), 87; Whittaker (1994), 237; Percival (1992), 159; Percival (1997), 3; 5–6; Arcuri (2009), 58–62. See Lewit (2003) for a cogent survey, but note the response and critique of Bowes and Gutteridge (2005). Also Wickham (2005b), 465–81. Note, however, that it is impossible to quantify this process, particularly given the difficulties of determining the proportion of early medieval villages that lie under sites still inhabited today: Périn (2004); Arthur (2004); Durand and Leveau (2004); Wickham (2005a); Cheyette (2008).

[111] Mattingly with Flower in Barker ed. (1996).

[112] For farmsteads and other dispersed settlements in the diocese of Oriens, cf. Decker (2009), 44–8. It is possible that there was some territorial reorganization in the period: Sanders (2004). Note, however, Pettegrew's critique of survey sampling and the possible biases that those problems may have caused: Pettegrew (2007).

particularly strong for the Methana Peninsula in Greece and the Mareotis region around Alexandria, where the upturn can be dated to the fourth and subsequent centuries. Likewise, sites abandoned in earlier centuries appear to have been reoccupied in Boeotia in the period. We should not attribute this surge in settlement to generalized patterns of prosperity, however, for the experience of northern Syria and the Hauran was of a slightly later economic surge, which endured into the late sixth or seventh century.[113] Narrowing our focus still further, it is possible to identify villages that simply failed in the period. The rural settlements around Petra, for example, appear to have fallen victim to the same economic trends that doomed the town in the period, as trade routes shifted elsewhere.[114] By contrast, we may also observe the emergence of concentrated settlements for the first time, as for example, in the desert region east of Jerash, where it appears that the late Roman period saw the beginnings of a process of sedentarisation of the nomadic and semi-nomadic pastoralists, and corresponding changes in the size and composition of sites.[115] In these areas, then, existing sites continued, but the relative distribution of nucleated, clustered, and dispersed settlements changed.

It seems reasonable to assume that these physical settlements were home to communities, made up of households and families that were involved in a complex collection of alliances, relationships, and interactions with one another. The "small politics" of these types of communities has been the subject of much scholarship in comparative contexts, and it will, in part, form the subject-matter of the chapters that follow. But communities defined by coresidence were not the only types of community in the countrysides of the late Roman world, and the inhabitants of these types of communities were not limited to their immediate vicinities. On the contrary, the landscapes of the late Roman Mediterranean were peopled by travelers. Skilled urban craftsmen could be sent long distances to carry out a job. On his way to Ravenna shortly before his death, for example, St. Germanus of Auxerre encountered a group of artisans crossing the Alps, who were on their way home from Gaul to Italy.[116] Likewise, in Cappadocia, Gregory of Nyssa sent to his friend and fellow-bishop

[113] Greece: Mee, Gill, Forbes, and Foxhall (1991), 227. Cf. Alcock (1993), 56–8. Alexandria: Haas (2001), 50–3. Boeotia: Bintliff (1991), 124–7. Hauran: Villeneuve (1985), 63; Tate (1992), 243. Also Sapin (1998), 129 with note 44 for the central basin of the Wādī Sahbān in Arabia. For broader synthetic treatments, cf. Laiou (2005); Wickham (2005b), 442–65; Haldon (2007); Decker (2009), 18–27.
[114] Fiema (2001), 121–2. [115] Sapin (1998), 122–3.
[116] Constantius, *V. Germani* 31; with Mathisen (1981), 153–4; Garnsey and Whittaker (1998), 325, observe that "geographic mobility among urban craftsmen and traders was certainly not a new phenomenon."

Amphilochius of Iconium, asking that he be sent some skilled stonemasons to help build his church.[117] Itinerant traders moved with ease between urban and rural market sites, and will have been responsible for the spread of information from community to community.[118] In his *Edict on Maximum Prices*, Diocletian acknowledges the wide geographical range of some of these traders, and we must countenance the possibility that some peasants, too, traveled quite long distances in order to participate in market activity.[119] Clergymen and pilgrims, soldiers, brigands, and nomads wandered the landscape.[120] These habitual travelers might be joined by occasional travelers – a young woman, a peasant or tenant farmer with a grievance, a slave traveling on his master's business.[121]

Mobility of the rural population is reflected in legislation concerning the movement of registered *coloni*, where it is portrayed as flight from fiscal obligations, but we should be wary of assuming that the motivation ascribed by the state was shared by the individuals in question.[122] Agriculturalists clearly traveled for reasons which had nothing to do with a crushing tax burden. We catch glimpses, for example, of men and women hailing from different regions or communities getting married, such as the couple who are the subject of a letter of Sidonius Apollinaris to his friend Pudens.[123] Another couple, mentioned in the will of Remigius of Rheims, also came originally from estates owned by two different landowners. Upon their marriage the woman moved in with her husband, though she appears to have remained technically under the *dominium* of her landlord until his death.[124] In both cases we are left none the wiser as to the circumstances in which these couples first met, or whether wider circles of family and kin were involved, but we may imagine that a periodic regional cycle of markets and festivals might have presented opportunities for contacts of this sort.[125] Alongside these regular patterns of movement may be observed more

---

[117] *Ep.* 25.1; MacMullen (1964), 53.

[118] *V. Sim. Styl. (S)* 34. Theodoret, *Hist. Rel.* VII.2; *Nov. Val.* XXIV.1.1 (447); MacMullen (1970), 335 note 11 provides further references. Cf. also MacMullen (1974), 25 with note 82.

[119] Long-distance traders: *Ed. Diocl.* 17. Peasants traveling to trade: *SEG* 20, 372 (342, Kefr Haya).

[120] Theodoret, *Hist. Rel.* XVII.2; Paulinus of Nola, *Ep.* 12.12; 17.1; 22.1; Augustine, *Ep.* 22.6; Gregory of Tours, *Virt. Jul.* 9; *Virt. Mart.* 1.31; *V. Sim. Styl. (S)* 35; Jerome, *V. Malchi* 4.

[121] *V. Sim. Styl. (S)* 35; 39; Symmachus, *Ep.* v.48; VII.56; Sidonius, *Ep.* II.10; VI.3; VI.12; Paulinus of Nola, *Ep.* 23; Sulpicius Severus, *Ep.* 3. For attribution of this correspondence to Severus and Paulinus, cf. Lepelley (1989), 236–8.

[122] E.g. *Brev.* v.9.1 = *CTh* v.17.1 (332, *ad provinciales*); Whittaker (1997), 301–3. Grey (2007a), 158. Fuller discussion below, 193.

[123] Sidonius, *Ep.* v.19.   [124] *Testamentum S. Remigii*, 66–7.

[125] Frayn (1993), 133. For further discussions of the socio-economic role of markets in rural economies of the period, see, for example, MacMullen (1970); Mitterauer (1973); Shaw (1981); de Ligt and de Neeve (1988); Hodges (1988); de Ligt (1993); Kaplan (1992), 94–5.

immediate circumstances for relocation. Peasants might flee because they had stolen from their landlord, or committed some other crime to arouse his wrath.[126] The *coloni* of the *fundus Thogonoetis* in North Africa threaten to abandon their tenancies and move if an unpopular bishop is imposed upon them, and the fact that their grievance against the man is taken seriously by both their landlord and Augustine, bishop of the nearby see of Hippo, reveals that this was no idle threat.[127]

Threats of this sort reveal the mutually implicated nature of relations between landlords and their tenants. In such circumstances, the high incidence and regularity of movement by agriculturalists speaks to the advantages that it provided both for landowners and for peasants. For both parties, it was part of an environment in which casual or seasonal labor was both available and needed at crucial times of the year. It seems that that availability could within certain limits be predicted and exploited regularly.[128] As a consequence, we need not assume that agriculturalists simply picked up and moved against the will of their landlord, patron or master.[129] Rather, aristocratic landowners might aid or even initiate movement by their dependents, and there survive a small number of letters written in such circumstances. Thus, for example, Sidonius Apollinaris writes a letter on behalf of a rural laborer traveling from one of his estates to Vaison, a journey involving up to two weeks' travel on foot. While the circumstances are somewhat obscure, it would appear that Sidonius expects the man to return to his estate in the future. Certainly, there is no indication that relations between the two are terminated by this journey.[130] We may therefore imagine that some, at least, of the peasants who traveled the roads of the late Roman Empire alongside soldiers, itinerant artisans, Imperial officials, and the holy did so clutching letters from landlord or patron.[131]

This context of mobility forces us to expand our perspective beyond the boundaries of the village, hamlet, or estate, and embrace the notion of the rural community as a regional phenomenon.[132] Certainly, individual members of a village or hamlet maintained links with other communities

---

[126] Ruricius, *Ep.* II.20; 51.
[127] Augustine, *Ep.* 20*.10; Whittaker (1997), 302, with further references. Fuller discussion below, 145–6.
[128] Banaji (1992), 379–81; Wickham (2005b), 274–6.
[129] Although some, of course, did: Sidonius, *Ep.* III.9 provides an example.
[130] *Ep.* IV.7; cf. VII.4. Fuller discussion of the identity of Sidonius' estates and the distances involved in Grey (2004), 27.
[131] Further discussion below, 157–8.
[132] DeWindt (1987), 191–2. Note, by contrast, Wickham (2005b), 470, on the village community and territorial identity as coterminous notions.

through tribal affiliations, kinship bonds, and economic connections.[133] We are better informed as to the form that these relations might take in the eastern provinces of the Mediterranean world. The papyrological evidence from Egypt, for example, reveals family members residing in different regions writing to each other with news, requests for particular goods or items, and exhortations to travel.[134] Cult sites could act as a focus for a collection of village communities, linked by tribal affiliations or quasi-familial bonds.[135] Inscriptions at a religious site in north-eastern Nuqrah in Syria, for example, commemorate the common religious building activities of four different villages, whose members come from the same two tribes. It appears that this was a site which united these villages and served as a focus for worship.[136] Cult sites might also serve as spaces for managing tensions between different groups in the landscape, as in the case of El-'Ain, which occupied a position that was both the symbolic boundary between sedentary and nomadic populations in the desert east of Jerash in northern Jordan, and a locus where they could meet.[137]

Comparable phenomena are visible in the western provinces, although the emphasis is less on the connections between discrete communities in the rural landscape or their inhabitants, and more upon the ways in which particular religious sites created communities. Thus, for example, the late fourth-century Italian poet Prudentius describes a procession to the cult site of St. Hippolytus just outside Rome in terms that celebrate the mixture of urban and rural, rich and poor, noting that the festival drew devotees from as far afield as Picenum, Capua, and Nola.[138] Similarly, Paulinus of Nola reveals the role of the cult site of Felix of Cimitile as a focal point for both sedentary and pastoral inhabitants of Campania when he celebrates his own patronal beneficence towards tired, hungry drovers who had traveled far to celebrate the feast of the saint.[139] In Gaul, religious sanctuaries and sites occupied focal points in the landscape, and might be attended by small rural settlements in a pattern that is archaeologically attested as far back as the

---

[133] Lambert (1953), 200; 204; Whittaker (1978), 360–1; Sartre (1982), 85; 87; MacAdam (1983), 107–8; 111. Cf. Whittaker (1994), 24–5, discussing the incorporation of tribes into the fiscal structure of the municipalities in North Africa. Also Wickham (2005b), 469, who emphasizes economic implications of a regional perspective upon the notion of community. Economic connections: e.g. *P. Sakaon* 69 (331); 70 (338).

[134] E.g. *P. Mich.* 3.214 (c. 296–7); *P. Wisc.* 2.74 (third/fourth century); *SB* 14.11437 (fourth/fifth century). Cf. Harris (1982), 146–7.

[135] MacMullen (1970), 336; MacMullen (1974), 19–20; 24–5; de Ligt and de Neeve (1988), 392–6; Frayn (1993), 133.

[136] Wadd. 2393–8, with MacAdam (1983), 109–10.   [137] Sapin (1998), 113; 123.

[138] *Peristephanon* xi.199–202; 205–8.   [139] Paulinus of Nola, *Carm.* xxi.542–67. Also Brown (1981), 43.

Iron Age.[140] Gregory of Tours, for example, notes the centripetal pull of a certain lake in the region of Poitiers, which attracted a crowd of *rustici* who collectively offered libations and celebrated a feast there.[141] With the spread of Christianity, cult sites attached to saints also dotted the landscape of Gaul, attracting beggars and penitents, pilgrims, artisans, and sellers of trinkets.[142]

In both eastern and western provinces, then, religious sites drew devotees.[143] Interactions with these strangers may not always have been entirely positive experiences for the local inhabitants, but rural communities could exploit the presence of strangers in the area, too, particularly if they were able to act together.[144] The cult site of St. Menas in the Mareotis region of Egypt was so famous between the fourth and seventh centuries that pilgrims traveled there from as far afield as Marseilles, Cologne, and Jerusalem. The settlement at the site developed considerably as the cult of St. Menas grew, and came to include a large pilgrims' court, storerooms, bathhouses, and a covered market.[145] One can assume that the *ampullae*, or souvenir flasks, which traveled such distances with returning pilgrims were produced locally. Feasts held at the site required considerable supplies of foodstuffs, which would also have been drawn from the surrounding countryside.[146] These economic benefits, and the enhanced regional prestige that might attach to the community hosting a religious festival of this sort will not have been lost on the local residents. It is therefore not surprising to observe fierce and sometimes violent contests between villages in Syria over the bodies of holy men, for those bodies could be used as a focal point for establishing a festival celebrating his life and death.[147]

These vignettes of conflict and tension between particular types of communities emphasize the multiple scales at which our analysis must operate. The "village community," the "peasant community," and the "rural community" were not coterminous phenomena in the late Roman world, but rather three examples of the multiplicity of communities that

---

[140] Mitterauer (1973), 71–7; Drinkwater (1983), 179–82.   [141] Gregory of Tours, *Glor. Conf.* 2.
[142] Augustine, *Ep.* 22.6; Gregory of Tours *Virt. Jul.* 9; *Virt. Mart.* 1.31; Brown (1981), 44–5 with note 117 gives further references.
[143] Paulinus of Nola, *Carm.* XIV.55–70.
[144] Negative experience: *CIL* III.12336 = *IGBulg* IV.2236 (238, Thrace). Work together: cf. the attempts of some villagers to con the holy man James of Nisibis by pretending that one of their number was dead and required money to pay for his burial: Theodoret, *Hist. Rel.* 1.8.
[145] *Apa Mena: Miracles*, 8, 108; 13, 112. See the discussion of Drescher, in his foreword to *Apa Mena*, XI. Also Kiss (1991), 116–17. Grossmann (1991), 24–5; Haas (2001), 54–5.
[146] *Apa Mena: Encomium*, 68, 145–6, a feast held in the reign of Theodosius, Arcadius, and Honorius.
[147] Theodoret, *Hist. Rel.* XV.4; XVI.4.

coexisted simultaneously, encompassing a multitude of membership groups with a variety of communal activities and interests. In the eastern provinces, at least, village communities are likely to have been involved in disputes with neighboring villages on a relatively regular basis, particularly over land or access to resources.[148] Equally, however, we should expect some awareness of a regional community that encompassed all the villages in the landscape, and revolved around shared religious and ritual practices, relatively regular economic contact at markets and fairs, and relations based upon marriage and bonds of kinship.[149] As we shall see, these different types of communities complemented each other in an individual's network of socio-economic interaction, but they are likely also to have created tension and discord when an individual was forced to prioritize resources or choose one community over others.[150] In the following chapters, I explore the collection of compromises and negotiations that attended communal living, the considerations that both served to bind those communities together and threatened to tear them apart, and the complex mechanisms that existed for managing and defusing the tensions and disputes that inevitably arose.

---

[148] E.g. *Hist. Mon. in Aeg.* VIII.30–1; 36; *P. Sakaon* 35 (332); Theodoret, *Hist. Rel.* XV.5; XIX.3; XXI.9.

[149] E.g. Theodoret, *Hist. Rel.* IV.1; VII.2; Sulpicius Severus, *V. Mart.* 13, with further discussion below, 154–5.

[150] Cf. Bowdon (2004), 418.

CHAPTER 2

What really matters: risk, reciprocity, and reputation

The peasant households of the late Roman world were flexible and dynamic entities, whose fortunes rose and fell according to their capacity to maintain an equilibrium between their resources and their needs.[1] A change in the composition of the household – the birth of an infant, the marriage of a child, the death of an elderly member of the family – will have impacted upon both a household's capacity to exploit its economic resources and its needs for sustenance. A bad harvest or a collection of adverse climatic fluctuations placed economic pressure upon the household, and might have tipped the fragile balance between subsistence survival and crisis. Equally, a series of good years, or a little good fortune, could have enhanced the household's wealth and provided an opportunity to climb the social ladder, but may also have exposed the household to jealousy and gossip within the community of which it was a part.

Dearth and prosperity alike were potentially disruptive of a peasant household's equilibrium and were likely in addition to place pressure upon the cohesion and character of the community more generally. Therefore, both may be categorized as a type of risk. Comparative literature suggests that peasant households and communities develop and maintain a sophisticated apparatus of strategies for mitigating and managing both phenomena, and we witness some, at least, of these strategies among peasants in the late Roman world.[2] Peasants practiced complex crop and field rotation regimes, and farmed fields spread widely across the landscape,

---

[1] Above, 34–5. See also the classic account of Chayanov (1966). Cf. the elaborate model constructed by Gallant (1991), 60–112, but note the critique of the life-cycle as a heuristic tool by Verdon (1998), 41–2.
[2] For a representative sample of recent studies of risk and its management, see Kimball (1988); Cashdan (1990); Lupton (1999); Hovelsrud-Broda (2000); Sobel and Bettles (2000); Bliege Bird, Bird, Alden Smith, and Kushnick (2002); Tulloch and Lupton (2003); Richardson (2005); Molm, Collett and Schaefer (2007); Molm, Schaefer, and Collett (2007); Biele, Rieskamp, and Czienskowski (2008); Brennan, González, Güth, and Levati (2008); Clement (2008); Zinn (2008).

in order to minimize the chance of a single disaster wiping out their entire year's produce.[3] They periodically modified the composition of their households, removing dependents in response to productive downturn, and adding labor to supplement the household's resources and utilize its economic assets in times of plenty.[4]

We may assume also that they developed and maintained a complex network of mutually supportive reciprocal relationships, both symmetrical – between individuals and households on more or less equal standing – and asymmetrical – between individuals and households of differential wealth and status. These relationships characteristically rested upon the ethos of mutual obligation and collective solidarity, but they also served subtly to emphasize divisions and inequalities within a community. In this chapter, I begin to explore these networks of alliances in the rural communities of the late Roman world. I argue that we should regard the maintenance of socio-economic relationships within those communities as the primary aim of such strategies. That is, it is the negotiation and resolution of tensions between the objectives of an individual, household, or family on the one hand, and the cohesion of the group on the other, which is the principal concern of these communities. Therefore, those strategies for managing a community's social risk which revolve around the community and its members should be treated first, before relationships contracted with powerful outsiders, which I leave for a later chapter.

We should not expect complete uniformity in the structure, composition, or experience of peasants and peasant communities in the period. But comparative evidence suggests that some phenomena, at least, were more or less universal. I emphasize three in particular. The first is a preoccupation with the management of risk, within both individual peasant households and the communities to which they belonged. Second, the members of rural communities characteristically participate in an elaborate and complex collection of exchanges that may be conceptually grouped together under the rubric of reciprocity. Finally, the social position of a particular household within a community rests in large part upon the reputation it enjoys, and as a consequence individuals are perpetually engaged in a process of reputation construction and management. In what follows, I illustrate the

---

[3] Fragmented landholdings: e.g. *P. Cair. Isid.* 3 and 5 (299); *P. Sakaon* 2–3 (300); 69 (331); 70 (338). Crop and field rotation: fuller discussion in Grey (2007b), 364–7. Also Forbes (1976), *passim*; Gallant (1991), 36–57; Hamerow (2002), 125–47.

[4] Removing dependents: e.g. *Nov. Val.* xxxiii.1 (451); *Concilia Galliae*, 262 (Vaison, 442); Cassiodorus, *Variae* viii.33.4. Adding members of the household: *Testamentum S. Remigii* 57–63 with discussion above, 43–4.

broad range of expression that each might take in the villages, hamlets, farmsteads, and towns of the late Roman world.

RISK AND ITS MANAGEMENT

Risk has long been a staple concept among economists, but in recent decades, the subject has generated debate in various other fields in the social sciences. To date, no general consensus exists as to the best way to define the concept, although in very broad terms, scholars agree that it entails a state of uncertainty over future outcomes, usually connected to unpredictable variation in some environmental or ecological condition.[5] Recent scholarship has sought to expand this definition so that it is not limited to phenomena that satisfy a narrowly focused economic understanding of risk. Scholars have included under the rubric of risk factors such as social discord, cultural loss, and danger to life and limb.[6] In what follows, therefore, I examine not only instances where a household or community may be observed seeking to ensure its subsistence survival by safeguarding or augmenting its productive capacity, but also examples where what is at stake is the social cohesion of the group, or the place of an individual or household within that group. I focus here upon strategies of alliance-building and relationship-maintenance that are designed to ensure that a household and its inhabitants can make claims upon their fellows at times of need. In particular, I explore the creation of inter-family connections through marriage and friendship.

The advantages of adopting a broadly focused concept of risk are clear, for it allows in turn for a more complex understanding of the ways in which vocabularies and practices of reciprocity may be enacted in its management, and the crucial role played by the politics of reputation in forming a bridge between the two. I treat each of these concepts in turn after a discussion of risk and the strategies for managing it in the rural communities of the late Roman world. In what follows I adopt a deliberately broad definition, moving backwards and forwards between two types of risk: first, risk of subsistence failure, which carries with it the dangers of poverty and starvation; and second, risk of social discord, which entails a disruption of the fragile equilibrium between conflict and cooperation within a community.

---

[5] See the classic treatment of Knight (1921), and the recent account of Haimes (2009). For the breadth of treatments in contemporary scholarship, see Cashdan (1990); Zinn (2008). In her introduction to the volume, Cashdan provides a succinct statement of the definitional issues: Cashdan (1990), 2–3.

[6] See the detailed typology of Baksh and Johnson (1990). For the specter of death and the obsession with health in Egyptian letters, at least, cf. Bagnall (1993a), 184–8.

As we shall see, these two types of risk are intimately connected: the threat of subsistence failure will expose pre-existing fault lines and fissures within a community, or shatter fragile accords, leading to social discord and conflict that require a swift communal response.

Risk is an all-pervasive phenomenon in pre-industrial agrarian contexts. The threat of subsistence failure hangs like a shadow over those whose resources and composition render them particularly vulnerable, but even the relatively well-to-do are haunted by the danger of hunger, poverty, or worse. Scholars working on contemporary agrarian societies have identified an array of techniques that are characteristically employed in response to that threat. In broad terms, these techniques may be divided into risk-response strategies on the one hand, and risk-management strategies on the other. The former are reactions to an immediate subsistence crisis, and include mechanisms for adjusting either the productive or the consumptive aspects of the peasant economic unit: sowing of "crisis crops," for example, the sale of farm equipment or livestock, turning to foraging, or shedding members of the household on a temporary or permanent basis. These mechanisms can be arranged into a loose hierarchy, which can be linked to the seriousness of the subsistence crisis being experienced.[7] Risk-response strategies, then, amount to a carefully calibrated collection of mechanisms for dealing with a subsistence crisis once it is upon the peasant household. They focus in particular upon manipulating the productive or consumptive capacity of the household itself.

Risk-management strategies are designed to forestall or avoid such a crisis. These strategies can be further divided into those which are carried out within the household and revolve around its productive resources, and those which involve connections outside the household and entail the creation and maintenance of resources that rest primarily upon social or socio-economic relationships. The first can be dealt with relatively quickly here. Peasant households characteristically practice a variety of agricultural strategies in order to minimize the risk of subsistence crisis. These strategies include the regular rotation of fields and crops, intercropping of legumes, pulses, and grains, and fragmentation of landholdings in a mixed-farming regime which combines animal husbandry and agriculture in a symbiotic relationship.[8] Additionally, a peasant household might remove dependents

---

[7] Baksh and Johnson (1990), 217–18. Gallant (1991), 113–42 offers a detailed account, with further references.

[8] Cf. the classic treatment of Forbes (1976), 236–8; 248–9. Also Gallant (1991), 36–45. Further discussions in Grey (2007b); Grey (forthcoming).

from the household, either permanently or temporarily, by placing them in other professions. Shepherding, the military, and service as a sailor are typical occupations.[9] Peasants might also enter the ranks of the clergy, or send a member of their household into a monastery.[10] In most cases, we need not imagine the move to be permanent or to lead to the severing of family ties.

Alongside risk-management strategies within the household itself may be placed strategies that involve embracing the advantages of participation in a community, while acknowledging also its potential for frustration and conflict. While the members of rural communities publicly espouse an ideology of mutual cooperation and emphasize the benefits of communal living, this impression of harmony coexists alongside factionalism, competition, and petty jealousies. Rural communities are heterogeneous collections of alliances and loyalties, groups of households aware that they may at any moment find themselves in conflict with their neighbors for resources.[11] As we shall see, the villages of the eastern Mediterranean in particular emerge as stages for internecine disputes, violence and crime.[12] While our evidence for rural communities in the western Mediterranean is less forthcoming in this regard, this is in part a product of the nature of our sources, and we should not expect that this absence of evidence speaks to a marked difference in the character of regular interactions in the countryside. On the contrary, we should imagine that the occasional mentions of petty crime, assaults, and waylaying of travelers in the western sources are merely hints of a more general character that is not so very different from that attested in Egypt, Syria, and the other eastern provinces.[13]

This background noise of violence and contestation suggests that the impression of group solidarity sat somewhat uneasily alongside marked

---

[9] Shepherding: *CTh* IX.31.1 (409, Italy). Cf. Le Roy Ladurie (1978), 69; 72–3. The military: Vegetius, *Epitoma Rei Militaris* 1.7; *CJ* XI.48.18 (426, Italy), explicitly forbidding enrollment of *coloni*. Sailors: *SB* XXII.15620 (425).

[10] Clergy: e.g. *CJ* 1.3.16 (409, East). *Oblatio* to a monastery: cf. discussion above, 39–40.

[11] Keenan (1985); Drinkwater (1983), 175; cf. Aguilar (1984), 8–9; Gallant (1991), 143–6; Anderson (1997), 506–7; Bowdon (2004), 418; Blanton and Fargher (2008), 12.

[12] E.g. Besa, *V. Shen.* 14–6; *P. Cair. Isid.* 68 (309/310); *P. Princeton* III.119 (early fourth century, Karanis); *P. Cair. Isid.* 79 (early fourth century, Karanis); *P. Sakaon* 46–7 = *P. Abinn.* 44 (342); *P. Mich* XVIII.793 (381); *P. Cair. Masp.* 1.67087 (sixth century, Aphrodito). Note Wickham's argument that village communities in Egypt were particularly characterized by violence, because of the higher incidence of both risk and reward: Wickham (2005b), 426, and further references at 543 note 43. Also Jaillette (2005), 203 with note 51. For a detailed discussion of the phenomenon of violence in Egyptian villages during the Roman period, and further references, see now Bryen (2008b).

[13] Crimes: Constantius, *V. Germani* VII.19–27; Sidonius, *Ep.* III.9.2; Ruricius of Limoges, *Ep.* II.20. Assaults and waylaying: Sulpicius Severus, *V. Mart.* 5; Constantius, *V. Germani* 10; 20; Sidonius, *Ep.* III.12.

divisions in status, power, and access to resources within a community. In such circumstances, the ethos of inclusiveness and shared endeavors existed in a permanent state of tension with a tendency among wealthier members to exclude their poorer or less powerful neighbors from full participation in the political, social, and economic affairs of the community.[14] I will argue in the following chapter that these tensions hold a community together, for they force that community to create strategies for mitigating and managing the pressure they create. We observe, for example, communal building projects, which function simultaneously as expressions of group solidarity and commemorations of the differential contributions of the various members of that community. We witness also the exchange of gifts during religious festivals, which serve to bind the community together as well as emphasizing marked disparities in wealth. We catch glimpses, too, of internal regulation mechanisms for managing situations of conflict, and moments where a community has called upon an outsider to resolve a dispute which has caused its consensus to break down. We may surmise from the existence of these mechanisms that individuals, their households, and families habitually and regularly accessed a range of social resources in the management of their social and subsistence risk, and it is to those resources that we now turn.

ACCESSING AND MANAGING SOCIAL RESOURCES

The management of both subsistence and social risk rests in large part upon the peasant household's circle of contacts. An individual household characteristically stands at the center of a web of social connections, comprising relations with family and kin, links of friendship, and mutual obligation with other households in its immediate vicinity and in the wider regional community, and informal risk-pooling collectivities, which are characteristically embedded in cooperative economic ventures and activities.[15] Together, these alliances create a network of contacts that the household can reasonably expect to call upon in a crisis, and who can, in return, call upon the household in their own hour of need.[16]

This web of connections also serves to insulate the community collectively against the risk of social conflict leading to a complete and permanent collapse of internal harmony and cohesion. We need not imagine that

---

[14] Cf. Schofield (2003), 5–6; Axelby (2007), 48.   [15] Galbraith (2003), 78; Wickham (2005b), 552.
[16] Gallant (1991), 143–69.

mediation or resolution was desired or even sought in all conflict situations. Nor should we expect the parties involved to have restricted themselves to finding other members of their community to address their differences. Indeed, it is becoming increasingly clear that in Egypt, at least, the legal apparatus of the state was not simply a last resort, but could instead be strategically accessed at different points in a conflict or ongoing feud.[17] Nevertheless it is likely that, should mediation be desirable, an individual with links to both parties could be found to at least attempt to do so. However, the maintenance of such collections of potentially contradictory relationships is likely to have been a fraught undertaking at times, and will no doubt have entailed dissatisfaction, jealousy, and conflict in some circumstances. In what follows, I examine such evidence as survives for friendships, marriages, and small socio-economic collectivities in the rural communities of the late Roman world. I pay particular attention to the glimpses that we catch of the tensions that might arise when an individual chose to privilege one connection over others, or a household sought to replace one type of alliance with another that better suited its particular circumstances.

It is not always the case that family and kin are a household's automatic first port of call in a crisis, but there is no doubt that tribal affiliations and kinship bonds characteristically constitute a key resource in both the short and the longer term, and allow the household to maintain links to households both within their own communities and with households in other communities, sometimes located at a considerable physical distance.[18] In particular, marriage alliances are a key strategy for forging links with a wealthier family in the community, or establishing mutually beneficial kinship bonds in another community.[19] There exists a small amount of evidence for peasant marriages in the late Roman period, which reveals that these could occur both within a community and between different communities in a region. An early fifth-century law, for example, putatively dealing with the recovery of fugitive *colonae* and their progeny, reveals

---

[17] Cf. Bryen (2008a), 25–8; 170–80, with fuller discussion of the relevant literature. Also Bagnall (1993a), 161–2.

[18] Tribal and kinship bonds in Africa: Lambert (1953), 200; 204; Whittaker (1978), 360–1; Wickham (2005b), 333. In Syria: Sartre (1982), 85; 87; MacAdam (1983), 107–8; 111. Cf. Whittaker (1994), 24–5, discussing the incorporation of tribes into the fiscal structure of the municipalities in North Africa. Ambivalence towards kin and intra-familial conflict: See the discussion below, 69–71. Cf. Aguilar (1984), 17; Schofield (2003), 87–9. Also, for a detailed study of kinship bonds beyond the household in nineteenth-century Italy, cf. Kertzer, Hogan, and Karweit (1992).

[19] Le Roy Ladurie (1978), 25; 32; Gallant (1991), 154–5. Cf. Schofield (2003), 90–104, for the variety and diversity of peasant marriage strategies in medieval England.

peasant families transacting marriage alliances not only with peasants on other rural estates, but also with residents of cities.[20]

Our most detailed evidence for peasant marriages comes, unsurprisingly, from Egypt. In the archive of Aurelius Sakaon, for example, we observe a series of marriages with members of other families in the village of Theadelphia. Sakaon himself remarried after the death of his first wife, and this marriage led to an attempt to dissolve an existing marriage arrangement that had previously been made with one of his neighbors, a certain Aurelius Melas. The result of this attempt appears to have been the precipitation or exacerbation of a conflict between these two families.[21] Melas is explicit about his attempts to create a marriage alliance with Sakaon. As he tells the story in a petition to the Prefect of Egypt, he had agreed upon such an alliance between his son, Zoilos and Taues, the infant daughter of his aunt, Sakaon's first wife. Upon the woman's death, Melas took the girl and raised her as his own, then married her to Zoilos in a ceremony that, he claims, involved everything that is customary in such circumstances. However, Sakaon's second wife Kamoution wished to marry Taues to her nephew Sarmates, and so Sakaon took the girl back to his own house, citing as a pretext the fact that he had not received any marriage gifts. Melas then goes on to explain that he had already sought the aid of the *praepositus pagi* and pursued mediation through the agency of a resident of the nearby village of Dionysias and a soldier from the camp stationed outside Dionysias. He stresses that Zoilos currently serves as a *sitologos*, or tax collector, for the village, notes the risk of Zoilos abandoning this position as a result of the wrong done him, and hints at the possibility of further violence between the two families.

This petition is carefully crafted, and Melas connects the conflict that has resulted from Sakaon's apparent change of heart to a possible interruption to the flow of this village's taxes to the state. In doing so, he demonstrates a keen sense of what, in his view, at least, is most likely to pique the Prefect's interest and encourage him to intervene in this affair, and we will have occasion to explore this strategy in greater detail in a later chapter.[22] The petition also reveals the multitude of options that Melas has employed in seeking a satisfactory resolution to this conflict. We witness both formal and informal avenues of redress being accessed, and we may imagine that these were preceded by some attempt to reach an agreement directly with Sakaon. The petition contains a subscript directing that if the girl is happy living

---

[20] *CTh* v.18.1.3–4 (Ravenna, 419).   [21] *P. Sakaon* 38 = *P. Flor.* 36 (312).
[22] *P. Turner* 44 = *P. Sakaon* 44, discussed below, 220–1.

with her husband she should be returned to him, but there is no further evidence to determine whether the marriage between Zoilos and Taeus did in fact survive Sakaon's attempts to bolster connections with members of his second wife's family.

There is much else besides that remains unclear. We do not know, for example, whether Sakaon was the father of Taeus. We have no further information about her age relative to Zoilos at their marriage, although it is possible that there was some significant gap between them if Zoilos is currently serving as a *sitologos*. We are also left wondering about the positions of the two families within the socio-economic hierarchy of the village and the ways in which this marriage alliance might have intersected with or contradicted other interactions between them. Melas and Sakaon may be observed partnering with several other members of the village to borrow grain from the state, so it is clear that their relations were not always entirely antagonistic.[23] It is clear also that both families were members of the village's elite. We observe Sakaon serving as komarch of the village alongside another son of Melas named Aoug, and two years later Sakaon's son Pennis sharing the position with Zoilos.[24] It is possible that, later again, Sakaon accuses this same Aoug of illegally acquiring two and a half *arourae* from his landholdings.[25] We may therefore surmise that the families were more or less coeval, prepared to cooperate in some circumstances, but that relations between the two were far from straightforward.

Further, this was not the end of Zoilos' matrimonial travails in relation to Sakaon and his family. Some thirty years later, we witness him petitioning the *praepositus pagi* to complain about the actions of Sakaon in the aftermath of another marriage alliance between the two families, this time between his son, Gerontios and Nonna, daughter of Annous.[26] This is the same Annous who was the aunt-in-law of Sakaon's wife Kamoution, and who was the subject of petitions from her sister-in-law, Aurelia Artemis and from Sakaon himself in his role as guardian to her great-nephew Aithiopias.[27] However, in this case Sakaon and Annous are depicted acting in concert to forcibly remove Nonna from Zoilos' house following the death of her husband Gerontios. While Zoilos professes outrage at this act, he admits that it was not until another son, Pasis, intervened in a dispute on the street between his grandfather and Sakaon and was set upon with axes

---

[23] *P. Sakaon* 49 (314).
[24] Sakaon and Aoug: *P. Sakaon* 23; 51 (324). Pennis and Zoilos: *P. Sakaon* 52 (326).
[25] *P. Sakaon* 43 (327), with further discussion below, 222.   [26] *P. Sakaon* 48 (343).
[27] *P. Sakaon* 37 (284); 40 (318–20), above, 37–8.

and clubs that Zoilos decided to take the matter to the *praepositus*. He further accuses Sakaon and his confederates of stealing sheep, oxen, and asses from him and his other sons, before requesting that the *praepositus* intervene so that Sakaon may first receive retribution and then make restitution for his acts.

Zoilos' tale is a tangled one, and we should not expect him to be telling the whole story. It is not necessarily the case that all of these acts are connected, but by placing them together in this way, he certainly seems to imply that they are part of the same sequence of events. If this is the case, we may wonder what prompted Sakaon and his kinsmen to confront Pasis' grandfather in public, and to come to such a confrontation armed with axes and clubs. While Zoilos naturally seeks to place himself in the role of the injured party, it is possible that we observe here a series of attempts by the family of Nonnas to retrieve the dowry that was rendered up to the family of Gerontios when the two were married. Viewed in this way, the gradual escalation from "kidnapping" through physical confrontation to theft of property has a certain logic, and reveals also that in this instance Sakaon preferred to settle matters himself rather than call in an outsider for adjudication or mediation. The full details and realities of these disputes are, of course, impossible to recover, but we observe here some hints, at least, of the tangled skeins of interpersonal relations that existed inside an Egyptian village community, and of the role that marriage might have played in both alleviating and provoking tension within such a community.

In western Europe, our sources are far less forthcoming. Peasant marriages appear in evidence principally concerned with registered *coloni*, which represents a point at which those strategies came into contact and potential conflict with the fiscal concerns of the state and the socio-economic expectations of a wealthy landlord. From Gaul, a letter of Sidonius Apollinaris concerning the elopement of the daughter of his nurse with an *inquilinus* of his friend Pudens offers tantalizing glimpses of the ripple effects that peasant marriage practices might have upon an aristocrat's social relationships, familial strategies, and techniques of self-representation, but provides only the barest information about the circumstances of the elopement itself.[28] Our ignorance about the circumstances in which the two young lovers met and decided to elope together appears to have been shared by both Sidonius and Pudens. Indeed, in excusing the latter of any culpability, Sidonius is careful to emphasize that he had no knowledge of the affair, and he certainly appears to be none the wiser himself. It is possible that this is the heart of the

---

[28] Sidonius, *Ep.* v.19, with Grey (2008).

matter. Indeed, it has been plausibly suggested that this event, and others like it in the late Roman sources, are evidence of a culture where parents customarily participated quite heavily in the negotiations over marriage between their children.[29] The object of those negotiations was, no doubt, the resulting alliance between families as much as it was the feelings of the individuals involved. We may therefore imagine that, in some situations, a couple might take matters in to their own hands and concoct a situation where the suitor appeared to forcibly abduct the girl, and in the process to irrevocably besmirch her honor. As a consequence, the only option available to the families involved was for the two to marry – precisely the result that the couple had in mind.

It is striking that, in this instance, the family of the girl seems to include Sidonius, for whom the principal problem seems to be that the legally binding relationship between Pudens and his *inquilinus* presents insurmountable barriers to a lawful marriage between the two. He therefore demands that Pudens remove those impediments so that the girl in question – and, by extension, Sidonius himself – will not be burdened by a shameful association. We return to this letter in a later chapter, where we will explore Sidonius' techniques of self-representation further. Here, it is sufficient to note that, for Sidonius, this elopement provides an opportunity to display his literary skill and to emphasize his own role in the affair by foregrounding his own relationship with both the girl and Pudens. The point is hammered home by the neat rhetorical flourish with which he ends the letter: "I am content to make this concession to your prayers and to our friendship – that, if freedom releases the husband no punishment shall fetter the ravisher."[30]

A comparable case is provided by the will of the sixth-century bishop Remigius of Rheims, who bequeaths to Lupus, one of his heirs, a woman named Edoveifas who has married one of Lupus' dependents.[31] Once again, we have no way of knowing how far apart Edoveifas and her husband originally lived, and no further information about the circumstances in which they met and married. Their legal status is unclear, and consequently we can only speculate about the foundations upon which Remigius' act of bequeathing Edoveifas to Lupus might rest. In any event, the two appear to have been residing together since their marriage, but Remigius' will provides him with an opportunity to formalize whatever arrangement had been

---

[29] Evans Grubbs (1989), 61; Evans Grubbs (1995), 187 with note 146. Cf. Grey (2008), 288.
[30] Sidonius, *Ep.* v.19.2.   [31] *Testamentum S. Remigii* 66–7.

made, and in the process to present himself as a benevolent patron to both Edoveifas and Lupus.

Both the will of Remigius and the letter of Sidonius suggest that peasants did not always transact marriages with households in their immediate vicinity. Indeed, we may place the hints contained in the western sources alongside the more detailed evidence that can be gleaned from the papyrological sources, and surmise that marriages were usually regarded as entailing some measure of ongoing cooperation between the two families involved, and could be entered into on the basis of quite pragmatic considerations of the utility and benefits to be derived. Further, it seems that where communities separated by distance were involved, it was the woman who tended to move. We may imagine that in such circumstances, links between the daughter marrying out and her natal household remained strong, and in this way connections between the two families were maintained and sustained.[32]

Studies of friendship in rural communities reveal a broad range of expectations, expressions, and examples of such relationships. Anthropologists often measure the degree to which friendship is valued within a community with reference to visits between neighbors, the incidence of shared meals, and the degree of intimacy that informants admit to within individual friendships.[33] This information is unavailable to scholars of the late Roman world, and examples of friendship or discussions about the nature of such relationships among the upper echelons of society are of only limited use. Nevertheless, we can, with caution, identify friendships between peasants. Evidence from two quite different physical and socio-economic contexts reveals the broad contours of such relationships, and the fundamental contradictions inherent in them. The papyrological evidence is richly populated by individuals acting alongside their friends and associates. Often, it is true, their behavior is held up for censure, as in a curious case of breaking and entering that survives in the archive of Aurelius Isidorus of Karanis. Isidorus complains to the *praepositus pagi* that a group of drunken youths broke into his house, vandalized it, and stole whatever they could lay their hands on, before finally being scared off by the female members of his household.[34]

It seems unlikely that this is a completely straightforward case of a drunken prank that has got a little out of hand. Isidorus identifies each

[32] Harper (forthcoming), citing further comparative literature. Cf., for medieval France, Le Roy Ladurie (1978), 33; 43–4.

[33] Sommier (1996), 482–4. Also Heppenstall (1971), 151; Aguilar (1984), 19–20. Cf., for the early medieval period, Wickham (2005b), 390–1.

[34] *P. Cairo Isid.* 75 (316).

member of the group by name, stresses that they had no grievance against him, and emphasizes his own blamelessness in the affair. While we should be suspicious of his protestations, there is no way of tracing his relations with the individuals in question. Nevertheless, we may imagine that there was history of some sort between him and one or more of his attackers.[35] We may imagine also that some, at least, among this group had misgivings, second thoughts, or regrets after the fact. We catch glimpses here of the contradictory expectations and assumptions that friendship carries with it. On the one hand, friends cooperate with each other regardless of the circumstances. On the other, they are acutely aware of the potential for disagreement or conflict amongst themselves, and torn by complex, perhaps even contradictory, collections of loyalties and connections. Simeon the Stylite's hagiographer preserves a curious tale of a group of men destroying the cucumber garden of one of their neighbors. Ultimately, the group is caught and punished one by one. Credit for this is, naturally enough, attributed to the holy man, but it is possible that we observe here the disintegration of the group's solidarity as a result of some internal conflict or disagreement in the aftermath of their attack upon their neighbor.[36]

The same spectrum of cooperation and competition, trust and distrust is found in the comic text commonly referred to as the *Querolus*. The protagonist is largely a stock character of comedy, bad-tempered and gullible. But his relationship with his neighbor is nevertheless instructive, and may reasonably be taken as representative of the types of relationships that might exist in the smaller, more dispersed communities of the western Mediterranean. Querolus evinces a deep hostility to the members of his community in general, and his closest neighbor, Arbiter, in particular. However, these statements sit uneasily with comments made by his slave, Pantomalus about the close connections between Querolus and Arbiter, and we must imagine that the two attitudes are complementary aspects of a complex relationship.[37] Indeed, when conmen convince Querolus to allow them access to his home, ostensibly to consult with and appease various spirits who are responsible for his misfortune, but in reality to steal his inheritance, he sends for Arbiter to be his companion while he waits for the ceremony to be concluded. By the time Arbiter arrives, the con has been

---

[35] For identification of these individuals elsewhere in the papyrological sources, see the editors' introductory comments on this text.

[36] *V. Sim. Styl. (S)* 39.

[37] *Querolus* 27; 30; 73. Cf. Santos-Granero (2007) on friendship as a mechanism for neutralizing potentially antagonistic relations.

revealed, and Querolus enlists him as an ally against the outsiders.[38] Conflict and cooperation are interdependent elements in the relationship between the two men. Even as they consider themselves to be friends, they are simultaneously in a constant state of competition over resources and social position.[39]

Personal relationships between family and friends bring with them a degree of intimacy and expectation that are potentially as disruptive as they are supportive.[40] Alongside these types of relationships, peasants often join groups within their communities whose explicit or implicit aim is mutual insurance against risk, or participate as business partners in cooperative economic ventures.[41] We catch fleeting glimpses of these ventures in the late Roman world, in the form of *pittakia* and other types of agricultural partnerships, commercial contracts, and the collective ownership of plow animals.[42] In addition, we may assume that the *capitula* and other fiscal collectivities of the late Roman tax system also contributed to a household's capacity to manage its subsistence risk, for the principle of collective responsibility for taxes is likely to have fostered some impulse towards mutual aid. Indeed, the state's practice of assigning liturgies and other portions of a municipality's total tax burden to particular areas of land is likely to have expanded the options available to some small landowners, at least. We may take as an example the *capitulum*, a geographically contiguous area of land that was held responsible for the supply of a military recruit or sum of money in lieu of such a recruit. Consequently, small and large landowners might find themselves held collectively responsible for this liturgy, and we may imagine that the former could, perhaps, call upon the latter for aid based on this connection.[43]

Occasionally it is possible to gain some further information about connections between the participants in these collective ventures. A series of *pittakion* lists in the collection of Aurelius Isidorus, for example, reveal a certain amount of continuity in the membership of the group from list to

---

[38] *Querolus* 65–6; 92–100.   [39] Cf. Bailey (1971), 18–9; Hutson (1971), 49; Heppenstall (1971), 141–2.

[40] Cf. Aguilar (1984), 24; Chong (1992), 689.

[41] Cf. Ligon, Thomas, and Worrall (2002), 210; Richardson (2003), 301–2; cf., for a detailed discussion of such institutions in medieval English agriculture, Richardson (2005).

[42] *Pittakia*: see, e.g., *P. Cair. Isid.* 24–6 (first quarter fourth century); *P. Col.* 7.159 (344–5, Karanis); *P. Mich.* 12.651 (360, Karanis). Collective tenancies and leases: e.g., *P. Cair. Isid.* 98 (291); 103 (early fourth century). Collective ownership of land: *P. Sakaon* 3 (300). Commercial contracts: e.g. *P. Oxy.* 1896 (577). Cf. Lirb (1993), 280; 284–7; 293. Collective ownership and use of resources: Ulpian, *Dig.* xix.5.17.3; Justinian, *Inst.* iii.24.2; *P. Ness.* iii.32 (sixth century). Cf. Foxhall (1990), 107; Lirb (1993), 279–84.

[43] *Capitula*: e.g. *CTh* vii.6.3 (370). See in particular Carrié (1993c), 121–30. Further discussion below, 214–16.

list.[44] Isidorus and his brothers Heras, Heron, Demetrius, and Pancratius appear in each list, together with one of their nephews and another man, also named Demetrius. This Demetrius' connection with the other six is otherwise unclear, and it is possible that his relationship with them was restricted to their co-membership of this *pittakion*. Beyond these seven, however, there is considerable variation in the composition of the list. In one, the group seems to be more or less completed by the addition of other members of the families of the original seven. But in others, it is more difficult to trace connections between the extended family of Isidorus and the individuals named. A fragmentary contract between Isidorus and Tanouphis, the only woman appearing in these lists, seems to suggest that her son had stood in for Isidorus in the fulfillment of some kind of liturgy, but we have no way of knowing whether there was any connection between this and her participation in the *pittakion* under Isidorus' name.[45] It seems clear that undertakings such as this agricultural collectivity could, and perhaps frequently did, include a mix of close kin, friends, and others whose social links were somewhat more tenuous.

A further example of mixed membership in an economic collectivity is provided by a contract for a loan of seed from the state, contained among the documents of Aurelius Sakaon. In all, sixteen men are named. Of these, we can with a certain degree of confidence trace familial relationships of one sort or another that link nine together. Alongside Sakaon and two of his brothers are a brother-in-law, a nephew, and two great-great-nephews, while Melas is also involved, as well as a nephew and one of his grand-children. A further three comprise a family group of their own, made up of two brothers and the son of one of them. Of the remaining three men, one, Arion, had previously acted as surety for Sakaon on a loan and may have later served alongside his great-great-nephew Alypios as *sitologos*. He also acts alongside Sakaon here as surety for this loan. Another, Hatres by name, may have had some kind of connection of friendship with the family of Melas, for he could be the same Hatres mentioned alongside Aoug in a complaint of Sakaon.[46] The group is completed by an individual named Pasis, who may be the same man whom we witness in another document selling wool. But any explicit connections with his fellows in this loan are now lost to us.[47]

---

[44] *P. Cair. Isid.* 24–6 (first quarter fourth century), with the commentary of Boak and Youtie in their edition of the papyri.

[45] *P. Cair. Isid.* 123 (317).   [46] *P. Sakaon* 43 (327), with further analysis below.

[47] *P. Sakaon* 95 (301); 96 (303). Cf. *P. Sakaon* 97 (305–7), where he is identified as a shepherd on the estate of a certain Alypios.

The documents in the collections of both Isidorus and Sakaon suggest that family and friends did participate in business ventures together, and it is not difficult to imagine that in such circumstances issues of trust and accountability might be considered slightly less pressing than in cases where the participants were not as well known to one another. For our current purposes, however, it is the individuals whose connections are the most tenuous that are of most interest to us, for their presence in this group offers hints of the ways in which familial bonds and friendships might be complemented by alliances that revolved more around shared financial or business interests. Those alliances could then function as a further mechanism for mitigating risk, for participants were mutually implicated and, in the case under discussion here, responsible to the state for the repayment of their loan. The role of the state in creating tax collectivities and determining the composition of collective tenancies has already been noted, and it receives further attention in a later chapter. Here, it suffices to observe that such groups are likely to have had certain positive impacts upon the capacity of peasant households and communities to manage their subsistence risk, but may also have increased the potential for tension and disagreement. As we shall see, the tangled webs that connected the various members of these collectivities will also have rendered the decisions of both individuals and groups complex and fraught exercises.[48]

The potential benefits of these collectivities for the management of subsistence risk have already been noted. They spread a household's web of contacts more broadly, and, in the case of *capitula* at least, may also have brought them into partnership with wealthier landowners, who might as a consequence look with more favor upon any request for aid. But these groups can also be sources of dissatisfaction and conflict between their participants. More fortunate or careful members of the collectivity may come to resent the disparity between their contributions and their returns, and seek to leave the group. Individuals may happily receive the benefits of membership but be unwilling or unable to meet the attendant obligations.[49] It is possible that something of this sort lies behind an assault on the property of Sakaon by four men whom he identifies by name: Heron, Hatres, Pennis, and Aoug.[50] It is unlikely that there is a direct connection between this particular attack and the shared loan agreement that may have

---

[48] Below, 103–4.
[49] Aguilar (1984), 10; Smith and Boyd (1990), 179; Biele, Rieskamp, and Czienskowski (2008), 90.
[50] *P. Sakaon* 43 (327).

included Sakaon, Hatres, and Aoug's father, Melas, for the two events are separated by over a decade. Nevertheless, we should certainly not believe Sakaon's protestations that he has no idea why these men sought to take two and a half *arourae* from his landholdings, for no doubt he knows very well and is consciously choosing not to divulge that information here. It is therefore tempting to interpret the act as an attempt by these men to recover or secure Sakaon's promised portion of some collective endeavor. In any event, from the willingness with which Sakaon goes to the *praepositus pagi* here, we may surmise that there was a legal apparatus available for settling disputes within collectivities such as this. That apparatus is likely to have complemented communal mechanisms for enforcing or encouraging conformity with the aims of the group. In these ways some, at least, of the risks associated with shared economic activities of this sort will have been mitigated.

Together, these social strategies provided a web of contacts and connections, who could be called upon at times of economic need in order to minimize the risk of subsistence crisis. Fostering personal relationships is also likely to have functioned as a buffering mechanism against social risk, serving as a brake upon the fissile tendencies and the potential for conflict within a community, and providing a means for settling disputes through the mediation of individuals with links to both parties. The precise configuration of an individual household's network will depend upon a variety of factors including the makeup of his or her household, the availability and proximity of neighbors and kin, its social standing and economic resources. The will of Remigius reveals a certain Iovia, for example, who appears to be a single woman holding a tenancy in northern Gaul. She will have required an entirely different network of support from collections of veterans and their families, who might form joint households in order to open up marginal lands in frontier regions.[51] One feature common to all, however, is that they carried with them the need to strike a balance between the best interests of the household on the one hand, and the obligations and responsibilities attendant upon participation in a group, on the other. It is here that we encounter the phenomenon of reciprocity, a concept that, like risk, covers a broad semantic field and defies simple or succinct definition.

---

[51] Northern Gaul: *Testamentum S. Remigii* 69. Veterans and marginal lands: *CTh* VII.20.8 (364, *ad provinciales*); 11 (368/370, to Jovinus, *magister militum*). Also *De Rebus Bellicis* v.5, suggesting turning veterans into agriculturalists. Cf., for Egypt under the High Empire, Alston (1995), 39–52; and, for comparative perspectives, Ring (1979), 17–8; Goldschmidt and Kunkel (1971), 1066.

VOCABULARIES AND PRACTICES OF RECIPROCITY

What is reciprocity? In his account of the life of the Syrian holy man Publius, the early fifth-century hagiographer Theodoret of Cyrrhus demonstrates a clear, if theoretically unsophisticated understanding of the phenomenon:[52]

> Just as in city markets one sells bread, another vegetables, one trades in clothes while another makes shoes, and so supplying their needs from each other they live more contentedly – the one who provides a piece of clothing receives a pair of shoes in exchange, while the one who buys vegetables supplies bread – so it is right that we should supply each other with the precious components of virtue.

Theodoret's picture is undeniably an idealized version of the internal workings of urban communities, but it nevertheless provides a useful point from which to begin a discussion of reciprocity in rural contexts as well. His account highlights a series of analytical problems that have been the subject of considerable debate in contemporary scholarship on the subject. Scholars generally agree that reciprocity entails a system of exchange that is not principally governed by the commercial logic of the marketplace, but disagree over the extent to which reciprocity and market exchange might coexist in the same community. They acknowledge that the system contains a collection of expectations and obligations that together constitute a set of social rules, but are divided over the role that those rules play in ensuring that an individual embraces the obligations as well as the benefits of reciprocity. They concur that power structures and reciprocal relationships are likely to be interdependent aspects of a community's social matrix, but differ over the relative influence that the two might have in determining the structure and nature of the community in question. These debates hinge, ultimately, on whether reciprocity is to be regarded as a mechanism for ensuring social cohesion, or a tool for perpetuating the reproduction of social inequality.[53] In what follows, I engage briefly with each problem, before proposing a strategy for analyzing reciprocity that consciously

---

[52] Theodoret, *Hist. Rel.* v.4, trans. Price. See the discussion of de Ligt (1991), 38; de Ligt (1993), 132–3. Cf. Patlagean (1977), 261–77.

[53] Social cohesion: Durkheim (1933); Malinowski (1922); Mauss (1923–4); Polanyi (1944), (1977); Molm, Collett, and Schaefer (2007), 205–6. Ultimately, this position derives from Hobbes's notion of the social contract. Social reproduction: Gouldner (1960), 164; Foucault (1982), 226; Bourdieu (1977), (1990); Narotzky and Moreno (2002), 288; Galbraith (2003), 86. Note also Bliege Bird, Bird, Alden Smith, and Kushnick (2002), 317–18, who provide a collection of critiques by behavioral ecologists, experimental economists, and anthropologists of the very concept of reciprocity as a system of exchange.

embraces its ambiguous position as both a stabilizing and a disruptive force in a community.[54]

Scholarship on reciprocity may be traced back to the accounts of Malinowski and Mauss in the first quarter of the twentieth century, whose approaches may be characterized as, respectively, structuralist and relational. Malinowski sketched the structural components of the kula, an exchange system among Trobriand Islanders which involved the almost continual circulation of prestige goods as gifts, and served principally to enhance the social prestige of participants in the exchange.[55] Mauss focused upon pre-industrial societies more broadly, identifying a social universe characterized and underpinned by an ethos of exchange that entailed mutual obligations on both giver and receiver.[56] Mauss's analysis was adopted and given a more rigorous typological structure by Sahlins, who identified three distinct types of reciprocity: generalized reciprocity, whereby individuals share goods and labor with another without the explicit expectation of return; balanced reciprocity, between two individuals who implicitly or explicitly expect a future return; and negative reciprocity, which amounts to an attempt to get something for nothing, through such diverse means as barter, haggling, trickery, and theft.[57] Subsequent scholarship has augmented and refined Sahlins' typology. Bourdieu, for example, observed that the period of time between gift and counter-gift must be carefully negotiated, since the initial giver should be compensated for the length of time during which he or she has been deprived of what was lent. This has important implications for the nature of the relationship between the participants, and the balance of power between the two.[58] In an equally influential modification of structuralist approaches, Lévi-Strauss distinguished between direct exchange, involving individuals in a dyadic relationship with one another, and indirect exchange, in which an individual might share goods or labor with another individual, only to have that contribution returned eventually by a third party.[59] Forty years later, however, Sahlins' analysis remains largely intact, and has been adopted as a typology for

---

[54] See now the detailed and systematic argument for this interpretation of reciprocity in Narotzky and Moreno (2002).

[55] Malinowski (1922). For a recent restatement of the utility of a structural approach to reciprocity, see Molm, Collett, and Schaefer (2007).

[56] Mauss (1923–1924).   [57] Sahlins (1965), 147–9.

[58] Bourdieu (1977); (1990). Bourdieu regarded this as another way in which relations of power, inequality, and exploitation could be perpetuated. For implications and applications of this insight, see, for example Galbraith (2003), 78–9; Ferraro (2004), 83; Wickham (2005b), 538–9.

[59] Lévi-Strauss (1969). Lévi-Strauss's typology has been the subject of much debate in the scholarly literature. Cf. the discussion of Molm, Collett, and Schaefer (2007), 206–11.

characterizing reciprocal exchange, and determining the particular form that reciprocity takes in a given context.

This approach seems to be unnecessarily limited. Sahlins' three forms of reciprocity should properly be regarded as ideal types, heuristic tools that function to organize the empirical reality, but neither describe that reality in its entirety nor prescribe what form it should take.[60] Viewed in this way, general, balanced, and negative reciprocity can be interpreted as three abstract forms of reciprocal exchange that represent a hypothetical, notional set of interactions. The reality of exchange within a rural community or communities is unlikely to be restricted to one form or the other – indeed, we may imagine that all three forms of exchange coexist in most contexts. In particular, we should expect the members of rural communities in the late Roman world to have participated in complex systems of direct and indirect reciprocal exchange of goods and services, at the same time as they were enmeshed in market-based exchange involving money. Each form of exchange entails a distinct moral code, with the result that within a single community a variety of moral economies operate concurrently.[61] The mix of the three forms of exchange and their attendant sets of moral expectations is likely to differ from community to community, in response to local socio-economic conditions, and will serve as an indicator of what we may call the social health of each community – that is, its capacity to maintain a balance between the impulse towards communal cohesion and the tendency for conflict and fission.

I suggest here that reciprocal relations in rural communities are the subject of constant, ongoing negotiations. Those negotiations are carried out in both words and deeds, as an established vocabulary of reciprocity is accessed by various actors with diverse purposes. An individual such as Publius, for example, might embrace the vocabulary of reciprocity in pursuit of his purpose to encourage the monks under his care to undertake the obligations of communal life. A relatively humble peasant might seek to establish a friendship with a more influential figure in his community by recourse to elaborate gifts, invitations to dine, and expressions of affection in public.[62] Villagers could entrust the care of their sheep to certain

---

[60] Sahlins himself observes of his typology that "it is bogus, really just a metaphor of exposition, not a true history of experiment": Sahlins (1965), 145. Cf. Hovelsrud-Broda (2000), 194.

[61] Shared moral codes ensure the perpetuation of reciprocal systems: Narotzky and Moreno (2002), 290. Multiple moral codes and exchange systems: Codd (1971), 189–90; 200–1; Aguilar (1984), 6; Parry and Bloch (1989), 9; Hovelsrud-Broda (2000), 195; Narotzky and Moreno (2002), 295; Galbraith (2003), 73; Ferraro (2004), 78–9.

[62] Cf. Aguilar (1984), 15–16; 23.

individuals, who acted as shepherds for the whole community, or undertake to compensate or partially support the potter or blacksmith who plied his trade on a full- or part-time basis within the community. A fisherman might count on catching enough fish to exchange for other foodstuffs. Itinerant woodchoppers and professional reapers, living either within the community or on its margins, might also legitimately expect to be included in a community's web of reciprocal interactions.[63]

In each case, the actors reveal that they have a relatively clear understanding of the way that they wish reciprocity to function. Equally, however, it is evident that the reality may be quite different.[64] Shepherds and agriculturalists might clash over access to land, for example, or damage to crops by livestock, and the papyrological sources betray traces of just such conflicts.[65] Overtures of friendship might be taken advantage of, rebuffed or not reciprocated, and we have, perhaps, already observed something of this sort in the petition of Melas against Sakaon's attempts to dissolve a marriage alliance between the two families. A similar case of an initial offer of friendship or hospitality being later withdrawn may lie behind an encounter between Martin and a householder in the city of Trèves. As Sulpicius tells the story, Martin was visiting this city, and had just entered into the dwelling of a certain householder when he discerned a demon sitting in the courtyard. The demon immediately possessed one of the householder's dependents, who raged at all and sundry, but particularly at the saint. Martin thrust his fingers into the demoniac's mouth, then exorcised the demon, who left the body as diarrhea.[66]

The story should be read on multiple levels. For Sulpicius, it provides an example of the miraculous powers of the saint, first in discerning the demon and then in successfully combating it. The focus of his attention is therefore upon the act of exorcism and the power of the saint that this act makes manifest. But this stock hagiographical trope of demonic possession resonated with its audience, for whom demons and demonic possession were recognized, recognizable, and tangible phenomena.[67] Therefore, for our

---

[63] Shepherds: Kaplan (1992), 195; 483–8; Neri (1998), 143–51. Blacksmiths and potters: Palladius, *Op. Ag.* VI.4.1; VII.2.1; Theodoret, *Hist. Rel.* XIII.1. Woodchoppers and reapers: *CJ* XII.33.3 (Arcadius and Honorius to Pulcher, *mag. mil.*); Gregory of Tours, *Glor. Conf.* 30; *V. Sim. Styl.(S)* 11. Cf. Montanari (2003).

[64] Cf. Bourdieu's notion of misrecognition, and note modifications and nuances of the concept in Narotzky and Moreno (2002), 287; 291; Galbraith (2003), 80–1; Voirol (2004).

[65] E.g. *P. Cair. Isid.* 78 (324); 9 (early fourth century). Fuller discussion in Keenan (1985).

[66] Sulpicius Severus, *V. Mart.* 17. Cf. Molm, Collett, and Schaefer (2007), 212.

[67] E.g. Constantius, *V. Germani* 13.7–10, 16.5–8; Salvian, *De Gubernatione Dei* VI.3.14. Cf. Flint (1991), 20; 101–8; Stancliffe (1983), 209; 215–27; 252. Note the slightly more nuanced and cautious observations of Horden (1993), 182–4. Also Grey (2005), 52–3.

current purposes, it is the demonically inspired attack upon Martin and the motivation behind this attack that are of most interest, for the expected norms of hospitality appear to have been completely abandoned here. We might simply dismiss the story as an example of a medical condition being couched in terms appropriate to the times, for the symptoms described seem quite reminiscent of an epileptic fit of some sort. But to do so misses the point, for our ancient sources reveal both an awareness of the distinctions between "medical" and "demonological" afflictions and a tendency to blur the boundaries between the two.[68]

We should not be surprised, therefore, if individual actors, either consciously or unconsciously, did the same. It is therefore possible that the motif of demonic possession here provided a convenient vocabulary for expressing a potentially unwelcome or unpopular emotion, one which, moreover, was likely to channel responses down a clearly defined, controllable path. Further, if the householder in question did have a change of heart over an offer of hospitality to the saint, he is not alone in transferring the physical expression of that change of heart on to a member of his household. Indeed, Sulpicius preserves a parallel story involving a certain Tetradius, who sought the saint's aid in curing a member of his *familia*. Martin agreed, but only on the condition that Tetradius convert to Christianity. Here, we may interpret the motif of demonic possession functioning as a mechanism for a pagan aristocrat to present his abandonment of his old religious convictions in favor of Christian beliefs as a product of his sense of duty and obligation towards members of his family.[69]

At any rate, figures such as Martin may be observed causing disruption and conflict within the small communities that are the focus of our study, and we will explore some of these conflicts in the pages that follow. Most particularly, we will see that claims or expectations of interpersonal interactions, on the one hand, and the realities of those interactions, on the other, coexisted in a state of perpetual tension. This tension is critical to our understanding of reciprocity as a fundamentally ambiguous and contingent phenomenon, simultaneously fostering social cohesion and emphasizing deep divides within a community.[70] The vocabulary of reciprocity could be consciously or unconsciously misapplied to a given situation, in order to give the impression of a mutually binding interaction, when the reality was of mutual distrust or exploitation of one party by the other. It could be exploited in order to make claims upon another, as in the case of petitions to

---

[68] Grey (2005), 45–7.   [69] Sulpicius Severus, *V. Mart.* 17, with Grey (2005), 66–7.
[70] Narotzky and Moreno (2002), 282; 288; 301.

Imperial officials, which often stress both that official's obligation to behave in the way that the petitioner expects and the petitioner's gratitude to him for doing so.[71]

The diverse objectives of these actors when accessing the vocabulary of reciprocity point to the multifarious ways in which that vocabulary can be manipulated. But they also prompt a more basic question: what motivates an individual or household to participate in reciprocal networks at all? Such a decision characteristically carries with it an undertaking to live as part of some kind of community. That decision, in turn, entails obligations as well as rewards, and exposes the household to an increased risk of social conflict, with the attendant disruptions and frustrations that such conflicts inevitably bring with them.[72] One factor, no doubt, is to minimize the risk of subsistence crisis.[73] By choosing to live in a community and acknowledge the reciprocal structures that are intrinsic to that community, individual households lessen the risk of subsistence crisis, and increase potential strategies for coping with such crisis. If a household in subsistence crisis calls on its neighbors for assistance, they will help – if they can – in order to safeguard their own survival when their own subsistence crisis arises.

However, scholars have long recognized that a purely economic explanation for the embrace of practices and vocabularies of reciprocity is insufficient. Where they remain divided is over what other factors should be considered.[74] The problem can, in part, be circumvented through the adoption of a broadly focused understanding of risk, which allows us to envisage motivations that encompass maintenance of communal cohesion and individual standing within the community, as well as the avoidance of subsistence crisis.[75] Consequently, we should not be surprised to observe individuals consciously accessing the vocabulary and practices of reciprocity as a means for gaining prestige within the community, or establishing a reputation for generosity or trustworthiness. Equally, practices of giving may have less to do with explicit notions of reciprocal exchange and reputation management than with the acknowledgment and embrace of a

---

[71] E.g. *P. Sakaon* 36 (*c.* 280); 37 (284); 38 (312); 40 (318–320).

[72] Cf. Bailey (1971), 4; Heppenstall (1971), 141; Price (2003), 192; Nachi (2004), 292.

[73] Heppenstall (1971), 144; Aguilar (1984), 8; 20–1; Gallant (1991), 146–7; 156–8.

[74] Note the discussions of Smith and Boyd (1990), 174; Hovelsrud-Broda (2000), 193; Bliege Bird, Bird, Alden Smith, and Kushnick (2002), 298; Price (2003), 192; Molm, Collett, and Schaefer (2007), 205–6.

[75] Reyes-García, Godoy, Vadez, Huanca, and Leonard (2006), 83–4; Bereczkei, Birkas, and Kerekes (2007), 278; Molm, Collett, and Schaefer (2007), 210; Biele, Rieskamp, and Czienskowski, (2008), 101–3; 96.

particular communal code of morality.[76] On the other hand, we must also countenance a dark side to the decision to enact notions of reciprocity, as individuals attempt to make claims upon others for goods or services, without necessarily acknowledging the obligation that such claims place upon themselves. The success or failure of this strategy is connected in part to the effectiveness of a community's mechanisms for enforcing full participation in communal activities, and, in what follows, I explore the occasional, fleeting glimpses of those mechanisms in the late Roman sources.

It seems reasonable to suggest that motivations for participation in reciprocal networks will vary according to the individual and his or her objectives, and will characteristically comprise a mix of personal and communal factors.[77] The broad applicability of the notion of reciprocity, and the diverse ends to which it might be accessed may perhaps best be illustrated with reference to circumstances which might not, at first, seem to involve the vocabulary of reciprocity at all. In some situations, we observe a gift, or the appearance of a gift, being offered in order to ensure an individual's ability to make a claim upon others. A fourth-century law appears to provide one such example when it singles out for censure peasants who give gifts to powerful government officials for purposes of tax evasion.[78] While the object of the exercise may not in reality have been quite so directly instrumental, it seems reasonable to assume that there was some expectation of a return for the gifts in question.

Cases such as this emphasize the interdependence of giving and taking in reciprocal networks. They also reveal that the balance between the two favors the latter: one either gives with the explicit intention of receiving, or takes as a prelude to giving. In these instances, the giver gives, but is motivated as much by the desire to receive as by the impulse to give.[79] We may gauge just how deeply ingrained expectations of reciprocity were in late antique communities from the acts of the holy bishop Rabbula in the city of Edessa in the early fifth century. Rabbula's hagiographer lavishes particular attention upon his hero's spectacular acts of giving, observing that he even gave charity to Jews. He was as a result successful in winning over many converts, for his gifts to them were accompanied by constant exhortations to embrace Christianity.[80] The impulse to obtain a return from a gift that we might expect to have been given in a somewhat more disinterested

---

[76] Cf. Howe (1998), 535–6; Bliege Bird, Bird, Alden Smith, and Kushnick (2002), 316–17; Galbraith (2003), 79.
[77] Gintis (2003), 156; Reyes-García (2006), 82–4; Molm, Collett, and Schaefer (2007), 213.
[78] *CTh* XI.11.1 (368), with further discussion below, 164.
[79] Narotzky and Moreno (2002), 288–9; 301.   [80] *Heroic Deeds of Mar Rabbula*, 94.

fashion is clear: by making a direct, instrumental connection between charity and religious conversion, Rabbula's hagiographer – and, arguably, Rabbula himself – reveals that notions of reciprocity infused ancient understandings of interpersonal relations, even in circumstances where the familiarity and closeness of the relationship was open to question.[81]

A contrasting story, also connected with charity, comes from the Palestinian Talmud, where a certain Rabbi Hiyya bar Adda is reported to have remarked upon the fact that some among the elderly will happily accept charity in the months between Rosh Hashanah and the Great Fast, but will not do so at other times.[82] During these months, mutual gift-giving is an accepted practice, so it would appear that their aim here is to camouflage their receipt of alms under a more general and widespread practice of reciprocal generosity. While the reality is that they are receiving without giving anything in return, they seek to construct and participate in a fiction of reciprocity. The construction of this fiction speaks again to the powerful pull of reciprocity as a structuring principle and a force for social cohesion. But it also reveals some more unpalatable realities of reciprocal exchange, for differential giving can serve to perpetuate inequalities within a community.[83]

Fictions of reciprocity can be observed in other situations, too, where an individual may consider it expedient to give even to those who are unwilling or unable to return the gift. While Rabbula appears to have hit upon a strategy for turning even charity into a reciprocal exchange, the remarks of Rabbi Hiyya bar Abba reveal that this type of giving is usually interpreted as one such example. We may place alongside this instances of provisions for public feasting or offers of oil and grain to the village community at large.[84] Such acts of beneficence appear to come closest to resembling pure altruism, but in these circumstances, too, there are both tangible and intangible rewards to be gained. We may therefore surmise that the motivations of some individuals in these cases were mixed at best. Jerome provides a particularly telling example of the disjunction between the appearance of giving and the motivation underpinning it when he describes a contrived scene of public benefaction in the city of Rome:[85]

---

[81] Cf. Saller (1982), 15.   [82] *pPeah* 8.9.
[83] Cf. Maximus of Turin, *Serm.* xcviii, with further discussion below, 106–8.
[84] E.g. Theodoret *Hist. Rel.* xiv.2. See further below, 106.
[85] Jerome, *The Letters of St. Jerome* 22.32, trans. Mierow. For discussion of appearances and the importance of seeming to be generous, cf. Price (2003), 193; Wedekind and Braithwaite (2002), 1014; Bereczkei, Birkas, and Kerekes (2007), 277–8. On the strategic thinking behind these public acts, see Olsen (2009), 375–7.

Recently I saw the most prominent lady in Rome (I do not mention her name, lest you think I am writing satire) in St. Peter's Basilica, attended by her eunuchs. She was dispensing charity to the beggars, giving them a penny apiece. Meanwhile – as might easily have been expected – a certain old woman conspicuous for her years and her rags ran to the head of the line to get another penny. When she had reached the lady in due course, she received instead of the coin a blow with the fist. She was guilty of so great an offense that her blood was shed.

The context of this exchange is, of course, urban, and the focus of Jerome's attention is a member of the aristocracy. Nevertheless, the example high-lights the potential for acts of giving to be fundamentally public events, motivated as much by an estimation of longer-term gains as by a sense of compassion, generosity, or altruism. In this instance, as, no doubt, in others, the decision to share resources is predicated upon a conscious or unconscious calculation of the potential for future benefits, which is weighed against the short-term cost of the act. Those future benefits may include material goods, received either directly from the recipient, or indirectly from a third party. They are also likely, as in this case, to entail an enhancement of the individual's reputation and standing in the community.[86]

The constraints of living in a community might create situations where individuals find themselves participating in reciprocal or communal activ-ities that seem at first glance to be at odds with the best interests of their individual households. Enforcement of these expectations may take the form of social sanctions or legal structures. This phenomenon finds partic-ularly striking expression in a story related by Eugippius in his account of the life of St. Severinus of Noricum. The fortified settlement of Cucullis, we are told, experienced a plague of locusts, and the inhabitants called upon the saint for aid. In response, he exhorted them to gather together and pray, forbidding anybody to travel to his fields and attempt to stop the locusts alone. However, Eugippius reveals that a poor man left his prayers only half done, and sought to protect his small field. The next day it was discovered that all the fields of the community except his had been miraculously spared. The message that individuals must subjugate their desires to the common weal could not be more emphatically expressed. However, once the lesson is learned, the transgressor is quickly reintegrated by the very

---

[86] Longer-term gains: Price (2003), 192; Wedekind and Braithwaite (2002), 1014; Molm, Collett, and Schaefer (2007), 213; Biele, Rieskamp, and Czienskowski (2008), 101. Reputation-building as a strategy: Bereczkei, Birkas, and Kerekes (2007), 278; Sommerfeld, Krambeck, and Milinski (2008), 2529. For the continued emphasis on the giver rather than the receiver in the late Roman world, cf. MacMullen (1990), 265.

mechanism that he so recently scorned. His entreaties for aid are heeded, and the community contributes to his livelihood as an investment both in the individual's acquisition of humility and the group's collective cohesion.[87]

Several different systems of reciprocal exchange coexisted in the rural communities of the late Roman world.[88] It is important to recognize that the inhabitants of those communities were aware of this complexity, and sensitive too to the opportunities it provided for exploiting a variety of socio-economic networks, and ensuring their ability to call on a number of different resources when necessary. As we have seen, peasants may seek a marriage alliance with one household, be involved in multi-stranded relations of friendship and mutual insurance with another, and habitually take part in market exchanges with a third.[89] Whatever resources a household had available for such exchanges will have been limited, however, with the result that individual households needed to choose between a number of potential exchange partners, or were forced to distribute material or physical aid differentially. We may imagine that one criterion upon which such decisions were made was the relative standing of potential partners or recipients in the community, for reputation is a powerful component of an individual's apparatus of risk management, and a crucial factor in his or her ability to call upon neighbors, friends, and peers.[90]

THE POLITICS OF REPUTATION

The phenomena highlighted by Jerome's example of self-consciously public benefaction are equally valid when we turn to the small, face-to-face rural communities of the late Roman world. Scholars have long recognized the fundamental importance that individuals attach to their standing within such communities. Peasants guard their reputations jealously, and often, it seems, seek to assail those of their peers.[91] Even friends are not necessarily immune from this impulse, as the example of Querolus and his neighbor Arbiter reveals. Assaults upon the reputation of a neighbor, or attacks upon an enemy may focus upon a perceived unwillingness to recognize or conform to the expectations and obligations of communal

---

[87] Eugippius, *V. Sev.* 12.
[88] Cf. Hovelsrud-Broda (2000), 199; Narotzky and Moreno (2002), 295–8.
[89] *P. Sakaon* 3 (300); 23 (324); 49 (314); 51 (324).
[90] Cf. Chong (1992), 701; Galbraith (2003), 82; Biele, Rieskamp, and Czienskowski (2008), 102.
[91] Bailey (1971), 18–19; Hutson (1971), 49. With specific reference to Roman Egypt, Bryen (2008b), 184–5; 195–9.

existence. We observe, for example, accusations of grain-hoarding, theft of water resources, or damage to irrigation networks, as well as suggestions of physical and magical damage to crops.[92]

It is probable that, in most cases, both parties were in fact known to one another, for anonymous acts in such circumstances seem neither likely nor effective. Consequently, we may imagine that the decision to identify a culprit was a powerful weapon in the internecine struggles that lay beneath the surface of the vignettes that survive in our sources.[93] In a group of petitions sent within a fairly short time of one another, Isidorus moves from expressing ignorance about the identity of the men responsible for burning his threshing floor to identifying them explicitly by name.[94] Similarly, when a man comes to Simeon the Stylite complaining that his garden has been destroyed, the saint has no trouble in identifying the perpetrators and ensuring that they suffer horrible punishments for their act. While his hagiographer presents this as an example of Simeon's prescience, it is likely that, just as in the case of Sakaon's professed ignorance of the reasons behind an attempt by some of his neighbors to detach from him a portion of his landholdings, this man is perfectly aware of the identity of those responsible for the attack, and their motivations for doing so.[95]

The likelihood of victim and perpetrator knowing each other and the focus upon disruption or destruction of crops and water are eloquent testimony to the fine balance between subsistence and social risk in these communities, for both are imperiled in such circumstances. A threat to or attack upon a neighbor's means of subsistence is a powerful rejection of that neighbor's entitlement to enjoy the basics necessary for survival, and a blow struck at the place where he is most vulnerable. Further, an attack upon the community's agricultural resources amounts to an attack upon its economic lifeblood, and therefore an attack also upon its social fabric.[96] Therefore, by accusing an enemy of such an act, peasants reveal a clear understanding of the fact that an individual's reputation is likely to suffer the greatest damage in this particular context.

We may attribute the close attention paid to reputation in large part to the license a good reputation gives an individual to call upon others at moments of economic or social risk. In circumstances where resources are

---

[92] Grain-hoarding: Eugippius, *V. Sev.* 3 and below, 113. Water resources: *P. Sakaon* 33 (320); 34 (*c.* 332) and below, 113–14. Damage to crops: see, e.g., Bryen and Wypustek (2009), 34–5. Cf. also accusations of illicit sheep-shearing: e.g. *P. Abinn.* 48–9; *P. Sakaon* 31; 36; 46.
[93] Cf. Bryen (2008a), 170–80.
[94] *P. Cair. Isid.* 65 (298/299); 66 (299); 67 (299). Also *P. Cair. Isid.* 124 (298) and below, 115–16.
[95] *V. Sim. Styl. (S)* 39.   [96] Further discussion below, 116.

limited, and an individual's or household's choice to help one neighbor or friend will inevitably involve a corresponding decision to withhold from another, the benefits of a good reputation should not be underestimated. It is on the basis of reputation that an individual's capacity or justification to legitimately make a claim upon his or her fellows is judged. Consequently, recent scholarship has posited instrumental connections between reputation management, the ability to access or manipulate networks of reciprocity, and the successful maintenance of strategies for mitigating economic and social risk.[97] In what follows, I build upon these connections by turning attention to the mechanics of reputation construction and management in the rural communities of the late Roman world. In accord with the tenets sketched in the previous chapter, I adopt a relational perspective and suggest that reputation is not a resource owned by the individual, but rather a collection of qualities attributed to him or her by others.[98] Consequently, attempts to enhance one's reputation are only as effective as the impression they make upon one's fellows. In particular, I emphasize the role of gossip and rumor in constructing and maintaining an individual's reputation, whether good or bad.[99]

Reputation amounts to the collection of opinions that other members of a community hold of an individual. One may attempt to influence those opinions, and therefore that reputation, by actions and words. Public building, feasting, and other acts of generosity towards the community are part of an individual's repertoire of reputation management. Such behavior often entails compromise, as individuals trade short-term losses for longer-term gains, or indulge in behavior that appears to be contrary to their self-interest in pursuit of a broader strategy.[100] Sometimes the investment in one's reputation might not appear to be justified by the results. In the course of a discussion with the Lar of his household about what he would wish to be in order to make him happy, Querolus observes that he would like to have the good reputation enjoyed by an advocate. But, once the Lar outlines the sacrifices of his time, energy, and resources that go into building and maintaining such a reputation, Querolus quickly backs down

---

[97] Cf. Chong (1992), 689; Kollock (1999), 102–3; Bliege Bird, Bird, Alden Smith, and Kushnick (2002), 316–17; Bereczkei, Birkas, and Kerekes (2007), 277; Sharman (2007), 23; Clement (2008), 185; Sommerfeld, Krambeck, and Milinski (2008), 2529.

[98] Cf. Bailey (1971), 4; Chong (1992), 693–4; Sharman (2007), 20–1.

[99] Gossip and talk: Hunter (1990), 299–300; Gleason (1998), 503; Fenster and Smail (2003); Sommerfeld, Krambeck, and Milinski (2008), 2529. Impact of a bad reputation: Ligon, Thomas, and Worrall (2002), 213–14; Ferraro (2004), 89. Note, however, Bailey's argument that an individual with a bad reputation is nevertheless still part of the community: Bailey (1971), 7.

[100] Heppenstall (1971), 141–2; Chong (1992), 683.

and agrees that the cost is too high for him to bear.[101] We may place alongside Querolus' reluctance to invest in the construction of his reputation Jerome's aristocratic matron, whose actions reveal the potential for contradiction to exist between public actions and private motivations. Clearly, the woman wished to have a particular reputation, and sought to acquire it in a very public forum. But Jerome's anecdote reveals that this outward appearance of humility and generosity was not matched in her heart.[102]

Ultimately, an individual's reputation lies in the minds and mouths of others. Gossip – or, more neutrally, talk – fulfills a variety of functions. It may serve to bring the mighty back down. It can affirm group expectations or communal cultural practices and beliefs. It can also bolster an individual's standing, or enhance the possibility of trust. Information spreads quickly from one person to another in small communities, and performs both negative and positive functions in those communities.[103] On the one hand, we observe gossip serving as a mechanism for emphasizing the positive qualities of an individual, and singling them out as particularly praiseworthy. Accounts of the lives of the saints characteristically note that the fame of the holy man or woman spreads far and wide, with the result that all manner of pilgrims and petitioners flock to them.[104] In this case, gossip serves to enhance an individual's reputation, and distinguish them within the community, or as a figure who stands outside it.

Gossip may also serve as a mechanism for resistance to or critique of an individual who is deemed threatening, especially in circumstances where those responsible for the gossip feel themselves to have somewhat limited options. Daniel the Stylite's hagiographer notes the attempts of some of the holy man's religious rivals to besmirch his reputation by enlisting a harlot, who spread rumors that she had managed to seduce him.[105] Sulpicius Severus relates that, while visiting the city of Trier, Martin encountered a conspiracy of demoniacs, who admitted to spreading rumors in an attempt to drive the holy man from the city, and this story will receive more

[101] *Querolus* 31.
[102] Cf. Palladius, *Hist. Laus.* 6; 28, a pair of stock tales that warn of the perils of adopting an outward appearance of piety and humility while retaining arrogance in one's heart.
[103] Communal expectations: Bailey (1971), 2; 10–11; Codd (1971), 184; Hunter (1990), 322; Gleason (1998), 502; Wickham (1998), 11–12; 23. Positive and negative functions of gossip: Wickham (1998); Schofield (1998); Fenster and Smail (2003), 9, with further references.
[104] E.g. Theodoret, *Hist. Rel.* 1.7; 11.3; 13; IV.8; *V. Sim. Styl. (S)* 34; Constantius, *V. Germani* 14; 21; 30. Cf. Gleason (1998), 503.
[105] *V. Dan. Styl.* 39.

attention in the following chapter.[106] The resort by these individuals to gossip in their struggle with the saint is testament both to the potential effectiveness of the tactic in such circumstances and to their feelings of disempowerment and marginalization in the face of a new and potentially threatening figure of power.[107]

It is likely that Martin's position as a bishop accorded him a certain degree of institutional authority that complemented the reputation that he possessed as a holy man and wonderworker. By contrast, the ascetics, hermits, and holy figures of Syria and Egypt tended not to be part of the church's ecclesiastical structures, and consequently their reputations rested on somewhat different foundations: their spectacular acts of public self-abnegation, for example, their demonstrated piety and purity, their success as figures of healing, intercession, and exorcism.[108] The reputations of holy figures living in or on the margins of rural communities are therefore likely to have been somewhat more vulnerable to the scrutiny of other residents of those communities, who may in some instances have been unwilling to accord them the position of uniqueness that they claimed.

The experience of Palladius, a hermit living just outside the village of Imma in the Antioch valley, is salutary.[109] Theodoret of Cyrrhus relates that, following a fair in the village, a trader set off for his home carrying a considerable amount of money. He was attacked, robbed, and murdered, and his body was dumped at Palladius' door. The news quickly spread, and an angry throng gathered outside the holy man's dwelling. As Theodoret tells the story, the holy man was able to extricate himself from this predicament by calling upon the dead man to identify the true culprit, which the corpse duly did, to the astonishment of all assembled. But we should not lose sight of the normalizing force of rumor here, or of the object of that rumor. Here, we observe a religious fanatic living on the edge of the community, a man who evidently excited a certain degree of distrust and even envy, and whose claims to sanctity, distinctiveness, and the attendant reputation and respect were in this instance subjected to a powerful challenge. Such challenges are not uncommon in the hagiographical literature of Syria and Egypt, and it is tempting to interpret them as evidence for village

---

[106] Sulpicius Severus, *V. Mart.* 18.
[107] Further discussion below, 101–3. Cf. Wickham (1998), 5–6; 18.
[108] For a reflection upon the reputation and power of the holy man, see Brown (1998), with the collection of responses in the same volume. Also below, 131–2.
[109] Theodoret, *Hist. Rel.* VII.2–3.

communities denying the implicit or explicit claims made by these figures – or their hagiographers – to a position of special authority or influence.[110]

We should interpret these accounts as highly visible examples of a relatively common phenomenon: people talk in small communities, and generally one's private behavior as well as one's public reputation are common knowledge. Eugippius provides a neat encapsulation of the principle when he relates the experience of a paralytic healed by St. Severinus, who was forever afterwards the focus of public comment and discussion every time he was sighted in the town's market.[111] Of course, the potential for one's reputation to be affected by everything that one does can place the individual in an unenviable position. In such circumstances, one cannot afford to behave in one way towards some individuals, and another way towards others, for, as Jerome's example makes clear, the risks of being observed perpetuating such a double standard were high and the potential damage was huge.[112] Equally, holy figures of all stripes in the period needed to be careful lest acts performed in public be interpreted as aimed towards gaining a reputation rather than examples of their piety or the power of the deity. It is probably for this reason that some hagiographers chose to emphasize that their subjects performed healings and exorcisms in private rather than in public.[113] Similarly, in Palestine, Rabbi Liezer was forced to negotiate the implications of being named *parnas*, or benefactor of the poor, in his community. When greeted by the news that some poor people had prayed for him after eating their fill, he elicited disappointment. It was only when he was informed that some had eaten and drunk then cursed him that he expressed satisfaction at the reward he received for his trouble.[114]

These vignettes reveal that an individual's standing within his or her community was the subject of continuous negotiation, and required constant attention. The normative force of gossip and the potential for an isolated, private event to produce a ripple of public opinion and rumor is likely to have created a situation where social interactions within rural communities were charged with meaning, and public events were laden with a raft of expectations. It would be unnecessarily reductionist to interpret all such events as strategies for managing risk, perpetuating

---

[110] Palladius, *Hist. Laus.* 70. Cf. stories of women disguised as male monks, who were falsely accused of rape: e.g. the sixth/seventh-century *V. Mar.* 9–11. Also accounts of holy figures' extreme asceticism disturbing the harmony of their religious communities: e.g. *V. Sim. Styl. (S)* 17.

[111] Eugippius, *V. Sev.* 6.4.

[112] Cf. Chong (1992), 684; 696–7. Note, however, Bailey's observation that cheating in church or the Masonic lodge is regarded in a qualitatively different way from cheating the tax man: Bailey (1971), 8.

[113] E.g., Sulpicius Severus, *V. Mart.* 7–8; Paulinus, *V. Amb.* 14; 28.   [114] *pPeah* 8.7.

reciprocal networks, and negotiating the competing claims of individuals. But it was certainly the case that, for the individual households that comprised the rural communities of the late Roman world, communal living entailed compromise.

Attempts to minimize subsistence risk by participating in a community created a situation where the risk of social conflict was high. Seeking to ensure that one's household would be in a position to receive aid from other households at a time of need entailed participating in reciprocal networks as a giver, and weighing the short-term costs of such behavior against potential longer-term benefits. The business of reputation-management required a keen awareness of the relationship between one's own words and deeds and those of others. In all cases, however, we must assume that the peasants of the late Roman world were self-conscious actors, aware of the potential benefits and costs of their choices. No doubt some individuals were more effective managers of their reputations, more fortunate cultivators, more opportunistic in their responses to circumstances. However, their successes were likely to have been relatively fleeting.

We must therefore imagine that communities possessed mechanisms both for managing the relationship between conflict and cohesion, and for responding quickly when equilibrium between the two was lost. As we shall see in the following chapter, those strategies revolved around expressions and expectations of reciprocal exchange and the subsuming of an individual household's needs to those of the community. They were particularly visible at moments of subsistence or social risk. And they rested, ultimately, upon the capacity of the individuals most intimately involved to manage or exploit their reputation within the community.

CHAPTER 3

Small politics: making decisions, managing tension, mediating conflict

The literary and documentary sources of the late Roman world evince relatively little interest in the internal workings of rural communities, and reveal mechanisms of self-regulation only rarely. But we must assume a diversity in social structures and patterns of interaction that matches the physical diversity of settlements sketched above.[1] For analytical purposes, we may envisage two poles, and assume that in most cases a community will fall somewhere along the spectrum between the two. At one extreme may be placed the more or less egalitarian community of agriculturalists, characterized by relatively poorly developed structures of self-government, and collectively subject to a wealthy patron or landlord. At the other is the highly stratified village community, dominated by an exclusive oligarchy of wealthier peasants, who consciously excluded their less wealthy or powerful neighbors from the business of governing the community, and the status and recognition that this entailed. We should imagine also that the natural state of rural communities both large and small was a delicate equilibrium between the competing and largely contradictory needs of the individuals, households, and families that made up those communities on the one hand, and the cohesion of the group as an effective mechanism for the mitigation and management of subsistence and social risk, on the other. It will be the purpose of this chapter to explore the strategies available to communities in seeking to maintain this equilibrium.

To this end, I briefly sketch the evidence for social differentiation and self-governance within rural communities in the late Roman world. Next, I examine the decision-making processes of individuals and households in those communities, the constraints within which those decisions were made, and the collection of mutually contradictory demands that had to

---

[1] Above, 49–52.

be balanced and evaluated in the process. Then I outline the ways in which inequality and internal tension might be negotiated, paying particular attention to regular mechanisms for the periodic alleviation of jealousy and conflict. Finally, I explore some strategies that these communities might employ for resolving disagreements or disputes that have escalated to a point where they require a specific response or solution. Throughout, I focus principally upon structures that may be considered intrinsic to the community, leaving discussion of their interactions with outsiders for a later chapter. As we shall see, while such a strategy is in a certain sense artificial, it has the benefit of emphasizing the primacy of the community's cohesion and the subsistence survival of its members over the demands, perceptions, and desires of the powerful figures whose perspective has long dominated the study of rural communities in the period.

SOCIAL DIFFERENTIATION AND INTERNAL ORGANIZATION

The rural communities of the late Roman world were not merely collections of socially and economically homogeneous agriculturalists, whose world view was limited to and by the boundaries of their small settlements. As we have seen, those communities characteristically included among their number individuals who filled a variety of economic niches in addition to subsistence farming. They also interacted with both powerful and socially marginal figures living on the edges of their worlds.[2] However it is not easy to move beyond these relatively banal observations and flesh out the internal dynamics of these communities. Our evidence is somewhat fuller and more detailed for the internal organization of the villages of Egypt and Syria, but we should not imagine that differences in wealth and status were completely absent from the hamlets, estates, and farmsteads of the western provinces. There, as in the east, we should expect to encounter individuals with more or less favorable reputations than their fellows, managing more or less successfully to take advantage of opportunities for enrichment or advancement, coping more or less successfully with stresses or pressures upon their resources. In what follows, I explore the evidence for social differentiation in the rural communities of the late Roman world, and signal some implications that will be developed further in this and following chapters.

As we have seen, the countrysides of the western Mediterranean tended to be populated by relatively small communities of agriculturalists, who

---

[2] Above, 28–31.

lived together in hamlets and upon estates. The social matrices of these communities are likely to have been oriented more towards relationships of power, dominance, and dependence with the landlords and patrons who lived alongside them in these landscapes. In the countryside outside Milan, for example, Germanus encountered the retainers of a local *vir spectabilis*, who informed him that this man and his household had been struck down by various illnesses, and begged him to divert from his path and cure them. He agreed to do so, and ministered not only to the estate owner and his immediate household, but also the residents of the surrounding *tuguria*, or cottages. Constantius' description of these events assumes that these individuals were in some sense dependents of the man who sought the aid of the saint, and we observe less benevolent expressions of the same assumption in other western authors.[3]

Nevertheless, we may imagine that these communities had some forms of social differentiation and internal organization, however loosely structured, and we catch occasional glimpses of the mechanisms of self-governance that may have existed within them. While traveling through the small town of Arcis, for example, the Parisian virgin and saint Genovaefa is begged by the tribune to heal his wife, who has been suffering from paralysis for nearly four years. When the elders of the place (*seniores loci illius*) add their voices to the plea, Genovaefa agrees, and promptly heals the woman through prayer and the sign of the cross.[4] There are considerable difficulties with using this account as an accurate reflection of the internal mechanisms of rural communities in the period. Even if Genovaefa's hagiographer has reliably recorded the titles here, we can glean no further information about the role or standing of the *tribunus*, nor do we know whether he was externally appointed or elected from within the ranks of the town's elite. Moreover, while we have no way of quantifying the size of Arcis, its designation as an *oppidum* signals the danger of applying this evidence to the hamlets, farmsteads, and small villages of the Gallic countryside. But the council of *seniores*, at least, rings true and accords with other evidence for customary structures of self-governance that existed within the rural communities of the western Mediterranean.

Certainly, councils of *seniores* can be observed in at least some of the *castella*, *vici*, and *pagi* of North Africa.[5] We may imagine these groups to

---

[3] Constantius, *V. Germani* 33. Cf. below, 151.   [4] *V. Genovefae* 35.

[5] Shaw observes that it is only in North Africa that these groups are attested in the epigraphical evidence: Shaw (1982a), 207. In early medieval Italy, we observe occasional mentions of *priores vici* in rural inscriptions, and it may be possible to interpret these individuals in a similar light: cf. Sannazaro (2003), 44.

have comprised wealthier, more influential or charismatic figures in their communities, and we may posit also both connections of kinship and friendship, and the potential for competition and conflict, between their members. It is difficult to determine how open or closed these bodies might have been from generation to generation, but it seems unlikely that the position of *senior* was hereditary.[6] We might therefore expect these councils to have been relatively fluid in their constitution, according to the fortunes of individuals and households. In the late Roman sources, *seniores* are attested occupying a position of some small authority and respect within the Christian communities of the North African countryside, and it has been convincingly argued that this prominence may be attributed to enduring continuities in the social structures of the hamlets and villages of the region: that is, the respect accorded *seniores* in Christian documents, and the responsibilities attributed to them for enforcing directives concerned with religious matters, is a product of the long-established importance of such groups in rural contexts.[7] However, what precisely their role was, how they enforced compliance with their decisions, the limits and scope of their authority – all remain frustratingly elusive.

It is also possible that alongside these *seniores* were elected officials of one sort or another, although, again, very little epigraphical evidence for magistrates and councils in the *castella* and *vici* of the province has survived from the period.[8] Certainly, we may imagine that, regardless of the existence of formally recognized headmen or leadership groups, communities of this sort looked to an influential or authoritative figure to mediate their relations with outsiders. We occasionally encounter these figures elsewhere in the western sources, too. Constantius tells us, for example, that during Germanus' first visit to Britain, he was stricken by a foot injury and forced to make an unscheduled stop in a nearby settlement, where he convalesced for some period of time. The house in which he stayed during his recovery was thatched with reeds, and appears to have been a relatively humble abode. But we may surmise that, even if this householder lacked the standing of Germanus' other hosts during his travels around Britain, Gaul, and Italy, nevertheless he was a respected member of the community, who will have seized the opportunity to entertain such an exalted figure and garner the attendant prestige.[9]

---

[6] Cf. Shaw (1991), 29–30, hypothesizing a relatively closed group, as in pre-Roman times.

[7] Shaw (1982a), 222–3, and *passim*, provides references and full discussion.

[8] Shaw (1982a), 207; Dossey (2010), 102; 117–20. Cf., for evidence from Italy in the period, Ceccone (1994), 192–9; Sannazaro (2003), 45.

[9] Constantius, *V. Germani* 16. Cf. *V. Germani* 11, where Constantius describes Germanus seeking the hospitality of humble folks, which he greatly preferred over that of the powerful.

For rural communities in the eastern provinces, there is somewhat fuller evidence for social stratification. We may take as an example Egypt, which certainly contained the kinds of physical settlements that would foster communities with a relatively high degree of social differentiation, and we have already witnessed something of the jockeying for position that might go on in such communities.[10] Disputes in these circumstances could take a multitude of forms, and we catch glimpses of one such dispute between Aurelius Isidorus and Acotas, son of Germanus. In Isidorus' presentation, at least, this dispute encompasses both arson and extortion, and we may imagine that ongoing disagreements of this type might also entail physical attacks, theft, use of magic, and gossip.[11] The suspicion remains that the participation in these conflicts was restricted to the wealthiest members of these village communities, although it is possible that fluctuations in the fortunes of individual households meant that the wealthy elite of one generation was superseded by another in subsequent generations.[12] In interactions between these communities and outsiders, a headman or chief magistrate is occasionally visible, acting as spokesman for the community in such dealings, and functioning as an instrument through which the demands of those outsiders were met or mediated.[13] In a dispute before the *defensor civitatis* over who was entitled to enjoy the fruits of the harvest on land that had been abandoned by its owners but sown by members of the local village, it is the headman, speaking through an interpreter, who puts the case for the villagers.[14]

We should not overemphasize the distinction between rural settlements in the west and the east, for these contrasting types of community could coexist in the same landscape.[15] The archive of Aurelius Sakaon, for

[10] Above, 46. Cf. *P. Cair. Masp.* 1 67002 (567, Aphrodito). Bagnall (1993a), 112; 133–6, provides a succinct summary. Competition within village communities: see discussion further below, 105–12, as well as references in MacMullen (1974), 23–4 with notes 72–7. Cf. de Ligt (1990), 49–51.

[11] Isidorus and Acotas: *P. Cair. Isid.* 65–7 (298/299); 69–70 (310). Theft: *P. Abinn.* 45 (343, Arsinoite nome); *P. Abinn.* 47 (346, Arsinoite nome); *SB* XIV.11380 (c. 346, Hermoupolis); *SB* XVIII. 13158 (fourth/fifth century, Oxyrhynchite nome). Magic: Cf. Bryen and Wypustek (2009). Physical violence: e.g. *P. Sakaon* 38 (312). Note, in particular, Bryen (2008b), 184–5, arguing that violence is part of constantly evolving, contingent negotiations of relative positions in the community. Cf. Wickham (2005b), 415. Note also Giliberti's arguments for a diversity of statuses and conditions within these communities: Giliberti (1992), 177.

[12] Cf. Bagnall (1993a), 5; Keenan (2007), 226; above, 34–5.

[13] Headmen in Egyptian villages: e.g., *P. Sakaon* 46–7 (342) with Bagnall (1993a), 64; 134. Cf. Déléage (1945), 78; Carrié (1994), 46–7 with notes 66–8. Also Sarris (2006b), 97; 99; Trombley (2004), 75–81. For further references, MacMullen (1974), 23 with notes 69–72.

[14] *P. Col.* VII.175 (339), first published in Kraemer and Lewis (1937), and republished with English translation by Bagnall and Lewis in *P. Col.* VII (1979). Note now the textual corrections of Kramer and Hagendorn (1982). This text is also discussed below, 213.

[15] Above, 96–7.

example, reveals that the landscape around the village of Theadelphia contained both smaller settlements, or *epoikia*, and estates owned by large landowners. In a petition to the Prefect concerning the evasion of liturgies by certain of their fellow-villagers, Sakaon and two of his neighbors claim to have discovered some of these individuals living with their families on nearby estates, before being driven off by the landlord and some of his retainers.[16] In another petition, Sakaon accuses residents of the *epoikia* of Ptolemaios and Myron of stealing some sheep.[17] These documents not only reveal the complexity of settlement patterns in the immediate vicinity of Theadelphia; they also attest to a high degree of mobility within and between those settlements, and it seems that we are dealing here with a regional community comprising a variety of complementary settlements.[18]

A comparable diversity of settlement size and type may be observed in the countryside around Antioch, where Libanius draws a distinction between villages with one owner and villages belonging to many owners.[19] We should be cautious lest we map Syrian settlement patterns too closely upon Libanius' contrast, but it seems reasonable on the basis of the epigraphic, documentary, and literary evidence to distinguish in the landscapes of Syria independent communities, complete with their own councils and headmen, from communities beholden to a single powerful landowner and patron, whether a member of the local municipal aristocracy, a senator, or the emperor himself.[20] The former communities, at least, reveal how expressions of group solidarity could coexist with the impulse towards exclusiveness. Commemorative stones in these contexts characteristically mention "the inhabitants of the village" (*hoi apo tês kômês*), "the community of the village" (*to koinon tês kômês*), "the community" (*to koinon*), or "the villagers" (*hoi kômêtai*).[21] Alongside these expressions of collective identity, however, we observe also an exclusive group, comprising a headman and

[16] *P. Turner* 44 = *P. Sakaon* 44, with further discussion below, 218–21.
[17] *P. Sakaon* 39 (318).   [18] Cf. above, 46–9.
[19] Libanius, *Or.* XLVII.4. See the recent interpretation of the economic implications of this contrast in Wickham (2005b), 447–8.
[20] Liebeschuetz (1972), 67. Whittaker and Garnsey (1998), 298 note 89 agree with some reservations. Also Trombley (2004), 75–6. Independent villages with councils and headmen: e.g. *IGLS* 376 (224, Jabal Simʿān); *IGLS* 1908 (344, Misrifah, Syria); *IGR* 3.1187 = Wadd. 2546 (282, Syria); also MacAdam (1983), 107–8 with notes 20–2; Grainger (1995), 193 with Table 8. Villages beholden to a single figure: Theodoret, *Hist. Rel.* XIV; XVII.4. Also Tate (1992), 257–70, Tchalenko (1953), 404–21. Villages belonging to the emperor or the *res privata*: e.g. *IGLS* 1232 = *SEG* 42.1364 (sixth century), with Trombley (2004), 76.
[21] Wadd. 2209, Syria; *IGR* 3.1187 = Wadd. 2546 (282); Wadd. 2129, with Jones (1931), 272; MacAdam (1983), 107. *AE* 1996.1566 (mid fifth–early sixth century, Orvat Beʾer-Shemaʾ in the Negev). MacAdam (1983), 107–8, collects further references; Rey-Coquais (1993), 145, alludes to more examples of communal religious construction from Middle Syria.

council of elders, which affirms its unity in conscious opposition to those less wealthy, less powerful members of the village at large, whom it excludes from its ranks.[22]

In seeking to elucidate further the internal organization of these communities, it is difficult to move much beyond the impressionistic and hypothetical.[23] The physical remains of these villages demonstrate a considerable degree of homogeneity in their size and the material used in their construction, and very little inscriptional evidence for individuals distinguishing themselves as benefactors of or leaders within their communities has survived. This has led some scholars to suggest that the communities themselves were similarly homogeneous and socio-economically undifferentiated.[24] Caution is necessary, however, for as we have seen socio-economic differentiation can be expressed in forms that will not show up readily in the material record: provision of feasts and gifts to the community, for example, or deference and respect in social and ritual circumstances.[25] We may imagine also that here, too, there was a certain amount of fluidity and dynamism in the fortunes of individual households, which served as something of a brake upon the creation of a circumscribed, self-contained village elite.

In any event, it seems clear that, regardless of the size and composition of rural communities in the late Roman period, their inhabitants were connected to one another in complex patterns of cooperation and conflict. In some circumstances, as we have seen, those connections may be defined as friendships, and we have also observed family members both cooperating and squabbling amongst themselves.[26] Alongside these ongoing and multidimensional relationships may be placed the business partnerships discussed in the previous chapter, as well as casual acquaintances, friends-of-friends, and so on. The almost infinite complexity of these patterns of connection will impact upon both individual and communal decision-making, for in many cases, such decisions amount to privileging one relationship over others and therefore involve a complex set of calculations and negotiations.

---

[22] Council of elders: e.g. *V. Sim. Styl. (S)* 29; 105. Headman: Libanius, *Or.* XLVII.7. Cf. Trombley (2004), 75–6; Decker (2009), 38; 41–4; MacMullen (1974), 16; 23 with notes 73–7. Also Keenan (1985), 253; de Ligt (1990), 50–1 with notes 82–8; Giliberti (1992), 177.

[23] Cf. Trombley (2004), 80.

[24] Equation of physical homogeneity with socio-economic homogeneity: Tate (1997), 65; 67; Tate (1998), 923–4. Also Foss (2000), 796–800.

[25] For balanced analysis of the debate over social structures in the villages of the Syrian Limestone Massif and the eastern Mediterranean more generally, cf. Wickham (2005b), 443–9; Decker (2009), 33–44.

[26] Above, 37–8; 69–71.

RATIONALITY, AGENCY, AND DECISION-MAKING

The evidence we possess does not lend itself easily to the contemplation of decision-making in the rural communities of the late Roman world. Where motivations are imputed to *rustici*, they are characteristically generated by our aristocratic authors, and revolve around their concerns or respond to the interests or perspectives of their audiences and subjects. Scholars have been justly cautious of these ascribed motivations, and have in any event tended to regard with suspicion the project of reconstructing the social goals and objectives of small agriculturalists. Instead, they have concentrated upon the economic considerations underpinning their decisions, which have been the subject of much debate. Both in ancient studies and in the study of the peasantry, there exists a long-standing disagreement over the rationality underpinning peasant economic decision-making. We may briefly characterize that disagreement as a contrast between the assumption that peasants were motivated purely by the desire to maintain their subsistence livelihood, on the one hand, and the contention that notions of profit and the pull of the marketplace impacted upon their decision-making, on the other.[27] This debate, in turn, may be placed within the context of ongoing arguments over the nature of the economy in antiquity. In recent scholarship, however, this apparent dichotomy has been challenged and, to a certain extent replaced by a more nuanced, multidimensional understanding of the economic factors motivating economic behavior.[28] In what follows I assume the utility of this position but focus instead upon complementary aspects of decision-making within rural communities.

In particular, our interest here is in the processes whereby impulses become acts, and the relationships between those impulses or acts and the socio-cultural matrices within which they occur. We encounter here the problem of agency. Recent social scientific debate on the subject has been characterized by a reaction against the tendency in some fields to downplay the role of agents in decision-making, in favor of the broader structures that define or shape the form that their actions take.[29] However, restoring a role to agents is a difficult task, not least because the concept of agency does not lend itself easily to clear and concise definition.[30] Intuitively, agency rests most easily in the individual, but as we have seen, individuals are

---

[27] Above, 26–7.
[28] Saller (2002) is a landmark in reconstituting this debate. See also the new approaches taken to the problem by the contributors to Scheidel, Morris, and Saller (2007).
[29] Surveyed by Mutch, Delbridge, and Ventresca (2006), 608.
[30] Emirbayer and Mische (1998), 962 speak of the term's "elusive, albeit resonant, vagueness."

characteristically part of families and households, which themselves combine to form communities. At each analytical level it is possible to speak of
agents making decisions: that is, agency is a characteristic of both an
individual and a group.

Our sources describe families, households, and communities making
decisions that appear to be analogous to the decisions made by single actors:
a village decides to undertake a building project, to call in workmen to
repair a canal, or to petition a holy figure for intercession in a dispute or aid
against an external threat;[31] a community of tenants decides to resist the
authority of an unpopular bishop;[32] a family decides to take a sick child to a
healer;[33] a household decides which crops to sow, and how to exploit its
labor resources most effectively.[34] In each case, the apparently straightforward recording of the decision masks immense diversity in the processes
leading up to that decision. We should not, of course, expect every act to
have been preceded by a self-conscious, deliberate decision-making process,
and we must acknowledge also the possibility of actions having consequences that were entirely unintended by their agents.[35] Nevertheless, whether
conscious or not, any act is part of an ongoing series of practices that
collectively restate, reproduce, and renegotiate a community's collective
experience and the place of the individual actor within that experience.[36]

Recent scholarship on agency in sociology and related fields has revolved
around two sets of problems that may be regarded as complementary. First,
scholars have sought to elucidate the links between individuals as agents on
the one hand, and the structures that constrain or determine their capacity
to act, on the other. Second, attention has focused upon determining
whether a group decision is shared among members or made by a single
individual who asserts or is granted sole responsibility for that decision.
These two sets of debates may at first sight appear to be entirely incompatible, for one explores the extent to which actions may be regarded as

---

[31] Building: see the discussions and collections of references in MacAdam (1983); Sartre (1993);
Trombley (2004), and further discussion below, 107–8. Canal: *V. Sim. Styl. (S)* 64; 85; *V. Theod.
Syc.* 43. Dispute or aid: Eugippius, *V. Sev.* 3; *Hist Mon. in Aeg.* IV.3; *V. Sim. Styl. (S)* 60; 86. For the
implications of regarding communities as social actors, see Carroll (1999); also Olsen (2009), 381.

[32] Augustine, *Ep.* 20*, with fuller discussion below, 145–7.

[33] *V. Sim. Styl. (S)* 33; Paulinus, *V. Ambr.* 28; Constantius, *V. Germani* 15. For the decision-making
processes in these circumstances, see Grey (2005), 44–7.

[34] Crops: the economic strategies of peasants in the period are largely opaque, but may be gleaned from
the writings of Palladius and legislation putatively concerned with *agri deserti*; see, for fuller
discussion, Grey (2007b). Labor resources: *Nov. Val.* XXXIII.1 (451); *Concilia Galliae*, 262 (Vaison,
442); *CJ* VII.51.2; Cassiodorus, *Variae* VIII.33.4. Note also the discussion of *oblatio* above, 39–40.

[35] Cf. Giddens (1976), 78; Giddens (1984), 14; Bourdieu (2000), 127–8; Adams (2006), 513.

[36] Cf. Harding (2005), 98.

unconscious or habitual, while the other explicitly credits individuals with a high degree of reflexivity and deliberation. However, this distinction can be effectively collapsed if we acknowledge that thought-processes occur along a continuum of consciousness from fully reflexive and conscious to completely unconscious. They can therefore only with difficulty be distinguished from one another.[37] That is, by placing these debates in dialog with one another, we escape the methodological conundrums of agency versus structure and reflexivity versus habitus, in favor of an account that envisages actions as the outcomes of an ongoing, complex interplay between these phenomena. In what follows I expand briefly upon this proposition, with reference to a series of vignettes which reveal individuals and groups within the rural communities of the late Roman world making decisions in a variety of ways.

Controversy over the relationship between agents and structures has long been a staple in social-scientific literature.[38] In broad terms, scholars generally agree that individuals do not act in isolation, but, rather, are necessarily a part of broader social, economic, cultural, and political structures. Collectively, these structures have been dubbed a community's habitus, although the concept has been the subject of much debate in the scholarly literature and should be regarded as a convenient, but imperfect, label.[39] In particular, scholars disagree over the extent to which agents are able to act independently of their habitus, or to manipulate or shape it to their own wills.[40] This disagreement rests, ultimately, upon a difference of opinion over whether the social world should be analyzed by focusing upon entities, which are static and isolated from one another, or relations, which unfold dynamically and continually between those entities.[41] In what follows, I argue that neither the self-conscious agency of individuals nor the constraints of the structures within which they exist are sufficient to explain the process of decision-making. Indeed, agents and structures are not two opposite, mutually exclusive analytical poles, but rather a pair of inseparably

---

[37] Cf. Adams (2006), 516–21, who posits a hybridization of habitus and reflexivity. Also Elder-Vass (2007), who reconciles the consciousnessless habitus of Bourdieu with Archer's emphasis upon conscious reflexive deliberation into what he calls an "emergentist theory of action."

[38] See now the surveys of Davis and Fisher (1993); Emirbayer (1997); Emirbayer and Mische (1998); Elder-Vass (2008).

[39] A succinct statement of the habitus as "a system of dispositions acquired by internalizing a determinate type of social and economic condition" may be found in Bourdieu (1992), 105. Cf. the modifications of the concept offered by O'Mahoney (2007) and note in particular Olsen's critique of the habitus as a highly restrictive notion: Olsen (2009), 380.

[40] Note the survey of Elder-Vass (2007), 326–9.

[41] Emirbayer (1997), 281–2. Also Verdon (1998), 33–4.

connected concepts which exist only in relation to each other.[42] Our task, therefore, is to account for the influence of both, and to explore the nature of the relationship between the two in specific circumstances.

Such an approach entails acknowledging that agents are perpetually involved in the process of constructing and modifying structures, while at the same time being constrained by them.[43] That is, any single act is simultaneously acknowledging, reconstructing, and challenging existing expectations, mores, and understandings. We may usefully map these processes by introducing a temporal aspect to our analysis, for no act occurs in isolation from the past or the future. Rather, agents draw upon established norms, habits, and expectations; evaluate their present circumstances and adapt their negotiating strategies accordingly; and assess or anticipate particular outcomes or implications of their acts.[44] Past, present, and future are therefore mutually implicated. A curious account of an encounter between Martin of Tours and a conspiracy of demoniacs in the city of Trier, preserved in Sulpicius Severus' account of the saint's life, demonstrates this mutual implication neatly, as well as revealing the interpenetration of agents and their habitus.

Sulpicius relates that, while Martin was visiting the city of Trier, a rumor began to circulate that the barbarians were poised to attack. In response to this rumor, Martin had a demonically possessed person summoned before him. He questioned the man, who "admitted that there had been ten demons with him who had spread this rumor through the population, in the hope that by the ensuing panic, at least, Martin might be caused to flee the town."[45] The story operates on several levels concurrently, and we may envisage a corresponding multiplicity of motivations and interpretations. For Sulpicius, this event reveals the perception and power of the saint, and therefore functions as part of his project of constructing Martin as the embodiment of the Christian struggle against paganism and the forces of the supernatural in the period.[46] It serves also to identify Martin as a figure

---

[42] See the full and detailed discussion of Emirbayer and Mische (1998), *passim*. Cf. Emirbayer (1997), 287–8; 294; Harding (2005), 90; Olsen (2009), 369; 383, arguing for a "tolerant pluralism" when it comes to theories of agency. Also Foucault (1982), 219; Ortner (1995), 186; Howe (1998), 546–7; Seymour (2006), 305; Axelby (2007), 72.

[43] Cf. Emirbayer (1997), 307; Olsen (2009), 372; 381.

[44] Emirbayer and Mische (1998), *passim*, summarized succinctly at 970–4; O'Mahoney (2007), 491; Harding (2005), 89.

[45] *V. Mart.* 18, with the discussion of Grey (2005), 59–61. Fontaine has suggested that this incident takes as its context one of a number of visits by Martin to the city of Trier in the mid 380s, when he participated in a series of embassies by bishops to appeal to the emperor for judgment against adherents of the heretical teachings of Priscillian: Fontaine (1968), 815.

[46] Cf. Grey (2005), 48–9.

of power and authority, for in Sulpicius' account, Martin's exposure of the conspiracy assuages the fears of the community.

When we turn to the collective experience of the community, the laconic nature of the reportage reveals that for Sulpicius and his audience, as for Martin and the other participants in the story, the existence of demons and the ready identification of the demonically possessed were relatively unremarkable. It was accepted and expected in the period that boundaries between the natural and supernatural worlds were permeable, and demons were a real and recognizable presence. Further, and as Sulpicius reveals here, the connection between possessed person and possessing spirit was difficult to disentangle.[47] Therefore, we may interpret the existence of this conspiracy of demons-cum-demoniacs as consistent with the psychological and cultural contexts of the late Roman world.

However, these individuals are not simply responding to those contexts, for, simultaneously, they may be observed seeking to exploit them in order to achieve their ultimate objective of driving Martin – and, perhaps, others – from the city of Trier. The decision to pursue that objective by recourse to both the vocabulary of demonic possession and the threat of a barbarian invasion need not have been consciously made by these individuals. Indeed, we may imagine, rather, that demonic possession here represents a culturally appropriate vocabulary for the expression of distress, alienation, or exclusion.[48] Nevertheless, we observe both an appreciation of the opportunities that the former provided in directing and shaping the responses of others, and a keen awareness of the frisson of fear that might be expected to accompany news of the latter. These individuals are inextricably bound with their habitus here, and responding to it in a complex collection of ways.

Further, the objective itself arguably betrays how enmeshed these individuals were in the collection of dispositions and expectations that characterized social interactions in the period. We may, perhaps, place this story within the same context of concern over power, status, and authority that was identified in the Introduction to this study as fundamental to the world-views of our authors and their fellow aristocrats.[49] We might, for example, suggest that the members of this conspiracy were a group of local aristocrats, progressively marginalized within the city of Trier by the presence of the imperial court and the burgeoning influence of bishops and other members of ecclesiastical hierarchies. Their response to that marginalization may be

[47] Grey (2005), 52–5, with fuller discussion and further references.   [48] Grey (2005), 62.
[49] Above, 9–10. Fuller discussion and argument in Grey (2005).

interpreted as an attempt both to claim power and influence in an alternate sphere, and to remind those whose position was eclipsing their own of their capacity still to impact upon the destiny of their city.

We observe in this vignette the interpenetration of agency and structure, but Sulpicius leaves unexplored the process through which the collective decision was reached by these conspirators, and the ways in which any potential conflicts of interest were resolved. These aspects of decision-making among groups have long been a topic of debate in the social scientific literature. Much attention has focused in particular upon the processes whereby individuals cooperate in order to make collective decisions, and scholars have identified two poles around which these decision-making processes may be arrayed. At one extreme are "shared decisions," where the group arrives at a decision by some process of collective agreement, while at the other stand "unshared decisions," which involve one dominant member of the group making a decision on behalf of all.[50] For our current purposes, the most important aspect of this debate is the light it sheds upon the relationship between the individual and the community, for the two emerge here not as dichotomous entities to be analytically distinguished from one another, but rather as participants in a shifting series of negotiations over the balance between individual interest and mutual benefit in any particular circumstance.[51] Further, in any specific situation, the factors influencing an individual's decision to cooperate with the group, dissent, or seek to dominate it will vary according to a variety of factors including the strength and nature of his or her investment in that group, possible or expected outcomes of the decision, and the existence of other groups also demanding investment or involvement.[52]

We may observe one such constellation of negotiations in a petition from a group of taxpayers from the village of Theadelphia, in the Fayum, preserved in the collection of Aurelius Sakaon. The petition is dated to 331/2 CE, and is addressed to the Prefect of Egypt by three members of the village, who represent themselves as acting on behalf of the whole community.[53] The three claim to be the only contributing taxpayers remaining in the village, before going on to identify by name and location eight men who, they assert, are evading their fiscal obligations. We may imagine the decision to send this petition to have involved a careful weighing of the

---

[50] Review of the literature in Conradt and Roper (2009), 807–9.   [51] Cf. Axelby (2007), 49.
[52] Cf. Siegel (2009), 122–3; also King, Douglas, Huchard, Isaac, and Cowlishaw (2008) on collective decision-making and despotism by the dominant male among social primates.
[53] *P. Turner* 44 = *P. Sakaon* 44.

hoped-for benefits against the potential costs of exposing the internal workings of the community to the scrutiny of outsiders. It is probable also that
these men took account of their past experiences of interactions with
imperial officials, although it is difficult to determine what those experiences were. At any rate, the papyrological evidence suggests that recourse to
the law was an established pattern of behavior in a variety of situations, so
we should not be surprised to witness these individuals seeking to enlist the
legal machinery of the state in the present context. Further, by choosing to
present their case using the vocabulary of taxation and tax evasion, they seek
to manipulate the state's interest in ensuring that revenues continued to
flow from contributing taxpayers and their communities.[54]

However, such a strategy was not without its risks, and it is likely that
there was a certain amount of debate between the three over the advisability
of this petition and the form it should take. While we have no way of
connecting the eight named men to individuals identified in other petitions,
it is likely that Sakaon and his fellow petitioners were involved in a range of
interactions and relationships with some of them, at least. By choosing in
this instance to privilege the desire to deliver themselves from an apparently
unreasonable portion of the community's tax burden over such obligations
as they might have to these individuals by virtue of friendship, kinship, or
other mutually cooperative, reciprocal relationships, Sakaon and his fellow
petitioners opened themselves up to the possibility of future conflict within
their community. Consequently, we should interpret this petition as the
result of a careful decision-making process, which entailed both an assessment of the potential outcome based on past experience and present
circumstances, and a series of explicit and implicit negotiations between
the participants over their respective aims and positions. Given the provenance of this petition in the collection of Sakaon, it is possible that he took a
leading role in the decision and retained a copy for his records, although
such a conclusion would be somewhat speculative. At any rate, it is likely
that a decision represented here as emanating from a group representing the
entire community had a considerably more complex genesis in reality.

The multidimensional calculus that goes into any single decision is
impossible to recapture in anything other than isolated fragments for the
rural communities of the late Roman world, but it is possible at least to
sketch the form that those processes took and the factors that might be
involved in a particular decision. In pursuit of this project, we must assume
that there is characteristically a rationality or rationalities to decision-

---

[54] Going to the law: below, 204–5. Vocabulary of tax evasion: below, 216–24.

making, and set ourselves the task of recovering the strategic decisions that both shaped and constituted those rationalities.[55] We must also acknowledge the existence both of collective action and of individual decision-making, operating in a state of mutual tension and dialog. In the discussions that follow, attention shifts, deliberately, backwards and forwards between the individual, the family, the household, and the community as actors and decision-makers. This perpetually shifting focus reflects the constant, ongoing tension between these phenomena.[56] That tension is manifested in continuing negotiations and renegotiations of boundaries, connections, and mutual interests, and it is to those negotiations that we now turn.

NEGOTIATING INEQUALITY

Inequalities in wealth, status, access to resources, and power lead a community to develop strategies for affirming its ideological unity and managing internal antagonisms. Communal activity, such as participation in religious festivals, civic and religious building, is an affirmation of the ideology of reciprocity and equality within the community. These projects present members of the "exclusive" community with a stage upon which to display their status and wealth, thereby perpetuating and affirming their position of power and privilege. They also benefit the entire community, affirming those communal links which may prove to be the difference between survival and extinction, and releasing jealousies and rivalries which might result from differential access to resources and disparity in wealth and status. Again, tension engendered by such imbalances of wealth is characteristic of rural communities. This tension must simultaneously be negotiated, neutralized, and emphasized if a community is to continue to function successfully.

Communal participation in religion clearly provided a forum for such strategies of negotiation.[57] In the village communities of the eastern Mediterranean, religious festivals simultaneously affirmed the status of the wealthiest members of that community and constrained them to behave in ways which were beneficial to the entire group. Libanius, harking back rhetorically to a pagan past of recent memory, provides an example from the villages of the Antioch valley when he remarks upon the practice of country

---

[55] Cf. Olsen's "theory of strategies": Olsen (2009), 384; 386–7. Note also Wegren (2004), 555–6, with specific reference to the rationalities implicated in agriculturalists' adaptations to change.
[56] Cf. Anderson (1997), 506–7; Hovelsrud-Broda (2000), 197; Reyes-García, Godoy, Vadez, Huanca, and Leonard (2006), 96; Axelby (2007), 49.
[57] Wolf (1966), 97–9; Hutson (1971), 44–5; Ferraro (2004), 84–5.

folk assembling at the houses of their wealthiest members at festival times, where they would sacrifice and hold a feast.[58] Libanius' image of communities united by common ritual observances and mutual expectations may be extended to encompass villages of Christians and Jews as well. In the sources for the eastern Mediterranean, benefaction by the wealthier members of the community towards those less fortunate than themselves is a common theme. Discussions in the Palestinian Talmud reveal, for example, that one criterion upon which Rabbi Eliezer was selected as *parnas*, or charitable overseer, of his community, was the resources he possessed.[59] Similarly, when selected as priest of an unnamed village near Antioch, the Christian holy man Maësymas is reported to have kept jars of oil and grain outside his house for the use of villagers and strangers alike.[60]

Our evidence for religious festivals in the western provinces comes largely from the disapproving pens of church leaders, and is principally directed at activities that take place in urban contexts. However, in many cases it is clear that rural inhabitants traveled to the city to participate in these events. It seems reasonable to suggest that in Gaul, Africa, and Italy too, religious festivals provided communities with a context for affirming communal integrity through exchange of presents, communal feasting, and dancing.[61] These activities served as statements of the equality and integrity of the community, in much the same way as communal worship.[62] They also subtly emphasized inequalities, a fact not lost on Maximus of Turin, who remarks upon the practices of gift-giving that accompanied the annual festival of the Kalends. In Maximus' construction, the exchanges of gifts that characterize this festival mark a moment where the desire to receive has superseded the impulse to give, and the commercial logic of the marketplace has tainted reciprocal interactions. What is more, the expectation of gift-exchange presents problems for the less wealthy, who are expected to give gifts to their wealthier neighbors, but might be forced to enter into debt in order to do so. Meanwhile, the wealthy give extravagantly, for they crave the resulting reputation for generosity.[63]

Maximus presents these phenomena in extreme terms, in order to make the rhetorical point that the festival of the Kalends is immoral, and disrupts

[58] Libanius, *Or.* xxx 19. Cf. Julian, *Misop.* 15 (346c).

[59] *pDemai* iii.23. Cf. Kindler (1989), 55 with n. 15.

[60] Oil for the community: Theodoret *Hist. Rel.* xiv.2. Cf. *V. Sim. Styl. (S)* 29. Cf., for the role of festivals in uniting communities regardless of religious affiliation, Belayche (2007), 37.

[61] Augustine, *Ep.* 22.6; Caesarius of Arles, *Serm.* xl.7; cxcii.3; cxciii.3. Also Rutilius Namatianus, *De Red. Suo* 1.371–6.

[62] Caesarius of Arles, *Serm.* vi.3. Cf. Wolf (1966), 7.

[63] Maximus of Turin, *Serm.* xcviii.2. Giving in order to enhance reputation: cf. above, 82–3.

the proper rhythm of communal interactions.[64] But the strategy of exploiting imbalances in wealth, while also affirming the ideology of reciprocity, was effective for both rich and poor. For the former, participating in structured reciprocal exchanges of this sort allowed them to maintain a reputation for generosity and public-spiritedness, and perpetuated their position of influence and standing in the community. For the latter, it provided a mechanism whereby they could legitimately expect to receive more than they gave while also behaving in ways that accorded with accepted norms of communal behavior.[65] In these ways, both social and subsistence risk could be mitigated and managed.

Building projects also provided a series of opportunities for the community to emphasize its collective identity, as well as for individuals to make claims about their own distinctiveness or uniqueness within that community. Wealthy individuals might take responsibility upon themselves, dedicating buildings on behalf of the villages under their protection or control.[66] Alternatively, the community may commemorate a collective project. We observe, for example, a group of imperial tenants in Africa emphasizing their collective contribution to a building project when they commemorate their restoration of a temple "with their own money" (*sua pecunia*). Similarly, a fragmentary devotional inscription from Italy suggests religious building by Imperial tenants, although little further can be surmised about the nature of the project.[67] These small groups give the impression, at least, of cohesion, and offer no hints of differential contributions.

This evidence can be contrasted with inscriptions from the villages of the eastern Mediterranean, where imbalances in wealth and status could be acknowledged while at the same time the collective act of building was celebrated. In synagogue dedications, for example, alongside cash dedications of varying amounts from those able to afford such bequests, we witness laborers whose particular skills in constructing the building are commemorated.[68] Religious or communal building confirmed both the

---

[64] Cf. Caesarius of Arles, *Serm.* CXCII and CXCIII, with Klingshirn (1994), 216–18.

[65] Cf. Rabbi Hiyya bar Adda's observation about the elderly accepting charity only at certain times in the year: *pPeah* 8.9, and above, 82.

[66] Western provinces: *CIL* XIII.3475 (n. d., Gaul), for the *vicus Ratumagus*; *ILTG* 126 (n. d., Gaul), involving the *vicini Spariani*. Eastern provinces: Mouterde and Poidebard (1945), no. 30 (353, Chalkidike); no. 54 (Chalkidike). Also Mouterde and Poidebard (1945), no. 17 (553, Jabal Hass); *IGLS* 1490 (473, Sarjilla); cf. Trombley (2004), 77–8.

[67] Africa: *ILTun* 1568 (235). Note, however, Dossey (2010), 105 for the rarity of this kind of collective activity in the fourth and later centuries. Italy: *AE* 1995.553 (late third – early fourth century).

[68] Kindler (1989), 55. Cf. Trombley (2004), 74 note 5 for construction costs of village buildings in Syria. Also Decker (2009), 70–2.

solidarity of the group in the face of underlying tensions and the fundamental inequality of that group. The resulting monument was an acknowledgment of the importance of the physical space in which the community
lived, or a symbol of the geographical uniqueness of a particular shared cult
site in the landscape.[69] It was also a monument to the community's capacity
to negotiate and absorb imbalances in wealth.

Shared religious building projects may also, with caution, be taken as
evidence for religious solidarity within a community. Much recent attention has focused upon the Christianization of the countrysides of the late
Roman world, and the implication of the explosion of churches, shrines,
and other physical manifestations of Christianity in rural contexts.[70]
However, it is difficult to determine what impact the imposition of these
new Christian structures had upon the rural landscapes of the period and
upon the communities which resided there. Both Libanius and Maximus
have religious axes to grind in their presentations of the conflict and
inequality engendered by religious differentiation in the period. In drawing
a distinction between past and present practices, Libanius implies that, with
reference to the celebration of community, pre-existing pagan festivals were
in some sense incompatible with the new dictates of Christianity, which
served to fragment rather than cement the community. Maximus, for his
part, makes the opposite argument: in the community of Christ, there is no
place for the inequality and moral inversion that characterized pagan social
interactions.

It is true that our sources portray a fundamental struggle between
Christianity and paganism for control of the countrysides of the late
Roman world. In those sources, this battle is fought between the saints,
bishops, and churchmen who were to be recognized in later centuries as
heroes of the church on the one hand, and, on the other, the pagan priests,
soothsayers, and their adherents who played the role of villains in the
hagiographical literature and theological tracts of the period. These texts
take as their contexts a series of struggles between figures of power – or the
recorders of their deeds – for the right to exercise legitimate authority over
the somewhat simple-minded inhabitants of the countrysides of the late
Roman world. Those struggles will be explored in more detail in the
following chapters. For our current purposes, it remains to be seen whether

---

[69] Brown (1981), 86–8.
[70] A brief survey of recent literature must suffice. For Gaul: Terrier (2007); Codou and Colin (2007).
North Africa: Riggs (2006). Italy: Trout (1995), (1996). Syria: Caseau (2004). Egypt: Frankfurter
(2007), 184–5. Note also Chavarría and Lewit (2004), 38–43.

this antagonistic pattern was replicated or reproduced at the level of the rural community.

In fact, the somewhat meager written sources for the religious makeup of rural communities in the period suggest that the coexistence of a mixture of religions need not necessarily have led to conflict and disharmony. There survive some snippets of information about the dynamics of mixed-religion rural communities in both eastern and western contexts in the period, and these vignettes tend to present the members of those communities coexisting in relatively harmonious fashion. The general pattern that we witness in these accounts is that the community's internal harmony is disrupted by the attempt of a zealous Christian figure to proselytize the non-Christians in the community, or to effect a hardening in the attitude of its Christians residents towards their non-Christian neighbors. Thus, for example, John of Ephesus reveals the peaceful dynamic between nominal Christians and putative pagans in a mountain village in Syria, which is disturbed by the arrival of Simeon the Mountaineer, who seeks to inculcate a markedly stricter and less tolerant form of Christianity upon the inhabitants of the community.[71] Similarly, an anonymous fourth-century hagiographer emphasizes conflict between the holy man, Apollo, and pagan inhabitants of the villages surrounding the site he chose to settle.[72] The impression we gain is that these communities had not experienced a significant degree of religion-derived conflict until the arrival of the saint. Martin's experience in the countryside of Gaul reveals a similar pattern of relatively peaceful coexistence between Christians and non-Christians, which is fundamentally altered when the saint undertakes a program of aggressive Christianization.[73]

In each case, the authors of our texts focus upon the deeds of the holy man in effecting a fundamental shift in the religious sensibilities of the populations with whom he has come into contact. But in each case, we should concentrate rather upon the impression of relative peace and harmony that preceded that shift. This impression gains further support when we turn to current scholarship on the relationships between Christians and Jews in the period, which sees little in the way of open conflict at least until the end of the fourth century.[74] This proposition can be illustrated with reference to a variety of communities across the Mediterranean. The arrival of the relics of St. Stephen in Minorca in the early fifth century appears to

---

[71] John of Ephesus, *Lives of the Eastern Saints* 16: *PO* 17.241. Further discussion below, 144–5.
[72] *Hist. Mon. in Aeg.* VIII.24–9.   [73] E.g. Sulpicius Severus, *V. Mart.* 13–15. Fuller discussion below, 154–5.
[74] Schwartz (2003), 202–4 offers a balanced treatment of the issues.

have precipitated the miraculous conversion of the Jewish inhabitants of the island. But prior to that time, these individuals were so thoroughly integrated with their Christian neighbors that some among their number were recognized as patrons of the community. Similar arrangements emerge from inscriptional evidence in the cities of both the eastern and the western provinces in the period.[75] In Syria, John of Ephesus relates the experience of a certain Sergius, who encountered a village which included a community of Jews under the protection of the Christian church of the nearby city of Amida.[76] The appearance of relatively peaceful coexistence is further attested by phenomena such as the Godfearers of Aphrodisias, individuals who appear to have identified as Christians, but who observed certain Jewish religious rituals.[77]

The interweaving of putatively different religious observances and practices is particularly evident in exhortations by Christian bishops that their flocks no longer worship trees and mountains, streams and forest glades, but preserve themselves for Christ alone. These exhortations were, no doubt, part of the conscious efforts to Christianize the countrysides of the late Roman world that also engendered the building programs that have been the subject of so many recent studies. But we should not imagine that the presence of Christian buildings automatically created Christians in these landscapes. Our best evidence for the endurance of practices and rituals that were out of step with the beliefs of the bishops and church leaders who tried to stamp them out comes from the pen of Caesarius of Arles, who appears to have mounted a concerted campaign to attack these practices in southeastern Gaul.[78] Although Caesarius attempts to draw distinct boundaries between Christianity and paganism, the picture that emerges is of a certain pragmatic eclecticism among some, at least, of the inhabitants of the late Roman countryside. As Caesarius tells it, peasants might attend church on a Sunday and even count themselves Christians, without necessarily feeling the need to reject or cease long-standing rituals of observance of the natural resources and rhythms of the countryside in which they lived.[79]

---

[75] Minorca: *Epistula Severi*; Hunt (1982), *passim*. Inscriptional evidence for Jewish patrons: e.g., Noy (1993), 1.15 (Ostia, mid third century); 17 (Porto, fourth century); 20; (Capua, second–fourth century); 30 (Naples fourth–fifth century).

[76] John of Ephesus, *Lives of the Eastern Saints* 5: *PO* 17.90–1.

[77] Reynolds and Tannenbaum (1987), with the emendations and comments of Chaniotis (2002).

[78] Cf. the detailed discussion of Klingshirn (1994), 209–26.

[79] E. g., Caesarius of Arles, *Serm.* XIV.4; LIII.1; LIV.5. Note Klingshirn's tripartite division of the religion of peasants in the period into "pagan"; "Christian" in Caesarius' terms; and "Christian" in their own terms: Klingshirn (1994), 210–11. Cf., for a similar process of hybridization and (reluctant) tolerance in North Africa, Riggs (2006), 302–3, with further references.

We should be wary of taking Caesarius' account completely at face value, for it is clear that his knowledge and understanding of these practices was limited, and his attitude towards them constrained by a fairly narrow set of motivations.[80] Certainly, it does not appear that the individuals whom he censures experienced any intellectual or spiritual dissonance or angst about their hybrid religious observances. We may suspect, therefore, that notwithstanding the attitudes of Christian leaders to the somewhat lax and conditional Christianity of these *rustici*, their eclecticism was motivated, at least in part, by a sensitivity to the advantages of enlisting the Christian Church and its God within a household or community's apparatus of social and subsistence risk-management. We may surmise, further, that for the individuals and communities that are the subject of this study, religious difference was not quite so fraught a subject as it was for our aristocratic authors and the state. While we should not necessarily regard this apparent religious pluralism as a consciously embraced strategy, nevertheless it is likely to have offered a broader pool of resources to access in the management and mitigation of subsistence and social risk.

The rural communities of the late Roman world emerge from our sources as complex, multidimensional collectivities of individuals, families, and households. Those communities offered mutual insurance against economic disaster, for they provided opportunities to access and exploit a range of strategies for managing subsistence risk. But they were also characterized by inequality and tension, in the form of social differentiation, disagreements between closely coeval neighbors, and an array of mutually contradictory demands upon scarce social and economic resources. As a consequence, we may observe these communities participating in a variety of activities which functioned as brakes upon conflict, and safety valves for dissatisfaction and jealousy. Public or religious building projects and the celebration of religious festivals functioned in this way, for they provided opportunities for inequalities to be acknowledged within the context of shared endeavor. But imbalances remained just beneath the surface of the public face of the community, and emerged at moments when the community was most vulnerable. Instances of food shortage or famine loom large here, but the community's cohesion was also under threat every time collective action was necessary: the harvesting, threshing, and storage of grain, the construction and maintenance of irrigation works and other agricultural installations. In each case, latent tensions might erupt into open conflict, requiring swift activation of risk-response mechanisms.

---

[80] Klingshirn (1994), 210.

CONFLICT AND ITS RESOLUTION

Inclusion in a community involves interactions and activities which are theoretically voluntary but effectively compulsory.[81] These activities include communal harvesting, processing, and storage of grain; construction of agricultural buildings such as wells and cisterns, threshing floors, olive presses, and granaries; and the maintenance of irrigation systems, either by members of the community or by pooling financial resources to hire outsiders.[82] Additionally, and as we have already seen, groups within the community may cooperate for mutual economic benefit, undertaking a collective tenancy, borrowing or renting seed, grain, or money for a small business venture. We observe, for example, groups of peasants undertaking commercial contracts for the collection and processing of olives or vines.[83] Collective ownership of plow animals was also an established practice, as legal discussions of the practices of *communio* and *societas* reveal.[84]

The advantages of such behavior are clear. The construction or maintenance of large installations or owning a team of oxen represent investments which might be too great for one household to bear alone.[85] By collectively participating in seasonal, large-scale agricultural activities, members of the community are able to access a considerably larger supply of labor than would otherwise be available to them at relatively low, if any, extra labor cost to themselves. But each undertaking is fraught with tension. Who determines the order of plowing, of harvesting and threshing each household's grain? Who is responsible for recording the amount of grain each household stores in communal granaries? Who controls the release of that grain, and ensures that each individual takes only his share? Who regulates the irrigation system so that each plot of land receives its fair share of water? Who ensures that the terms of business agreements are met, and what avenues are available in the event that an individual member defaults on his or her responsibilities? The answers to these questions

---

[81] Aguilar (1984), 9; Reynolds (1997), lii–liii.

[82] Communal harvesting: Theodoret, *Hist. Rel.* VI.5; Eugippius, *V. Sev.* 22. Grain storage: Tchalenko (1953), 30; 41; 44. Communal processing: *P. Ness.* III.32 (sixth century); *PSI* VI.711 (311, Oxyrhynchus). In North Africa: *ILAfr* 7; 219; Kehoe (1988), 230–4. For northern Gaul, see van Ossel (1992), 143. Irrigation: *V. Sim. Styl. (S)* 64; 85; Shaw (1984), 169–70. Stone (2000), 721–2, provides a summary of recent historiography for North Africa.

[83] Above, 71–4. Cf. also *P. Cair. Isid.* 98 (291); 103 (early fourth century); *P. Oxy.* 1896 (577); Lirb (1993), 280; 284–7; 293.

[84] Ulpian, *Dig.* XIX.5.17.3; Justinian, *Inst.* III.24.2; *P. Ness.* III.32 (sixth century). Cf. Foxhall (1990), 107; Lirb (1993), 279–84.

[85] MacMullen (1974) 20 with note 61.

are elusive, since internal systems of regulation are only visible when they fail.

Failures in the regulation of communal strategies, and an accompanying escalation of tension are particularly evident in the cases of grain storage and irrigation systems. Communal storage and processing of grain is a crucial strategy for risk management, while in marginal desert regions, irrigation systems can only function if a community cooperates. But both are susceptible to abuse, particularly in times of stress. We witness, for example, a case of communal conflict in the town of Favianis, in Pannonia, which was suffering a severe famine while a member of the community hoarded a large quantity of grain.[86] Although the precise details of the conflict are unclear, the woman was evidently wealthy and of high status and appears to have owned the granary in question. We may imagine a number of possible circumstances. She may have refused to release the community's stores from her granary, or, alternatively, the granary may have been filled only with her own grain. She may have planned to hoard it for herself and her dependents, or intended to profit from the food shortage by selling it only at a ruinous profit.

Whatever the precise circumstances, her actions amounted to an instance of an individual stepping outside the accepted norms of communal behavior. It is likely that this moment of potential subsistence crisis exacerbated existing tensions between this woman and other, less well off members of the community. In Eugippius' account, the latter called upon Severinus, a figure well known in the region, but clearly an outsider to the community in question, to resolve the dispute. The depth of the conflict may be gauged by the lengths to which the saint was forced to go to resolve it: appeals to the ideology of reciprocity and the call of *humanitas* fell upon deaf ears, and it was only Severinus' threat of divine retribution that encouraged the woman to accede to the needs of the community.

Disagreement and disputes, jealousy and conflict also characteristically surround the construction, use, and maintenance of irrigation systems.[87] Such conflict is particularly visible in Egypt, where we may observe disagreements not only within communities but also between villages over the allocation of precious water resources and the responsibility for maintaining and managing those resources. The early fourth-century archive of Aurelius Sakaon from Theadelphia, for example, reveals ongoing tension

---

[86] Eugippius, *V. Sev.* 3. Cf., for a comparable case of tension between a prominent individual and the community, Bryen and Wypustek (2009), 544.

[87] Cf. Shaw (1982b), 69: "conflict is often endemic to irrigation systems."

and periodic disputes between members of his village and the inhabitants of villages between them and the ultimate source of their water. These conflicts revolve around the state of the irrigation canals and the failure of various liturgists to discharge their responsibilities for upkeep of those canals. Most explicitly, Sakaon and two of his neighbors accuse the residents of the villages of Narmouthis, Hermoupolis, and Theoxenis of siphoning off the water as it comes down the canal, with the result that none reaches their fields.[88] The petitioners here are the same three men whose denunciation of fellow villagers who had fled their responsibilities was discussed above, and the two events are closely contemporaneous.[89] We may therefore surmise that one effect of this conflict between villages was to raise tensions within Theadelphia itself, with the result that certain members of the community sought intervention from an external source.

A more local dispute is evidenced by a papyrus from the village of Karanis dated to 439. The text appears to reveal a similar case of siphoning, this time by members of the village from a reservoir that had been ceded to the local church. A dispute had also apparently arisen over rights to graze sheep on land belonging to the church. In response to a complaint from members of the clergy, the most prominent members of the community undertook on behalf of the entire village to cease illicit use of the water resources, and to police rights to pasturage.[90] Again, the precise details of the dispute are difficult to determine, but we witness here a small segment of the village community speaking for the whole group, and offering to regulate the behavior of its members. We may surmise that this text marks a point at which long-standing animosities bubbled over, but that the collective authority of the named individuals made it possible for the conflict to be resolved, and the community to be restored to its customary state of suspended tensions.

The nature of our surviving evidence gives the impression that the conflicts in question are isolated events, but it seems more likely that, in many cases, they represent merely one moment in a much longer series of disputes that might last years or even decades, and could be prosecuted on a variety of fronts simultaneously. We have already witnessed hints of just

---

[88] *P. Sakaon* 35 (c. 332?). Also *P. Sakaon* 32 (late third century); 33 (320).

[89] *P. Turner* 44 = *P. Sakaon* 44. Above, 103–4.

[90] *P. Haun.* III.58, with Rea (1993), 89–90, modifying the interpretations offered by Bonneau (1979), and by the editors of the text, although see the alternative interpretation offered by van Minnen (1995), 51. Pollard argues for a reinterpretation of the economic condition of late Roman Karanis, suggesting that, contrary to the *communis opinio*, the site was not declining throughout the fourth century and abandoned in the early fifth century, but remained occupied and relatively prosperous until at least the sixth: Pollard (1998), 148 and *passim*.

such a feud in the exchanges between Aurelius Isidorus and Acotas, son of Germanus.[91] We may imagine also that discontent, rivalry, and jealousy accompanied any mutual arrangement over the collective use of scarce resources, and in such circumstances these simmering emotions will not have needed much to boil over into open dispute. The fourth- or fifth-century Roman *agrimensor* Agennius Urbicus provides indirect evidence of the endemic nature of disputes over irrigation in rural North Africa when he comments upon the striking differences between the nature of these disputes and those with which Roman law was designed to deal: the latter were principally concerned with the diversion of water onto a neighbor's property, while in the arid environment of North Africa, the opposite was the case.[92] It may seem surprising that disputes between rural cultivators in the North African countryside should have come to the attention of a Roman *agrimensor*, but we should take this as evidence for the pervasiveness of these disputes and the broad range of strategies used by peasants in seeking to settle them.

Clearly, no single, established avenue existed for individuals or communities to seek redress of their grievances. On the contrary, our sources reveal immense variation in the strategies employed by peasants for the settlement of disputes, from actions that look very much like exercises in self-help or simple revenge, through mediation using neighbors, friends, or other local figures, to petitions directed at local figures of authority.[93] We may observe almost this complete range in a petition from Aurelius Melas, complaining about the attempts of Aurelius Sakaon to dissolve a marriage alliance between the two families.[94] Melas reveals that Sakaon had chosen to act on his own recognizance in seizing the wife of Melas' son, Zoilos, and taking her back to his own house. He notes further that he himself had already sought mediation from a resident in a nearby village and a member of the military stationed nearby, before finally undertaking a formal petition to the *praepositus pagi*. The diversity of this collection of strategies, revolving around a single dispute, bears eloquent testimony to the complex calculus involved in any instance of conflict.

This variation in strategies for obtaining redress of grievances may be mapped along a complementary axis as well, depending upon whether it is

---

[91] *P. Cair. Isid.* 65–7 (298/299); 69–70 (310), discussed above, 95.

[92] Agennius Urbicus, in *Corpus Agrimensorum Romanorum*, 24, with Shaw (1984), 138; 169–70. For dating, see Campbell in the introduction to his edition of the text: xxxi–xxxii.

[93] Note Hobson's careful typology of the stages of conflict resolution, which may be regarded as a little static: Hobson (1993), 199; cf. Gagos and van Minnen (1994), 35–46, particularly 45–6. Bryen (2008a), 25, offers further references and fuller discussion.

[94] *P. Sakaon* 38 (312), discussed above, 65–6.

an individual acting on his or her own, or a community acting collectively. The grievances of individuals appear, on the whole, to be motivated by a desire for justice or vengeance, or at the very least an impulse to highlight rather than conceal the conflict. In such circumstances, the petitioner names the perpetrators of the deed, uses language that evokes notions of justice, and calls for retribution and redress.[95] In a series of petitions whose recipients escalate steadily from the *stratêgos* to the Prefect of Egypt, Aurelius Isidorus complains about the burning of grain on his threshing floor. The first two petitions are separated by only a few days, and Isidorus gives the impression of having obtained quite a bit more information about the event and those responsible in the time between submitting the first and preparing the second. By the time he writes to the Prefect, the message has been honed: three named individuals burned his crop; he has no idea why; he seeks both punitive retribution and monetary redress.[96]

It is not surprising that Isidorus devotes such attention to an attack upon his threshed crops, for as we have seen, such attacks were a blow struck at the lifeblood of the community.[97] Theodoret of Cyrrhus relates an intervention by the holy man Symeon the Elder in a comparable dispute, which contrasts with Isidorus' account in illuminating ways.[98] As Theodoret tells the story, while the sheaves lay in heaps awaiting threshing on a village's communal threshing floor, one of the villagers stole some of his neighbor's and added them to his pile. Immediately lightning struck the threshing floor. The perpetrator then approached Symeon to inform him of the disaster, but sought to keep hidden his own culpability. Upon being confronted by the holy man, he confessed to his crime and was told to repay the sheaves he had stolen. Only in this way, he was told, would the fire be extinguished. The man promptly returned the sheaves to the individual he had robbed, the fire was miraculously quenched without water, and the community's grain was saved.

Theodoret emphasizes the way in which an entire community's internal equilibrium can be upset by the actions of one of its members. We have already encountered this fundamental tension between the individual and the community, for it underpins the complex set of interactions between risk management, reciprocity, and the politics of reputation explored in the previous chapter. The decision to live in a community acts as a form of

---

[95] Cf. Bryen (2008a), 64–5.
[96] *P. Cair. Isid.* 65 (298/299); 66 (299); 67 (299); 124 (298). Above, 85. Cf., however, Bagnall (1989), who discusses the role of arbitration in restoring equilibrium and the honor and standing of the complainant, rather than the punishment of crime per se.
[97] Above, 85.   [98] Theodoret, *Hist. Rel.* VI.5.

insurance against subsistence risk, but it heightens the potential for social risk. Vocabularies and practices of reciprocity are, at base, aimed at enhancing an individual's reputation within the community so that he or she may call on neighbors at moments of economic need, but they also contribute to a collective sense of communal cohesion. That cohesion is maintained only through the continual performance by the community and its members of the social rituals of community. It is therefore not surprising that it is the decay, corruption, or cessation of those social rituals that characterizes a community in crisis. Theodoret's near-contemporary Libanius offers a rhetorically overblown but nonetheless suggestive portrait of just such a community when he emphasizes the destructive consequences of the intervention of members of the military in the affairs of villages in the Antioch Valley: property boundaries and the possessions of one's neighbors are not respected, feasts are held by only a few and at the expense of their neighbors, violence erupts in the street, and irrigation is interrupted or entirely cut off.[99]

The village community which calls upon Symeon for intervention seems not to have fallen into such dire straits, and Theodoret's purpose in any event is to highlight the prescience of the holy man in identifying the perpetrator. But there is surely more to the story than meets the eye. In particular, it seems entirely too coincidental that the same individual responsible for the theft should find himself informing the holy man of the fire. Perhaps he was instead a figure with some measure of responsibility for regulating or supervising the communal use of this threshing floor. Perhaps also that role carried with it the responsibility for ensuring the security and safety of the facility, and for guaranteeing or recompensing other members of the community in the event of a disaster or dispute. In such circumstances, the role of the holy man is somewhat incidental to internal mechanisms for regulating the community's resources, and managing any conflicts that might arise. Conflict resolution in this instance is the responsibility of one of the community's wealthier members, drawing upon his personal reputation and resources in a manner comparable to the solution to the dispute over water in Karanis explored above.

There is precious little evidence for conflict resolution within the rural communities of the western provinces, although the suspicion remains that these communities could be riven by disputes every bit as damaging as those which threatened to tear apart certain villages in the east. We may imagine, for example, that in the arid desert of North Africa, irrigation was a potential

---

[99] Libanius, *Or.* XLVII.4–5.

flashpoint for communal conflict, and there survives an inscription outlining the settlement of one such conflict from the early third century CE.[100]
However, the fourth- and fifth-century sources are somewhat less forthcoming. In part, this is no doubt a product of a series of transformations in
the status and political identity of rural communities in the region during
this period, for it has recently been argued that these communities endured
a steady erosion of their independence, with a corresponding diminution in
the level and character of conspicuous collective action.[101] Still, it seems
unlikely that these communities magically became conflict-free in the wake
of these changes to their political position, so it is worth exploring this
apparent gap in our evidence in a little more detail.

The relative silence of the North African evidence is matched by similar
silences elsewhere in the western provinces. This may be attributed, in part,
to the differential nature of our sources for these regions. We possess
nothing comparable to the petitions preserved on papyrus from Egypt,
and the hagiographical texts are somewhat different in their focus.
In marked contrast to the eastern sources, saints, bishops, and holy
figures tend not to be described intervening in the internal disputes of
rural communities in the western provinces. Rather, the texts focus more
intensely upon relations of power between aristocratic landowners, agents
of the state, and religious figures on the one hand, and rural communities as
collectivities on the other.[102] Similarly, the letter collections of western
aristocrats do offer hints of a greater investment in the affairs of the *rustici*
who resided on and around their rural estates, and we may surmise that this
extended to the settlement of disputes between and among those *rustici*.[103]
But if this was the case, our authors are almost completely silent on the
subject. As we shall see in a later chapter, this contrast is in part attributable
to differences in the way that relations between peasantries and the powerful
are presented in our sources. But the silence is nonetheless striking, for it
would seem that, while intervention as a patron in the affairs of *rustici*
became a more important component in the self-representation of aristocrats in the western Mediterranean in the period, the settlement of disputes
between those *rustici* did not.

Of course, disputes are not completely absent from the Latin hagiographical sources, and Eugippius' account of the experience of Severinus in

---

[100] Cf., in particular, the case of Lamasba: *CIL* VIII.18587 = *ILS* 5793 (early third century), with Shaw
(1982b).
[101] Dossey (2010), 114–18.   [102] Focus on relations of power: below, 161–2.
[103] Greater investment: below, 138–9.

Favianis has already been mentioned. But even there, the suspicion remains that the dispute rests fundamentally upon the differential power, status, and wealth of the woman in question in the one hand, and the community more generally on the other. It would be overly credulous to infer that rural communities in the west did not approach figures of power to settle situations of conflict. But we cannot escape the impression that disputes within those communities were somehow less fraught, less visible than among the seemingly more fractious communities of Syria and Egypt. Attempts to resolve instances of conflict seem not to have involved quite the same jockeying for position between neighbors and rivals that is so evident in the eastern sources, nor do communities appear to be quite so likely to expose their internal workings to the scrutiny of powerful outsiders. Rather, their most typical engagement with those figures was collectively, as communities. In those interactions, western peasants appear to display a communal cohesion and capacity for manipulation and exploitation that are rather less in evidence in the east.[104]

At any rate, it seems reasonable to conclude that inequality, tension and division were fundamental to the structure of rural communities throughout the late Roman world. Individual members constantly negotiated and renegotiated their standing, and contributed to the negotiation over the positions of their fellows. Collectively, the communities of the late Roman world had recourse to long-established techniques for managing imbalances, and for maintaining the integrity of the community. Those techniques rested upon the assumption that, having enjoyed the benefits of communal living, all members of the community would acknowledge its obligations in moments of subsistence or social risk, and recognize that the needs of the community superseded those of the individual. Often, they rested upon the capacity of an influential individual or individuals to effect resolution of a conflict. While we should not expect that all the rural communities of the late Roman world were able to respond effectively to internal discord and to resolve tensions caused by inequality and competition, we should not assume uncritically that the political upheavals and religious conflicts that preoccupied our aristocratic authors were experienced in the same way by the inhabitants of the countrysides of the period.

It is clear that the communities of the late Roman world possessed mechanisms for integrating the contradictory and competing interests of the individual households of which they were comprised. In most cases, those communities were characterized by inequality, but devoted

---

[104] Scrutiny of outsiders: above, 104; below, 220–1. Manipulation: below, 145–6; 154–5.

considerable attention to managing that inequality. They were loci for conflict, but also for mechanisms designed to mitigate and resolve that conflict. A community's efforts to negotiate the tensions between individuality and communality, cohesion and conflict, fragmentation and fusion when faced with the demands of outsiders, may be observed in a continuous series of interactions both within the community and between members of that community and outsiders. Some degree of variation in the internal organization of rural communities is visible, particularly between economically diverse village communities, characterized by a comparatively high degree of social and economic differentiation, and smaller settlements revolving primarily around the relationship of their inhabitants to a powerful outsider. As we shall see in the following chapters, however, the orientation of these latter communities towards asymmetrical power relations need not entail their complete disempowerment.

CHAPTER 4

Power as a competitive exercise: potentates and communities

Alongside the collection of negotiations and interactions that made up the internal dynamics of their communities, the peasants of the late Roman world were enmeshed in a collection of complementary relationships with the powerful figures who lived on the margins of their world. These relations of power, authority, and dependence have long been regarded as the principal determinants of the socio-economic contours of the late Roman countryside. Certainly, such accounts as survive of interactions between peasants and the powerful in the period tend to stress the unthinking deference of the former and the unquestioned dominance of the latter. However, these narratives have, on the whole, been constructed by the powerful and for the powerful. When placed within the context of the strategies for the management and mitigation of subsistence and social risk that were outlined in the preceding chapters, interactions between peasants and aristocratic landowners and soldiers, bishops and holy figures take on a subtly different valence.

In this chapter, I sketch the array of powerful figures who interacted with rural communities and their inhabitants in the period. I begin from two propositions which appear at first blush to be contradictory, but which should in fact be regarded as complementary. On the one hand, relations of power are fundamental to an understanding of the structure and functioning of rural communities in the late Roman world. Patrons and would-be patrons operated within a competitive environment, expressing their claims to power and, by extension, authority using a variety of subtly different vocabularies, both familiar and unfamiliar to the peasants who served as their interlocutors. Their capacity to exercise their power effectively rested upon their ability to obtain or elicit an acknowledgment from subordinates that that power was legitimate, and therefore carried authority. This reliance upon the peasantry as a source of legitimacy granted the latter, both singly and collectively, a certain amount of agency in both initiating and structuring their interactions with the powerful.

On the other hand, it is probable that the instances of direct or indirect confrontation or collaboration between peasants and potentates that emerge from our sources were in some sense unusual or unique events, which were acted out against a backdrop of relatively limited contact between the two. That is, it is unlikely that the everyday rhythm of rural life in late antiquity was quite so charged with power, or quite so focused upon the wielders of that power, as our aristocratic authors would have us believe. Rather, we should expect that their ability to follow through on and enforce their claims to authority was somewhat circumscribed, and their interest in doing so rather limited in any event. Consequently, the networks of power that our aristocratic authors work so hard to construct and maintain in their writings are likely to have been, in reality, somewhat incomplete and largely incoherent.[1] The implications of this proposition will be explored in more detail in the following chapter. Here, I outline the various identities of figures of power in the period, the foundations upon which their power and claims to authority rested, and the nature of their interaction with one another.

PEASANTS, POTENTATES, AND PATRONS IN LATE ANTIQUITY

If our sources are to be taken at face value, the countrysides of late antiquity seethed with an extraordinary variety of potentates, their claims to power and authority based on a wide diversity of foundations, the scope and extent of their activities serving as compelling evidence for the fundamental transformation of the social contours of the late Roman world. We should be careful not to overemphasize the novelty of this competition among would-be patrons in rural contexts, for peasants characteristically find themselves interacting with their wealthier, more powerful neighbors in arrangements of tenancy, wage labor, and patronage. However, the sheer weight of evidence from the period suggests that local structures of power were disrupted and transformed over the course of the fourth and fifth centuries. These transformations had tangible, if imperfectly understood, effects upon local aristocrats, who found themselves alternately competing and cooperating with figures whose claims to power and authority were

---

[1] Cf. Certeau (1984), 24–8; 38; 95; Morrow (1996), 420; Schilling (2003), 36–7; Campbell and Heyman (2007), 7.

subtly different from their own. We should expect also a series of ripple effects upon the more humble inhabitants of the municipalities and their hinterlands, who were presented with both a greater number of options for the satisfaction of their own needs and an increase in the potential for conflict and oppression. In what follows I briefly survey the evidence for patrons and would-be patrons in rural contexts in the late Roman period, before reflecting upon the extent to which the resulting landscapes of power can be regarded as new and different.

Scholars now agree that the impression of an impoverished, vestigial curial class, shorn of its most capable or connected members as the latter steadily entered the ranks of the imperial bureaucracy or abandoned their responsibilities, is overly dramatic.[2] Likewise, it would be simplistic to assume uncritically that we are witnessing a universal process of usurpation of the authority and power of local landowners in the municipalities by more powerful outsiders.[3] However, it is clear that they experienced challenges to their position as natural patrons and intercessors in rural contexts. In a long and detailed oration aimed at exposing perversions of existing patronage relations caused by the protection rackets of local military figures in the hinterland of Antioch, Libanius offers a heartfelt plea that existing patrons not be supplanted or abandoned in favor of these figures, but rather be approached by their clients to act as intercessors with them. Libanius portrays *curiales* continuing, or attempting to continue, to act as landlords, patrons, and intercessors for the inhabitants of the city's hinterland, and his request provides an inkling of the important place that the role of patron played in a local aristocrat's armory of self-representation, as well as an appreciation of the capacity of potential clients to pick and choose between patronal figures in the period.[4]

The military figures to whom Libanius alludes were one group among a number of powerful outsiders whose claims to authority rested upon a variety of foundations in the period. We observe, for example, current and former members of the imperial bureaucracy exercising or attempting to exercise power and authority in the countrysides of the late Roman world. Legislation putatively concerned with tax evasion among the peasantry of Egypt holds up for censure a bewildering array of current and former members of the state's administrative and fiscal bureaucracies, who

---

[2] Petit (1955), 333; Lepelley (1981a), 338 and *passim*; Wickham (1984), 14; Brown (1992), 19; 26–7; Laniado (2002), 4–9; Wickham (2005b), 199. This is not to say that *curiales* did not enter the ranks of the imperial bureaucracy: cf. Garnsey (2010), 52 for this phenomenon.

[3] Detailed discussion in Wickham (2005b), chapter 4. Cf. Harper (2008), 97.

[4] Libanius, *Or.* XLVII.19–22.

are accused of facilitating the resistance by villagers of their compulsory liturgies.[5] Libanius offers the story of a comparable figure, whom he describes competing with local aristocrats for the patronage of villages in the hinterland of the city.[6] The power of these individuals, and therefore their claims to authority in the municipalities rested, at least in part, upon their ongoing connections with the imperial court. But it would appear that those claims were expressed and negotiated using strategies and practices with very localized resonances: intercession on behalf of tenants and clients with other powerful figures; loans of money or equipment; euergetism or beneficence to the community as a whole.

As Libanius' oration makes clear, members of the military, too, appeared as figures of power, seeking or claiming authority in rural contexts, and, in the eastern provinces at least, vigorously pursuing wealth in the form of land.[7] Libanius' vision of these individuals is somewhat jaded, and he seeks to portray their presence in rural contexts as calamitous for existing members of the municipal aristocracy, the majority of agricultural residents not under their protection, and the state's fiscal machinery alike. In Libanius' account, villagers under the protection of the soldiers plundered their neighbors, pelted the curial tax collectors with stones and threatened even worse. This may indeed have been the case, but we should be careful about accepting his account in its entirety, and in recent scholarship it has been situated within the context of a socio-economic competition between *curiales* and military men – in particular a competition over land and the workforce that went with it.[8] Further, by Libanius' own admission, the presence of the military in rural contexts is equally likely to have resulted in the oppression and exploitation of the rural population.[9]

No doubt a military presence in a region could bring with it both positive and negative effects for local populations.[10] Elsewhere in Syria, for example, inscriptional evidence attests the prominence of military personnel in the countryside, and documents their involvement in the construction of

---

[5] *CTh* xi.24.3 (395); 4 (399). Jaillette's account of these texts is now essential: Jaillette (2005), 206–8; 214. Also Giliberti's brief comments on these texts: Giliberti (1992), 206–7. The legislation also suggests that palatine officials took advantage of postings to their home provinces – as a law banning their being assigned to duty in those provinces reveals: *CTh* viii.8.4 (386, Italy and Illyricum).

[6] Libanius, *Or.* xxxix.6; 10. The man's name, Mixidemus is generally understood to be a fictitious name: Liebescheutz (1972), 199 with note 1.

[7] Libanius, *Or.* xlvii.4; 11. Cf. *CTh* i.21.1 (393, a general edict *comitibus et magistris utriusque militiae*).

[8] Carrié (1976), 174; 166–7; Krause (1987), 86. Petit, too, interprets Libanius' evidence in the context of a competition, but in his opinion, this competition is purely political, rather than socio-economic: Petit (1955), 376–7.

[9] Libanius, *Or.* xlv.5; Petit (1955), 189 and note 8; Krause (1987), 85–6 and notes 68–9.

[10] Cf. Fulford (1996) for economic benefits to regions with a military presence.

fortresses, towers, and, possibly, local churches as well.[11] A further counter-point to Libanius' rather pessimistic view of the impact of the military upon a region comes from Egypt, where an accident of survival has preserved a series of papyri which document the activities of a small-town garrison commander named Flavius Abinnaeus.[12] These petitions offer fleeting glimpses of the role that the inhabitants of rural communities in Egypt, at least, might expect members of the military to play in resolving their disputes. We observe, for example, a villager from Hermoupolis asking Abinnaeus to intervene in the apprehension of a man who, he claims, stole some pigs from him.[13] We may place alongside this purely internal conflict an accusation by an inhabitant of the village of Berenicis that a resident of the nearby village of Philagris robbed him in his house. Again, the perpe-trator is named, and the expectation that Abinnaeus will apprehend and punish the wrongdoer is clear.[14]

In this instance we lack the perspective of a figure comparable to Libanius, but Abinnaeus certainly does not appear to be acting in a manner calculated to offend or usurp the authority of local aristocrats. The partic-ulars of rural power structures in the countryside of Egypt in the fourth and fifth centuries have been the subject of considerable attention in recent scholarship, although those studies have tended to focus upon political domination and economic exploitation, rather than the social matrices that are the subject of the present study.[15] At any rate, for our current purposes it suffices to note that, in Egypt at least, members of the military had long exercised functions comparable to those expected of Abinnaeus.[16] In particular, the documents contained in this archive offer hints of the role of a figure such as Abinnaeus in mediating relations between soldiers, veterans, and their families on the one hand, and the inhabitants of the villages in and around which they lived, on the other. In this regard, it is worth observing that soldiers and veterans appear as petitioners themselves as often as they are the subject of petitions.[17] It seems reasonable to suggest, therefore, that the presence of the military in this instance did not inevitably entail an overwhelming rise in violence visited by soldiers upon the

[11] Trombley (2004), 83–7 collects references and offers further discussion.
[12] Teeter (2004), 31; Jaillette (2005), 204 with note 54. Accident of survival: Rathbone (2008), 195.
[13] *P. Abinn.* 53 (346).   [14] *P. Abinn.* 55 (351).
[15] See the detailed account of Banaji (2001), chapter 5. Cf. Banaji (2009), 62–3. Also, focused principally on the late fifth and sixth centuries, Wickham (2005b), 411–19; Sarris (2006b), particularly chapters 2–3. Political and economic rather than social focus: cf. Grey (2003), 379.
[16] Cf. Aubert (1995), *passim* and the brief comments of Palme (2007), 256.
[17] Petitioners: *P. Abinn.* 45; 47; 51–2 (daughter of a veteran). Perpetrators: *P. Abinn.* 46; 48; 49.

peasantry, nor did it necessarily cut across existing relations between local aristocrats and peasants.

Soldiers and garrisons are visible in the western provinces also, particularly in those which served as borders for the empire. As in the east, those regions with a military presence are likely to have experienced something of an economic boom by comparison with their non-militarized neighbors, although it is difficult to transform this economic data into evidence for the impact of soldiers upon local power structures.[18] Our most detailed evidence for the presence of members of the military derives from instances of settlement of barbarian soldiers and, sometimes, their families in regions of Gaul, Spain, and Africa over the course of the fifth century. The evidence is by no means unproblematic, and debate continues to rage over the precise terms of those settlements, but it seems likely that land was involved in many cases.[19] These figures are presented in our sources as strange and foreign, their dress, habits, and appearance marking them out as fundamentally different.[20] However, we should be careful not to overemphasize the degree to which they did, in fact, differ from existing elites, and cautious about overstating the disruption that their settlement caused for rural populations.[21] It is likely that some, at least, came to act as landlords to peasant tenants in the period. It is possible also that the presence of a barbarian *hospes* may have served to protect or insulate his host or tenant from the demands of the tax collector.[22] But our sources are largely silent about their impact upon existing power relationships in the countrysides of the western empire.

The consonance of tenancy and patronage that many of these examples reveal should not surprise us, for the two often go hand in hand in rural contexts. For peasants, certain advantages beyond access to land and resources attached to contracting a tenancy agreement with a wealthy landowner, whether that person was a member of the local curial

---

[18] Garrisons and soldiers in the western provinces: Wirth (1997); Visy (2001); Maas (forthcoming); Mathisen (forthcoming). References to the settlement of barbarians are collected by Ste. Croix (1981), 509–18. Note Whittaker (1994), 251–62; 271–4 on the effects of a military presence in frontier regions of the empire. Also Wickham (2005b), 476–7.

[19] Problems and concepts are summarized by Wirth (1997). See now Maas (forthcoming); Mathisen (forthcoming).

[20] E.g., Sidonius, *Ep.* IV.20; VIII.3.2.

[21] Degree of difference: cf. Sidonius *Ep.* I.2, depicting the Visigothic king Theoderic II in the mold of Suetonius' portrait of Augustus. Also Halsall (1992), interpreting the so-called *Reihengräberzivilisation* as a new style of self-representation among local aristocracies rather than evidence for the arrival and insertion of an entirely new elite. Minimal disruption: Garnsey (1996), 145. Cf. the summary of the debate over barbarian settlement in Wickham (2005b), 80–7.

[22] Cost of the absence of a barbarian *hospes*: Paulinus of Pella, *Euch.* 282–5.

aristocracy such as those whose demise in Antioch is lamented by Libanius, or a member of the senatorial aristocracy such as the Italian senator Symmachus or the individuals whose burgeoning influence in Egypt has recently been sketched.[23] For our current purposes, the most significant of these advantages is the opportunity that such an arrangement provided to the tenant for the cultivation of the landlord as an intercessor, protector, and buffer against subsistence and social risk – in short, a patron. The sources from the late empire betray a blurring of the conceptual boundaries between these two structurally distinct phenomena, with the result that arrangements of tenancy and relationships of patronage are interwoven, and appear in some circumstances to be interchangeable.

Perhaps the most explicit statement of this elision of the notional boundary between tenancy and patronage may be found in a pair of letters written to two high-ranking imperial officials by the Italian senator Symmachus, probably in 397. These letters were written on behalf of a *colonus* of Symmachus' fields who, it appears, was involved in some kind of legal proceedings concerning his taxes.[24] The language used is formulaic, as comparison with certain other letters of Symmachus on behalf of clients reveals.[25] Symmachus emphasizes his close relationship with this individual, and speaks of his personal obligation to the man. That obligation is expressed using the rhetoric of *humanitas* and debt that form such a fundamental part of a patron's self-representation. But what is unusual here is the emphasis Symmachus places upon his role as the man's landlord. The relationship he describes is not between *patronus* and *cliens*, or with a member of his own household, but between *dominus* and *colonus*. It is sufficient for Symmachus to describe their relationship as one of tenancy for his behavior in sponsoring his appeal to a pair of government officials to be comprehensible and justified.

Of course, the foundations of an individual's claims to power and influence over individuals or communities need not reside exclusively in the physical realm, or revolve around ownership of property or control over access to resources. Sorcerers and witches, shamans and healers, claiming special access to the supernatural or a unique set of skills had long been a feature of rural life in antiquity, where they might be found wandering the

[23] Sarris (2006b), 81–96; 115–30; Banaji (2001), 134–70. Cf. Wickham (2005b), 245.
[24] Symmachus, *Epp.* v.48, to Felix, *Quaestor Sacri Palatii*; vii.56, to Hadrianus, *Magister Officiorum*. For attribution of the addressee of the latter letter to Hadrianus, cf. Bonney (1975), 369–70. Fuller discussion of dating and subject-matter of these letters in Grey (2004) 29–30.
[25] E.g. Symmachus, *Epp.* ii.70; ix.57 (*c.* 402).

countryside or residing at the margins of a rural settlement. These figures
were often regarded with some degree of suspicion and fear, and their claims
to a position of privilege or influence over rural populations were frequently
the subject of negotiation or resistance. But they could also be approached
to act as mediators or intercessors for individuals or groups, or to adjudicate
disputes within the community.[26] The hagiographical literature of the late
Roman period provides some evidence for these figures, their actions,
motives, and legitimacy refracted through a particularly Christian lens. In
these texts, Christian holy men and women come into conflict with a wide
variety of pagan charlatans, whose claims are put to the test and ultimately
found to be without substance.[27] It is unlikely that the lines of battle,
drawn so starkly in these texts, were quite as sharp in reality, but these
sources do, at least, attest to the potential for the supernatural to function as
the foundation for an individual's claims to power and authority in the
period.[28]

The power of the supernatural might be complemented by the more
immediate influence that members of ecclesiastical hierarchies were able to
exert, backed up by the institutional resources of the Church. We may
sketch a bald trajectory over the course of the fourth and fifth centuries, as
the role of bishop was embraced first by relatively humble local figures and
then, as various privileges and immunities were attached to the office, by
men who might otherwise have served in the administrative bureaucracy of
their municipalities or the empire. By the early fifth century, we observe
some members of the senatorial aristocracy becoming bishops, and these
individuals brought with them the expectations and self-representational
arsenal of the Roman senatorial aristocracy.[29] These figures embraced, or
at least expressed, the particularly Christian vision of a community that
encompassed the poor as well as the rich, and in the process they created
social landscapes in the cities of the late Roman world that look fundamentally different from those which preceded them. While Jerome's scathing
vignette of charitable giving in the city of Rome reminds us that the
implications and realities of these transformations remain open to question,

---

[26] Suspicion and fear: e.g. Maximus of Turin, *Serm.* CVII.2; Theodoret, *Hist. Rel.* VII.2–3, with
discussion above, 88. Mark the Deacon, *V. Porph.* 17–19. Intercession and mediation: e.g. *Hist.
Mon. in Aeg.* VIII.30–7; Cf. Brown (1971), 87; 92–4; Mathisen (1996), 311.

[27] See, for example, the accounts of Ward (1981); Flint (1999). Also, more generally on figures of this sort
and the communities in which they existed, Kolenkow (2002).

[28] Cf. Ammianus Marcellinus, *Res Gestae* XVI.8.1, with Brown (1972), 124–5; Augustine, *Ep.* 11*.13.

[29] See the elegant summary of Van Dam (2007), 344–50. Also, the detailed study of Rapp (2005),
particularly 172–207.

there can be no doubt that Christian vocabularies had a profound effect on the self-representation of figures of power in the period.[30]

However, while we may with a certain degree of confidence comment upon the changes wrought by the Church and its bishops upon the social structures and ideological composition of the cities of the late Roman world, it is more difficult to determine the impact of the Church as an institution upon rural social relations. Peter Brown has argued that, over the course of the fourth century, the claims of Christian bishops to be "lovers of the poor" were predicated upon a new vision of the community that encompassed both urban and rural populations.[31] One important corollary of these claims was the establishment of hospices, hospitals, and *xenodocheia* from the second half of the fourth century.[32] These foundations were aimed, at least in principle, at the care of the disadvantaged and the stranger. They were located primarily in or on the immediate outskirts of cities, and tended to be associated with bishops or wealthy, pious laypersons. In Brown's construction, they were a crucial component in the self-representation of bishops in the period, functioning as a real source of relief and support for the community's poor and, as a consequence, bolstering the authority and legitimacy of the individual or individuals identified as responsible for their construction and maintenance.

But it is less clear what impact these institutions might have had upon rural populations.[33] Certainly, the abundant evidence for relatively free movement between city and countryside in the period allows for the possibility that some peasants might benefit, at least in a casual way, from these institutions, and I return to this point below.[34] On the other hand, there were certain limits to the ability of these institutions to minister to the needy, with the result that such care as was available tended to be directed towards individuals who were known to the administrator of the hospice or his associates, or could be vouched for. Our sources speak, for example, of travelers and supplicants needing some kind of chit or marker before they

---

[30] Jerome, *Ep.* 22.32; above, 82–3. Christian vocabularies of power: see, in particular, Brown (1992); Brown (2002). For some cautions about the realities of this transformation, cf. Grey and Parkin (2003), 289–91.

[31] Brown (1988), 75–103; Brown (2002), 5–6. Cf. Van Dam (2007), 359–60. For responses, nuances, and extensions, see, for example, Horden (2005), 362–3, with note 4; Corbo (2006), 170.

[32] The origins of these institutions are briefly sketched by Brown (2002), 33–5, who also provides further references. Cf. Mayer (2001), 62; Horden (2005), 364.

[33] To date, rural bishops have been the subject of only relatively limited study. Two recent treatments offer elegant surveys of the relevant literature and compelling arguments for granting them more attention: Dossey (2010), chapter 5 for North Africa; Bowes (forthcoming), for Italian contexts.

[34] Cf. above, 46–9.

were admitted.[35] We have no further information about how an individual might obtain such a thing, but it does not seem likely that humble *rustici* were very high on the list of recipients. I argued in the Introduction to this study that bishops and other Christian authors of the period spoke of the utterly destitute in an effort to excite the sympathy of their audience or flock, but tended to give to the known poor: individuals who had temporarily fallen from a position of relative ease, or who could be vouched for by other respected members of the community.[36] Peasants were neither one nor the other, and we should therefore be cautious about overemphasizing the influence of these charitable institutions and their impresarios upon the social matrices of the countrysides of the late Roman world.

Nevertheless, it is clear that over the course of the fourth and fifth centuries, the bishop emerges as a figure of power. In some circumstances, at least, his ability to claim authority over both urban and rural populations came to rest upon a combination of personal wealth and status, the institutional resources of the Church, and his capacity to inspire and mobilize his flock at times of crisis or need. Sidonius Apollinaris is a case in point, a man of considerable oratorical skills who had served as Prefect of the City of Rome before becoming bishop of Clermont-Ferrand in the Auvergne, the site of his ancestral holdings, where he was subsequently involved in both the relief of famine and the defense of his community from barbarian raids.[37]

Of course, contrasting figures are not difficult to find: Rabbula, for example, bishop of the city of Edessa in the early fifth century, whose background was not markedly different from Sidonius' but whose position as bishop rested upon fundamentally different foundations. He appears also to have been of relatively high birth, and might have pursued a career in the imperial bureaucracy. As bishop, he eschewed public building, in favor of an aggressive mission of ministry to the poor, sick, and disadvantaged of the city. One apparent consequence of this was that his bishopric was characterized by conflict with influential members of the church in the city, who challenged his authority and questioned his methods.[38] We should be

---

[35] E.g. Gregory of Nazianzen, *Orationes* 4.111. Cf. *Chronicle of Pseudo-Joshua the Stylite*, 42, for victims of a natural disaster being identified by lead seals around their necks, and provided with a small daily portion of bread. For a pagan perspective on the generosity of Christian practices of giving, see Julian, *Ep.* 22, also quoted in Sozomen, *Hist. Eccl.* v.16.

[36] Above, 11–12.

[37] For Sidonius' life and career path, cf. Harries (1994); Kaufmann (1995), 41–64. More generally, Brown (1981), 38–9 with notes; Lepelley (1998), *passim*.

[38] Care for the poor: *Heroic Deeds of Mar Rabbula*, 84; 88–90; 92–4. Conflict: *Heroic Deeds of Mar Rabbula*, 76–7; Drijvers (1996), 209. Discussed above, 81–2.

mindful of the particular objectives of our author in presenting Rabbula in this way, for his account is a particularly striking example of the hagiographical text focusing upon a moral exemplar rather than biographical particulars.[39] Nevertheless, when placed alongside Sidonius, the combination of parallels and contrasts between these two patterns of Christian behavior illustrates that bishops were far from a homogeneous phenomenon in the period. On the contrary, they made their claims to power and authority on the basis of a multitude of intertwined factors, emphasizing different aspects in different contexts, and to different interlocutors.

Variation in an individual bishop or holy figure's apparatus of self-representation can also be explored with reference to a broad contrast in the niches that these individuals occupied in the eastern and the western provinces. The eastern sources suggest that bishops were expected to live exemplary holy lives, but they were also recognized as notables in their cities, and came over the course of the fourth and fifth centuries to occupy important positions in civic hierarchies of power.[40] Charismatic holy figures tend to be portrayed evading or avoiding formal inclusion in ecclesiastical power structures. Instead, they withdraw from or even come into conflict with monasteries and the responsibilities of ecclesiastical office, and set themselves up either in deserts and caves or on the edges of small rural settlements. We should not be mesmerized by the illusion of isolation, for it was an important and fundamental topos of accounts of the lives of these holy figures in the period. In reality, it seems, these individuals were often heavily enmeshed in local power structures and broader networks of communication and influence. Holy men could and did become bishops and were as a consequence celebrated and commemorated in much the same ways.[41] Additionally, figures such as Pachomius and Shenoute presided over sizeable monastic communities in the desert of Egypt.[42] At any rate, we observe in the east immense variety in attitudes towards ecclesiastical hierarchies, and a correspondingly complex series of negotiations and

---

[39] Cf. Drijvers (1996), 207–8.   [40] Rapp (2005), 274–89. Cf., e.g., Mayer (2001), focusing on Antioch.

[41] Rapp (2005), Rubenson (2007), 641–2; 645–6; 661–2. The *locus classicus* for holy men in the eastern provinces remains Brown (1971), with his reconsideration of the phenomenon in Brown (1998). The motif of the holy man's withdrawal from civilization is established in Athanasius' *Life of Antony*, and becomes a stock topos in later literature. Cf. Elliott (1987); Frank (1998). Note also Kaplan (2004) for the ways in which ascetic withdrawal shapes sacred space. For representations of Egyptian ascetics as the "other," cf. Ševčenko (2000). Not all of these figures embraced power relationships, however: Whitby (1987).

[42] Pachomius: Rousseau (1999); Goehring (1996). Shenoute: Krawiec (2002); Emmel (2004). Cf. Rapp (2007), 551; Rubenson (2007), 650.

conflicts between individual holy figures and the bishops and other church
figures with whom they interacted.

In the west, by contrast, there was a little less heterogeneity in relations
between individual sanctity and ecclesiastical authority. The opportunities
for spectacular self-abnegation in harsh and inhospitable environments were
more limited and, arguably, the institutional influence of the Church
greater. As a consequence, saints tended also to be included within
Church hierarchies, or to function as the heads of communities of monks
or nuns.[43] This is not to say that claims to authority were any less complex in
the west. On the contrary, bishops came to be enmeshed in the affairs of
their cities in much the same ways as their eastern counterparts. In addition,
our sources reveal them playing a multiplicity of roles in connection with
the *rustici* who were part of their religious communities, or resided on or
around their estates. In letters written on behalf of small agriculturalists,
laborers, and tenants, we witness Sidonius Apollinaris behaving, in turn, as
an intercessory figure on the strength of his role as bishop; as a beneficent
patron to his dependents; and even as the head of an extended family group
which, in this case, includes both urban and rural members. We can explore
each example in a little more detail, for they illustrate the complex foundations upon which an individual figure of power's claims to legitimacy and
authority might rest.

Sidonius appears to have been a little reluctant to assume the role of
bishop, but once he did, he may be observed exploiting the vocabulary of
Christian piety and accessing the Church's networks of influence on behalf
of members of his congregation as well as other adherent Christians who
sought his aid. A letter to Bishop Censorius of Auxerre on behalf of a deacon
who had been forced to flee his home by the depredations of the Goths
illustrates Sidonius' skill at combining the two. As Sidonius tells the story,
this deacon had sown some seed on a partially tilled field belonging to the
Church of Auxerre, and now sought to be excused the obligation to tender a
tithe to the bishop. Sidonius adds a clever sweetener to his request on behalf
of the deacon, which places this interaction firmly within the context of the
Church: should Censorius agree to excuse the deacon his tithe, the resulting
letter will be cherished by the brethren at Clermont Ferrand as a blessing

---

[43] Dunn (2007), 671–2; Van Dam (2007), 348–9. Cf. MacMullen (1990), 264–71; Grey (2005), 56. For
networks of ecclesiastical authority, see in particular the influence of alumni of Lérins: Mathisen
(1989), 76–89; Anton (1993), 43–5; Miele (1996), 151–6; Gioanni (2000), 157–60. Note also Gregory of
Tours' account of the attempts of local bishops to rein in a would-be ascetic's behavior: Gregory of
Tours, *Historia Francorum* VIII.15, with Rapp (2007), 556–7.

dropped from heaven.[44] We witness Sidonius emphasizing another aspect of his apparatus of self-representation in a letter written to Riothamus, king of Aremorica. In this case, Sidonius intervenes on behalf of a man whom he describes as *humilis* and *despicibilis*. The man claims that his slaves have been lured away by certain of Riothamus' subjects, and seeks a fair hearing in the matter. Sidonius seems to know a little more about the man than in the case of intercession as a bishop just mentioned, for he offers a neat rhetorical flourish to the effect that the man's humble and unassuming nature might lead to the charge that he was, in fact, something of a naïve simpleton.[45]

More complex is the case of an elopement by the daughter of a *nutrix*, or wet-nurse residing on one of Sidonius' estates with the son of a *nutrix* from an estate belonging to a man named Pudens. Sidonius' attitude towards the matter appears to hinge upon questions of honor, for the young man in question was entered into the municipal tax rolls as an *inquilinus*, or registered tenant. In Sidonius' opinion, at least, this made marriage between the two problematic, and he instructs Pudens to change the legal status of the man to that of a legally free, taxpaying client rather than a bound, dependent tenant. The legal intricacies of the matter are difficult to untangle, and need not detain us here. For our current purposes, we should focus upon the vocabulary of personal shame that permeates the letter: Sidonius labels the young man a *raptor*, and speaks of *indignum*, *stuprum*, and *contumelia*.[46] It would appear, then, that this is a case not of patronage or intercession by a disinterested but pious bishop, but rather of the head of a household seeking to preserve his honor and that of his family. In this context, however, Sidonius' conception of his family has extended to encompass non-free dependents residing on his rural estates.[47] Of course, the boundaries drawn above between the three aspects of Sidonius' self-representation are artificial and difficult to maintain. But this difficulty is an eloquent illustration of the fundamental point: figures of power were able to call upon a range of vocabularies in making their claims to authority and legitimacy in the period.

The experiences, effectiveness, and strategies available to these would-be patrons and figures of power must be analyzed in the light of the social

---

[44] Sidonius, *Ep.* VI.10.2. Reluctance: cf. the career trajectory of Sidonius, as sketched by Harries (1994); Kaufmann (1995), 41–64. Further examples of intercession in the role of bishop: *Epp.* VI.3; VII.2. Cf. also, for example, Ruricius of Limoges, *Ep.* II.20, a letter written on behalf of a rural laborer who had fled his landlord's wrath and taken refuge in Ruricius' church.

[45] Sidonius, *Ep.* III.9.2. For further examples of Sidonius interceding in the role of a landlord or patron, cf. *Epp.* II.7; IV.7.

[46] Sidonius, *Ep.* V.19. Full discussion of this letter in Grey (2008).   [47] Cf. Grey (2008), 298–300.

matrices sketched in the preceding chapters. I suggested there that the rural communities of the eastern provinces were, on the whole, somewhat more complex, more characterized by internal tensions, and possessed of a more clearly expressed communal identity than their smaller counterparts in the west. This contrast has implications for the strategies available to peasants in their interactions with powerful figures which appear on the surface to be contradictory. On the one hand, the loose networks of villages that dotted the provinces of the east created a series of foci for the social dynamics that characterized the small worlds of peasants to play out. We may expect the inhabitants of these villages to have been in a somewhat stronger bargaining position as a result of their greater sense of corporate identity. But, it seems, the attending social complexity, and the need to balance competing and contradictory tensions within those communities hampered their capacity to manipulate effectively vocabularies of power. Further, the predominance and centripetal pull of cities as residences for the aristocracies of the eastern Mediterranean produced a countryside that was less populated by figures of power. As a consequence, we may imagine that the inhabitants of the countrysides of the eastern Mediterranean were less adept because less practiced at interacting with those figures on a regular basis.

A series of exchanges between Simeon the Stylite and the inhabitants of a small village near Gindaris in Syria illustrates both aspects of interactions between rural communities and the powerful in the east. It also reveals something of the dynamics possible in interactions between a charismatic holy man and the elected or appointed representatives of the Church. When these villagers discovered that their water supply had dried up, they sent to Simeon for help. It emerged that one of their number had worked on a Sunday, in defiance of the saint's instruction. Initially, he reacted with anger and refused to help them, but when the priests of other villages were called in to help to sway him, he relented. The value that our author attaches to the holy man's reputation among the inhabitants of the Syrian countryside is here highlighted, as, too is the capacity for those in a position of dependence to take advantage of a powerful figure's vocabulary of self-representation. We observe also a clear, if perhaps rhetorically colored, statement of the relative positions of Simeon and local ecclesiastics. Simeon's next act appears to emphasize further the negotiated character of his interactions with these villagers, when he insists that they sign a covenant not to act in this way again before he consents to help them.[48]

---

[48] *V. Sim. Styl. (S)* 64. For the conditional and contested nature of a holy man's reputation, cf., for example, Theodoret, *Hist. Rel.* VII.2–3, with discussion above, 88; *Hist. Mon. in Aeg.* VIII.30–7.

We catch glimpses here of the complex internal dynamics and divisions within a village that were sketched in the preceding chapters. We may imagine, for example, that the decision to approach the holy man was taken by a small group of more influential individuals, although we have no way of determining what the impetus for that decision might have been. In the intervention of the priests of neighboring villages, we observe also something of the complex web of connections that linked this village with its neighbors in a larger, regional community. Of most interest in the current context, however, is the condition that Simeon places upon his resolution of the village's water problems. While our author is little interested in the particulars of this covenant, it seems reasonable to suggest that it is not in fact offered to the whole community, but rather to the same small group that decided to approach him – or, perhaps more likely, the representatives it sent to seek his aid.

Perhaps we should imagine a situation analogous to the one hinted at in the document commemorating the settlement of a dispute over water rights that was discussed in the previous chapter. In that instance, a small group within the village community appears to have undertaken to guarantee the behavior of their fellow-villagers, basing their capacity to do so upon their reputation and standing within that community.[49] If so, we observe here Simeon seeking to force a particular code of behavior upon this village, then placing responsibility for enforcing that code upon some small segment of the village's community. Such a strategy on the part of the holy man reveals a subtle understanding of the internal workings of a village community. Indeed, given the potential for conflict, tension, and competing interests that were observed operating within communities of this sort, we might expect this to have impacted in a variety of detrimental ways upon the village's mechanisms for maintaining its equilibrium and balancing internal tensions.

In the west, we observe a subtly different but equally telling set of contrasts. Arguably, relations of power are presented in our sources as more obviously those between unequals. In a sermon of Maximus of Turin, for example, delivered to a congregation made up principally of aristocratic landowners in the early fifth century, it is assumed that responsibility for the actions and beliefs of the peasantry rests firmly upon the shoulders of their landlords and patrons. Legislators, ecclesiastical figures, and aristocratic landowners elsewhere in the western provinces evince similar sentiments about the relative bargaining positions of powerful and

[49] Above, 114.

less powerful figures.[50] These expressions of dominance can, perhaps, be connected to the more dispersed patterns of settlement evident in the western empire, for in such circumstances, we may posit closer proximity between aristocrats and *rustici* than in the east and therefore a more explicit set of expectations about the nature of interactions between the two. This is not to say that powerful figures in the west necessarily had a greater knowledge of or interest in peasants than their eastern counterparts: on the contrary, I argued above that our authors are largely ignorant of the motivations and world view of *rustici*, and I return to this proposition below.[51] But if there was greater physical proximity in the western provinces, with the corollary of more regular contact between peasants and the powerful, it may be the case that the former had more regular experience of accessing, negotiating with, and exploiting the vocabularies of power used by the latter.

Unsurprisingly, our western authors are somewhat less than forthcoming on the subject of *rustici* exploiting or manipulating aristocratic claims to authority. But, in the pages that follow, peasants of the western provinces can be observed manipulating the powerful in a variety of subtle ways. We will encounter, for example, a rural laborer extracting a letter of recommendation from his landlord, even though the latter's opinion of him can at best be described as extreme distaste; tenants on an African estate manipulating both their landlord and the local bishop with threats to leave if an unpopular bishop is not removed; small agriculturalists seeking out powerful aristocrats and initiating tenancy contracts with them in order to safeguard their subsistence livelihoods; and *rustici* expressing skepticism about the efficacy of the Christian God, and baiting a holy figure into a life-threatening test of faith.[52] These examples are suggestive rather than conclusive, but they offer hints that contact between the powerful and the relatively powerless was somewhat more mundane in the west than in the east, and therefore more open to exploitation from below.

We may surmise that this greater familiarity among peasants in the west with the experience of interacting with the powerful gave them a greater

[50] Maximus of Turin, *Sermones* 53. Cf. *CJ* iv.25.5 (294, provenance unknown), with Aubert (1994), 109 and note 282; *CTh* ii.31.1 = *CJ* iv.26.1 *mut.*; *CTh* ii.30.2; *CTh* ii.32.1 = *CJ* iv.26.13 (422, West). These laws together constitute evidence for the history of the *actio quod iussu* in the period: cf. G. and M. Sautel (1959). Also the anonymously authored *Ep. ad Salv.* 2.9; Salvian, *De Gubernatione Dei* iv.15.74–5, with further discussion below.

[51] Above, 5–15; below, 167–75.

[52] Letter of recommendation: Sidonius, *Ep.* iv.7, below, 157–8. African tenants: Augustine, *Ep.* 247, below, 145–6. Tenancy contracts: Salvian, *De Gubernatione Dei* v.8.38–45, below, 210–12 and cf. Grey (2006), 176–80. Skepticism: Sulpicius Severus, *V. Mart.* 13, below, 154–5.

adeptness – or at the very least, more confidence and insistence – in those interactions. We may compare, for example, the exasperated tone adopted by the Italian senator Symmachus when speaking of a rural dependent's demands that he intervene in a legal dispute with the unquestioning manner in which the residents of a village in the Antioch valley accede to the somewhat haughty demands of their landlord for their rents.[53] Cumulatively these vignettes offer glimpses of a western peasantry that was able to manipulate the claims to authority and legitimacy of a variety of powerful figures with a degree of sophistication that arguably exceeded the capabilities and ambitions of peasants in the eastern Mediterranean.[54]

COMPLEMENTARITY, COMPETITION, AND THE LIMITS OF NEGOTIATION

While some of these patrons and would-be patrons were clearly new and without precedent, they were not in every instance as markedly different from existing patrons as they appear in the sources. In many cases, the novelty lay in the vocabulary of power that these individuals adopted, and the role that rural populations played in their armories of self-representation. It seems, for example, that rural patronage became a more important element in the self-representation of some figures of power in the fourth and fifth centuries. Simeon the Stylite's biographer places a premium upon the role that his hero adopted as defender and champion of the poor, emphasizing repeatedly the authority and legitimacy that Simeon enjoyed as a result.[55] Of course, intercession on behalf of the poor becomes a motif of Christian hagiographical literature in the period, and, in a manner similar to Gregory of Nazianzen's portrait of the poor, Simeon's hagiographer performs something of a sleight-of-hand in equating the inhabitants of rural communities with the destitute. Nevertheless, Christians were not alone in seeking out new, rural contexts for expressing their power and authority in the period. Libanius, for example, attests to the aggressive attention paid by both *honorati* and members of the military to cultivating relations of patronage with the inhabitants of the villages and hamlets that dotted the hinterland of Antioch.[56]

---

[53] Symmachus, *Ep.* IX.11, below, 159. Theodoret, *Hist. Rel.* XIV.2–4, below, 145; 152.
[54] Contra Wickham (2005b), 471, who argues for the relative weakness of rural communities in the western provinces.
[55] *V. Sim. Styl. (S)* 39; 42–3; 56–8.　　[56] Libanius, *Or.* XXXIX.6; 10; *Or.* XLVII.

Likewise, the letter collections of both Christian and non-Christian aristocrats in the western provinces reveal these individuals reconfiguring their armories of self-representation. These changes are subtle, but tangible nonetheless. We glimpse in those letter collections a small but significant number of letters written for tenants, rural laborers, and farm managers. We may imagine that, occasionally, similar letters were written by Cicero or by Pliny the Younger – men whose published collections were the model for letter writers in late antiquity. But their subjects were not deemed appropriate for publication, and so they were not preserved in those collections. By contrast, authors of the fourth and fifth centuries do, occasionally, preserve such letters in their own collections. The interest taken by Symmachus in the legal travails of one of his tenants has already been mentioned. We may place alongside it, for example, a letter written at the urging of a rural dependent of some sort, named Amazonius. This letter was also apparently written in connection with a legal dispute, involving another *rusticus* named Ursus. The letter is fragmentary in places and the nature of the dispute is unclear, but it would appear that the recipient is again an Imperial official. In this particular instance, as we shall see, the pious expressions of beneficence on behalf of Ursus are in marked contrast to his attitude towards the go-between in the affair, Amazonius.[57]

A letter of Ausonius of Bordeaux is even more revealing of the contradiction that might exist between distaste and obligation in relations of this kind. The letter is a rarity in Ausonius' collection, for his correspondence does not on the whole concern itself with identifying or even acknowledging the existence of letter carriers. Here, as elsewhere in his collection, Ausonius is principally concerned with demonstrating his literary sophistication and wit, and his attitude towards the petitioner and subject of this letter is rather condescending. In this letter, written for his former bailiff, Philo, he derisively labels the man a *graeculus*, or "Greekling" and mocks him for his desire to be styled an *epitropos* rather than simply a *vilicatus*. Nevertheless, he writes the letter, and, even more surprising, preserves it in his letter collection. In the process, he appears to betray his interest in at least seeming to be sensitive to the needs of his rural clientele.[58] Alongside these few hints of a greater attention among aristocratic landowners to playing the role of patron in rural contexts in the period may be placed

---

[57] Symmachus, *Ep.* IX.11. It is possible that Amazonius is a bailiff on one of Symmachus' estates. For possible implications of this for the nature of their relationship, below, 143.

[58] Ausonius, *Ep.* 26.

other letters of Christian bishops and landowners, who we have already observed intervening in the affairs of their flocks, dependents, and tenants in a variety of ways in the period.

Additionally, we witness some aristocratic landlords, at least, taking a more active interest in the management of their estates in the period. The impulse has its most explicit expression in the handbook of agriculture written by the Italian or Gallo-Roman agronomist, Palladius. We should not accept at face value Palladius' claim that the treatise was written specifically for *rustici*, but there are hints that it was intended as something more than merely a philosophical treatise or an exercise in demonstrating his command of technical arcana. The work is organized month by month, which leads to a certain amount of repetition, but also makes for a manual that might be somewhat more useful in a practical sense than those of his predecessors. While Palladius pays relatively little attention to the man-power resources attendant upon the agricultural enterprises he describes, his interest in matters rural is nevertheless palpable, and it is echoed in other authors of the period.[59] It would seem, then, that over the course of the fourth and fifth centuries, we witness some aristocratic landowners, at least, focusing more carefully upon their rural estates, their personal exchange networks in rural contexts, the role they could play as patrons of the communities that inhabited those estates and the surrounding countryside, and the benefits that might accrue from playing that role in contestations with other potentates over status and power.[60]

For existing patrons and landlords, this new attention to rural clienteles by other figures of power was potentially threatening, and elicited a range of responses. Resistance was one such response. We might call to mind, once again, Martin's encounter with a conspiracy of demoniacs in Trier, and place alongside that incident a series of stories in the hagiographical literature that revolve around the demonic possession of children or dependents of local aristocrats and imperial potentates. For the authors of these stories, the saint's ability to cure these children, and their parents' acknowledgment of that power were eloquent statements of the legitimacy and authority of their heroes. But recent medical anthropological literature has drawn

---

[59] Written for *rustici*: Palladius *Op. Ag.* 1.1. For Palladius' reputation as an author and his engagement with his predecessors, see Grey (2007b), 364, with further references. Interest in agricultural matters: e.g. Paulinus of Pella, *Euch.* 198–200, with MacLynn (1995), 477–8; Drinkwater (2001), 140–1. For a more general survey of aristocrats' closer attention to the management of their estates in the period, see Wickham (2005b), 268–72.

[60] For more general comments on the impulse among new figures of power to embrace local power structures, see Silverman (1977), 17.

connections between particular types of bodily dysfunction and feelings of anxiety about dislocation and disempowerment. It is therefore tempting to interpret the fact of demonic possession among these particular children as indicative of a deeper unease with their place in a world that was rapidly changing its contours of power and authority.[61] These implicit expressions of distress about their circumstances may profitably be placed alongside more explicit statements in our literary sources to reveal the broad spectrum that expressions and perceptions of conflict might take.

In his oration to the emperor against the protection offered by military men to the residents of villages in the surrounding countryside, for example, Libanius emphasizes the illegitimacy of these new patronal figures by focusing upon their role in preventing the taxes of the villagers under their protection from being collected. As we have seen, this is only part of the story, and Libanius' portrait of an oppressed curial class is somewhat overblown. Nevertheless, the antagonism he sketches accords with the more subtle expressions that we can glean from the hagiographical sources, and we may imagine a range of strategies open to local aristocrats. While we should not imagine wholesale flight from curial obligations in the period, there is no doubt that some *curiales*, at least, were able to evade their responsibilities and the potential for conflict that came with them, either through physical relocation or through attempts to obtain the privileges, if not the obligations, of inclusion in the imperial hierarchy of offices and statuses.[62]

Alternatively, however, existing potentates might choose to accommodate new figures of power, and cooperate with them. Such a decision is likely to have involved a certain amount of negotiation between the two parties. One such negotiation is preserved in the account of the life and career of Daniel the Stylite, who set himself up on an elevated platform on the outskirts of Constantinople in the middle of the fifth century. Our author hints at conflict over Daniel's choice of site when he observes that a companion of the holy man and a group of workmen erected the platform at night. The next day, they discovered that residents from the surrounding region had made plans to knock the column down, and the conflict escalated further when the owner of the nearby property, a member of the imperial bureaucracy named Gelanius, learnt of Daniel's actions from a

---

[61] E.g. Sulpicius Severus, *Dialog.* III.2; Paulinus, *V. Amb.* 28; Constantius, *V. Germani* 15; 26–7; 38–9; Theodoret, *Hist. Rel.* III.22; *V. Sim. Styl. (S)* 33; 81; *V. Dan. Styl.* 37. Bodily dysfunction and anxiety: e.g. Csordas (1990); Lock (1993); Migliore (1994). For applications of these insights in late Roman contexts, see Horden (1993), 187; Grey (2005), 61–7.

[62] Jones (1970) collects legal references. Cf. *V. Sim. Styl. (S)* 60.

group of peasants. After an unsuccessful appeal to the emperor, Gelanius approached the holy man in person, setting the scene for a spectacular confrontation. However, rather than carry through on his threats to evict the holy man, Gelanius engineered a situation whereby the holy man seemed about to descend from his column, only to be stopped, invited to re-ascend and asked to pray for Gelanius' sins.[63] This carefully orchestrated performance of accommodation provided the interloper with a degree of legitimacy, since his right to remain was tacitly acknowledged by the owner of the land. Meanwhile, the landowner himself was able to maintain his reputation as an effective protector of his dependents while at the same time bolstering his credentials as a pious man. Gelanius immediately undertook to provide the saint with a higher and more elaborate column, thereby seeking to establish himself in the role of patron to the holy man, although in our author's account it is the holiness of the saint and the will of God that prompted these actions. The ambiguity of relations between different figures of power, claiming authority in different ways, is here clearly revealed.

Established figures of power in local contexts might seek to reposition themselves in the changing power landscapes in other ways, too. We observe, for example, men of curial status acting as farm managers or bailiffs, *procuratores* or *actores* of private estates in the period.[64] Farm managers were by no means a unified or homogeneous category in the Roman period, but in late antiquity as in earlier periods, such individuals functioned as the fundamental linking mechanism between an aristocratic landowner and the labor force on his fields, and as a consequence, there were certain ambiguities to the position that might be exploited.[65] It is likely, for example, that the rhetorical stance taken in certain landlords' letters of close, personal relations with the inhabitants of their rural estates

---

[63] *V. Dan. Styl.* 25–8.

[64] This was forbidden in the legislation, and equated with accepting a servile status: *CTh* XII.1.92 = *CJ* X.32.34 *mut.* (382, East); *Nov. Theod.* IX.1.1 (439). Cf. Augustine, *Ep.* 24*.2, who regards accepting a position as a bailiff as tantamount to becoming a slave. However, Lepelley (1983a), 338–9 demonstrates that free *actores* were not at all unusual.

[65] Various statuses: Cf. Lepelley (1983a), 338, discussing legislation of Septimius Severus that forbade the auction of *vilici* of estates confiscated by the Fisc (*Dig.* XXXIX.4.16; XLIX.14.30). Carlsen (1995), 92, argues for a hierarchy of *dominus–procurator–vilicus* or *actor*, but this does not appear to hold into the late Roman period, and distinctions between the functions of different types of bailiffs are difficult to sustain: cf. *CTh* XVI.5.65 (428); *Nov. Maj.* VII.4 (458). The latest attestation of *vilicus* in a rural context in the legislation is *CJ* VII.38.2 (292), and note also Symmachus *Ep.* VI.81. Vera has argued on the basis of Ausonius' *Ep.* 26 that bailiffs came to oversee *coloni*: Vera (1997), 217–18. This might also be inferred from the *Ep. ad Salv.* The approach followed here is that of Teitler (1993), 210–11, who suggests treating all of these roughly synonymous terms under the same general heading of farm managers.

was in many instances mediated in reality through a bailiff or farm manager.[66] The bailiff was therefore simultaneously the agent of the landlord, an intermediary through which petitions or complaints from tenants or laborers could pass, and a dependent of that landlord. As such, he was able to take advantage of the opportunities the post offered to exploit both the role of a client and the privileges of a patron. As clients and agents, estate managers could trade upon the wealth, standing, and influence of their landlords.[67] As mediators and figures of power on and around their estates, they are likely to have garnered a certain amount of reputation and influence from successful instances of mediation between tenants and laborers on the one hand, and the landowner on the other.[68]

Equally, estate managers might exploit their role as both the landlord's agent and the closest figure of power, to the detriment of landowner and tenant alike. One such opportunity for exploitation was provided by the fiscal system. The *actor* was characteristically responsible for collecting rents of his landlord's tenants, and legislation of the period reveals that he might also collect the taxes owed by those tenants.[69] The opportunities for abuse of this responsibility are clear, and may be observed in a letter of Augustine to a landowner named Romulus. The exact circumstances of this letter are somewhat obscure, but it appears that Augustine had been approached to intercede on behalf of Romulus' tenants, who claimed that they had been forced by Romulus' bailiff to pay their taxes twice.[70]

Augustine's carefully worded rebuke to Romulus reveals the autonomy with which a bailiff might be expected to act, and in recognizing this he is not alone. A law censuring the holding of heretical assemblies on rural estates, for example, acknowledges that a bailiff could act with a considerable degree of independence when it imposes different penalties according to the landlord's degree of involvement and knowledge.[71] Romulus' involvement in this case is difficult to determine, and we may envisage a multitude of possible scenarios. Augustine seems to hint at two in

---

[66] Augustine, *Ep.* 20*.17; *PSI* IX.1081 (late fourth century, Oxyrhynchus). Also, perhaps, Symmachus, *Ep.* IX.11. Cf. MacMullen (1990), 255.

[67] Cf. Ausonius, *Ep.* 26.

[68] Cf. *PSI* IX.1081 (late fourth century, Oxyrhynchus), where a farm manager mediates the request by a group of tenants for a loan from their landlord. Note also evidence from the Appianus estate in third-century Egypt: Rathbone (1991), 71.

[69] *CTh* XI.1.14 = *CJ* XI.48.4 (371, East); *CTh* VI.2.16 (395, Rome).   [70] Augustine, *Ep.* 247.

[71] *CTh* XVI.5.57 (415, East). The *procuratores* in this case may have been of curial status. The punishment of exile here may be compared with that of deportation threatened in *CTh* XII.1.92 = *CJ* X.32.34 *mut.* (382, East). See also *CTh* I.16.14 (408, Italy); *CTh* XVI.5.65.3 (428, East); *Nov. Maj.* VII.1.4 (458, Italy). For economic independence of bailiffs, cf. *P. Oxy.* 1126 (fifth century); Foxhall (1990), 103; 105.

particular. In the first instance, Romulus simply instructed his bailiff to extract double the customary or agreed amount of rent from his tenants. Legislation survives directing that in such circumstances, tenants had a right to legal redress, although interestingly they have chosen in this instance not to exercise it.[72] In the second instance, the *actor* in question embezzled the tenants' contributions, then, finding himself at risk of being discovered in this fraud, later extracted the same amount again. In these circumstances, too, we may imagine that there was an avenue of legal redress open. Consequently, the choice of Augustine as an intercessor may betray a reluctance to take the matter to the courts. But it also reveals a keen awareness of the possible benefits of pitting two figures of power against one another.

No doubt, relations between some landowners and their bailiffs were fraught at times. In addition to situations such as the one that Augustine hints at, we may imagine that in some circumstances bailiffs might overstep or overestimate their position in relation to their landlord. This might create conflict, both in the cases censured in the legislation where men of relatively high status turned to farm management, and in contexts where a relatively humble individual seeks to overplay his hand, such as Ausonius' bailiff, Philo. Additionally, different attitudes towards the needs of the farm could lead to tension. Symmachus complains bitterly about the condition of one of his rural estates, which appears to be in a sorry state as a result of the cropping decisions made by his bailiff.[73] We can glean no further information about this particular individual, but, in another letter, Symmachus appears also to be speaking of a bailiff when he complains about the doggedness with which a certain Amazonius is pursuing him to intervene in a dispute involving a *rusticus* named Ursus. It is possible that here, as also in the letter of Ausonius for Philo, we are witnessing the implications of the sometimes close and quite regular interactions between an involved landowner and his farm manager.[74] Clearly, for landowners, those interactions might carry with them a certain amount of distaste and frustration.

Other figures may be observed attempting to impose new vocabularies of power and, by extension, authority upon rural populations, with varying degrees of success. Martin's hagiographer Sulpicius Severus portrays the saint converting the rural inhabitants of Gaul to Christianity, but we are struck by the fact that his hero's attempts to eradicate the worship of pagan

---

[72] *CJ* XI.50.1 (325, East); 2 (396S, East). Vera notes that this legislation, too, is concerned with behavior that affects the transition of revenues to the Fisc; Vera (1997), 206 with note 69.

[73] Symmachus, *Ep.* VI.81.   [74] Symmachus, *Ep.* IX.11, discussed further below, 159.

deities was marked by as many failures as successes. Indeed, Sulpicius offers eloquent testimony for the sometimes violent nature of interactions between a new potentate and the inhabitants of rural communities when he describes *rustici* attacking the saint with swords and knives as he attempted to destroy temples and shrines in the region.[75]

John of Ephesus' account of the actions of Simeon the Mountaineer in the mountain village of M'rbn' in the Euphrates region reveals that inter-actions of this sort might have costs for the community itself. While wandering in the mountains as was his habit over the summer months, Simeon encountered a group of shepherds, cattle herders, and agricultur-alists who lived in a loosely agglomerated collection of hamlets. While these men claimed to be Christians, their Christianity was not sufficiently organ-ized for Simeon's liking, and their church exhibited signs of neglect and disrepair. After stealthily gathering information about the children of the community, Simeon seized them all, forcibly tonsured thirty of them, and released the others to spread the news of his actions. The villagers responded with anger, and seized two of the children back, in spite of the holy man's threats that they would die if they were not returned to him. When the children did indeed die, the inhabitants of the village succumbed to Simeon's claims to exercise authority over them. Ultimately, he remained in the community for twenty-six years, cowing the residents of the sur-rounding mountains.[76]

Questions can be raised about this story at almost every point, and the picture that emerges of interactions between Simeon and his flock is some-what unsettling. Although his actions are presented as entirely praiseworthy, they were underpinned by violence and intimidation, and appear to have resulted in an ongoing relationship of antagonism between him and his flock. While his hagiographer presents his legitimacy and authority as entirely unproblematic, we gain the impression of a reign of terror rather than a reciprocal relationship of patronage. We may, perhaps, place this and other stories which appear to celebrate violent resistance to the actions of saints alongside the accounts discussed above of fundamental disjunctions between existing familial structures and the new family that the Christian community offered.[77] Certainly, by stressing the degree of resistance and the unwillingness of the community to embrace the saint, hagiographers were able to emphasize their heroes' success when it came. I return to this

---

[75] Sulpicius Severus, *V. Mart.* 14–15.   [76] John of Ephesus, *Lives of the Eastern Saints* 16: *PO* 17.232–7.
[77] Above, 38–40.

point briefly below in discussions of relations of dominance and resistance between potentates and *rustici*.

Simeon's hagiographer John presents the village of M'rbn' as entirely separated from interactions with other powerful figures, but this is unlikely. In fact, we should imagine that most rural communities entertained one or more patrons as a matter of course. In such circumstances, the community might exploit competition between those patrons to its own advantage.[78] Two examples, one involving a village community in Syria and one the residents of an estate in North Africa, illustrate the possibilities and the limits of such negotiations, and the stakes for the participants. In his account of the life of Maësymas, a Syrian holy man residing in a village in the hinterland of Antioch, Theodoret relates a confrontation with the master (*despotês*) of the village, a pagan *curialis* by the name of Letoius.[79] The foundations upon which Maësymas' authority rested in this situation are unclear, but we are told that he had been entrusted with the care of this village, and functioned as their priest. Letoius visited the village, and demanded the fruits of the field from the villagers with more severity than was necessary. When the great man attempted to depart, having rebuffed the holy man's pleas that he show a degree of kindness and pity, his carriage became stuck fast and would not move, despite the efforts of the villagers to extricate it. Eventually, he prostrated himself before Maësymas and asked forgiveness for the manner of his actions. He was subsequently allowed to depart. This seemingly conventional narrative of the agent of Christ's confrontation with and triumph over paganism masks a complex situation. The community is not attempting here to replace or defy their *despotês*, and at no point is the legitimacy of Letoius' authority over the village challenged. Nor is it the fact of Letoius' demands that are at issue, merely their manner. Maësymas' intervention may have been requested by his flock, or he may have done so of his own accord, but in either case, the result for the village is not a change in circumstances, simply a change in the character that their interactions took with Letoius. The presence of two complementary figures of power in their orbit allows these peasants to negotiate the terms, but not the fact of their subjugation.

By way of contrast, Augustine's account of a dispute over a wildly unpopular bishop named Antoninus in the region of Fussala in North Africa reveals

---

[78] Garnsey and Woolf (1989), 164–5, with specific reference to competition between imperial and curial elites. Cf. Jaillette (2005), 204 with note 54 for Egypt. Inscriptional evidence from Timgad in North Africa shows who is involved in local power politics: *Album ordinis Thamugadensis*; *Ordo Salutationis*, with Lepelley (1981a), 338 and *passim*. Cf. Salvian, *De Gubernatione Dei* v.4.18, with Lepelley (1983b), 144; 149.

[79] Theodoret, *Hist. Rel.* XIV.2–4. This is not the Letoius of Libanius' *Or.* XLVII: Petit (1955), 349; 399.

a community turning to complementary figures of power in order to exploit fully their value as tenants and clients.[80] As Augustine tells the story, upon his ordination as bishop of Fussala and its surrounds, Antoninus immediately began to deport himself in a manner that was inconsistent with the expectations of both his superiors and his flock. He rejected the obligations placed upon a bishop to see to the spiritual and material wellbeing of his congregation, and instead created a climate of violence and fear to facilitate his pursuit of wealth and power. Augustine's account is a litany of the illegitimate exercise of power: robbery and plunder, eviction and appropriation of material resources, the breaking of contracts, theft of the fruits of the harvest.[81] For our current purposes, however, it is the responses that Antoninus' behavior elicited that are of most interest. We observe, for example, an accusation of adultery being pursued against him through the courts, as well as a letter to the primate of Africa from the inhabitants of Fussala.[82] When he sought and obtained a position over the tenants residing on the nearby *fundus Thogonoetis*, they wrote both to their landlord and to Augustine in protest, threatening to leave if he was confirmed as their bishop. They also staged a public demonstration against Antoninus in the presence of the primate of Africa, and were promptly excommunicated.[83]

The stakes in this matter are clearly high. For their landlord, of course, their potential departure threatened to damage her revenue flow and, by extension, might have impacted upon her capacity to fulfill her obligations for the payment of taxes. Her reputation among both her peers and in the eyes of other tenants and clients was also under threat. Similarly, Augustine's reputation, legitimacy, and authority, both as Antoninus' superior and as the titular head of the church in the region were at risk, as he acknowledges implicitly in his account when he describes his desire to offer a justification for his actions to a synod convened in the town of Tegulata.[84] Indeed, Augustine's reputation was already shaky in the town of Fussala as a result of his imposition of Antoninus upon them in the first place.[85] In such circumstances, it is therefore not surprising that Antoninus was ultimately removed, although it is difficult to determine the weight that the displeasure of his intended flocks ultimately carried.[86]

---

[80] Augustine, *Ep.* 20*. For detailed treatment of the particulars of this letter, see Lancel (1983). Also Whittaker (1997); Dossey (2010), 130–1. Cf. Wickham (2005b), 473, who accepts only reluctantly the coherence of this community.

[81] Augustine, *Ep.* 20*.46.   [82] Adultery: *Ep.* 20*.8. Letter of complaint: *Ep.* 20*.13.

[83] *Ep.* 20*.10; 20.   [84] *Ep.* 20*.12.   [85] *Ep.* 20*.15; 23.

[86] It seems that this was precipitated more by the complaints of the owner of the estate than by the actions of Augustine himself, and the situation is further complicated by her claims that Antoninus had asked her not to agree to his being installed as bishop over the estate: *Ep.* 20*.14; 17–19.

The late Roman sources portray a multitude of interactions between established figures of power and other individuals, who are alternately presented as illegitimate interlopers or new and wholly beneficent patrons over the rural communities of the period. We should be cautious about accepting either the essential continuity in the role of a local aristocrat such as the *curiales* whose demise Libanius laments, or the startling novelty of a figure such as Maësymas, who is described occupying a new niche as an intercessor between Letoius and the villagers under his power. In both cases the contrast is probably overdrawn. It seems more likely that local landscapes of power retained their basic structural features. With the apparent exception of the hamlets discovered in the hills near the Euphrates by Simeon the Mountaineer, the inhabitants of rural communities characteristically interacted regularly with a range of powerful figures. Often those interactions were deliberately described by one or both parties as single moments that were part of ongoing relations of patronage. Libanius provides an example when he elicits distress at the acts of his tenants, who, he claims, took him to court in a situation where the informal negotiations characteristic of relations between patrons and clients would have been more appropriate.[87] Alternatives were possible, however. Some individuals may be observed deliberately employing a novel vocabulary of power to make claims to legitimacy and authority. Such a strategy was potentially fraught and the stakes were high, for it rested upon the willingness of a potential client or client community to acknowledge the legitimacy of that vocabulary. As we shall see, novel or unfamiliar vocabularies were often met with resistance.

At any rate, the increased visibility of these figures highlights disjunctions between competing ideologies of patronage, and between those ideologies and the functioning of patronage relationships in reality. Our sources reveal a spectrum of possible interactions, from the "monogamous," traditional relationship revolving around tenancy envisaged by Libanius to the exploitative, amoral behavior of *potentiores* censured so virulently by Salvian.[88] The coexistence of this multiplicity of possibilities reveals the dangers of narrowing our focus to concentrate solely upon patronage *tout court*, for rural socio-economic relations were far more complex and variegated. In the following chapter, I explore the multitude of possible interactions between peasants and the powerful.

---

[87] Libanius, *Or.* XLVII.13–16.   [88] Libanius, *Or.* XLVII.19–22; 24; Salvian, *De Gubernatione Dei* V.8.42.

CHAPTER 5

Resistance, negotiation, and indifference: communities and potentates

Relationships between peasants and the powerful varied considerably in form and nature, and displayed great diversity in their terms and the foundations upon which they rested. In some circumstances, a group of peasants may be observed interacting as a collectivity with a figure power, while in others the influence of a powerful outsider might be enlisted by an individual in order to gain some advantage over his fellows. When these relationships are described in the sources, it is often in terms that evoke the concept of patronage, an enduring, mutually binding, intrinsically unequal relationship, underpinned by an ethos of reciprocity.[1] This conscious enlistment of the language of patronage, evidenced in texts produced by both the powerful and the relatively powerless, amounts to one element in a continuous process of construction and reconstruction of relations between the two.[2] However, these negotiations must be situated within the context of a broad range of interactions between peasants and the powerful, including the naked exercise of force to achieve domination, which can be met only by capitulation or compliance; overt or covert resistance or subversion on the part of subordinate populations; mutual manipulation, collusion, or collaboration; and purely incidental contacts between the two, which have consequences that are both unforeseen and unintended.

In this chapter, I will argue that the inhabitants of rural communities in the period did more than merely suffer the depredations of the military, accede to the wishes of the clergy, or satisfy the demands of the state and its aristocracies for taxes and rents. Rather, they emerge as conscious actors,

---

[1] Studies of patronage in the Roman world continue to rest fundamentally upon the work of Saller: (1982), (1989). For patronage in rural contexts, cf. Garnsey and Woolf (1989). See also the recent reappraisal of the problem by Garnsey (2010). The relational approach adopted here complements the structural typology of patronage in the late Roman period provided by Krause (1987).

[2] Cf. Emirbayer (1997), 291–2; Braddick and Walter (2001), 3; 8–9.

both individually and collectively, whose decisions and behavior were able to impact upon the more powerful individuals with whom they came into contact. I will suggest, further, that their interactions with the powerful were characteristically motivated by a certain logic. That logic revolved around an individual's impulse to obtain leverage against his fellows, a household's imperative to balance its needs against its resources, and a community's desire to maintain or regain its internal cohesion. These factors should be privileged over both the motivations of the potentates with whom these individuals, households, and communities came into contact, and the motives that those potentates impute to peasants in their accounts of those encounters.

In what follows, I explore the full complement of interactions between peasants and figures of power in the countrysides of the late Roman world. For purposes of analysis, I identify three complementary types of interaction, which, I suggest, existed simultaneously and were mutually interdependent. I argue that no single analytical position is sufficient to capture the complexity of asymmetrical relations in the period, and we must instead develop a dynamic, multidimensional approach to the problem.[3] The first type, which I label "dominance, compliance, and resistance," encompasses the explicit or implicit tension between an expectation that subordinates will accede to domination and internalize the claims of their superiors, and an assumption that they will resist those claims in a variety of subtle and not-so-subtle ways.[4] The second, "negotiation, collusion, and manipulation," places the employment by the powerful of specific vocabularies of authority and legitimacy alongside instances of effective manipulation of those vocabularies by the relatively powerless for their own ends, and collusion between the two parties in constructing and conducting the relationships in which they are involved.[5] The third, "the incidental and the accidental," involves instances where the actions of both the powerful and the relatively powerless impact upon one another only indirectly or in unanticipated ways.[6]

---

[3] Interdependent and complementary axes of power: cf. Abu-Lughod (1990), 42; 48; Reed-Danahay (1993), 223–4; Anderson (1997), 505; Howe (1998), 546; Braddick and Walter (2001), 1; 4; 42; Campbell and Heyman (2007), 4; 25–6. Also, with specific reference to sixth-century Egypt, Wickham (2005b), 419.

[4] Domination: Gramsci (1971); Foucault (1979); Giddens (1984). Cf. Morrow (1996), 406–7. Resistance: Scott (1985), (1986); Certeau (1984), 39–42. Cf. Reed-Danahay (1993), 222–3, drawing parallels between the approaches of Scott and Certeau, and labeling these strategies "cunning." See also the detailed survey of Seymour (2006).

[5] Negotiation: Braddick and Walter (2001), 6–8. Manipulation: Certeau (1984), 24–8; Collusion: Herzfeld (2005), 371.

[6] Cf. Campbell and Heyman (2007).

The relative balance between these three analytical axes will have varied from context to context, and circumstance to circumstance. It is the second set of relations that most closely resembles patronage in its ideal (and idealized) form, while, arguably, the first fits best the received picture of relations between landlords and their registered tenants that long dominated studies of rural socio-economic relations in the period. However, to focus solely upon creating a contrast between relations of dominance and antagonism on the one hand, and instances of negotiation and mutual exploitation, on the other, is to miss the bulk of interactions between individuals of differential wealth and standing in the late Roman world. Indeed, while the third analytical type of interaction is the least represented in our sources, it is likely to have constituted the bulk of everyday contacts between the two.

DOMINANCE, COMPLIANCE, AND RESISTANCE

There can be no doubt that an immense social and economic gulf separated a wealthy aristocratic landowner from the peasant who worked on his field as a tenant or laborer. In many cases, the former was also in a position to exercise force, either by recourse to members of the military, who were expected among other things to help enforce the collection of taxes, or by calling upon his own band of armed retainers, who appear to have become a more visible presence in the period. Similarly, a government tax official, with the full resources of the state behind him, was an intimidating figure to the relatively humble inhabitants of the villages, hamlets, and farms of the late Roman world.[7] With limited or no resources available to them, we should expect that in some circumstances peasants had no other option but to comply with the demands of these individuals. The acts of Simeon the Mountaineer have already been discussed, and further examples of the illegitimate use of force by the powerful and capitulation by the victims of their actions are not difficult to find in the sources. In legislation aimed at curbing the excesses of palatine officials, for example, these figures are depicted roaming the countryside demanding taxes of the peasantry with menaces.[8] Likewise, Libanius portrays the peasantry of the Syrian

---

[7] Soldiers in the tax-collection process: E.g. *P. Abinn.* 46 (343); Libanius, *Or.* XLV.5; *CTh* XI.7.16 (401, Italy and Africa). Cf. Petit (1955), 189 and note 8; Krause (1987), 85–6 and notes 68–9. Armed retainers: Cf. Whittaker (1993), 294–8. Intimidation: Constantius, *V. Germani* 7.19–27. Cf. Wickham (2005b), 66–7.

[8] *CTh* 1.16.11 (369, Italy). Cf. *CTh* VIII.8.6 (395, *ad provinciales et ad proconsules*); *Nov. Maj.* III.2 (458, West).

countryside traveling to the city of Antioch, where they are oppressed by the soldiery, despoiled by the keepers of the city gates, and forced to transport rubble from civic building projects outside the city.[9]

Alongside these overt examples of the use of force may be placed more mundane instances, where a powerful figure casually expresses his position of dominance over his dependents, or merely assumes that his will is superior to theirs. In a letter to a certain Salvius, an anonymous African landowner describes the tenants of his fields as *ruricolae mei*, "my rustics," and *coloni mei*, "my tenants," before warning Salvius not to try to remove them from his estate, or pretend to be the rightful owner of the land upon which, it appears, they were registered.[10] The potentially harsh realities of relations between tenants and landlords hinted at here are given more explicit recognition in legislation concerned with defining the legal status of registered tenants. The law acknowledges that such a relationship might consist of both an impulse towards solicitude (*sollicitudo*) and a capacity to exert force (*potestas*), and instructs *domini* to exercise both in ensuring that tenants registered on their fields fulfill their responsibilities.[11] The casualness with which a figure of power might exercise that power is visible also in Salvian of Marseilles's sustained and detailed diatribe against the despicable acts of the rich and the catastrophic decline in morals of his age. Salvian describes the plight of a poor man who is being ruined by a man he describes as a *praepotentior*, or powerful figure. When Salvian confronts the aggressor, he is informed that his pleas on the pauper's behalf cannot be satisfied, because the man had sworn an oath to ruin him.[12]

It is difficult to determine the extent to which the victims of these actions were complicit in their subjugation. We should be wary of assuming that our authors have accurately represented the motivations of the peasants whose actions they describe, just as we should resist the urge to supply those motivations ourselves. We should also be cautious about interpreting compliance with authority as equivalent to passivity.[13] But it is certainly possible to argue that peasants' active participation in the ongoing structures of

---

[9] Libanius, *Or.* L.33–6.

[10] *Ep. ad Salv.* 2.9. This letter was long attributed to St. Martin's hagiographer Sulpicius Severus. Such an attribution was challenged by Lepelley, and remains controversial in current scholarship. For particulars, see Lepelley (1989), 238–9; Sirks (1999), 94–5. For our current purposes the problem of authorship is less important than the dispute to which this letter refers, and the assumptions that underpin the dispute. Cf. the debate between Lepelley and Sirks: Sirks (1982), (1999), (2001); Lepelley (1989). Sirks seems to overplay the legal aspects of the case slightly.

[11] *CJ* XI.52.1 (396S, Thrace). Cf. Grey (2007a), 166–7.   [12] *De Gubernatione Dei* IV.15.74–5.

[13] Giddens (1984), 309. Cf. Ortner (1995), 182; Morrow (1996), 405–8; 420; Braddick and Walter (2001), 6.

dominance that form the backdrop for these events signals acceptance of those structures, or at the very least an assumption that they are somehow natural and inevitable.[14] Our aristocratic authors clearly assume as much. In his account of the confrontation between Maësymas and Letoius, for example, Theodoret portrays the villagers as passive participants in the story, who submit to the demands of their *despotês* and even go so far as to help him in his attempts to dislodge his carriage and leave the village.[15]

Similarly, when Salvian of Marseilles attempts to portray the response of the poor to the ambition and greed of the wealthy, he mixes sarcasm and complaint with resigned acceptance. Elsewhere in his work, he appears to acknowledge the agency of the peasantry, and identifies a range of responses available to them when faced with the demands of the tax man and the depredations of the rich. He arrays these options in a loose hierarchy, listing flight to the barbarians, as well as joining a shadowy band of outlaws on the margins of the empire before he depicts peasants giving themselves over to the domination of a landlord.[16] The terms in which he describes this last strategy confirm his view of it as a counsel of desperation: "Some of those of whom I speak, who are either wiser than the rest or necessity has made them wise, having either lost their homes and farms. . ., or fled before the tax gatherers. . . , seek out the farms of the rich and great, to become their tenants [*coloni*]." While it is possible to offer alternative explanations for this behavior, for Salvian, these peasants consciously, if reluctantly, acknowledge their role as subordinates with few if any opportunities for amelioration of their lot.[17]

However, alongside examples of peasants appearing to accept their subjugation, albeit with resignation, may be placed instances where they resist the demands of the powerful either overtly or covertly. We should not interpret these instances of resistance as motivated by a uniformly held, universally embraced, coherent set of principles or attitudes towards the power of an individual or group or the hegemony of the state. Rather, it is more likely that they constituted a loosely articulated collection of responses to individual circumstances.[18] As a consequence, we may imagine that

---

[14] Cf. Foucault (1986), 233. Also Lemert and Gillan (1982), 226; Yanagisako and Delaney (1995), 1; Gramsci (1971).

[15] Theodoret, *Hist. Rel.* XIV.2–4.

[16] Salvian, *De Gubernatione Dei* V.5.22–6.27. In mentioning bandits on the Loire, Salvian appears to be referring to the Bagaudae, a shadowy and ephemeral group of outlaws who recur periodically in our sources for the third to fifth centuries. See fuller discussion of this account and the phenomenon of the Bagaudae below, 187–8.

[17] *De Gubernatione Dei* V.8.43. For fuller discussion of Salvian's account, see now Grey (2006), 175–80.

[18] Scott (1986), 23–9; Abu-Lughod (1990), 43–7; Reed-Danahay (1993), 223; Ortner (1995), 190; Howe (1998), 546–7.

resistance took a variety of forms in the period, and was motivated by a variety of objectives. At its most overt, it might entail violence, both threatened and real; the threat to leave one's tenancy; the rejection of a patron or would-be patron's claims to power by recourse to an alternative vocabulary of power. More subtle forms include tardy rent payments; slow or poor-quality work; rumor and gossip.[19] In what follows, I explore a series of vignettes that reveal peasants, both collectively and individually, resisting the powerful, or at the very least behaving in ways designed either to subvert or to circumvent their claims and demands. I note both the risks and the potential rewards of such acts, and argue that they are inextricably linked to the instances of dominance and compliance sketched above.[20]

Violence is never very far from the surface of power relations in the countryside, particularly when we turn to the realm of tax collection.[21] While the bulk of that violence is, no doubt, perpetrated by agents of the state upon those from whom taxes are to be extracted, an individual or community might successfully resist the tax man, at least for a time. An early fifth-century letter from an unidentified tax official to his superior, reporting upon events in the village of Karanis is a case in point. The author complains that a member of the village not only refused to pay his taxes, but also threatened him with violence and later gathered a group of associates together to savagely beat the local *eirênarchos*, who was responsible for liaising with him over the collection of the village's *merismos*.[22] The full details of this event are impossible to reconstruct, for the papyrus is fragmentary and we possess no information about the response that these actions provoked. The victim of the violence in this instance seems to have been a member of the village community as well as an agent of the state. It is therefore possible that the root of this conflict was not an individual's desire to evade his tax burden, but, rather, a personal grievance against his neighbor. Even so, it is difficult to imagine the villager acting in the way that he did if he was convinced of the state's ability to respond effectively. In this instance, then, we observe the limitations of an agent of the state's capacity

---

[19] This notion of resistance was advanced in its most complete form by Scott: Scott (1985), 6–9; Scott (1986), 14–7. Note Seymour's succinct definition: Seymour (2006), 305. Also Abu-Lughod (1990), 44; Ortner (1995), 174–5; Braddick and Walter (2001), 8; 28. For gossip and rumor, cf. above, 86–9.

[20] Cf. Foucault (1978), 95–6; Abu-Lughod (1990), 41–2; Reed-Danahay (1993), 222; Groves and Chang (1999), 237; Braddick and Walter (2001), 7. Note, for the problems that historians encounter in recovering these strategies, Walter (2001), 145.

[21] Cf. Wickham (2005b), 71–2. Further references for the earlier imperial period are collected by MacMullen (1974), 36–7 with notes 28–9.

[22] *P. Col.* VIII.242 (fifth century, Karanis). Cf. Wickham (2005b), 414–15 for comparatively greater incidence of violence in Egyptian village communities.

to impose his will by force. Those limitations opened up a space for the less powerful to act, if not with complete impunity, then at least with the reasonable expectation that their acts would not elicit the full penalty prescribed by the law.

Slightly more subtle in the form the resistance takes is an early fourth-century letter sent by the inhabitants of the village of Euhemeria to a certain Nechos, whom they address as both *despotês* and *patrônos*, before offering a carefully worded protest against his recent attempts to ensure that they pay their yearly taxes (*entagion*) by seizing some of their children.[23] The exact circumstances of this text and the identity of its recipient have been the subject of much debate. Most recently, it has been proposed that Nechos was not their landlord and patron, but rather the local *praepositus pagi*, charged with the task of enforcing their payment of their taxes, and seeking to do so by obtaining sureties in the form of hostages.[24] In this reading, the employment of the term *patrônos* signals not an ongoing relationship of patronage between the two parties, but rather the village community's intention to employ the vocabulary of patronage in a closely connected, but analytically separate context, in order to signal certain expectations of their interlocutor.[25] The use of this honorific marker contrasts with the tone of protest that the letter takes, and the implicit suggestion that Nechos' actions are in some sense unreasonable and therefore illegitimate. We observe here a village community, united in its dealings with an agent of the state's fiscal and administrative bureaucracy, self-consciously employing a vocabulary of power that contrasts in subtle but significant ways with the realities of the current interaction between the two. In employing this vocabulary they are, arguably, seeking to dictate or influence the course that that interaction will take.

While the examples of Karanis and Euhemeria reveal resistance to an established, long-standing power structure, Sulpicius Severus' account of the experience of St. Martin of Tours when he attacked the worship of pagan deities in the countryside of Gaul may be taken to illustrate the collective unwillingness of the rural population to accept a new figure of power, exercising a novel vocabulary. That unwillingness is manifested in a number of ways, from direct, violent resistance to more subtle, sophisticated means. Sulpicius relates that in a certain *vicus*, Martin destroyed an ancient

---

[23] *P. Ross. Georg.* III.8 (early fourth century).
[24] Rathbone (2008), 201–4. Van Minnen (1997), 67–70 succinctly summarizes previous scholarship on this text.
[25] Rathbone (2008), 196–7. Cf. Walter (2001), 128; 134–5.

temple then turned his attention to a sacred tree that stood nearby. The local peasants appeared to accept with resignation his destruction of the temple, but they were less willing to allow him to cut down the tree. Martin offered a series of reasoned arguments in support of his actions, and in reply was invited to prove his God's efficacy and power by standing under the tree as it fell. Sulpicius remarks upon the peasants' glee at the impending death of the holy man, before describing his miraculous repulsion of the tree by employing the sign of the cross, just as it threatened to crush him.[26]

We should be wary of taking Sulpicius' narrative completely at face value. Leaving aside the curious matter of the tree changing its direction mid-fall, his interpretation of the peasants' attitudes and motivations is, of course, open to question, as too is his image of an undifferentiated, homogeneous rural population, possessing a common purpose and united in the face of an unwelcome interloper. Further, by focusing upon the end point of this story and its result – namely, the conversion of the whole community – Sulpicius constructs a narrative of triumph. Nevertheless, we may with caution interpret his account as offering a plausible version of reality. In that sense, the verbal exchange between Martin and the villagers is of particular interest, for it reveals a sophisticated approach to resistance. For all that it was ultimately unsuccessful, the challenge to the holy man here amounted to the use of his own vocabulary of power against him.

The strategic employment of a specific vocabulary is also visible, albeit in a slightly different form, in accounts of demonic possession preserved in the hagiographical literature of the period. Recent scholarship on the subject has suggested that, in some circumstances at least, demonic possession can be interpreted as a mechanism for expressing and contextualizing fear and anxiety over disempowerment and marginalization, externalizing misfortune and articulating envy and dissent.[27] The vocabulary of demonic possession provided an individual who had few other resources with the opportunity to express emotions or opinions that were dangerous or unpopular, or even to manifest those feelings purely psychosomatically through a violent and shocking loss of control over his or her body. Thus, for example, we witness demoniacs screaming invective at the saint or attacking him in public; a habitual thief and known demoniac stealing a purse belonging to a member of the imperial bureaucracy, before he is

---

[26] Sulpicius Severus, *V. Mart.* 13.
[27] Cf. Kapferer (1997), 224–5; 234–5; Van Ommeren, Sharma, Komproe et al. (2001), 1260; Bax (1995), 53–4; 61–2; Herzfeld (1986), 108–9. For the Roman world, see, for example, Brown (1971), 88–9; Smith (1978), 437; Dickie (1995), 11; Grey (2005), 53.

publicly chastised and exposed; and a conspiracy of demoniacs spreading rumors of an impending barbarian raid in an effort to drive the holy man from their city.[28] While instances of exorcism are often spectacular and public acts of confrontation, they also form one element in the ritualistic performance of possession, which involves a carefully stage-managed progression from transgression through healing to reintegration of the cured demoniac into the community. In this sense, demonic possession may be interpreted as a means by which the relatively or newly powerless can express anger or distress at their subordinate position, or resist the encroachment of a new figure of power.[29] By accessing the vocabulary of demonic possession, an individual may seek to control or determine the form that responses to his or her transgressive behavior can take.

Of course, active resistance carried with it certain risks. Peasants were still overwhelmingly disadvantaged when it came to resources, support networks, and the capacity to exercise force. It is unlikely that the actions of the reluctant taxpayer at Karanis could be sustained in the longer term, and it is not difficult to imagine a visit from the recipient of the letter or a subordinate, with a group of soldiers at his back.[30] Equally, the decision by the residents of Euhemeria to appeal to notions of legitimacy and fairness bears eloquent testimony to the fact that they had little tangible power in their interactions with Nechos. Even in the case of demonic possession, where it may have been possible to control or manipulate the form that their interaction with a figure of power took, peasants' attempts to attain a semblance of parity, power, or freedom of expression are unlikely to have produced more than fleeting success. It is therefore probable that the bulk of peasant resistance to the claims of the powerful was more mundane or subtle.

Glimpses of these small acts of defiance or subversion emerge occasionally from our sources. Symmachus comments with exasperation about the persistent problem of rent arrears, a phenomenon which in some circumstances may have less to do with economic straits than with a keen appreciation of where a landlord is particularly vulnerable.[31] Malingering, surliness, and deliberate obtuseness might also function as a form of

---

[28] Invective: Constantius, *V. Germani* 32; Sulpicius Severus, *V. Mart.* 17. Thief: Constantius, *V. Germani* 7. Conspiracy: Sulpicius Severus, *V. Mart.* 18 and above, 101–3.

[29] Fuller discussion in Grey (2005), 58–68. Cf., for exorcism as imitation of Christ, Aune (1980), 1523; 1525–6; Adnès and Canivet (1967).

[30] The enlistment of the military in the collection of taxes: Brown (1992), 19; 26–7; Aubert (1995), 260–1. Cf., for the limits upon resistance, Herzfeld (2005), 370.

[31] Symmachus, *Ep.* VI.81; IX.6. This was certainly not a new complaint. Cf. Pliny, *Ep.* III.19; IX.37; X.8; Ste. Croix (1981), 257.

resistance, for they are designed to frustrate, impede, or disrupt a patron, landlord or employer's objectives. A playful letter of Sidonius provides a curious twist on the response that we might expect to such behavior.[32] Sidonius presents the bearer of the letter as something of a troublemaker on his estate, whose rude manners, vulgarity, and general demeanor mark him out as occupying a very different world from that of Sidonius and his kinsman Simplicius, the recipient of the letter. It is possible that Sidonius' choice of letter carrier here is some kind of deliberate insult to his kinsman, although the two appear to have been on generally good terms, and we might equally imagine that Sidonius is playing some kind of elaborate joke upon the bearer, for he emphasizes the shock that the man will receive when offered the full extent of his kinsman's hospitality.

These contradictions and uncertainties leave us wondering why Sidonius agreed to write the letter, and why he did so in this form. The humiliation a humble peasant would experience by being welcomed into the home of an aristocrat might have been Sidonius' object here. But, given the likely imbalances in wealth, power, and status, such an elaborate exercise was surely unnecessary. Of course, Sidonius may simply be displaying a measure of opportunism: he observes that, while the bearer of the letter requested the letter from him, he would himself have wished to send a letter with the man once he found out where he was going. We should not dismiss practical considerations such as this, particularly in the light of the distance involved. Perhaps Sidonius saw here an opportunity to nourish his relationship with Simplicius with no cost to himself and little effort to find a bearer. In that case, the contents of the letter are less important than the physical fact of it. But we should not lose sight of the initiative shown by this man in seeking the letter, and his success in obtaining it in spite of his somewhat unflattering reputation.[33] True, Sidonius expresses, or at least projects, distaste for him and his unappealing qualities, and he is clearly considered completely unimportant as anything other than an opportunity to display some literary and comic talent. But he has succeeded in exploiting his landlord's networks of friendship or kinship, and secured for himself some kind of introduction to Simplicius, which is at the very least likely to have raised him above certain other petitioners or potential laborers who lacked such a letter.[34] We observe here a relatively humble *rusticus* betraying a sophisticated attitude

[32] Sidonius, *Ep.* IV.7.
[33] Cf. Reed-Danahay (1993), 224 on the simultaneous expression of accommodation and resistance in a single vocabulary of power. Also Howe (1998), 532.
[34] For fuller discussion of this and other examples of dependents accessing their patrons' and landlords' social networks, see Grey (2004), 26–31.

towards the manipulation of relationships of power, and I return to the strategies employed in manipulation of this sort below.

At any rate, it is not difficult to observe peasants involved in antagonistic interactions with agents of the state, landlords, employers, and even patrons. Those interactions might be predicated upon the very real disparities in wealth, power, and status between the participants, or rest upon different interpretations of the mutual obligations of patron and client, landlord and tenant. It is impossible to quantify the frequency of these encounters by comparison with instances of negotiation or cooperation, and unnecessary to attempt to do so. It suffices to observe that to focus solely upon relations that are characterized by dominance and resistance is to produce a monochrome picture of rural socio-economic relations, which assumes the essential homogeneity of both powerful and relatively powerless as socio-economic groups, and ascribes a degree of class-consciousness to the latter that is difficult to sustain in reality.[35] Further, the attempt by the residents of the village of Euhemeria to present their interaction with Nechos using the vocabulary of patronage signals the ways in which vocabularies of power were malleable, adaptable, and adoptable by both parties in a given situation.

NEGOTIATION, COLLUSION, AND MANIPULATION

Essentially, the examples of dominance and resistance explored in the previous section reveal relationships lacking legitimacy, a quality fundamental to the successful transformation of a claim to power into the establishment of authority. Legitimacy can be asserted by the powerful, but it must be granted to them from below. Consequently, negotiations over the authority of the former can take one of two forms, both of which revolve around the pursuit of mutual consent. In the first instance, elites proffer a persona to their subordinates, entailing both claims to authority and implicit promises to behave in conformity with certain established paradigms. In the second instance, the subordinates themselves may attempt to initiate a relationship with a powerful figure, drawing upon the vocabulary of patronage in order to signal their intentions and their expectations.[36] Both sets of negotiations are visible in the sources of the late Roman world, and I explore them in turn.

---

[35] Cf. Gal (1995), 409; Ortner (1995), 175; 183; Anderson (1997), 506; Howe (1998), 532; 542–3.
[36] Cf. Chong (1992), 697; Braddick and Walter (2001), 8–9.

We may take as an example of the first type the letter collection of the late fifth-century Gallo-Roman landowner and bishop Sidonius Apollinaris, which preserves a small but significant number of letters written on behalf of tenants and laborers on his rural estates. The language he employs in some, at least, of those letters may be compared with the language of more conventional letters for aristocratic friends and clients: Sidonius tends to construct his relationship with the bearer as close, enduring, and personal. He speaks of the man's good character, their mutual obligations, and his gratitude to his correspondent for the latter's actions on the bearer's behalf.[37] As we have seen, however, there are, in addition, subtle differences, for alongside these pious expressions of affection and responsibility we catch glimpses of his distaste for these individuals.

This distaste is echoed in the letters of other western aristocrats in the period. In a letter written to Marcellus, who probably held the post of *magister officiorum* in the east in the mid 390s, for example, the fourth-century Italian senator Symmachus dispenses altogether with the conventional niceties of affection and obligation, in favor of language that emphasizes his frustration and annoyance at the continual requests by a certain Amazonius for his intervention in the affair.[38] It is difficult to untangle the particulars of the affair, for Symmachus is not particularly interested in spelling them out. Instead, he emphasizes his annoyance at the burden placed upon him by Amazonius. Nevertheless, he does write the letter, and expresses his support for Ursus in terms that are similar to those used by Sidonius in his letter to the Aremorican king, Riothamus: the man is a poor rustic, he has been a dependent of Symmachus' family for some time, and he should not be punished because of his ignorance of the law and his timidity. It would seem that Symmachus' anger at Amazonius has not prevented him from offering support to the man on whose behalf Amazonius has provoked that anger. It is worth exploring further the impulse that lies at the heart of this act.

The carefully constructed figures of power, authority, and intercession that emerge from these letters were aimed principally at the authors' peers and posterity. But the letters preserve a record of actions, and the actuality as well as the reportage of those actions will have had a lasting effect upon the beneficiaries of their interest and those individuals' circles of contacts. A figure such as Sidonius' legitimacy among his rural dependents rested, at

[37] E.g. *Epp.* II.7; III.4; 9. Cf. Symmachus *Ep.* II.70; IX.57 (*c.* 402).
[38] Symmachus, *Ep.* IX.II. For Marcellus' office, cf. Roda (1981), 113; Callu, in his commentary to his edition of Symmachus' correspondence (Symmachus, *Ep.* vol. 4, 100).

least in part, upon his reputation as an effective intercessor, a generous benefactor, and a reliable source of insurance against subsistence and social risk. In order to establish and maintain that reputation, Sidonius, like other patronal figures, was required to invest energy and resources in the constant, ongoing business of acting like a patron, and it is for this reason that, notwithstanding their contempt, distaste, or detached amusement, our authors appear to have acceded to the wishes of these petitioners and written letters on their behalf.[39] We may imagine, further, that, in addition to the instances of intercession that we witness in these letters, our authors may have held markets or feasts on their property;[40] provided loans of grain to individuals who found themselves in difficulty and, perhaps, money to those who wished to speculate on a business venture or purchase a new piece of equipment;[41] mediated disputes that the members of a community could not settle on their own;[42] and protected their clients from the unwelcome attentions of other potentates in a variety of ways.[43]

Such acts functioned as ongoing expressions of the legitimacy of these individuals as figures of both power and authority.[44] But legitimacy is an intensely context-specific phenomenon, highly dependent upon the point of view of the reporter, and the circumstances in which the actions occur. The multiplicity of possible opinions about an individual's claims to legitimacy may be gleaned from evidence for tax evasion in the late Roman sources, most specifically in the phenomenon labeled Patrocinium in modern historiography. If the legal sources and the testimony of Libanius of Antioch are to be believed, patrons in the eastern provinces systematically protected their clients, both individually and collectively, from the attentions of the imperial and municipal tax collectors. These actions are portrayed in the sources as inconsistent with the behavior expected of a patron, although it seems clear that the perspective taken here is that of the state rather than the peasants themselves. By contrast, comparable actions of tax evasion in the western provinces are depicted by Salvian of Marseilles as

---

[39] Cf. *CTh* II.31.1 = *CJ* IV.26.1 *mut.* (422, West). For figures of power constantly playing the role of patron, see Braddick and Walter (2001), 9–10; 12; 27.

[40] MacMullen (1970), 333; Shaw (1981), 53–4; de Ligt and de Neeve (1988). Cf. *P. Ross. Georg.* II.41 (second century, Fayum), with the comments of Eitrem (1937), 45–8.

[41] *CTh* II.33.1 (325, East); 2 (386, East); 4 (405, East); Hamel (1990), 156. Cf. *PSI* IX.1081 (late fourth century, Oxyrhynchus), a fourth-century papyrus from Egypt which reveals some residents of the village of Paomis petitioning their landlord, Limenios through his steward, Ammonios, for a loan.

[42] Cf. Eugippius, *V. Sev.* 3, with discussion above, 113.

[43] *Ep. ad Salv.* II.9; 14; *P. Sakaon* 56. This text is lacunose, and it is difficult to determine the exact nature of the intercession here: see the discussion of Bagnall (1993a), 221.

[44] Cf. Braddick and Walter (2001), 9–10; 12; 27–8.

ruinous to the peasantry, as powerful figures deflect the attentions of the tax collector onto the very individuals whom they might be expected to protect, or at least shield from illegitimate or excessive fiscal demands.[45] Much ink has been spilled in attempts to resolve the tensions between these perspectives, and place them within a single analytical framework, but such an exercise ignores the fundamental differences in the perspectives of our sources. For our current purposes, we should concentrate rather upon the contingent and contested nature of a patron's legitimacy, and the fundamentally different valences that could be placed upon the same actions by different observers. Clearly, one man's patron was another's illegitimate potentate.

We may also analyze the contrast between the testimonies of Libanius and Salvian in another way. The evidence is patchy, and it would be naïve to attribute these differences merely to differential processes, structures, or power relations in the eastern and western provinces of the empire. Nevertheless, it may be possible to draw some subtle contrasts between the behavior expected of patrons in these two regions. In the letters of Symmachus, Sidonius, Augustine, and Ausonius, we catch glimpses of the range of circumstances in which clients, tenants, and dependents in the western Mediterranean might seek the intercession of a figure of power, and the arguments that might surround the claims of the latter to hold legitimacy in a particular interaction. As we have seen, two of Symmachus' letters reveal a slippage between a tenancy arrangement and a relationship of patronage, while Sidonius moves across a broad semantic field in the presentation of his interest and involvement in the affairs of the *rustici* who came to him for aid.[46] These examples suggest that, in these figures' self-representation, their responsibility as a patron is difficult to distinguish from their role as landlord, local potentate, bishop, or household head. These slippages in the type and nature of acknowledged relationships between aristocrats and their rural dependents are attested elsewhere in the letter collections of the late Roman west, and offer hints of a subtle series of realignments in the interests of those aristocrats in the period.

These realignments provided opportunities for dependents to manipulate the self-representation of their landlords and patrons in a variety of ways.[47] In addition, they might at times reveal an equally keen awareness of

---

[45] Salvian, *De Gubernatione Dei* IV.6.30; V.7.31; V.8.42.

[46] Symmachus, *Epp.* V.48; VII.56, above, 127. Sidonius, *Epp.* III.9; V.19; VI.10, above, 132–3.

[47] Cf. Dossey (2010), 122–3, who makes a complementary argument about the avenues and vocabularies available to peasants in North Africa in the period.

the added weight that an appeal to self-interest might carry. In a letter to Paulinus of Nola on behalf of a former bailiff named Philo, who had set himself up as a grain merchant, Ausonius betrays a complex collection of motivations for seeking the intercession of his correspondent on behalf of his client. He displays a mixture of amused contempt and pious concern for Philo's economic wellbeing which bears some similarities to Sidonius' letter to Simplicius for the vulgar resident upon his rural estate, and Symmachus' letter in response to the pleas of Amazonius.[48] But Ausonius betrays also the extent to which his own economic interests are implicated when he notes that his own estate at Lucaniacus is beset by a food shortage, and desperately in need of Philo's grain for its deliverance. In this instance, then, Philo is exploiting his former employer as much as he is petitioning him for aid.

Further, while our authors are keen to emphasize the vast social and economic gulf between themselves and the peasants who occupied the hamlets and farms surrounding their estates and worked on their fields, they cannot disguise the fact that they considered these individuals worth cultivating, and were prepared to do so using persuasion and argument. We may assume that in such circumstances the persona proffered by a patron or would-be patron was met by his potential client or clients either with consent or with a counter-argument, refining the terms of the existing vocabulary of power or drawing upon an alternative.[49] We catch occasional glimpses of these interactions in the sources from the western empire. Martin's recourse to persuasion when faced with resistance over his attempts to cut down a sacred tree in Gaul has already been mentioned, and we may place alongside it evidence from the letter collection of Augustine, who reveals his awareness of the utility of communicating directly with the rural inhabitants of North Africa when he emphasizes the need for Punic translations to convince them of the truth of the orthodox Christian faith.[50] Although Augustine is here speaking specifically of preaching to these individuals, we need only recall his exhortations to landlords that they take responsibility for ensuring the religious orthodoxy of their *coloni* to see that he considered shared faith and reciprocal relations to be closely connected.[51] It would seem, then, that peasants in the west might be accorded a certain amount of freedom in the nature and number of relationships they entertained with powerful figures, and some degree of latitude in their capacity to exploit and manipulate those relationships.

---

[48] Ausonius, *Ep.* 26; Sidonius, *Ep.* iv.7; Symmachus, *Ep.* ix.11.
[49] Howe (1998), 533; Braddick and Walter (2001), 15.   [50] Augustine, *Ep.* 66.2.
[51] E.g., Augustine, *Epp.* 57; 58; 89. Riggs (2006), 303.

The sources from the eastern provinces are less forthcoming, but the picture that emerges is subtly different. We may imagine that the Egyptian peasants depicted in the legislation abandoning their fields and flocking to a new landlord did so partly in response to a proffered persona that promised to satisfy their subsistence needs more effectively, and perhaps also to provide them with more opportunities for employment, more effective intercession, and more resolute protection from the illegitimate (and legitimate) demands of other figures of power. But, in general, the interactions that we are able to observe most closely take place between a village community and a figure or figures of power, and are somewhat less multidimensional and dynamic than comparable interactions from the western provinces.[52] The exchange between Letoius and the villagers under his control is a case in point. It is clear that the villagers possess only a limited scope for negotiation, and the vocabulary that they proffer is little different from the one already exercised by Letoius. It is possible that, in the figure of Maësymas, they acquire a more effective intercessor, but that intercessor appears largely to have interacted with their *despotês*. Similarly, while Libanius can be observed interceding on behalf of the peasantry, his actions are somehow less immediate, intimate, and involved. True, he delivered an oration against Icarius, *Comes Orientis* regarding forced liturgies, which focused upon the plight of the peasantry of Antioch's hinterland.[53] But his commitment to the day-to-day business of being a patron is less easy to observe.

It seems also that the comparatively stronger collective identity of the village as a community in the eastern provinces served to focus interactions with a figure of power principally upon resolving, mediating, or intensifying conflicts within the community itself. The seventh-century account of the life of Theodore of Sykeon falls slightly outside the temporal horizon of this study, but events preserved in this text illustrate the principle eloquently. In the village of Buzaea, for example, a conflict arose over the behavior of a group of workmen who had been hired to build a bridge. Some members of the community called upon Theodore for mediation in the dispute, but others hurled abuse at the holy man when he arrived.[54] Similarly, the village

---

[52] Cf. Banaji's argument for the elusiveness of peasants as a class in the early Byzantine east, and their comparative weakness in their negotiations with landlords and other powerful figures: Banaji (2009), 79–81. While Banaji's analysis concentrates principally upon economic factors, the insight is illuminating.

[53] Libanius, *Or.* L.

[54] *V. Theod. Syc.* 43. Cf. Horden (1993), 180–5 for an account of the social and cultural context of these events. Also, for a more detailed exploration of the light this text sheds on the social contours of the region in the period, Wickham (2005b), 406–10.

of Eukraae found itself embroiled in internecine conflict, possibly over buried treasure. Certain villagers resorted to violence and terror, and the internal order of the village broke down. Some members of the community beseeched Theodore to intervene, but again he was roundly cursed by the possessed members of the community when he arrived.[55] In each case, through the ritual of exorcism, Theodore restored order. But behind the theatricality of that exorcism lay a divided community, one which was not unilaterally in favor of the holy man as a patron or mediator. We witness here the pressure placed upon communities already predisposed to conflict by the claims of a new figure of power, providing an alternative option for mediating internecine disputes but demanding in return a different set of reciprocal services.

The eastern sources do reveal rural communities and their inhabitants attempting to initiate a particular type of relationship with a powerful individual, but in these instances they draw upon the vocabulary of services and the exchange of goods, rather than moral obligation or the expectations that one party might reasonably expect to have of the other. There survives legislation concerning the extortion of labor, goods, services, and gifts from *rustici* by municipal and imperial officials. The law also censures *rusticani* who present themselves voluntarily for such services, or who offer *xenia* or *munuscula* of their own accord to these figures. The primary objective of this legislation appears to be curbing abuses of power, and it appears to imagine, further, that the principal aim of *rusticani* in offering gifts or services is to commit fraud. It may therefore be linked with other legislation which makes this accusation explicit, and placed alongside Libanius' description of his tenants seeking out a local military commander and offering various gifts of produce.[56] Libanius explicitly suggests that the gifts are in effect bribes, for they lead directly to the perversion of justice, but there may be more to this phenomenon than he is prepared to admit. Certainly, it is likely that in some circumstances there were immediate and instrumental connections between a gift and an expected return. But there were also considerable advantages to be derived from initiating and maintaining a longer-term relationship, and peasants were quick to recognize those advantages and act upon them.

---

[55] *V. Theod. Syc.* 116.
[56] *CTh* XI.11.1 (368, Illyricum). Cf. *CTh* XI.24.2 (368). Libanius, *Or.* XLVII.13. For peasants initiating relationships with the powerful during the Principate, cf. Veyne (1981), 245–52. For the late Roman period, Krause (1987), 79–80. In comparative literature, it has been observed that the likelihood of subordinates offering gifts increases in situations of competition: Waterbury (1977), 332.

We witness, for example, communities raising honorific inscriptions or stelae to patronal figures, continuing a practice that was of great antiquity. Some of these monuments, at least, may have amounted to protreptic honors rather than purely acknowledgments of services already rendered.[57] Both parties stood to gain from a mutually exploitative, mutually beneficial arrangement of patronage, the patron through the prestige he garnered from a grateful community's public commemoration in stone, or the enhancement of his reputation among his peers and neighbors, his clients through the transformation of a disinterested outsider into a stakeholder in the community or a personal benefactor.[58] But, again, the contrast between these somewhat more sterile arrangements in the eastern evidence and the more dynamic, contingent interactions of the western sources is striking.

Attempts to honor a powerful figure as a communal patron might be part of a conscious attempt on the part of a community to draw that individual into a community's orbit, or to elicit a response from him that indicated his willingness to act in the manner of a patron towards them. But the approach of peasants in the east may again be contrasted with that of peasants in the west, who emphasize slightly different aspects of the relationship they are seeking to initiate. Arguably our most detailed evidence for this kind of proactive behavior on the part of peasants comes from Salvian of Marseilles, who portrays small landowners seeking out the wealthy and undertaking some kind of mortgage arrangement with them, which entails the initiation of a tenancy agreement and carries with it the explicit obligation upon their new landlord to provide care and protection. We should be cautious about accepting too readily the picture that Salvian paints of these tenants effectively losing their rights of citizenship as they suffer oppression, dispossession, and exploitation at the hands of an aristocracy interested only in commercial gain, for it is aimed principally at strengthening his rhetorical argument against the sinfulness of the Roman upper classes.[59] However, in explicitly linking tenancy and protection he echoes Symmachus' assumption of the role of a patron based on his involvement in a tenancy arrangement, and in locating the impulse for these transactions with peasants

---

[57] E.g. *IGLS* 1490 (Sarjilla, 473). Trombley (2004), 78–80 provides further references. Communities seeking out patrons: cf. Harmand (1957), 9. Building activity by these figures: Wadd. 1984b (c. 270, 'Ayun'); *ILS* 11.6093–120.

[58] E.g. *CIL* x.5349 (408); *CIL* viii.989 (fourth/fifth century). Cf. Marcone (1998), 362. Also Carrié (1976), 173–4; MacAdam (1983), 113–14; Garnsey and Woolf (1989), 164. Harmand (1957), 332–44, gives a catalog of inscriptional commemorations of patrons. MacMullen (1967), 113, for further examples of this kind of patronage, particularly by veterans.

[59] Salvian, *De Gubernatione Dei* v.8–9, with Grey (2006), 176–80.

themselves, he offers glimpses of the extent to which the relatively powerless might be able to initiate, exploit, or manipulate such a relationship.

The sources of the period reveal yet another locus around which claims and counter-claims about proper patronal behavior could be arrayed, for individuals and communities in both the east and the west were also able to exploit the ideology of care for the disadvantaged that was embraced and promulgated by the Church and its officers. The impulse is clearest at times of generalized subsistence crisis, where monasteries and bishops can be observed providing aid to the needy and mobilizing resources to help the starving.[60] We may discern this aspect of Christian rhetoric being exploited in other circumstances, too, although it is once again difficult to gauge the extent to which we may extend these accounts to encompass rural as well as urban contexts. Although ultimately unsuccessful, the poor old woman whom Jerome describes seeking a second coin in the city of Rome and receiving a blow instead was certainly awake to the possibility of taking advantage of a public display of charity.[61] The ecclesiastical historian Socrates of Constantinople preserves a similar example, albeit with a slightly different focus, when he describes a Jew who had made a habit of approaching each of the various sects of Christianity in the city and seeking baptism. Socrates notes with disapproval that, in each instance, the man received gifts or money, and as a consequence he had amassed a good deal of wealth. The purpose of the anecdote is to emphasize the prescience of the bishop, Paul, who was able to uncover this man's dishonesty, and who subsequently publicly exposed him as an impostor. But in the process Socrates reveals glimpses of the opportunity that affiliation with a particular sect, or, more broadly, conversion to Christianity may have offered the disadvantaged for amelioration of their condition.[62] It is unlikely that the Jew held up for censure here was the only one to spot and exploit these opportunities.

Although the physical and demographic landscapes of the eastern and western provinces of the late Roman empire were in many ways quite different, we should be careful not to overemphasize apparent contrasts between the experiences of rural patrons and clients in the two regions. It is possible, for example, that differences in the nature of the sources themselves have created a distorted and unevenly balanced picture of patronage relations in the east and the west. Nevertheless, both written and archaeological evidence suggests that the communities of the eastern Mediterranean

---

[60] *Hist. Mon. in Aeg.* VIII.44; Sidonius, *Ep.* VI.12; Mathisen (1993) discusses the mobilization of Christian clergy and laymen in response to the Gallic famine of *c.* 470.
[61] Jerome, *Ep.* 22.32, with discussion above, 82–3.   [62] Socrates, *Hist. Eccl.* VII.17.

were relatively more robust and visible than their smaller, apparently less autonomous western counterparts. Equally, while the peasants of the west appear to have been more enmeshed in asymmetrical relations, the evidence offers hints that they were as a consequence able to exploit figures of power more effectively, both as individuals and as collectivities. The stronger internal dynamics of the villages of the eastern provinces arguably provided them with a more complex and sophisticated collective identity in their interactions with powerful figures, but also rendered those interactions more static and one-dimensional, for they were characteristically focused upon mitigating or emphasizing internal tensions. Nevertheless, regardless of the axis along which they may be arrayed, instances of direct engagement between peasants and the powerful are characteristically played out against a backdrop of mutual indifference and ignorance. That context is crucial for our understanding of the contours and distribution of power structures in the countrysides of the late Roman world.

THE INCIDENTAL AND THE ACCIDENTAL

The texts that survive from the late Roman world suggest that power, legitimacy, and authority were subjects of immense importance for authors of the period. Whatever the foundations of an aristocratic letter writer's power, his apparatus of self-representation rested in large part upon his capacity to act as an effective patron, which provided him with the legitimacy that was essential for transforming his claims to power into authority. At the heart of the hagiographical texts of the period lie assumptions about the superiority of one form of power over others, and the effective exercise of that power by charismatic figures. Challenges to the legitimacy of agents of the state revolve around examples where those individuals exercise power in inappropriate ways, with consequences for both the victims of their actions and other figures, who might compete or cooperate with them. Power is therefore taken to be manifest both in the most spectacular confrontations and in the most intimate moments. It pervades accounts of ongoing relationships and chance encounters between rich and poor, aristocrat and peasant, powerful and relatively powerless.

We should not be mesmerized by the intensity with which the written sources focus upon power, legitimacy, and authority. For all that our authors emphasize the cohesion and integrity of the structures they describe, it is unlikely that those who wielded power in the period possessed either the will or the means to back up their claims quite as effectively as the sources seem to suggest. There existed a range of physical and structural limitations. The state and its agents relied upon the impression of all-encompassing power. But communications were slow, distances immense, and the personnel involved in enforcing the state's directives quite limited and unevenly dispersed across the empire. We need only recall the complaints of the tax collector regarding his experience at Karanis to observe that, while no doubt the state would ultimately have the upper hand in its dealings with its citizens, its control over the countryside on a day-to-day basis might be quite fragile.[63]

Similarly, an aristocratic landlord customarily owned a number of estates, spread over distances that were sometimes vast. In such circumstances he could never expect truly to function as an effective, present patron, but relied instead upon information supplied to him by his agents. A bailiff might deliberately falsify or manipulate information to his own advantage, or choose to act in ways that he knew to be out of step with the wishes of his employer. It is likely also that these individuals were sometimes able to take advantage of their position as the hub through which information flowed, and exploit the customary absence of their landlords in a way that undermined the exercise of effective power and authority by the latter.[64] We may suspect, finally, that the influence exercised by officers of the Church and holy figures was not quite as coherent and structured as our hagiographical sources suggest, and it was certainly anything but universally accepted and acknowledged in the period. Alongside the examples of resistance and conflict experienced by Martin, for example, may be placed the experience of Barochas, an officer of the Church charged with collecting rents from a village in the hinterland of Gaza, who was beaten and left for dead outside the village.[65] Evidently the power of the Church was as limited as that of the state in the period.

We should also be wary of interpreting every instance of the abusive exercise of power as somehow reflecting upon the power structure that underpinned and supported the individual in question. Simeon the Stylite, for example, was party to the after-effects of a particularly egregious, if not necessarily uncommon, instance of abusive behavior by an agent of the state. Simeon's hagiographer relates the story of a soldier who raped a young woman while traveling on the road, and immediately shriveled up and lost the ability to speak or walk. As a consequence, he was brought before the

---

[63] Contra Wickham (2005b), 66. Cf. Wickham's discussion of these issues as they apply both to "strong" and to "weak" states: Wickham (2005b), 56–7. Cf. Scott (1998), 49; Blanton and Fargher (2008), 18.

[64] Augustine, *Ep.* 247, above, 142–3. Symmachus, *Ep.* vi.81, above, 143.

[65] Mark the Deacon, *V. Porph.* 22.

saint who, after healing him, warned him never to perform such a wicked act again.[66] Certainly, the events described here could be placed alongside other examples of soldiers exercising their power in ways that are illegitimate or illegal. But in this instance the soldier's capacity to visit violence upon the girl is incidental to his role as an agent of the state.

It seems reasonable to suggest, therefore, that, notwithstanding the attention they receive in our sources, power structures in the period were in reality imperfectly formed and incompletely applied. In such circumstances, the actions of subordinates are likely in some instances to have interacted only obliquely with those power structures.[67] That is, peasants undertook certain actions that were designed to achieve objectives that had nothing to do with the claims or vocabularies of figures of power, but were motivated rather by the subsistence needs of the household or the impulse to maintain cohesion within the community. This proposition underpins the discussion of the tax system in the next two chapters. It may be briefly illustrated here with reference to two phenomena that emerge from the legal sources as key problems for the state in the period: mobility of labor and flexible crop rotation and field-management practices. In both cases the legislation gives the impression of widespread and deliberate resistance to the directives of the state. In both cases that impression must be tempered by an appreciation of the aims of the peasant economy, for each strategy possessed an internal logic that revolved around insulating the household against catastrophic subsistence failure.

Legislation concerned with taxation in the late Roman empire displays an impulse to identify and concretize connections between land and the individuals who could be held responsible for the fiscal burden assessed on that land, in their capacity as laborers, tenants, or owners. Purchasers of land were instructed to request that their names be entered in the municipal rolls as owners of that land, and a landowner's tax declaration might include, in addition to the number and nature of fields and other material assets, the number and names of laborers and tenants currently working or residing on those fields.[68] Once registered in the tax rolls in connection with that land, these individuals became visible to and identifiable by the tax collector, and could be placed within a hierarchy of liability for the land's taxes. As a consequence, the state attempted to limit their capacity to move from that land, instructing, for example, that registered tenants found to

---

[66] *V. Sim. Styl. (S)* 35. [67] Cf. Ortner (1995), 179; Campbell and Heyman (2007), 7; 17–8.
[68] *Dig.* L.15.4; V.I.55; XLIII.7.26; XLVII.15.7; XLVIII.18.1.20. Cf. *CTh* IX.42.7 = *CJ* IX.49.7 (369, Illyricum, Italy, Africa).

have left their tenancies be bound in chains and returned to the estates from which they had absconded.[69] Landowners, too, lost certain rights vis-à-vis laborers and tenants registered in the tax rolls, including the right to replace existing tenants and to move laborers or tenants from one field to another.[70]

From the point of view of the economies of landowners and peasants, these legal restrictions might be somewhat problematic, for in both cases, they were at odds with long-established practices of risk and estate management. Large landowners customarily employed complex, complementary systems of labor for exploiting their rural properties.[71] We catch glimpses of the complex manpower arrangements that might be employed on a single estate from legislation determining who is responsible for repaying the debts of various members of an estate's personnel. The law mentions registered and unregistered tenants, slaves and casual or permanent laborers alongside a farm manager who could be a slave, freedman or freeborn.[72] For their part, peasants regularly employed strategies for periodically modifying the productive capacity or personnel of the household. A household might rent additional plots of land in order to employ its labor force fully or ensure more produce.[73] Adolescent or adult members of the household might become specialist rural laborers, such as reapers.[74] In such circumstances, it is unlikely that an individual would expect to remain cultivating the same field from year to year. Rather, he would move from field to field – even estate to estate – according to the demands and resources of his household and the availability of labor or tenancies in his locality. These flexible, dynamic practices are likely to have come into conflict with the more static picture envisaged by the legislation, but neither peasants nor landowners were self-consciously resisting the state in this instance. Rather, some aspects of their economic decision-making suddenly became problematic for the state's new fiscal system, and therefore became the object of legislation.

The legal sources also betray an impulse to determine and concretize the productive capacity of particular fields, and to ensure that those fields

---

[69] E.g. *CTh* v.17.1 (332); *CTh* xi.24.2 (360, Egypt).

[70] E.g. *CTh* xiii.10.3 (357, to Dulcitius *consularis Aemiliae*); *CJ* xi.48.7 (371, Gaul); *CJ* xi.63.3 (383, East).

[71] Jones (1964), 788; Finley (1976), 103; Garnsey (1980), 34; Foxhall (1990), 97–8; Banaji (1992), 380; Carlsen (1995), 57; Grey (2007b), 364–7.

[72] *CTh* ii.31.1 = *CJ* iv.26.1 *mut.* (422, West). Cf. *CTh* xi.7.2 (319, Britain), which acknowledges that responsibility for an estate's taxes could fall upon a landowner, *vel colonus vel tributarius suus*. For variable statuses of bailiffs, cf. above, 141 with note 65.

[73] *P. Cair. Isid.* 98 (291); 99–100 (296); Palladius, *Op. Ag.* 1.6.6; *CTh* xi.1.14 = *CJ* xi.48.4 (371S, East). Cf. Gallant (1991), 82; 87–9.

[74] *CIL* viii.11824 (fifth century, Mactar); *CTh* xvi.5.52 (412, Africa).

continued to provide a defined proportion of a landowner's total tax burden from year to year. The resulting picture was also static, requiring constant year-by-year updating to take account of crop rotation and field-management strategies, which entailed a regular alternation of arable cultivation, fallow, and pasture. In the event that those updates were not carried out, there might develop a disjunction between the legal picture and the economic reality. In such circumstances, we may expect problems for both the state and the cultivator, as the former demanded revenues from the latter on the basis of inaccurate information, while the latter protested that land listed as under cultivation was, in fact, currently lying fallow. In a petition to the *praeses*, for example, a certain Valerius from the village of Karanis complains that uncultivated as well as arable land in his possession has been entered into the tax rolls as arable, with the result that he is being pursued for a heavier fiscal burden than he is able to support.[75]

This disjunction is particularly clear in the phenomenon of *agri deserti*, fields that were entered into the tax rolls as yielding a particular portion of the municipality's taxes, but in reality currently not providing revenues to the state. There survives, for example, legislation inviting new cultivators to return such fields to productivity, and censuring existing owners who attempted to reclaim them. This legislation appears to misunderstand long-term fallowing practices, whereby land might lie uncultivated for a period of years without actually being abandoned.[76] It should be stressed that those practices were not rendered illegal by these laws. Rather, the new fiscal system appears to have relied more heavily than in the past upon the regular updating of the information contained in the tax rolls. In circumstances where that information was not updated, what was recorded in the tax rolls came to be out of step with the actual state of an individual landowner's collection of holdings. As in the case of legislation attempting to bind tenants to the land upon which they were registered in the tax rolls, the economic practices of cultivators here were not motivated by an explicit desire to resist or defraud the state. Rather, they were predicated upon an understanding of the importance of returning nutrients to the soil and maintaining a regular, balanced cycle of cultivation. Once again, however,

---

[75] *P. Col.* VII.172 (341–2, Karanis).

[76] E.g. *CTh* VII.20.8 (364, *ad universos provinciales*); 11 (368, to Jovinus, *magister militum*); *CJ* XI.59.7 (386, East); *CTh* V.11.8 (365, Italy); 9 (365, Italy, Illyricum, and Africa); 11 (386); *CTh* XIII.11.13 (412); *CJ* XI.59.8 (388–92); 11 (400). Full discussion of these and other texts in Grey (2007b), 371–3. For comparable problems of translation between local practices and the state's fiscal concerns in other contexts, cf. Scott (1998), 34; 39–41.

that impulse appears to have become problematic for the fiscal system of the state.

The extent and nature of these misunderstandings or miscommunications between the state and agriculturalists can be partially explicated by turning to an observation of Augustine in a recently discovered sermon. In his description of the baptism of Donatist heretics, Augustine draws a comparison with small landowners who erect the marker of a powerful neighbor on their own fields, with the intention of protecting it from the attempts of more powerful individuals to seize it illegally and by force. There is some legal evidence for the phenomenon against which they are attempting to insure themselves, which is termed *invasio*.[77] Augustine reveals that in order to protect himself against such actions, a small landowner might pretend that the property belongs to another. That pretence involved erecting a boundary marker naming another individual as owner. It is difficult to determine precisely the circumstances of such an act. Augustine observes merely that the object is to ensure "that through that deed the one shall possess the land, and the other shall be the source of terror."[78] It would appear, then, that the principal intention was not to evade taxes, but, rather, to safeguard the small farmer's own fields from forcible seizure by a powerful neighbor. The problems that this caused for the municipal and imperial tax collectors, by creating a situation where the *gesta municipalia* listed one person as owner of a property and the boundary marker identified another, were of secondary importance to that aim. We may wonder, however, whether the individual whose name was raised on the boundary marker was complicit in the small farmer's actions or not, although both scenarios appear to have been possible. In this instance, once again, peasant survival strategies intersect only obliquely with the fiscal needs of the state, and only partially with the aims, desires, and objectives of local figures of power.

It seems reasonable to suggest that a significant proportion, indeed most likely the majority, of interactions between powerful and relatively powerless figures in rural contexts were neither overtly antagonistic nor carefully negotiated, but rather, relatively inconsequential and fleeting: a chance meeting on the road; an encounter between a traveling aristocrat and the proprietor of an inn or tavern; an economic exchange in the marketplace. Interactions such as these were often underpinned by mutual distrust and even distaste, but the impact of disparities in status, wealth, and power upon

[77] *CTh* 11.26.1 (330, East). See now the detailed discussion of terminology by Jaillette (1995).
[78] Augustine, *Dolbeau* VI.2.

the form that they took is less clear than in the case of a soldier's violent oppression of a hapless taxpayer or a beneficent landlord's letter of recommendation on behalf of a tenant.[79] Two brief vignettes, drawn from the hagiographical literature and bearing certain formal similarities, offer illustration. They reveal also the lengths to which Christian authors, at least, might go in attempting to enlist such meetings in the project of emphasizing the power of their heroes.

In his account of the deeds of the Egyptian holy man Apollo, who lived in the Hermopolis region of the Thebaid, an anonymous fourth-century monk relates an encounter between Apollo and the celebrants of a ritual to ensure the fertility of the Nile. The author emphasizes the chance nature of this encounter, observing that Apollo happened to be passing when this ritual was taking place. However, upon observing the rite, he immediately prayed to God, and the celebrants were rooted to the spot where they remained until they sent an embassy to the holy man pleading with him to free them, and promising to convert to Christianity if he did so.[80] Sulpicius Severus preserves a similar story in his account of the life of St. Martin, who once came across a funeral procession in the countryside of Gaul. Mistaking the procession for a pagan ritual, Martin stopped the participants in their tracks by making the sign of the cross in the air before them. When informed of the true nature of the procession, however, he immediately released the crowd of peasants and allowed them to continue. Sulpicius observes that Martin was able both to compel them to stand and to permit them to depart at his pleasure.[81]

In both cases, the author focuses upon the end result of the encounter. In Egypt, the conversion of the peasants in question serves not only to stamp out the cancer of paganism but also to enhance the fame of the holy man throughout the region. In Gaul, the vignette is imbued with a sense of the saint's power over both the natural and the supernatural worlds. Further, by emphasizing Martin's ability to grant these peasants permission to continue with their rite, Sulpicius elevates the saint to a level far above the miserable creatures with whom he comes into contact. But for our current purposes it is the accidental nature of both encounters that is of most importance. The aim of these peasants was neither to resist the power of the holy man nor to engage in some type of negotiation with him. Equally, while the power of

---

[79] Meeting on the road: Fronto, *Ep. ad M. Caesarem et invicem* 11.16; *pPeah* 8.9; Constantius, *V. Germani* 31. Chance encounter at an inn: Constantius, *V. Germani* 20. Cf. Rutilius Namatianus, *De Red. Suo* 1.381–6; Grossmark (2006). Exchange at market: *CTh* XIII.1.3 (361); Cassiodorus, *Variae* VIII.33.4.

[80] *Hist. Mon. in Aeg.* VIII.25–9.   [81] Sulpicius Severus, *V. Mart.* 12.

the holy men to influence proceedings is presented in the text as vivid and spectacular, the extent of their authority in reality is open to question. While our authors squeeze narratives of power, authority, and Christian triumph out of these stories, we are left with the impression that the holy figure in both cases was entirely incidental to the events being described. Indeed, funeral processions and communal ceremonies to ensure the Inundation may best be interpreted as exercises in emphasizing a community's internal cohesion and shared values, and therefore as exercises in the management of social risk at a local level.[82]

We should not be surprised by this. It is not difficult to find examples of subordinates being entirely incidental to the figures of power around whom the bulk of our sources revolve. While it is acknowledged in the legal sources that the agents of aristocratic landowners may display a certain amount of autonomy, nevertheless it is assumed that, on the whole, they will be doing the will of their principal, and therefore responsibility for their actions ultimately devolves upon the latter.[83] Certainly, Symmachus, Ausonius, and Sidonius are not alone in belittling the character, standing, and importance of the individuals who carried their correspondence to their kinsmen and friends, and in the letter collections of the period, they are characteristically dismissed summarily, or omitted entirely. Tenants and laborers, clients and dependents appear in the hagiographical literature as mere ciphers, bearing messages between their landlord or employer and the saint, or providing an opportunity for the power of the latter to be revealed to the former in a way that results in his or her conversion to Christianity.[84]

A curious story in Sulpicius Severus' account of the life of St. Martin is a striking reminder of the marginality of the peasantry to the affairs and concerns of elites in the period – even members of the Christian elite, who professed a greater degree of care and interest than their pagan predecessors and peers. Sulpicius observes that, since the devil found himself unable to escape detection by Martin, he instead chose to taunt and insult the saint at every opportunity. On one occasion, he burst into the saint's cell, exulting at having just killed one of his people. A hurried search of the monastery revealed no dead monks, but it was later discovered that a peasant who had been hired to transport wood for the monastery had been gored to death by one of his oxen.[85] No emotion is wasted upon the peasant, either by the monks or by Sulpicius – indeed, the only individual in the story who seems at all interested in his fate is, paradoxically perhaps, the devil himself. The

[82] Cf. above, 105–7.   [83] E.g. *CTh* 11.31.1 = *CJ* iv.26.1 *mut.* (422, West).
[84] E.g. Sulpicius Severus, *V. Mart.* 17.1–4; *V. Dan. Styl.* 25.   [85] Sulpicius Severus, *V. Mart.* 21.

death of this man serves solely as an indication of the saint's ability to perceive events before they happened and call them to the attention of the brethren.

Occasionally our texts reveal fleeting glimpses of chance encounters between peasants and the powerful, but on the whole moments of oblique contact, incidental and accidental interactions are under-represented in the written sources for the late Roman period, for they offered little of substance to the authors of those sources. Where these kinds of encounters do receive attention, they are characteristically interpreted or represented as examples of resistance, futility, or desperation, or opportunistically adopted in order to emphasize an individual's power or prescience. The silence of the sources presents a twofold problem. It is tempting to follow the lead of our aristocratic authors and dismiss as meaningless all encounters between peasants and the powerful that are not laden with clear, coherent resonances of power. Equally, it is possible to embrace the silence too enthusiastically and portray interactions between dominant and subordinate individuals in the late Roman world as essentially random and meaningless in reality, only receiving a semblance of meaning and cohesion through their later inclusion within narratives and contexts that are explicitly motivated by the desire to emphasize their heroes' power, legitimacy, and authority. Both impulses should be avoided. It has not been my intention here to deny that power, dominance, and patronage were real, meaningful, and fundamentally important elements of socio-economic interactions in the late Roman world. Rather, it has been to offer two suggestions. First, a more nuanced and inclusive reading of interactions between peasants and powerful out-siders reveals an infinitely broader spectrum of possibilities than conventional narratives of the devolution of patronage in the period would allow. Second, the sharper and more intense focus in our sources upon the nature, extension, and expression of power in rural contexts still had as its backdrop a general tone of mutual misunderstanding, distrust, and ignorance, which were based upon lack of contact rather than increased contact.

The immense variation in the nature and form of interactions between peasants and the powerful in the late Roman world signals the inappropri-ateness of focusing merely upon defining the form, origins, sources, and fate of patronage relations in the period. We may, with caution, separate instances of patronage proper from examples of dominance or resistance and from casual encounters with reference to the phenomenon of legiti-macy, on the one hand, and the expectation of continued contact, on the other. However, both criteria are problematic. In the first instance, legiti-macy is not intrinsic to an individual. Rather, it is negotiated and contingent, located in the moment, subject at any point to a breakdown in communications or a change in the relative positions and perceptions of participants. The boundary between antagonistic and negotiated relations is therefore fluid and permeable.

Likewise, it is difficult to quantify or define the nature of ongoing relations in the period. In spite of their protestations of perpetuated inter-generational contact, the residents of the village of Euhemeria are likely to have encountered Nechos perhaps three or four times a year. Their strategy of presenting their relationship with him in terms that evoke a patronage relationship is, in reality, an admission of the very tenuousness of their contact with him and therefore, the limitations upon their ability either to resist his demands or to appeal to his sense of fairness or legitimacy. Similarly, notwithstanding their presentation of their relations with their rural dependents as ongoing and mutual, we should regard the claims of Symmachus, Sidonius, and their fellows with some degree of suspicion. It seems more likely that instances of intercession were brokered or mediated by some kind of middle man – most likely a bailiff or farm manager. Moreover, the impression of distaste or frustration alongside the pious expressions of affection and responsibility that we might expect in letters of recommendation and intercession reveals something of the tension between the carefully constructed ideal and the cold, mechanical realities of these relationships.

This gap between the ideological representation and the lived experience of relations between peasants and the powerful was, of course, recognized by all participants. So, too, was the instability of boundaries between legitimate and illegitimate behavior. A man such as Symmachus, Libanius, or Martin is likely to have been simultaneously implicated in antagonistic and nego-tiated relations, as well as experiencing his fair share of incidental, accidental contacts. We cannot be surprised that they – or, in Martin's case, his hagiographer – chose to focus upon those moments that showed them in the most favorable light. We may assume that the relatively powerless were also habitually involved in the full complement of interactions with power-ful figures, and heavily engaged in the project of presenting and interpreting those interactions in ways that made them more palatable and less threat-ening. As a consequence, to focus solely upon relationships that conform to an idealized and therefore largely unrealizable notion of the behavior expected of clients and patrons is to apply an overly limiting lens upon the evidence.

Further, we must acknowledge that the interactions of the relatively powerless with the powerful are likely to have been refracted primarily through the lens of their interactions with other members of their communities, and the imperative of negotiating the constantly shifting balance between the needs or demands of the individual, family, or household, on the one hand, and the cohesion and coherence of the group, on the other.[86] We may contrast, for example, the apparent cohesiveness and unity of the village of Euhemeria with the somewhat more fractured and internally divided communities that Libanius observes in conflict with their fellows. Contrasts are possible, too, between the factors surrounding and motivating the actions of the *rustici* whose collective anticipation of the death of St. Martin were so cruelly dashed, and the circumstances that impelled those described by Salvian to break ranks with their fellows and seek out the individual protection of a powerful landlord. In each case, while the communities themselves were to a certain extent comparable in their demographic and socio-economic makeup, the particular characteristics of the interaction with a figure of power were determined by entirely different sets of circumstances. A multitude of comparable tensions between individuals and the groups of which they were a part are starkly highlighted in our sources in connection with responses to the demands and personnel of the new tax system instituted under the Tetrarchy, and modified over the course of the following centuries. Those interactions constitute the subject-matter of the following chapters.

[86] Cf. Ortner (1995), 176–7.

CHAPTER 6

Creating communities: taxation and collective responsibility

In the late third century, the emperor Diocletian and his colleagues in the Tetrarchy instituted a series of reforms that ushered in a new system of tax assessment, and produced a fundamentally different administrative landscape. This new tax system provided authors of the period with a rich rhetorical vocabulary, and an infinitely exploitable set of images and moral topoi. It emerges from the sources as corrupt, burdensome, and intrusive, an unwieldy monster that ultimately brought about the downfall of the Roman *res publica*. The individuals involved in its apparatus of assessment and collection appear little better than bandits, their attentions unwelcome, their actions the very epitome of the abusive exercise of power and the illegitimate use of force, their demands eliciting fear, flight, and active resistance.[1]

Scholars have long debated the extent to which the changes implemented under the Tetrarchy impacted upon existing networks of asymmetrical and symmetrical relations in the countrysides of the late Roman world. These debates have tended to revolve around two quantitative measures. First, attention focuses upon the tax burden itself, which appears to have grown in the period as the fiscal demands of the state increased.[2] Second, our evidence gives the impression that the personnel involved in the assessment and collection of taxes expanded dramatically as well.[3] Caution is necessary,

[1] See the list of complaints in Demandt (1984), 248. Also Krause (1987), 233–43; Wickham (2005b), 62–3.
[2] Carrié (1993a), 767–8; Garnsey and Whittaker (1998), 318 note 13; Lepelley (1999), 247. Cf. Wickham (2005b), 64–6; 108, with the criticisms of Shaw (2008), 97. Also the cautions of Jaillette (2005), 205; Ando (2008), 45.
[3] Cf. Lactantius, *De Mortibus Persecutorum* VII.3. For a brief statement of the problem, see Garnsey and Humfress (2001), 36–8. Cf. *CTh* XII.6.3 (Egypt, 349). The *Ordo Salutationis* of Ulpius Mariscianus (*CIL* VIII.17896 (361–3, Timgad)) also presents a register of the *sportulae*, or *commoda* to which each member of the municipal and provincial *officia* was entitled: see the commentaries of Leschi (1948), 71–100 and Chastagnol (1978), 75–83.

however, lest we overstate the scale and impact of these increases. Certainly, complaints about heavy taxation in the period are common, but orders of magnitude are impossible to recover, and complaints by themselves are a somewhat unreliable marker.[4] When we turn to the bureaucratic machinery of tax assessment and collection, we are similarly hampered by unreliable figures. In Egypt, the only province where sufficient evidence exists for statistical arguments to be made, the administrative bureaucracy of the period does not appear to have been an overwhelming presence – on the contrary, a recent study has put the proportion of *officiales* to provincials at 1 to 2,400.[5] Therefore, while it seems reasonable to posit some quantitative increase in the imperial bureaucracy of the period, that increase was perhaps not as massive as was once thought.

At any rate, for our current purposes it is the qualitative rather than the quantitative effects of the new system that are of most interest. Certainly, it seems that the new tax system was considerably more intrusive than the practices of previous centuries – although, again, we should be wary of overstating this case, particularly in Egypt, where the state had long had a hand in directing the apportionment of the tax burden in the localities.[6] Some new types of relationship emerged in the period while others were subtly transformed, and in both cases it is possible to connect these changes to pressures created by the new tax system. However, to refract the entirety of socio-economic interactions in the late Roman world through the lens of taxation is to distort and narrow our view of those interactions.[7] Further, to interpret the fiscal system of the period as solely an oppressive, constricting imposition upon rural social systems is to ignore evidence for exploitation of the personnel, structures, and vocabulary of taxation by peasants in the period. Rural social relations in the period were not simply epiphenomena of the state's fiscal demands and the structures put in place to satisfy those demands.

I argue here that, instead, we should view the contours of the new fiscal system in the light of the social networks outlined in the preceding chapters. I suggest that a study of interactions between the two provides a useful test case for assessing the responses of small-scale agriculturalists to the pressures

---

[4] Cf. Whittaker (1980), 8: "bitter complaints about taxation may occur also in periods of unparalleled prosperity." Also Jones (1959), 39.

[5] Palme (2007), 251. Cf. Bagnall (1993a), 66 and, for the relatively low incidence of officials across the empire as a whole, Noethlichs (1981), 159.

[6] Cf. Wickham (2005b), 71.

[7] Cf. Shaw (2008), 97; contra Wickham (2005b), 56; 72; 520; 529; 544. Note also Sarris (2006a), 409; Kehoe (2007), 164. Cf. Galbraith (2003), 85–6; Axelby (2007), 57.

and opportunities that attend large-scale, relatively sudden institutional change. In such circumstances, to regard compliance with or resistance to those changes as mutually exclusive alternatives is to offer a somewhat blunt analysis. We should expect, rather, a complex, perhaps even mutually contradictory, collection of responses. Those responses focus principally upon the small politics of the individual, his household, family, and community, rather than the aims and objectives of the agents or initiators of those changes.[8] I will argue below that to a certain extent, the picture that we receive from our sources of an oppressive, pervasive system and personnel of taxation is valid. But at the same time, the system contained a considerable degree of flexibility and adaptability to local circumstances.[9] As a consequence, it provided opportunities for peasants to adapt to and adopt structures, relationships, and vocabularies in pursuit of their own subsistence and social goals.

We should also resist the urge to place too great an emphasis upon the novelty of the new system and the relationships that it engendered. Rather, what is particularly striking in the period is the visibility and explicitness of certain types of relationship, and the refraction of those relationships through a fiscal lens. We may, at least in part, ascribe this new visibility of social relations in the countrysides of the late Roman world to the new interest of the tax system in identifying and defining those relationships. But it is less easy to determine whether there were fundamental shifts in the nature of the relationships themselves. In the analysis that follows, particular attention will focus upon the ways in which the fiscal system adopted and was co-opted within existing social matrices. I explore two connected but distinct sets of phenomena which emerge from the written sources. First, we witness the authors of our texts seeking both to prescribe the form that interactions between tax collectors and citizens should take and to adopt existing vocabularies of patronage and tenancy, mutual obligation and collective responsibility for describing the forms that those interactions actually took. Second, we observe peasants, both individually and collectively, adopting and adapting the structures of the new system, and placing those structures alongside existing strategies for the management of subsistence and social risk. In both cases, the vocabularies, strategies, and practices that attended the reciprocal relations outlined in the previous chapters are accessed and manipulated in instructive ways.

---

[8] Cf. Axelby (2007), 62; 72. For a brief summary of this debate, cf. Bernstein and Byres (2001), 30–2. See also Breman (1982), 190–2; Wegren (2004), 555; Grischow (2008), 65; 88.

[9] Flexibility: Grey (2007b), 369–70; 373. Local circumstances: cf. Harper (2008), 85; below, 190.

Clearly, interactions between the tax system and local social structures were dynamic, negotiated, and centered as much upon the small politics of the localities as upon the fiscal demands of the state. In what follows, I explore the various forms that those interactions might take in the period. I begin with some general comments about taxation as a means by which states and their citizens interact, and a brief sketch of the fundamentals of the new system as they impacted upon rural communities. These comments serve to frame the subsequent discussion. I then assess the extent to which we should expect the vocabulary and structures of the late Roman tax system to have shaped and determined rural social relations in the period, and detail a series of contexts where we may observe the fiscal system complementing, adapting, or conflicting with existing symmetrical and asymmetrical relationships. I focus in particular upon two phenomena: first, the interweaving of arrangements of tenancy and relationships of patronage, and the attending fuzziness of boundaries between the extraction of rents and the exaction of taxes; and second, the creation of new tax collectivities, which simultaneously constrained communities and provided new opportunities for peasants to manage their subsistence and social risk.

STATES, PEASANTS, AND TAXATION

Taxation is the principal point of contact between a state and its citizens. But it is not merely an economic drain upon the resources of taxpayers, extracting revenues that would otherwise be taken up as rents by a landlord or used by the taxpayer to satisfy social, ceremonial, or subsistence needs. It also represents a contract or negotiation of sorts between the two parties.[10] In the late Roman world, that negotiation is clearest between the state and its urban-dwelling provincial aristocracies, for the administrative organization of the Roman Empire revolved around its urban centers.[11] The *iugationes*, or tax declarations, of provincial landowners were lodged in their nearest city, and these individuals continued to count as their *origo* the urban centre that was closest to the bulk of their rural landholdings.[12] The cities functioned as economic, religious, and political foci for their

---

[10] Cf. Leroy (1992), 324–5; Lieberman (2002), 92–3; Hahamovitch and Halpern (2004), 5; Axelby (2007), 58–9; Blanton and Fargher (2008), 14–15. The form of that negotiation can vary: cf. Mann (1986), 144–50; Jacoby (2008), 269–70. For the late Roman world in particular, see Wickham (2005b), 64; 145.

[11] Cf. Wickham (2005b), 58–9; 61.

[12] Cf. *CJ* III.24.2 (Valens, Gratian, and Valentinian *ad senatum*), seeking to determine where senators should be held liable for taxes. See fuller discussion of Nörr (1963), 531–8. Also Sirks (2008), 126.

surrounding countrysides. They were also loci where imperial and municipal power structures came into contact, and where both interacted with
the rural populations that are the principal focus of this study.

In this period, the cities of the Mediterranean world experienced a
homogenization of their legal statuses, and a minimization of their role in
the administrative structure of the empire. The reforms of the Tetrarchy
included an expansion in the number of provinces and the creation of new
levels of administrative bureaucracy between the municipality and the
central government.[13] As a consequence, the municipalities gradually lost
their position as the minimal unit of administration, and were replaced by
the province.[14] A law of 380, for example, encourages the municipalities to
act in concert as a province when petitioning the emperor, and to choose as
their delegates members of the provincial assemblies.[15] These individuals
are most likely to have been *honorati*, men who had at one time served in
the imperial bureaucracy before gravitating back to their municipalities.
In the late Roman period, they were officially recognized, *ex officio*, as the
most important members of municipal society, and their local prestige was
enshrined in imperial statutes.[16] Of course, the respect accorded members
of the senatorial aristocracy in their municipalities is no new phenomenon
of the fourth century. Throughout the imperial period, senators customarily
held a position of influence and honor in their home provinces if they
chose to return there, and were routinely patrons of their municipalities.[17]
The novelty lies in the conscious incorporation of these *honorati* into the
governance of the municipality and, by extension, the province. We may
imagine, in addition, that there were attendant changes in the roles available
to municipal aristocrats in the administration of the empire, and in the
degree to which they were able to compete and cooperate with current and
former imperial officials.[18]

---

[13] Lactantius, *De Mortibus Persecutorum* VII.4. Lactantius is of course a hostile source, but cf., for
example, the *Laterculus Veronensis* of the early fourth century (Jones (1954) suggests *c.* 320). For further
discussion, see Barnes (1982), 201–25.

[14] Cf. *CTh* XI.1.33 (424, Illyricum); *CTh* XII.1.186 (429, Africa); Liebeschuetz (1959), 344; Lepelley
(1999), 242.

[15] *CTh* XII.12.7 (380, Illyricum). Jones (1964), 763 6; Heather (1998), 207.

[16] *Honorati* stand at the head of the *Ordo Salutationis* from Timgad in Numidia, which regulates the
order in which the provincial governor was to receive visitors. For textual tradition, Chastagnol
(1978), 75. They also take pride of place in the *Album Ordinis Thamugadensis*, the same city's
commemorative plaque to its municipal dignitaries. Cf., also, for Egypt, Banaji (2001), 134–70.

[17] Harmand (1957), *passim*. Cf. now Jaillette (2005), 197–8; 214 for further discussion.

[18] For this process of negotiation and renegotiation between municipal and imperial power structures,
see Heather (1998), 204–5. Cf. Goffart (1974), 94. For economic data for and implications of this
competition, see now Harper (2008), 97.

The legal sources also reveal that the state intervened in the affairs of the municipalities in a variety of new ways in the period. Cities lost control of their municipal revenues, the *vectigalia publica*.[19] Limitations were placed upon who was entitled to lease municipal lands, a process which amounted to a circumscription of the ability of the municipalities to draw revenues from those lands.[20] The emperor installed imperial officials in supervisory positions to allocate that land, assess the tax burden upon it, and control the revenues gained from it.[21] He also imposed imperial officials upon the municipalities and assumed responsibility for appointing the highest curial magistracies.[22] Further, inscriptional evidence suggests that from around the middle of the third century, prestige for building works within municipalities came increasingly to be claimed by or attributed to the provincial governor and his representatives, rather than municipal aristocrats themselves.[23]

Nevertheless, alongside this collection of changes to the nature of municipal governance, the collection of taxes continued to be essential for both the imperial administration and the municipalities, and the role continued to be fulfilled largely by members of the municipal aristocracies. While we may imagine that some of the poorest provincial aristocrats, at least, did seek to evade service on the municipal *curiae*, we should be wary of embracing uncritically the impression of *curiales* evading and fleeing their municipal

---

[19] It appears that they were confiscated by Constantine, before being restored to the control of the municipal *curiae* by Julian: Ammianus Marcellinus, *Res Gestae* XXV.4.15. In 374, Valentinian and Valens once again appropriated them: *CTh* IV.13.7 (374, Africa). Cf. Jones (1964) vol. III, 18 note 73; Garnsey and Whittaker (1998), 330 with note 59. The complexity of this process is sketched by Heather (1994), 23–4, who suggests that in the early fourth century, over three quarters of a city's *vectigalia* were taken by the imperial government. Lepelley maintains that many cities remained wealthy in spite of this: Lepelley (1999), 247.

[20] *CTh* X.3 *passim*.

[21] *CTh* XIII.11.10 (399, Italy); *CTh* XI.16.3 (324, Chalcedon and Macedonia); 4 (328, West).

[22] Imperial officials: Note, for example, the post of *defensor civitatis*, which appears to have originated in the reign of Constantine: *CTh* 1.29.1 (364, Illyricum); *CJ* VI.1.5 (319, Moesia); *P. Col.* VII.175 (339), with the corrections of Kramer and Hagendorn (1982). Cf. *P. Oxy.* 1470 (336); *P. Oxy.* 4082 (330); 901 and 3771 (336); *P. Oxy.* 4366 (336); *CTh* XI.7.12 (Pontus). For the origins of the *defensor civitatis* see Frakes (1993/1994), 338 with note 6. For palatine career paths more generally, Delmaire (1989), 138–45. Curial magistracies: Note the case of the *curator rei publicae*, which had become by the time of Constantine the culmination of a curial career path: *CTh* XII.1.20 (331). Cf. *Gesta Apud Zenophilum* 186–7; *AE* 1991.1643–4 (375–8, Africa Proconsularis), which describe *curatores* as *flamines perpetui*, a curial honor. The *Album ordinis Thamugadensis* places the *curator* after *viri clarissimi*, *perfectissimi*, and *sacerdotales*, but at the head of the municipal magistrates. See also the collection of *logistai*, with discussion in *P. Oxy.* 222–9. For the historical development of the office, see Lepelley (1979), 185; Lepelley (1996), 216; Burton (1979), 478–9.

[23] Nutton (1978), 220 with note 68, observes the origins of this practice in the middle of the third century; Lepelley (1999), 235, dates it to the period following Diocletian's reforms.

obligations wholesale in the period.[24] In fact, it seems likely that a significant number of curial magistrates continued to fulfill their obligations to their cities: holding traditional offices, performing customary liturgies and following the established *cursus honorum*. Indeed, members of the municipal councils appear in the literary sources as figures whose power in local contexts was relatively secure, and whose role had changed little in the period.[25] Querolus, the hero of an anonymously authored fifth-century comedy, regards their position with a certain degree of envy, before he is reminded that along with privilege and status came responsibility for collecting and paying taxes.[26]

In any event, those *curiales* who continued to fulfill their responsibilities to their municipalities became increasingly liable to oversight and intervention by members of the imperial bureaucracy.[27] Indeed, imperial officials and agents of the Roman state are highly visible in the cities of the late Roman world, and we may imagine that their presence created a certain amount of tension for existing provincial and municipal aristocracies.[28] The new fiscal system brought with it elaborate, overlapping hierarchies of assessment, collection, and enforcement, and the impression we gain is of an administrative landscape that was much more heavily populated than in earlier centuries. Further, it was characterized by a fundamental tension between an impulse to compartmentalize responsibilities and define roles, and a tendency for confusion and ambivalence at the boundaries of each individual's area of competence. This system of checks and balances permeated each level of administration.[29] A single example will suffice. An individual tax payment required separate officers to receive, record and confirm receipt, and each municipality's tax register was copied in quadruplicate and lodged in four different offices.[30] Imperial officials were

---

[24] Whittaker and Garnsey (1998), 299; Garnsey and Whittaker (1998), 324; Garnsey (2010), 52. Cf. above, 123.

[25] Cf., for example, *CTh* xiii.10.8 (383, *ad populum*); with the comments of de Zulueta (1909), 12 and note 1. On the crucial role of *curiales* in tax collection in this period, as well as the processes by which they gradually lost this responsibility over the course of the period under discussion here, cf. Wickham (2005b), 68–70; Harper (2008), 89.

[26] *Querolus* 29.

[27] Oversight: Note, for example, the role of imperial *mittendarii* in supervising tax collection by municipal *apparitores*, *discussores*, *susceptores*, and *tabularii*: *CTh* 1.22.1 (316, Africa); *CTh* viii.4.7 (361, Italy and Africa); *CTh* 1.16.5 (365, East); *CTh* xi.26.1 (369, Spain); 2 (400, Italy and Africa); *CTh* xii.6.30 (408, to Lucius, *CSL*); *CJ* xi.1.1 (Anastasius). Cf., in the realm of tax assessment, relations between imperial *censitores* and municipal *praepositi pagorum*: *AE* 1984.250 (368–5, Italy). Cf. *AE* 1994.1790 (Tetrarchic, Arabia); *P. Vindob.* L.132 (345–52), in Sijpesteijn and Worp (1986). Also Whittaker and Garnsey (1998), 303; Lepelley (1996), 220.

[28] Cf. above, 123–4. Also Ando (2008), 45.   [29] Kelly (1998), 170–1. Cf. Kelly (2004), 208–9.

[30] Separate officers: *CTh* xi.4.1 (372, East). Four different offices: *CTh* xi.28.3 (401, Gaul).

involved in the tax process at every level, as overseers, enforcers, or collectors themselves – and in many cases, the distinction between these three roles were unclear. The very mundaneness of imperial intervention in the municipalities is illustrated by an anecdote of Ammianus. Describing the cunning tricks employed by the Maratocupreni, a tribe of brigands living in Syria, he tells a story about a ruse they employed to gain entry into a nearby city. They did so, he observes, disguised as a governor (*rationalis*) and his retinue, complete with herald.[31]

Ammianus' vignette illustrates an imperial official's expectation that his claims and demands would be accepted and met without question in the municipalities. It is also emblematic of a vision of relations between the state and its municipalities that is heavily weighted in favor of the former. Interactions between the state and its subjects were assumed to be characterized by antagonism and violence. An eloquent, if somewhat shrill expression of this assumption may be found in the fourth-century Christian polemicist Lactantius, who describes census officials swarming across the landscape, their actions comparable to those of an enemy army, their impulse to record and categorize absolutely everything an encapsulation of the intrusiveness of the Diocletianic state.[32] While we might expect these relations of conflict and intrusiveness to have extended down the social scale and included peasants and peasant communities, it is difficult to assess the degree to which this was the case.

Certainly, in the eyes of our aristocratic authors, the peasantry was oppressed by the fiscal demands of the state in the period, and subjected to violence at the hands of its agents, and it is no doubt true that attempts by the state and its agents to collect its taxes were often accompanied by and met with force.[33] But it is less clear whether this amounted to systematic institutional oppression of the peasantry, for in general, and unlike the aristocracies of the Roman world, rural communities and their members did not experience the state as an institution, but as an individual.[34] The peasant

[31] Ammianus Marcellinus, *Res Gestae* xxviii.2.13. Cf. Delmaire (1996b), 43–4 on entry by imperial officials into cities by night.
[32] Lactantius, *De mortibus persecutorum* vii.4; xxiii.1–2. Cf. Wickham (2005b), 145 on tax officials as emblematic of the state's control.
[33] Cf. above, 153–4.
[34] Cf. Wickham (2005b), 72 on the Roman tax system as "oppression in a recognized institutional framework," but note Wickham (2005b), 418 on tax officials as individual oppressors. See also Ando (2008), 44, for a "widespread understanding of the state as a depersonalized institution whose primary role was the cultivation of social order within the empire, and peace with the powers without." Blanton and Fargher (2008), 17–18 address problems attending theories of the role of coercion in ensuring cooperation.

interacted with the state in a localized and intensely personal way, as the local aristocrat who had been charged with responsibility for collecting his taxes; the clerk who received and recorded those taxes; the soldiers who aided or hindered that process.[35]

Regardless of the foundations of these individuals' power, therefore, interactions between them and peasants tended naturally to be presented and transacted using the vocabulary of patronage. Peasants may be observed offering gifts to municipal tax collectors, government officials, and soldiers, and even to relatively lowly functionaries in the *officia* of the municipalities. When we can see them addressing these figures, they do so using terms of deference and dependence that are identical to the language that a tenant or client might use of his landlord or patron. In petitions for intercession and judgment, they emphasize the moral qualities and moral obligations of the recipient just as strongly as matters of law and justice.[36] They do so not because they sought to corrupt these individuals, nor because their horizons were so precipitously narrowed in the period that patrons of these sort were their only remaining options, but because these strategies were both an expected component of interactions between the powerful and the relatively powerless and the most effective means of turning interactions with government officials to their own advantage.[37] Scholars have long recognized that the late Roman state was intensely personal in its character and structures.[38] We observe here the implications of this for the form taken by both ongoing and more isolated interactions between its agents and the rural cultivators that constituted the bulk of the population.

Two consequences follow. First, it is difficult to speak of the state as a separate and identifiable entity in the imagination of rural communities and their inhabitants in the period, particularly in the light of the continuing heavy involvement of local municipal aristocrats in the mundane business of collecting taxes. It is therefore difficult also to gauge the extent to which

---

[35] Local tax collectors: *CTh* XII.6.6–7 (364–5, Italy, Illyricum, and Africa); *CTh* XII.6.20 (386, East). Municipal clerks (*tabularii*): *CTh* XII.6.15 (369, Illyricum, Italy, Africa); *CTh* XII.6.27 (400, Africa); *CTh* XI.28.3 (401, Gaul). Soldiers: Libanius, *Or.* XLVII.4; 11; *Or.* XLV.5; above, 156. Cf. Wickham (2005b), 63; 66, who prefers the more systemic account of Salvian to those which focus principally upon the moment of taxation. For cautions about the extent to which Salvian's moral and rhetorical purpose shapes the evidence he provides, see Grey (2006), 175–8.

[36] Gifts: e.g. *CTh* XI.11.1 (368, Illyricum); *CTh* XI.24.2–4 (368; 395; 399); Libanius, *Or.* XLVII.13, with discussion above, 164. Deference: e.g. *P. Ross. Georg.* III.8 (early fourth century). Morality: e.g. *P. Sakaon* 42 (*c.* 323); *SB* XVIII.13768 (fourth century); *PNYU*, 1a (318–20, Karanis); *P. Col.* VII.173 (342, Karanis). Cf. Connolly (2010), 138–40 for the vocabulary that could be used to make claims upon the emperor.

[37] Above, 154.

[38] Garnsey and Humfress (2001), 41–6 provide a useful synthesis. Also, recently, Palme (2007), 250.

the state existed as an institution independent of the individuals who constituted both its most intuitive representatives and its most visible consumers: the military and the administrative bureaucracy.[39] That is, while contemporary scholars cleave naturally towards viewing the state as an institution, it is not at all clear that *rustici* in the late Roman world would have shared their views.

Second, we should not assume that every interaction between agents of the state and peasants was an expression of the state's power, or, by contrast, an exercise in the rejection of that power. We should expect that some tax officials did oppress the peasantry on behalf of the state, some colluded with the peasantry against the state, and some pursued self-interest to the detriment of both. But their motivations for doing so were not always tied to their attitude towards the state, and the pursuit of one course of action in one context did not preclude the pursuit of others at other times. Indeed, we may imagine that these strategies were pursued concurrently in different circumstances, in pursuit of objectives which may be opaque to us, but were no doubt informed by decision-making processes that are comparable to those of the inhabitants of rural communities explored above.[40]

This personalization of the state's interest in raising taxes in rural contexts is likely to have been one factor in the relative absence of large-scale revolts against taxation, for it is difficult to identify such revolts in the countrysides of the late Roman world. Rather, the sources suggest that resistance to the tax collector among the peasantry of the late Roman world was essentially atomized, ad hoc, and personal.[41] Such evidence as there is for concerted, coordinated resistance concentrates around southern Gaul and northern Spain, and is connected, either explicitly or implicitly in ancient writing and modern scholarship, with a shadowy group of individuals collectively labeled the Bagaudae. The identity, aims, cohesion, and social program of these individuals remain hotly debated. Some scholars have chosen to interpret them as a peasant movement, consciously rejecting the Roman state and all it stood for, while others dismiss descriptions of their "un-Romanness" as deriving ultimately from a misunderstanding of their objectives by the authors of our sources, and portray them instead as local

---

[39] Personnel only with difficulty separated from state: Brown (2003), 55. Dangers of privileging the state: Shaw (2008), 99.

[40] Above, 103–5. Note also 168–9 for contacts between agents of the state and peasants that are not conditioned by existing power structures. Agents and officials exploiting incoherence of state structures and systems: Scott (1998), 24. Cf. Herzfeld (2005), 373 and *passim* for an important retrospective and critique of Scott's argument.

[41] Cf. the case of the unwilling taxpayer in Karanis: *P. Col.* VIII.242 (fifth century, Karanis), with discussion above, 153–4.

aristocrats and their clienteles, trying to carve out some semblance of *Romanitas* in their own local contexts.[42]

Clearly, the two positions cannot be resolved, and the distance between them illustrates the limitations of the evidence upon which they have been constructed. It is not my intention here to attempt a solution to this vexed problem, far less to combine these scattered references into a coherent picture of peasant resistance. Rather, it is to observe that, whatever the realities of resistance, revival, or self-removal among the rural inhabitants of the Loire and Ebro valleys, the sources betray a sense of "otherness" in their descriptions of the actions of these individuals. The anonymous author of the *Querolus*, for example, speaks of a society that consciously rejects existing Roman distinctions of wealth, status, and power, while Rutilius Namatianus speaks allusively about an inversion of normal relations between masters and their servants. Salvian's description of the Bagaudae revolves around a series of linked opposites: men prefer to live free under the appearance of captivity than to continue as captives in a situation of seeming freedom; the Bagaudae themselves have been oppressed by cruel judges, and called rebels and outsiders by the very people who have forced them to become criminals.[43] A society characterized by such inversions might be either utopian or dystopian, according to the predilection of the author, but at the very least, it was decidedly different from the society in which he found himself. It is tempting to ascribe this difference, and the resistance to or subversion of the social order that it represented, as manifesting an aristocratic fantasy of sorts, one generated in part by the immense transformations in socio-economic structures and relations of power that both local and senatorial aristocrats experienced in the period.[44]

However, it is less clear that *rustici* experienced the same upheavals in the same ways, and difficult also to ascribe with any degree of confidence their supposed withdrawal in this instance to a conscious decision to avoid or evade their fiscal responsibilities. Further, given the complex social matrices sketched in the foregoing chapters it seems something of a stretch to suggest

---

[42] Wickham (2005b), 530–4 provides a useful summary of the historiographical debate, although in identifying these figures as revolting against the tax machinery of the late Roman state, he seems to overplay his hand slightly. Note the detailed exploration of the relevant sources by Neri (1998), 400–17. Also the brief comments of Shaw (2008), 102. For a comparable example of multiple responses to the state's fiscal regime that stop short of large-scale rebellion, cf. Cronin (2005), particularly 30–3. For localized resistance, lacking a shared consciousness of resistance, Kim (2007), 1010–1. Note also Popkin's argument that the nature of peasant society militates against concerted action, particularly rebellion: Popkin (1979); cf. Anderson (1997), 506–7.

[43] *Querolus* 30; Rutilius Namatianus, *De Red. Suo* I.213–6; Salvian, *De Gubernatione Dei* v.5.22–6.27.

[44] Cf. Wickham (2005b), 433–4; 531; Banaji (2009), 63.

that their interactions with both local and senatorial aristocracies were fundamentally structured by the aims and constraints of the taxpaying and tax-collection process. It is more likely that the relations of power which infused the system of tax assessment and collection were mapped out along lines established by existing structures of dominance and resistance, mutual exploitation, and incidental contact. I return to this point in the following chapter, where I assess the novelty of the strategies that the new tax system provoked among the peasantries of the late Roman world. First, however, I outline the fundamentals of the new system as they impacted upon existing rural social matrices.

THE TAX SYSTEM OF THE LATE ROMAN EMPIRE

We observe both fundamental changes and broad continuities in the fiscal practices of the late Roman period.[45] On the one hand, the tax system instituted under the Tetrarchy emerges from our sources as markedly different from that of the Principate. Most significantly, it is presented as considerably more intrusive. The imperial administration was no longer satisfied, as it had been in earlier centuries, to assess a total tax burden upon a municipality, and leave it to the municipality itself to determine how the taxes were raised. Rather, the new assessment system was designed to facilitate the identification of particular plots of land, from which precise proportions of a community's tax burden could be expected to be drawn. This shift in the state's attitude towards the taxing of its municipalities took as its context the intrusion of the imperial bureaucracy into the municipalities which was sketched above, and a connected series of changes to the balance of cooperation and coercion in relations between the state and its municipal aristocracies.

On the other hand, long-established principles continued. In particular, land continued to be the principal focus of taxation, and the principle of collective responsibility continued to underpin the state's attitude towards the taxes it assessed upon the provinces. Indeed, it is likely that these principles were, if anything, emphasized under the new tax system. There were further continuities. While communities and individuals continued to be taxed on the basis of both the number of taxable individuals and the amount of their landed assets, the number and type of obligations incumbent upon land increased markedly in the late Roman Empire, as a variety of

---

[45] For a fuller exposition of the principles outlined here, see Grey (2007a), 170–1; Grey (2007b), 368–9. Cf., for slightly differing accounts, Wickham (2005b), 63–7; Kehoe (2007), 165–91.

liturgies and military *annonae* were incorporated into the fiscal system.[46]
The heterogeneity of local tax assessment and collection practices also
continued in the period, but a new system of "macro-fiscalité" was introduced, which was designed to render the multiplicity of local systems
mutually comparable and comprehensible.[47] Communities continued to
be held collectively responsible for their taxes, and the wealthiest members
of those communities remained the principal focus of taxation, but the
nature and implications of each of these impulses underwent subtle
changes, which may also be placed within the context of changes in the
state's attitude towards its relationship with the municipalities. In particular, we observe the state reaching into the municipalities to direct and
determine the allocation of their fiscal burdens, by identifying a diverse,
complementary collection of sub-municipal tax collectivities.[48]

The impulse towards systematization may be most clearly observed in the
introduction of the *caput* and the *iugum* as abstract measures of assessment,
and the combination of the *tributum soli* and the *tributum capitis* of the
High Empire under the rubric of the *capitatio*, an assessment of a community's total tax liability. These abstract units of assessment underpinned
the new system, in which the ad hoc requisitions in kind of the third
century were scrapped and all *munera*, liturgies, and burdens, including
military recruitment and supply charges, were incorporated into a single,
unified fiscal vocabulary.[49] A municipality declared its assets as a number of
iuga. This figure was arrived at on the basis of individual tax returns
(*iugationes* or *professiones*) submitted by residents of that municipality.
The resulting figure was used by the imperial *censitores* in their assessment
of that municipality's total tax burden (*capitatio*) as a number of abstract

---

[46] Déléage (1945), 29; Jones (1964), 60; Carrié (1994), 46. Cf. Wickham (2005b), 67; Kehoe (2007),
165–6. Cf. P. *Princ.* III.119 = *SB* XII.10989 (325) for a dispute over whether a particular parcel of land
was registered, and for what use.

[47] Heterogeneity: *CTh* VII.6.3 (377, East); *CTh* XII.4.1 (428, East); *Nov. Val.* X.3 (441). Cf. Jones (1957),
88; Brunt, in *Addendum II* to Jones, *The Roman Economy*, 183; Cérati (1975), 419–28; Goffart (1974),
128 note 15*. Macro-fiscalité: Carrié (1993c), 139. Such a strategy amounted to an exercise in gross
over-simplification: cf. Scott (1998), 24–9.

[48] Collective responsibility: *Pan. Lat.* VIII(V).11 (311); see the discussion of Nixon in Nixon and Rodgers
(1994), 255 with note 4; *ILS* 6091 = *FIRA²* 1, 95 (323–31); *CTh* XI.12.1 (340); *CTh* V.11.9 (364–5, Italy);
CTh XI.24.2 (368, East); *CTh* XI.13.1 (383, Illyricum, Italy, Africa); *CTh* XII.6.27 (400, Africa). Also
Giliberti (1992), 177. Wealthiest carry greatest burden: *CTh* XII.6.8 (365, East); 20 (386, East) and
Interp.; 25 (399, to Firminus, *CSL*); Jones (1964), 456; Durliat (1993), 31. Not all taxes were collected
by *curiales*: Delmaire (1996a), 60. For limitations upon a premodern state's capacity to intervene
effectively in local tax-apportionment practices, cf. Scott (1998), 33.

[49] *CTh* XI.7.6 (349, Italy). The incorporation of this law under the rubric *De Exactionibus* reveals that, in
the understanding of the compilers of the Theodosian Code, the *annona* was part of the regular tax
system.

units (*capita*).[50] Each of those *capita* could be earmarked as fulfilling a particular charge or liturgy.[51] Conversion between the *iugum* and the *caput* on the one hand, and the measure of assessment which continued to be used in the provinces, on the other, was effected by means of conversion tables.[52]

The fundamental aim of the system was to establish the productive capacity of each field as a basis for tax assessment, and to identify the individuals who could be held responsible for the tax burden assessed upon that field. The system of *capitatio–iugatio* was designed to facilitate the first of these aims, while the second was to be achieved by means of the *origo*, an administrative unit which could be laden with a proportion of a community's tax burden or a specific liturgy.[53] Under the High Empire, a provincial or Senatorial aristocrat's *origo* was the municipality to which he belonged, and where he was registered as a landowner. Over the course of the second century it came more specifically to denote the place in which he could be expected to fulfill *munera*.[54] By the late third century, the term continued to denote an aristocrat's links to a particular municipality, but its ambit also expanded.[55] In the period following the reforms of the Tetrarchy, the principle of the *origo* was enlisted in attempts by the imperial administration to ensure the fulfillment of fiscal obligations beyond the *munera* owed by members of the *curia*.[56] The *origo* also came to denote a particular region, village or estate, in connection with which members of the rural population were registered in the census.[57] This understanding of the *origo* is therefore analogous to the notion of the *idia* in Egypt, which had since at least the early Roman Empire denoted a region in which an individual

---

[50] Cf., for a marginally different analysis, Carrié (1994), 45–6 with note 61.

[51] *CTh* XI.16.4 (328, Italy).

[52] See, for example, the *Syro-Roman Lawbook* (*Leges Saeculares* 121 = *FIRA²* II, 795–6). Cf. Carrié (1994), 48–9; Jones (1953). Note also the collection of inscriptions from Thera and elsewhere, now exhaustively analyzed and redated to the late fourth century by Harper (2008), 86–90; 92–3 and *passim*. Barnes (1982), 231 observes that the existence of a similar schedule for Gaul, the *Gallicani census communis formula*, may be deduced from *Pan. Lat.* V(VIII).5.5. Conversion between local and state measures is likely to have entailed a considerable degree of simplification, and to have engendered a certain amount of confusion: cf. Scott (1998), 24.

[53] Fuller discussion in Grey (2007a), 170–5. Note the alternate position of Sirks (2008), 126–8, who concentrates particularly upon the legal situation in the reign of Justinian.

[54] Nörr (1963), 529–31.

[55] *CJ* X.39.*passim*; *CJ* X.40.*passim*. Also *Brev.* XII.1.2 = *CTh* XII.1.12 = *CJ* X.39.5 (325, East); Isid. *Etym.* IX.4.22. Cf. Jones (1964), 68–9.

[56] Cf. *Brev.* V.9.1 = *CTh* V.17.1, which directs that *coloni iuris alieni* should be returned to their *origo*. Imperial estates as a type of *origo*: *CTh* IV.12.3 (320, *ad populum*), with Rosafio (2002), 154.

[57] *CTh* VII.21.3 (396, Rome); Carrié (1983), 217–18. Theoretically, an individual could change his *origo*: cf. Sidonius, *Ep.* V.19; *CJ* XI.48.22 (531, East); Carrié (1983), 222–3 with note 78.

could be held responsible by the provincial administration for his fiscal obligations.[58]

By means of these *origines*, the landed wealth of the municipalities could be compartmentalized, categorized, and laden with a variety of liturgies, *functiones*, or fiscal burdens. Individuals identified in the census declaration as owner of, resident upon, or cultivating a particular *origo* could be held responsible for its burdens, their obligation reinforced by the principle of collective responsibility. It is not surprising, then, that in the eyes of the administration, an individual's withdrawal from his (or, more rarely, her) *origo* or *idia* branded that individual as an outsider. He was a dispossessed person, one who would most likely join a group of bandits, or become a beggar in the city.[59] He was unable to purchase land, since the purchaser was required to state his *origo* in the document of sale, and publicly acknowledge the tax burden of the land through entering his name into the municipal records.[60] He was also excluded from certain benefits of participation in public, official structures of society. For example, individuals proven to be *vagi* – that is, living illegally outside their *origines* – could legitimately be recruited into the army without diminishing the workforce registered on the land of a particular region.[61]

The impulse to define fiscal obligation and, by extension, an individual's standing in the community, with reference to his *origo* is particularly evident in the legal sources concerning registered *coloni*. Consequently, some scholars have posited the emergence of a *ius* based on the *origo* in the period, and identified that *ius* as crucial in the deterioration of the condition of *coloni*.[62] It certainly appears that the *origo* was recognized in the legislation as having some kind of legal identity, but we should be careful not to overstate the ambit and objectives of the *ius* which pertained to it. We should be wary, too, of limiting the ambit of the *origo* to registered tenants, for the legislation

---

[58] See now the detailed discussion of Braunert (1955). Nörr (1965), 447–8, posits a connection between the two, although we should be cautious about accepting the assumptions underlying this suggestion. Cf. also the brief comments of Giliberti (1992), 182.

[59] *P. Cair. Isid.* 127 (310); *CTh* XIV.18.1 (382, Rome). Cf. *P. Oxy.* 3364 (209), with Lewis (2000), 96. For general comments, Shaw (2000), 383–8. Also, for Egypt, Lewis (1937), 68–9, with references. For Campania, Rougé (1975), 343.

[60] Note the impulse to ensure that the purchaser of an estate's name be entered into the tax rolls as the new owner: *FV* 35.3–4; 249.5–8; *CTh* XI.3.5 (391, East); *P. Oxy.* 3583 (444); *P. Ness.* III.24 (569). Cf. requests for registration of houses in the possession of new owners: *P. Wisc.* 2.58–9 (298, Arsinoite nome); *P. Mich.* 12.627 (298, Arsinoite nome); *SB* 10: 10728 (318). Cf. Wickham (2005b), 70.

[61] *CTh* VII.13.6 (370, East); *CTh* VII.18.10 (400, Gaul); Neri (1998), 137. It seems that in reality this type of recruitment was not particularly successful: *CTh* VII.20.12 (400, to Stilicho, *magister utriusque militiae*); VII.18.17 (412, to Constantius, *magister militum*).

[62] Goffart (1974), 71–2 with note 14; 77 note 39; 81; 84–5; 87; Sirks (1993b), 344 note 43; Banaji (2001), 211–2; Rosafio (2002), 12; 177–214; Koptev (2004), 287–8.

of the fourth and fifth centuries reveals that the terms *origo, originalis*, and *originarius* could be applied in a variety of contexts, and across a broad semantic field. It was the nature and location of an individual's *origo* that determined his or her liability for such liturgies as the supply of recruits, ships, or pork, the production of bread and service on the municipal *curia*.[63]

Scholars now generally agree that the interest shown in the legislation to define a relationship between registered tenants and their *origines* should be located firmly and solely within the internal logic of the new tax system.[64] The visibility of these tenants in the legal sources is therefore best interpreted as a product of the contradiction that existed between the fiscal system, which created a static, idealized picture of agricultural activity, and the realities of economic behavior in rural contexts, which relied fundamentally upon the capacity for mobility of labor and the regular rotation of fields through a cycle of productivity and fallowing.[65] In this regard, the legislation was of only limited effectiveness at best, for the sources reveal that agriculturalists continued to move around the rural landscape, and peasants can be observed living, working, and taking tenancies in regions outside their *origo*.[66] It is therefore difficult to infer the socio-economic, or even the legal, realities of registered tenancy from the normative and idealized language of the legislation. It is also unlikely that the preponderance of legislation concerned with this phenomenon reflects the dominance in reality of arrangements of this type. Rather, we should interpret this evidence as documenting legal problems connected to the particular exigencies of the new tax system of the period.

Consequently, we should not seek in the legislation concerning obligations for liturgies and taxes evidence for the social dynamics of the countrysides of the late Roman world, far less an indication of the fundamental orientation of rural society along lines of power and dependence determined and driven by the tax system and its demands. The objectives of the state, and its impact upon existing social matrices in rural contexts in the period, were considerably more circumscribed. Fundamentally, the state sought

---

[63] Cf. the full and detailed discussion of Sirks (1993a). Also, for briefer statements, Grey (2007a), 171–5; Sirks (2008), 126–7.

[64] Carrié (1983), 220–5, drawing upon Goffart (1974), 67; 70–1; 78. Also Lepelley, (1989), 246 with note 37; 250–1. Cf. Carrié (1997), 101–3; Kehoe (2007), 168–71; Sirks (2008), 141.

[65] Grey (2007b), 365–7, and above, 171–2. Contra Wickham (2005b), 520, who argues that agriculturalists were particularly targeted and affected by the tax system of the period. For the potential economic costs of this, cf. Kehoe (2007), 173–7.

[66] Cf. *Brev.* v.9.1 = *CTh* v.17.1 (332, *ad provinciales*); *Brev.* v.9.2 = *CTh* v.17.2 (386, East). Note the role of marriage in effecting a change of *origo*, too: *CTh* vii.13.6 (370, East); *CTh* vii.18.10 (400, Gaul); *CTh* xi.24.6.3 (415, Egypt); *CTh* v.18.1.4 = *CJ* xi.48.16 *mut.* (419, Italy).

simply to define the fiscal responsibilities of its citizens. It did this by attaching those responsibilities to the land in a variety of ways. But even here the principle was not as coherent and cohesive as some scholars have suggested. A series of laws concerning the responsibility of the inhabitants of the municipalities for fulfilling their various urban and rural responsibilities illustrates both the fundamental importance of the *origo* in the new fiscal system and the inexactness with which the concept was understood in the period.[67] Far from a series of discrete, coherent micro-regions within a municipality and its hinterland, the *origines* of these texts seem to weave together in somewhat muddled and confusing ways.

These texts also hint at the difficulties attendant upon any attempt to divide the inhabitants of the municipalities and their hinterlands into a series of discrete economic units based solely upon the location of the land that they owned, resided upon, or cultivated. Indeed, the laws reveal once again the limitations of an abstracted and simplified administrative system in dealing with the complexity and flexibility of agricultural practices. We may therefore justifiably quibble over the effectiveness of these measures in reality. But their intent, at least, is clear. In the introduction of the system of *capitatio–iugatio* and the extension of the concept of the *origo* to meet the needs of the imperial administration as well as the claims of a civic community, we witness the intervention by the Roman state into the internal organization and fiscal practices of the municipalities.

The responsibility for collecting and paying a municipality's burden continued to rest ultimately upon the wealthiest members of the community, who were expected to acknowledge their responsibility for their community's fiscal obligations in the same spirit, and with the same motivations, as the provision of games, the staging of shows, and the erection of public buildings. Roman law recognized a multiplicity of social and legal obligations towards state, public provincial authorities, and the *municipium*.[68] These obligations, which fall under the broad heading of *munera*, could take many forms.[69] Under the High Empire, tax collection was considered a civic *munus*, one which was owed more to the municipality itself than to the state. It fell upon members of the *curia*, which traditionally

---

[67] Cf. *CTh* XI.10.1 (369, Gaul); *CTh* XII.19.1–3 (400, Gaul), with Grey (2007a), 163. Also *CTh* XII.18.1 (367, Egypt); *CTh* XII.18.2 = *CJ* X.38.1 (396, Illyricum). On mobility, see above, 47–9.

[68] Sirks (1993a), 164.

[69] Arcadius Charisius, *Dig.* L.4.18. Note, however, the limited application of some *munera*: *Nov. Val.* X.3 (441); *CTh* XI.16.15 (382, Italy); 18 (390, East). The clergy were also immune from service in municipal *curiae* and taxation: *CTh* XVI.2.10 (320/3); *CTh* XVI.2.14 (356, West); Basil of Caesarea, *Ep.* 104 (372) with Gascou (1997), *passim*. Cf. Jones (1964), 182–3 with note 52; Hunt (1998), 263–4, with further references.

comprised the municipality's wealthiest and most prominent citizens.[70] In the period following the Tetrarchic reorganization of the tax system, this principle continued, although it is possible that some limitations were placed upon the extent of these individuals' collective responsibility.[71] It is likely also that some, at least, sought to avoid their responsibilities to their municipalities, although as already noted we should be wary of assuming widespread abandonment of the *curiae* in the period.[72] At any rate, the impulse to reach into the municipalities and police the apportionment and distribution of their fiscal burdens is once again evident, as, too, is the importance of precisely determining the extent and nature of an individual's share of the collective responsibility for a particular portion of the community's tax burden.

This impulse was part of a transformation in the state's attitude towards taxing the municipalities. From the reign of Augustus, at least, the main subject of direct taxation was the *civitas stipendiaria* rather than the *homo stipendiarius*. That is, Rome imposed its taxes on a municipality, not an individual, and once this assessment had been carried out, the interest of the state was restricted to the collection of a total. The municipality was left to apportion that total in its own customary way.[73] In the period following the Tetrarchy, the attitude of laissez-faire evaporated, and was replaced by a much more interventionist approach, as the state reached into those municipalities and became involved in the allocation of their assessed tax burden. Conceptually, the *civitas stipendiaria* was fragmented, and divided into a variety of different segments in the period.[74] In a corresponding fashion, *munera* and liturgies were divided into those pendant on urban populations and those pendant on rural populations. In the cities, the *munera* of *curiales* remained largely unchanged from the pre-Tetrarchic period.[75] But, as we have seen, they were now subject to imperial regulation, apportionment, and enforcement. In the process, those obligations were subtly transformed from civic liturgies into responsibilities to the Roman state.

---

[70] *Honores* (offices) and *munera* were intimately connected: *Dig.* L.4.17.1. Cf. Goffart (1974), 27–30.

[71] E.g. *Dig.* L.4.18.26; *CTh* xII.6.8 (365, East); 20 (386, East) and *Interp.*, 25 (399, to Firminus, *CSL*). Further references are collected in Jones (1974), 177 at note 121. Also Jones (1964), 456; Durliat (1993), 31; Sirks (1993a), 163–7; Delmaire (1996a), 59. Grelle (1963), 42 at note 47 comments, "I *municipes* sono obbligati al tributo nei confronti della loro communità, non di Roma." Not all taxes were collected by *curiales*: Delmaire (1996a), 60. Limits on collective responsibility: *CTh* xI.7.2 (319, Britain).

[72] Above, 123; 183–4.

[73] Abbott and Johnson (1926), 120–1; 185; Jones (1940), 144–5; Jones, *The Roman Economy*, 164; 177; Goffart (1974), 6–21, particularly 6; 19–20. Cf. Scott (1998), 37–8.

[74] Giliberti (1992), 183; Carrié (1994), 62. Cf. *CTh* x.7.6 = *CJ* x.19.4 (349, Italy). For limitations upon the success of this impulse in a comparative context, see Scott (1998), 39–44.

[75] *CTh* xII.6.20 (386, East); 27 (400, Africa). Cf. *CTh* xI.23.2 (362, Gaul).

Members of *collegia* and *corpora*, as well as members of the *plebs urbana* also continued to be held responsible for specific liturgies.[76] Here, too, we observe a subtle shift in the balance between city and state, as obligations formerly considered principally civic became part of a centrally administered system of liturgies. A comparable transformation is visible in rural contexts, too, where we observe the emergence of a variety of *origines*, operating both as sub-collectivities within the municipality and as completely separate areas of land. Imperial estates, for example, were envisaged as a specific type of *origo* which carried with them a unique collection of rights and obligations, including exemptions from certain other liturgical responsibilities. The legislation concerned with defining those rights and obligations reveals that this proliferation of *origines* could be exploited by the residents of the municipalities and their hinterlands, when it censures tenants of imperial land seeking to evade other liturgies for which they were also responsible.[77] Again, the intrusiveness of the new system is evident, as, too are some unintended consequences of that intrusiveness.

The administrative landscape that the new system produced was characterized by a greater degree of detail and visibility than ever before.[78] But the new attention to detail brought with it problems as well as providing the opportunity to tax the provinces more effectively. A constant stream of information was required from taxpayers, recording changes in land ownership and land-use patterns. The initiative for providing that information rested with the taxpayers themselves. Individuals were expected to lodge changes in the amount, distribution, and nature of their possessions in the *gesta municipalia*. Provisions also existed for individuals or communities to request a tax equalization, or *peraequatio*, if they felt that distribution of their assets or the burden of taxation to be unfair.[79] In the event that neither of these things happened, any disparity between what was recorded in the

---

[76] *Navicularii, suarii,* and *pistores* were apportioned certain *munera,* and even exempted from the performance of others by way of compensation: e.g. *CTh* XIII.5.5 (326); 7 (334); 16 (380). Jones (1970) remains seminal. Also Sirks (1993a); Déléage (1945), 38. *Plebs urbana:* Lactantius, *De Mortibus Persecutorum* XXIII.2; XXVI.2 claims that they were registered in the empire-wide census of 306; cf. *Pan. Lat.* VIII(v).5.4. But the measure was later repealed, at least in the east: *CTh* XIII.10.2 (313, Lycia-Pamphylia). Cf. Jones (1964), 464. Also Nixon in Nixon and Rodgers (1994), 257–63; 272 note 5.

[77] Imperial estates a particular type of *origo*: *CTh* XII.1.33 (342, to Rufinus, *Comes Orientis*), with Grey (2007a), 161–2. Imperial *conductores* and *coloni* must share the municipality's burden: *CTh* XI.7.6 = *CJ* x.19.4 (349, Italy).

[78] Jones (1957), 94. Note Goffart's arguments about the language and methods of military tacticians in the creation of Diocletian's tax system: Goffart (1974), 142–3.

[79] Fuller discussion in Grey (2007b), 369–70. It is difficult to determine the extent to which these provisions were actually effective or even accessible in reality. For limitations upon premodern states' capacity to finetune their fiscal policies, cf. Scott (1998), 23–4.

tax rolls and the reality on the ground was likely to create problems for the tax collector, and I return to these problems in the following chapter. But the potential for problems should not obscure the adaptability and sophistication of the system as it was envisaged, or the extent to which it responded to and took advantage of existing socio-economic structures.

We observe peasants of the late Roman period both responding to the new pressures that this system brought with it and embracing the opportunities that it provided. Those opportunities are visible in a variety of contexts. The incorporation within structures of tax collection of existing relationships between aristocratic landowners and their tenants subtly changed the nature of those relationships, and provided both parties with an expanded apparatus for mutual exploitation. The creation of new fiscal collectivities encouraged the development of mechanisms of mutual support and reciprocity within rural communities, and between the members of those communities and their more powerful neighbors. The impulse to micromanage the apportionment of a community's collective fiscal burden provided the members of those communities with a powerful vocabulary to enlist in internal disputes that in reality had little or nothing to do with taxation. In the following chapter, I explore each of these phenomena in turn. I argue that the state's exploitation of existing relationships and its creation of new ones in rural contexts had consequences that were both unexpected and beyond its control.

CHAPTER 7

Unintended consequences: taxation, power, and communal conflict

The tax system of the late Roman world does not appear to have fundamentally reshaped rural socio-economic relations in the late Roman period. Rather, it was modeled upon networks of mutual obligation and alliance that already existed. The novelties introduced under the auspices of the new tax system interacted with those networks, and in some circumstances created new relationships and connections between participants. By means of the *origo*, the Roman state sought to identify clearly or create *ex novo* a multitude of overlapping collectivities, which could be held mutually responsible for proportions of a municipality's total tax burden. Those collectivities might involve individuals of quite different wealth and status, as in the case of registered tenants and their landlords; or they might be comprised of individuals whose circumstances were relatively similar, such as we might imagine the proposed purchasers of patrimonial estates mentioned in an early fifth-century law.[1] In each case, these new configurations are likely to have created or fostered asymmetrical and symmetrical relations between their participants. Consequently, the opportunities available to small agriculturalists for managing their subsistence and social risk will have increased, and those small agriculturalists were not slow to exploit these opportunities. In what follows, I explore both the intended objectives of the state in creating tax collectivities and ensuring that their members be held mutually responsible for their fiscal burdens, and a series of unintended consequences of those actions.[2]

TENANCY, PATRONAGE, AND THE PAYMENT OF TAXES

The close connection between tenancy and patronage in the understanding of both the powerful and the relatively powerless was emphasized in a

---

[1] *CTh* v.16.34 = *CJ* xi.68.6 (425, to Valerius, *CRP*).
[2] Cf. Wegren (2004), 555–6; 563–4; Axelby (2007), 37; 40–1.

previous chapter, where a blurring of the boundary between the two in the period was sketched. The legal sources reveal that the state attempted to exploit this partial merging of patronage with tenancy for its own fiscal purposes. A number of interconnected strategies are visible. First, there survives legislation which attempts to foster a relationship of patronage between large landowners and a variety of undesirable or threatening elements, by mandating the creation of an arrangement of tenancy between the two. A law addressed to the Prefect of the City of Rome, for example, directs that any beggars discovered to be sound of body and of robust years, and therefore to be begging illegitimately, should be given over to their denouncers in an arrangement of *colonatus perpetuus*, or perpetual tenancy.[3] At base, the law seems to be responding to a fear among the urban aristocracy of the threat posed by the unknown, unknowable urban mob, and a desire to neutralize that threat by attaching them to a member of the city's landowning aristocracy. Skepticism as to the practicality, effectiveness, and enforceability of such a law is warranted, but it reveals nevertheless an expectation that a relationship of tenancy will necessarily carry with it some measure of personal responsibility on the part of the landlord for the actions of his tenant.

Even more explicit in its connection of patronage, tenancy, and the late Roman tax system is a law concerning the settlement of a group of Sciri, who had been captured following the successful repulse of the Hunnish king Uldin in the early fifth century.[4] By this law, landowners are offered the opportunity to acquire these individuals under terms that resemble both the conditions attributed to the settlement of conquered barbarians in other circumstances and the limitations that surround the economic activities of landowners and their registered *coloni* elsewhere in the legal sources. In this case, landowners are offered tax breaks and other incentives to take on these cultivators, but at the same time stern warnings are issued about the parameters within which their labor can be exploited, and the regions in which they are permitted to reside. On the one hand, then, the law seeks to ascribe responsibility for these individuals to private persons in much the same way as the law for beggars outlined above. On the other, however, the arrangement between the landlord and his barbarian tenant appears, at least initially, to have been subject to certain oversights that betray the state's interest in maintaining some kind of control over the relationship.

---

[3] *CTh* xiv.18.1 = *CJ* xi.26.1 (382, Rome), with Grey and Parkin (2003).
[4] *CTh* v.6.3 (409, East), with Grey (2011a).

In both cases, the circumstances are somewhat unique, and the specifics of the solutions proposed should not necessarily be taken as exemplary of the state's attitude to these groups of people. But in each case the underlying assumption is the same: relations between *domini* and their *coloni* (whether registered or not) could be expected to display some of the same characteristics as those between *patroni* and their *clientes*. Such an assumption entailed a tendency also to blur the boundaries between the role of the *dominus* as a landowner, with rights over his landed property but only a relatively limited amount of power or authority over his tenants, and the rights of a *dominus* as slaveowner, who exercised a *ius in rem* over the slave's person, and possessed extensive powers to compel and constrain his actions. This impulse is clearest in laws concerned with defining the nature of the limitations upon registered *coloni* in the period, and the extent to which their landlords could or should be held responsible for their actions. Thus, for example, a law concerning labor relations in Thrace instructs landlords to deal with their *coloni* using both the *sollicitudo* of a *patronus* and the *potestas* of a *dominus*. The foundations upon which this *potestas* rested are not made explicit, although in a later law, his interest is identified as resting upon his ownership of the land to which the *colonus* is obligated in a "kind of slavery" (*quaedam servitus*). We observe here a certain semantic slippage, as the vocabulary of slavery provided a convenient but imperfect tool for describing the relationships that existed between these *coloni*, the land upon which they were registered, and the owners of that land.[5]

This vocabulary complemented, but also conflicted with, the terminology that landlords themselves used to describe their relationships with their tenants in the period. As we have seen, landowners of the western provinces, at least, may be observed writing letters on behalf of various tenants and laborers on their estates, in which they emphasize their sense of obligation towards these individuals in much the same way as they might in a letter of recommendation for a friend or client.[6] We observe also the state seeking to take advantage of these patronal impulses among landlords, and to encourage them to assume a greater degree of responsibility for their tenants. This strategy is clearest in legislation concerning the collection and payment of the taxes owed by the latter. Strictly speaking, rents and taxes should be regarded as distinct types of surplus extraction.[7] The two were clearly

---

[5] *Sollicitudo* and *potestas*: *CJ* XI.52.1 (393, Thrace). *Quaedam servitus*: *CJ* XI.50.2 (396, Asia). Fuller discussion in Grey (2007a), 166–7; Grey (2011b), 502–5.

[6] Symmachus, *Ep.* V.48; VII.56. Above, 127.

[7] Wickham (1984), 30. Contra Wolf (1966), 13; Patlagean (1977), 272; Krause (1987), 329.

separated, for example, in rent contracts from Egypt, which specified who was responsible for the taxes on the land.[8] However, for both peasants and the state, aristocratic landowners were a natural intermediary in the process. They fulfilled this function in their public capacity as municipal and imperial tax officials, and they also collected and transmitted taxes in their private role as landlords. The involvement of landlords as intermediaries in the tax-collection process suggests that, while in ideal terms rents and taxes were quite separate, the conceptual boundaries between the two could become blurred and they might in reality meld into one payment for the peasant household.

The legal sources of the late Roman period reveal the public recognition of this long-standing custom, and its adoption by the state in the interests of greater efficiency and accountability in the tax-collection process.[9] We may observe this impulse to take advantage of existing arrangements between landlords and their tenants particularly clearly in an early fifth-century law aimed at Egypt.[10] The law confirms the right of private landholders and the churches of Constantinople and Alexandria to absorb revenues from villages that had hitherto been part of municipal tax-collection hierarchies, provided they acknowledge and ensure the transmission of the liturgies due from those villages.[11] The law has been the subject of a certain amount of debate, with some scholars interpreting it as evidence of a capitulation by the government to the inevitable usurpation by *potentiores* of a quasi-feudal authority, while others argue that it is evidence of the state's success in suppressing a great number of claims to land through patronage.[12] In both cases, however, the assumption of an inherently antagonistic relationship between powerful landowners and the state seems something of an over-statement. Rather, we should place this law within the context of the devolution of responsibility for the collection and transmission of taxes onto local landlords and patrons. This phenomenon, in turn, was part of a process of acknowledgment, adoption, and incorporation of private structures of alliance and dependence by the Roman state in the period.[13]

---

[8] E.g. *P. Cair. Isid.* 100 (296).

[9] A long-standing custom: Sirks (2008), 139–40. Also Delmaire (1996a), 67–9. Cf. Durliat (1993), 41. Recognition: *CTh* xi.7.2 (319, Britain); Kehoe (2007), 167. Contra Goffart, this is not evidence that a tenant could pay taxes on his landlord's behalf: Goffart (1974), 134 note 5*; 42 note 3. Adoption by the state: *CTh* xi.1.14 = *CJ* xi.48.4 (371S, East).

[10] *CTh* xi.24.6 (415, Egypt), with Krause (1987), 79. Note also Giliberti (1992), 208–13.

[11] *CTh* xi.24.6.1; 6; 8.

[12] Quasi-feudal: de Zulueta (1909), 12; 21; Segrè (1947), 121; Andersen (1974), 59. Successful suppression of patronage claims: Johnson and West (1949), 22–3; 28.

[13] Grey and Parkin (2003); Grey (2007a); Jaillette (2005), 205 with note 61.

This process is visible also in the practice of seeking to identify the individuals directly responsible for the agricultural produce of the land, by creating discrete, recognizable, sub-municipal collectivities which were designated as the responsibility of an identifiable private individual.[14] This was to be achieved through registration in the tax rolls, but even here, the state was taking advantage of existing economic practices and strategies. A landowner acknowledged responsibility for the fields he owned when he submitted his *iugatio* or *professio*. He could, in addition, designate certain tenants or slaves as directly involved in the cultivation of those particular fields. It was not compulsory for a landowner to enter these individuals on his *iugatio*, and it seems that a significant proportion of the population was not registered in the census at all.[15] Those that were might in addition have been owners of their own small plots of land, which they would have been expected to declare in their own census declarations. Our best evidence for peasants as landowners comes from the papyrological sources of Egypt, but there are hints of a comparable situation elsewhere in the empire as well.[16] Given that peasant economic strategies for the management of subsistence risk are likely to have involved renting land in addition to any that they owned, we may imagine small landowners to have been involved in arrangements of tenancy also, and to have exploited those arrangements of tenancy in their social strategies for the management of risk.[17]

Here we observe the state exploiting these long-established strategies for risk management, for once an individual had been registered as a tenant in the tax rolls, the imperial administration sought to define the nature of his relationship with his landlord vis-à-vis the land in which they were mutually interested, and attempted to limit the economic decision-making and freedom of both parties.[18] Landowners were forbidden, for example, to expel or replace registered *coloni*, or to remove them from land that was sold or gifted

---

[14] Cf. *CTh* XI.7.2 (319, Britain).

[15] Limited application: *CTh* XI.1.26 (399, Gaul). Significant portion of the population not registered: *CTh* X.23.1 (369–70, East), which recommends that marines be recruited from among the *incensiti*.

[16] E.g. *P. Princeton* III.134 (early fourth century). Cf. *P. Cair. Isid.* 9 (post 309); *CPR* XVIIA.17 = *SPP* XX.80 (321?, Hermopolis); *BGU* IV.1049 (342, Arsinoe); *SPP* XX.86 (330, Hermopolis); *P. Oxf.* 6 (350, Heraclaeopolis); *SB* III.6612 (365); *P. Oxy.* 1470 (336, Oxyrhynchus); *P. Ness.* III.32 (sixth century). Also Bowman (1985), 143; 162–3 and Table VIII B; Bagnall (1993a), 72; Rowlandson (1996), 178–9. For elsewhere, Palladius, *Op. Ag.* 1.6.6; Libanius, *Or.* XLVII.4; *P. Ital.* 32 (540); 35 (572). Analogous evidence for a high turnover in land in Africa may be gleaned from *TA* 8.

[17] Renting land: E.g. *P. Cair. Isid.* 98–100 (*c.* 296); Palladius, *Op. Ag.* 1.6.6; *CTh* XI.1.14 = *CJ* XI.48.4 (371S, East); cf. Gallant (1991), 82; 87–9.

[18] Defining mutual responsibilities: *Brev.* V.9.1 = *CTh* V.17.1 (332, *ad provinciales*) with Carrié (1983), 223–4; 234. Cf. also Saumagne (1937), 510–12.

to another.[19] Registered *coloni* were subject to similar limitations upon their economic behavior. Their ability to move from a tenancy on one estate to another was curtailed. If they owned their own land, limitations were also placed on their capacity to alienate that land and other property in their possession.[20] The effectiveness of these limitations is debatable, but they reveal that, for the state, the object of registering tenants in the tax rolls in connection with a particular plot of land was part of a broader impulse to ensure that the public *munera* owed by a municipality, a village, or an estate on its land were acknowledged by its members. In the case of taxes on land, this was to be achieved by defining a hierarchy of responsibility, which extended down into the municipality, through the owner of the land to the individual responsible for its agricultural production. Thus, registration, like the tax system of which it was a part, was aimed at the collectivity, rather than at the individual.

It seems that the practice of registration could be undertaken voluntarily by a tenant, presumably in consultation with his landlord. Alternatively, we may surmise that it could be imposed upon him as part of a tenancy agreement. Once a tenant was entered into the tax rolls, *colonus* and *dominus* could be held mutually responsible for the tax burden assessed on the land. Their relationship was visible to the state, and a certain institutional inertia made it difficult (though not impossible) for the act of registration to be reversed or altered.[21] It was clearly in the interests of the state that relationships between individuals and land be established, acknowledged, and documented. Registration also provided a basis for assessing, among other things, extraordinary compulsory exactions.[22] Arguably, the collectivity, too, would benefit from such information being transparent.[23]

However, given the limitations that registration of a tenant placed upon their economic decision-making and the greater intervention that it represented into their private legal affairs, it is less clear what benefit individual landowners derived from such an arrangement. It is possible that

---

[19] Limitations upon expulsion: *CJ* XI.48.7 (371, Gaul); *CJ* XI.63.3 (383, East). Sitting tenants transferred with land: *CTh* XIII.10.3 (357, to Dulcitius *consularis Aemiliae*); *Nov. Val.* XXXV.1.18 (452, Italy and Africa). Cf. Vera (1997), 216; Grey (2007a), 168; Sirks (2008), 131.

[20] Limitations on movement: *Brev.* v.9.1 = *CTh* v.17.1 (332, *ad provinciales*). *Coloni* owning their own land: see, for example, *CTh* XI.1.14 = *CJ* XI.48.4 (371S, East). Alienation of property: *Brev.* v.11.1 = *CTh* v.19.1 (365, East).

[21] Grey (2008), 296–7. Also, for different dynamics in decisions to register a *colonus*, Sirks (2008), 129; 136.

[22] See, for example, *CJ* XI.17.4 = *CTh* XV.1.49 (408, Illyricum), a constitution published in the wake of Visigothic incursions in the province.

[23] Vera (1997), 206–7.

registration of tenants, and the visibility of the agricultural labor force that went with it, acted as a form of insurance against both the demands of the tax collector and a landlord's responsibility for collecting taxes himself. In such circumstances, the landlord arguably acquired additional leverage against recalcitrant tenants, and might also be able to mobilize the state's apparatus of force to compel the payment of rent arrears as well as taxes. However, it is unlikely that the use or threat of force could compel payment of rents or taxes from tenants who were simply unable to pay either. In such circumstances, landlords in the period display an attitude that was largely in tune with their predecessors in earlier centuries: better sitting tenants, with arrears, than no tenants at all.[24]

Paradoxically, therefore, it is possible that the greatest benefit of registered tenancy was enjoyed by those who appear on the surface to have been most disadvantaged by it: the tenants themselves.[25] It is true that registration in the census rolls pulled these individuals into the fiscal machinery and made them visible to the tax collector, often for the first time. Their taxes and arrears could be demanded from them or their landlord by the imperial, provincial, and municipal tax officials. On the other hand, in the eyes of the law, at least, registered tenants enjoyed certain protections that unregistered tenants did not. They were exempted from arbitrary impositions by imperial or municipal officials, and shielded from the performance of some liturgies. They were also granted legal remedy against the raising of their rents, and limitations were placed on the ability of landlords to expel or move them.[26] Of course, it is difficult to determine the actual impact of these limitations, for it is impossible to gauge the extent to which individuals chose to use the judicial system in settling their disputes. But the evidence reveals some hints, at least, of relatively powerless litigants as well as the more powerful figures who we might expect.[27] While we should not overstate the case, the very visibility that attended registration in the tax rolls may have been viewed by some small agriculturalists as an effective

[24] E.g. Symmachus, *Ep.* VI.81; IX.6. Cf. Pliny, *Ep.* III.19; IX.37; X.8. Also Ste. Croix (1981), 257.

[25] Cf. Kehoe (2007), 160–1. Note, by contrast Wickham (2005b), 525, who argues that it was the desuetude of these laws with the collapse of the Roman state in the west that brought the greatest benefit to the peasantry.

[26] Visibility and demands for arrears: *CJ* XI.55.I (Diocletian and Maximian, Syria); Goffart (1974), 47. Remedies against rent increases: *CJ* XI.50.I (325, East); *CJ* XI.50.2 (396S, East). Restrictions on removal or expulsion: *CTh* XIII.10.3 (357, to Dulcitius *consularis Aemiliae*); *CJ* XI.48.7 (371, Gaul); *CJ* XI.63.3 (383, East).

[27] See now the important summary of the state of this question by Bryen (2008b), 184 note 6. Also, more broadly, Connolly's study of petitions in the third-century *Codex Hermogenianus*: Connolly (2010).

strategy for managing their subsistence risk and insulating themselves against exploitation by larger landowners.

In many circumstances, no doubt, laws aimed at limiting the economic independence or mobility of registered tenants hindered these individuals in their interactions with their landlords, and it is reasonable to assume that, in general, the advantage in courts of law continued to lie with those with greater wealth and power. But landlords did not have it all their own way, as Libanius' travails with his Jewish tenants reveal. Libanius places his complaint about the behavior of these tenants within the context of a more general attack upon the illicit protection offered by military men to peasants, which allows them to resist the tax collector or their landlord, and to prey upon their fellows. But the linkage is slightly forced. While he offers considerable detail about the attitude and intentions of the general whom he accuses of perverting the course of justice, he gives no indication of what the court case was about, beyond a vague allusion to the dissatisfaction of his tenants with the terms of their arrangement with him. It is tempting to connect this impulse with the legal remedies open to registered tenants against their landlords, although such a connection would be speculative at best.[28]

At any rate, the registration of tenants in the tax rolls reveals again attempts by the imperial administration to regulate and oversee relationships that had previously been beyond its direct control. It also hints at the opportunities that the practice presented for both landlords and tenants to exploit the new relationship that might result. Certainly, it would appear that registered tenancy offered some advantages to peasants, in some circumstances. As we have seen, in his diatribe against the moral decline of contemporary Christians, Salvian of Marseilles provides evidence for small landowners deliberately choosing to become *coloni*. While we cannot be certain, the language he uses to describe the new arrangement hints at the fact that this decision involved registration and brought with it the expectation of greater mutual implication between the registered tenant and his landlord.[29]

We should not necessarily follow Salvian in interpreting such a decision as a counsel of last resort. Rather, we should focus upon the conscious decision-making process that Salvian identifies, and link this with the pious

---

[28] Libanius, *Or.* XLVII.13–16. On the opportunities for the relatively powerless to exploit the legal system in disputes with the more powerful, see Hobson (1993), 193–4; Harries (2001), 69; Kehoe (2007), 183–9. Cf. Cronin (2005), 8; 33–5.

[29] Salvian, *De Gubernatione Dei* v.8.43, with Grey (2006), 179–80.

observations of the Italian senator Symmachus about his relationship with his *colonus*. In seeking out an arrangement of tenancy, whether registered or not, peasants were able to take advantage both of the close conceptual links between such arrangements and the mutually binding links of patronage, and also, in the case of a registered tenancy, of some measure of legal protection in the period. These consequences were unintended by the promulgators of legislation concerning registered tenants in the period, to be sure, but no less real and exploitable for that.

TAXATION, OPPRESSION, AND PROTECTION

The coincidence of taxation, antagonism, and patronage in the sources has encouraged considerable scholarly debate over whether they provide evidence for the emergence of a new kind of patronage relationship in the period, and, if they do, what form or forms that new kind of relationship took.[30] Scholars are no longer convinced that relations between peasants and large landowners were universally characterized by the dispossession of the former and their inexorable slide into a state of quasi-servitude. They also acknowledge that the sources reveal a considerable degree of regional variation in the forms that interactions took between peasants, patronal figures, and the state.[31] Nevertheless, an explicit link continues to be made between the new tax system and new types of patronal relations, which were, it is argued, aimed at resisting its demands.[32]

This connection has probably been overstated. It is reasonable to suggest that patronage functioned as a mechanism through which the fiscal demands of the state could be negotiated with, ameliorated, or defused.[33] It is also likely that the state's increasing and increasingly intrusive demands produced a situation in which some patrons and clients conspired to hinder the transmission of the latter's fiscal burden to the state. However, it is less clear that these arrangements can usefully be gathered together and placed

---

[30] The literature is vast, and stretches back to the late nineteenth century. Among the earliest accounts, see, for example, Fustel de Coulanges (1890); Monnier (1900); Guilhiermoz (1902); de Zulueta (1909). The current state of the debate may be gleaned from Krause (1987), 81–2; Giliberti (1992), 197; Mirković (1997), 29–30; Marcone (1998), 362–3; Wickham (2005b), 521–7. Note also Fikhman (1978), citing a large number of Russian sources; Whittaker (1980), 14; Carrié (1983), 219; Gascou (1985), 27; Saradi (1994), *passim*.

[31] Segrè (1947), 120 and note 93; Ste. Croix (1954), 45; Hahn (1968), 275–6; Carrié (1976), *passim*; Krause (1987), 328.

[32] Most recently and explicitly, Wickham (2005b), 528–9. For caution and dissent, cf. Jaillette (2005), 205; Shaw (2008), 97 with note 18.

[33] Wickham (2005b), 143; 528.

under a single rubric. Further, and as we have already seen, we should be cautious about uncritically accepting the motivations that our aristocratic authors offer, or adopting the perspective of the state when it assumes that the only aim of peasants and patrons in the period was to evade their fiscal burdens.[34]

In the present context, the point may be illustrated with reference to the phenomenon of *possessio sub patrocinio*, or possession under protection, which is attested in the legal sources of the fourth and early fifth centuries. This practice existed in the grey area that was created by the impulse to establish ownership of property or relationship with the land as a basis for determining fiscal liability, and the tendency to ascribe to landlords and patrons responsibility for the collection and payment of the taxes of their tenants or clients. The legal sources imply or assume that, in some circumstances, peasants might transfer ownership of their property to a patron or landlord, who was in a better position to resist the demands of the tax collector. Scholars have long interpreted this arrangement as fundamentally disadvantageous to peasants, and part of the inexorable slide of the free peasant proprietor into the bonds of quasi-servitude.[35] Certainly, we should expect that in some circumstances, turning over the ownership of one's property to a powerful neighbor was a move born of desperation. But the evidence suggests that some peasants, at least, entered into the arrangement willingly and with a degree of planning and forethought. It is therefore worth investigating both the phenomenon of *possessio sub patrocinio* and the circumstances in which peasants and the powerful may be observed undertaking it.

Our best evidence for this phenomenon may be found in a series of laws aimed primarily at Egypt and collected together in the Theodosian Code under the rubric *De Patrociniis Vicorum*. These texts provide both explicit and circumstantial evidence for *possessio sub patrocinio*, but scholars are divided over whether they reveal patrons receiving the property of their clients in return for protection from the tax collector, or whether the clients continued to own the property themselves, but were able to take advantage

---

[34] Above, 169–72. For a call to explore the decision-making processes of agents of the state with the same sophistication that has been accorded peasants in recent scholarship, cf. Herzfeld (2005), 373–5.

[35] Monnier (1900), 103; 106; Segrè (1947), 118; 120; Krause (1987), 81. Cf., however, Hahn (1968), 268–9; Rowlandson (1996), 193, who sees little evidence of sale of land to cover rent arrears. See now Jaillette (2005), 205 with note 65; 216 with note 152. Also, for a comparative perspective on the heterogeneity of connections between dispossession of the peasantry, aristocratic power and the fiscal demands of the state, Cronin (2005), 9–10.

of the greater power of their patron in resisting the tax collector.[36] A further fault-line in the scholarship may be discerned, between those who regard this process as inevitably and universally leading to the dispossession of clients by their patrons, and those who limit the incidence of this phenomenon to the western provinces of the empire, and argue that peasants elsewhere merely lost their economic independence.[37] However, both the broad geographical delineation between east and west, and the proposition that patronage relations involved a transfer of property in the period are open to question. It seems rather that the legislation documents cases of fraudulent or fictitious transfers, which did not occur in accordance with existing regulations governing transfer of property, and therefore hampered the project of determining who should be held responsible for the tax burden assessed on that property. This phenomenon is visible in other sources, too, particularly from Gaul and North Africa. As we shall see, the motivations ascribed to such behavior in those contexts are very different from those found in the legislation.

Individuals were entered into the tax or census rolls on the basis of their relationship with land or the owner of that land, whether that be ownership, tenancy, usufruct, or any other right or obligation. Consequently, the clear definition of that relationship determined the extent to which an individual could be held liable for the tax assessed on the land. This was the driving force behind Constantine's reforms to the laws on sale and donation of land, which were concerned in particular with ensuring that the transfer be effected publicly in the presence of witnesses, who were also expected to attest to the vendor's ownership of the land.[38] In addition, these laws direct that the transaction be entered in the municipal lists (*gesta municipalia*), and the receiver publicly acknowledge the obligation to pay taxes.[39] In the cases censured in the legislation under discussion here, the arrangements whereby the transferor's responsibility for the land was made over to the transferee were not consummated in public, and were not recorded in any fiscal lists. Therefore, as far as the tax collectors were concerned, the transfer had not happened. It was fictitious, and conflicted with the information contained in the census rolls.

---

[36] Ownership by patron: de Zulueta (1909), 23–4, although he admits that this is the less convincing interpretation; Andersen (1974), 60. Ownership by clients: Krause (1987), 79.

[37] Not in eastern provinces: Petit (1955), 377–8; Krause (1987), 87 and note 76; Garnsey and Woolf (1989), 163. Loss of economic independence: Carrié (1976), 159. Cf. Carrié (1982); Carrié (1983). Krause (1987), 80–1, argues that *ländliche* Patrocinium developed in Egypt over the course of the fifth century, on the basis of *CJ* XI.54.1 and *Nov. Just.* XVII.13 (535).

[38] *FV* 35.5–6.

[39] *FV* 35.3–4; 249.5–8. The concerns of this legislation are prefigured in *CJ* IV.49.9 (293).

The most explicit treatment of *possessio sub patrocinio* may be found in an early fifth-century law directed to the Praetorian Prefect Aurelianus. The law is obscure in several places, but the intention to ensure that the name entered in the tax lists as owner of a landholding matched the individual who should be held responsible for that landholding's tax burden is clear. The law censures a fictitious transfer from client to patron, whereby the former retains possession, but the name of the latter comes to be entered into the tax lists as responsible for its tax burden. The law directs that such a transfer be reversed, and the person benefiting from the fruits of the land remain responsible for its *functiones*. The law concludes by confirming the *status quo*: landholders may retain their land provided they acknowledge the *functiones publicae* on that land.[40] The vocabulary used here is prefigured in a law in which *curiales* are forbidden to evade *munera publica* by pretended sale to bring their registered property below the 25 *iugera* necessary for membership of the *curia*.[41] It would appear that the result of such transactions was the continued possession by the transferor, although officially the transferee acknowledged ownership and, by extension, liturgical liability.

Strictly speaking, the transfer of ownership of land from client to patron was not illegal.[42] Cases of *donatio* are known, where gifts were given by *traditio*, but usufruct was retained by the donor.[43] But the transfers censured here were effected under pretext of a legally countenanced process, and are interpreted by the legislators to be motivated by a desire on the part of the transferors to evade their liability for the *functiones publicae* on the land. The legislation censuring fraudulent transfers of property in patronage relationships reveals the fiscal consequences of these fictitious *traditiones* of land. In the eyes of the legislators, peasants – whether tenants or small *possessores* – accepted the *patrocinia* of the powerful and transferred to them some form of responsibility for the tax burden on their land. Those individuals then resisted the tax collector.

In some circumstances, no doubt, the object of these fictitious transfers of property was to defraud the state. But, from the point of view of the peasant household, we may imagine there to have been a somewhat more

---

[40] *CTh* XI.24.6 (415, Egypt). See the detailed and perceptive analysis of Jaillette (2005), 209–10; 215–7. Cf. *CJ* XI.54.1 (468, East).

[41] *CTh* XII.1.33 (342, East).   [42] Cf. now Sirks (2008), 141–2 for corroborating evidence and discussion.

[43] Gordon (1970), 68 and note 6. He suggests that this may have been motivated by a desire to evade the *vicesima hereditatis*, since by this practice the property changes hands technically as a gift rather than a legacy or inheritance. *CTh* VIII.12.8 (415) forbade this practice, but was swiftly repealed in *CTh* VIII.12.9 (417).

complex calculus involving the management of subsistence risk, the effective marshaling and exploitation of the household's economic resources, and the mitigation or evasion of social risks such as the danger of injury or loss of property. In such circumstances, it is instructive to turn again to the analyses of comparable behaviors offered by the Gallic presbyter Salvian of Marseilles and Augustine, bishop of Hippo in North Africa. In Salvian's diatribe against the evils of his age, he speaks of poor landowners, laboring under an untenable tax burden, who seek out the rich and become their tenants and dependents, but in the process lose everything because of the rapacity of those same potentates.[44] Augustine, for his part, describes in a sermon about the pursuit of security small landowners erecting on their own properties boundary markers that bear the name of another, more powerful landowner. In each case, actions motivated by quite different imperatives, and effected in quite different ways, resulted in the same fundamental problem for the state: who was to be held responsible for the taxes of the land? In each case there is subterfuge. In each case, the object is to make it appear that one man is owner of the land while another continues in reality to enjoy all the rights of ownership. However, in each case, the evasion of taxation is not the principal objective. Rather, it is to ensure the financial and physical security of the household.

It would appear that the factors motivating peasant households to undertake a particular course of action did not begin and end with the fiscal imperatives envisaged by the drafters and promulgators of the legislation. We should expect, in addition, that those factors were specific to the particular circumstances in which a household found itself. These three accounts portray fictitious transfers of property in quite different lights, offering a multitude of motivations in a variety of circumstances. There are a number of reasons that we may adduce for those differences. In the first instance, the texts themselves are quite different, and have quite different objectives. The principal aim of the legislation is to ensure the smooth transition of tax revenues to the state, and as a consequence, any actions that hinder that objective are interpreted as deliberately fraudulent. This theme is particularly evident in a later law gathered under the same rubric, which censures *rustici* "who, for the purpose of cheating the taxes, with their customary fraud should flee for refuge to such protections."[45] It is therefore possible that in censuring relationships of protection or patronage, the

---

[44] Augustine, Dolbeau VI.2. Lepelley (1997), 205. Salvian, *De Gubernatione Dei* V.8.39–43. Cf. Scott (1998), 44.
[45] *CTh* XI.24.4 (399, Egypt). Jaillette (2005), 206; 215–16; 221.

legislators are identifying a convenient, but false scapegoat, or at the very least, ascribing explicit motivations to the participants on those relationships that were, at best, implicit or ancillary to their principal concerns.

The points of view that our two aristocratic observers possess are quite different, both from the drafters and promulgators of the legislation, and from each other. Salvian's account is contained within a blistering broadside aimed at the aristocracies of the late Roman world in general, and of Gaul in particular. Salvian presents a variety of peasant strategies as necessitated by a fundamental breakdown of social relations in his own time, largely as a result of the perversion of the tax system and its agents. Although it is difficult to determine how clearly he understands the actions he describes and the motivations behind them, we should at least give credence to his identification of them as novelties in the period. By contrast, Augustine's objective is to render the behavior of certain religious deviants comprehensible to his flock. He does this by making reference to a practice which, we may assume, was familiar to them. There is no hint that the simile he chooses is laden with any negative connotations. On the contrary, he appears to be offering some mitigation of the self-deception of these heretics when he observes that it is not the truth that impels their action, but rather the desire for safety.[46]

Both Augustine and Salvian purport to give the point of view of peasants themselves. We may justifiably doubt their capacity to recover the true motivations of small agriculturalists. Nevertheless, both authors focus upon self-protection and the pursuit of security, not the evasion of fiscal obligations. We should not be surprised by this. As we have seen, it is ensuring the subsistence needs of the household and managing any potential conflict within their communities that loomed largest in the decision-making of the peasantry in the period. Moreover, the capacity of the state to influence the behaviors of its inhabitants was circumscribed, and its interest in doing so limited. In the eyes of the legislators, to be sure, it mattered little whether a loss of fiscal revenues was motivated explicitly by a peasant's desire to evade his taxes or other, deeper factors. But from the peasant household's point of view, the defrauding of the state was most likely to have been an epiphenomenon of more fundamental concerns.

It would be difficult, if not impossible, to produce a homogenized picture from these disparate points of view, even if we wished to do so. In each case, the picture produced responds to and reproduces the particular context in which the author is writing and the quite different social matrices within

---

[46] Augustine, Dolbeau VI.2.

which the behaviors are embedded. The countryside of Egypt was dominated largely by the village, and it is the communal unity and integrity of this type of settlement that appears to be at stake as much as the fiscal objectives of the state. In another law included under the rubric *De Patrociniis Vicorum*, and directed at the Praetorian Prefect Helpidius, the physical fragmentation of communities is blamed upon powerful individuals who offer protection from the tax collector on their rural estates, and therefore encourage peasants to abandon their holdings and tenancies elsewhere, together with the mutual responsibility for the collectivity's tax burden that those arrangements entailed.[47]

The physical and socio-economic makeup of North Africa and Gaul were quite different. For Salvian, there is no real cohesion between small agriculturalists. Rather, their social matrix is dominated by the relationships that they are able to maintain with more powerful figures. In Salvian's estimation, those powerful figures have abused their position in the period, and it is this, rather than the defrauding of the state, which receives the bulk of his ire.[48] The portrait Augustine offers is subtly different, and he provides hints that not all small agriculturalists were tenants in the period when he reveals that small and large landowners could occupy or own plots of land adjacent to one another.[49] The landscape with which he is likely to have been familiar was characterized by estates populated by groups of agriculturalists, and probably also relatively small hamlets. Augustine shows no interest in the internal cohesion of these communities, choosing instead to emphasize their somewhat fraught interactions with local figures of power. But, as we have seen, these communities were characterized by an ongoing series of interactions and negotiations that had little to do with the state and its needs.

These phenomena further undermine the proposition that the tax system of the late Roman empire defined and framed socio-economic relations in the countrysides of the late Roman world. To be sure, our evidence reveals that the tax system, its agents and vocabulary did impact upon social and economic interactions in rural contexts. Equally, however, tax officials and the language of taxation could be accessed and employed by peasants, their patrons and landlords in a variety of ways, with a variety of motivations. We should also expect there to have existed a certain dissonance between the ideal functioning of the tax system, and the reality of practices of tax

---

[47] *CTh* xi.24.1 (360, Egypt). Cf. Giliberti (1992), 198; 201; 204–5.
[48] For these broad contrasts between eastern and western contexts, cf. above, 47–52.
[49] Cf. Palladius, *Op. Ag.* 1.6.6, with Vera (1997), 189 and note 14.

assessment and collection in the period. That dissonance opened up a series of spaces for taxpayers to exploit, and it is to those spaces that we now turn.[50]

THE *ORIGO*, TAX COLLECTIVITIES, AND GROUP RESPONSIBILITY

The legal sources attest the emergence of a variety of new sub-urban tax collectivities, based upon the principle of the *origo*. Just as in the case of the networks of alliance available to the inhabitants of rural communities, it is the groupings that fall along asymmetrical lines between individuals of differential power and status that can be discerned most clearly in the sources. However, alongside these collectivities may be placed groupings of taxpayers of comparable social status and economic circumstances. The evidence is limited and recondite, but some observations are possible. Again, the state can be observed both adopting or enhancing existing practices of collective responsibility, and creating new collectivities in the interests of ensuring that certain fiscal or liturgical obligations to the state would be fulfilled by rural populations. As we shall see, the creation of these collectivities provided peasants with further opportunities and options for managing both their social and their subsistence risk.

The principle of collective responsibility is clearest in Egypt, where the inhabitants of the villages had long been held collectively responsible for the taxes assessed upon their communities.[51] Acceptance of this principle is eloquently expressed in the proceedings of a court case that came before the *defensor civitatis* in the first half of the fourth century CE.[52] The dispute revolves around rights to property, and is brought by two sisters who, it emerges, had abandoned the property some years previously because they had been unable to afford the tax burden assessed upon it. They later returned and sought rents from the cultivators who had been assigned responsibility for the taxes by the *praepositus pagi*. The advocate for the cultivators acknowledges the right of the *praepositus* to ensure that the taxes are paid, observing that the act was valid both in order to safeguard himself and to ensure the transmission of revenues. Likewise, the peasants themselves, when questioned, admit that they cultivated the fields to safeguard themselves in the event that the taxes due devolved upon them.

We witness in this admission an awareness that the state's interest in enforcing a community's collective responsibility was linked to the practice

---

[50] Cf. Reed-Danahay (1993), 226–7; Galbraith (2003), 74; Cronin (2005), 24; Axelby (2007), 57; Campbell and Heyman (2007), 24–6; Kim (2007), 994.
[51] Giliberti (1992), 183–4.　　[52] *P. Col.* VII.175 (339, Karanis).

of attaching portions of that community's tax burden to particular plots of land. This connection is highlighted in legislation concerning tenancies on patrimonial estates, which came to be identified as one particular type of *origo* in the period. In this context we may observe the state attempting to employ both the principle of collective responsibility and the politics of reputation in a law which explicitly encourages the individual payment of portions of a collective debt in order that the example set by some will serve as a disincentive for others to default on paying their share.[53] A century later, a now-fragmentary law directed at the Thebaid returns to the problem of collective responsibility, and seeks to define more clearly the foundation upon which the principle rested in the period when it directs that the sale of a patrimonial estate should not be made to one *colonus*, but rather to a group from the same *origo*, in order that one individual not become a burden upon his *consortes*.[54] The language of this law suggests a link with the private law practice of *consortium*, whereby partners could jointly own or exploit land, as well as with the long-standing administrative principal of the same name, which functioned as a mechanism for describing the collective responsibility of village communities, at least in Egypt.[55] In the examples under discussion here, it appears that the principles of *consortium* and the *origo* have been linked together and applied in a new context. This is a further illustration of the opportunism and adaptation of the new tax system to existing practices, relationships, and structures.

We may also observe the state creating new tax collectivities. One such collectivity was implicated in the levying and collection of *prototypia*, the provision of recruits, and *protostasia* or *temo*, the recruit tax. The practice of ascribing corporate responsibility for provision of recruits or recruit taxes first appears in a law from the late third or early fourth century.[56] In a later law, responsibility for ensuring the fulfillment of the responsibility is placed firmly within the fiscal framework of the municipality, and described as a *munus curialium*. This understanding of this liturgy continued at least until the late fourth century.[57] The imposition was levied upon a *capitulum*, a

---

[53] Patrimonial estates as an *origo*: *CJ* xi.68.1 (325S, a general edict addressed to Constantius *PPO*); *CTh* xii.1.33 (342, to Rufinus, *Comes Orientis*). Collective responsibility: *CTh* xi.19.1 (321, Africa).

[54] *CTh* v.16.34 = *CJ* xi.68.6 (425, to Valerius, *CRP*).

[55] Private law: *CTh* ii.5 = *CJ* iii.40, *passim*. *Consortium vicanorum*: *CTh* xi.24 *passim*, with Jaillette (2005), 218–19.

[56] *CJ* x.42.8 (293–305); the provenance of this law is uncertain.

[57] *CTh* xi.23.2 (362, Gaul). For a short while, responsibility for collection passed to senators, but was quickly restored to *curiales* in the west, and eventually became part of the duties of *primipilii*, at least in the east: *CTh* xi.23.1 (361, *ad Senatum*); 2 (362, Gaul); 4 (396, Asia); for general discussion, Seston (1946), 367–72.

geographically contiguous area of land.[58] On the basis of a law concerning the supply of military vestments, Carrié has concluded that a *capitulum* was equivalent to 20 or 30 *iuga*.[59] The ratio of abstract fiscal *iuga* to physical *iugera* is the subject of much scholarly debate, and would in any event have varied according to the quality of the land in question.[60] For our current purposes, however, what is of most relevance is the enlistment of the principle of collective responsibility in this context and the implications of that strategy for socio-economic relations in the countrysides of the late Roman world.

In some cases one landowner might own the area of land in its entirety, and consequently be responsible for this charge on his own. Usually, though, the responsibility for supplying a recruit would be imposed in an alternating rota upon all the owners of the land.[61] In the event of the *capitulum* supplying a sum of money rather than a recruit, the nominal head for that year, or *capitularius*, was held responsible for the collection and payment of that sum to the *temonarius*.[62] According to the amount of property each owned, the various members of the *capitulum* would be responsible for different fractions of the recruit tax. There is therefore some analogy between the *capitulum*, the principle of the *origo*, and the practices of *consortium* outlined above. In each case it is the collectivity that is emphasized, but that collectivity operates at a level below that of the municipality, and is one of a number of possible groupings of taxpayers which will have operated concurrently.

---

[58] Delmaire (1989), 322.

[59] *CTh* VII.6.3 (370); Carrié (1994), 46. For a detailed analysis of the nature of the *capitulum*, see Carrié (1993c), 121–30. Cf. Delmaire (1989), 321–9; Delmaire (1996a), 62. For a reappraisal of the size of the *iugum*, however, see Harper (2008), 92–6.

[60] *Leges Saeculares* 121 (*FIRA*² II, 796). Cf. *P. Col.* VII.172 (341–2, Karanis); *CTh* VII.7.4 (415). For the focus in the new system upon type of land, rather than productive capacity or income, see now Kehoe (2007), 166.

[61] *CTh* VII.13.7.1b–c (375, East), providing that group did not contain both a father and a son still *in potestate*, in which case the latter was freed of the burden: *CJ* X.62.3 (286/93, Phoenicia). Similarly, villages in Egypt were expected to supply one recruit or his equivalent every other year: Bagnall (1993a), 175–7; Aubert (1995), 264.

[62] *CTh* VII.13.7.2. The individual fulfilling the *munus* of collecting these taxes or recruits is identified in some legislation as a *temonarius*: *CTh* VI.35.3.2 = *CJ* XI.28.2 (346/52, Illyricum); *CTh* VII.13.7.4 (375, East); *CTh* VII.18.3 (380, East). Cf. Souter (1949), 414. *Capitularius* and *temonarius* were complementary roles: cf. *CTh* XI.16.15 (382, Illyricum), which exempts those of high rank from the *capituli atque temonis necessitas*; also *CTh* VI.35.3 (319). Contra Jones (1964), index *s.v. capitularius (temonarius)*, Carrié (1994), 46 note 66 and Delmaire (1989), 322–3, who equate the *capitularius* with the *temonarius*. There is no evidence to support Carrié's suggestion that every *caput*, or "part fiscal" was under the control of a *capitularius*, who had a personal responsibility for guaranteeing its tax burden: Carrié (1983), 218. Rather, the term appears only in connection with the *capitulum*.

This has certain implications for our understanding of the functioning of the late Roman tax system, for, again, that system emerges as adaptable, flexible, and reactive. The small landowners involved in these *capitula* could, in addition, be enmeshed in a number of other complementary tax collectivities. They might be registered as resident in a village or hamlet of one of the *pagi* of the municipality, and thus expected to carry a share of the municipality's tax burden.[63] Within a village, they may be part of a group of small landowners who were responsible, along with their *consortes* or *koinônoi*, for a particular grain tax or liturgy.[64] They might rent an imperial estate as a group, each paying his share of the taxes and rents due on that land.[65] They might also be tenants, registered in the *iugatio* of their landlords. As a consequence, the fiscal machinery was able to reach a single rural cultivator in many ways in the late Roman period.

Equally, the flexible and reactive nature of the new tax system provided opportunities for small agriculturalists. The webs of fiscal obligations in which they now found themselves had as their corollary networks of socioeconomic alliances, for mutual responsibility for taxation is likely to have created an incentive for all parties to involve themselves to some degree in reciprocal relationships. We have seen how collectivities of this sort were characterized by suspended tension and competing interests, which might at any moment threaten the integrity of the group. In circumstances where tax revenues are involved, this potential for conflict was accompanied by opportunities for individuals to exploit their mutual responsibility for taxation in the eyes of the state. By enlisting the vocabulary of tax evasion in private, internecine squabbles, some peasants may be observed seeking to involve the state in those squabbles, and to ensure that any judgment or intervention was advantageous to them.

TAX EVASION AND INTERNECINE CONFLICT

As we have seen time and again, the vocabulary of tax evasion is an infinitely flexible, endlessly exploitable motif in the late Roman period. Tax evasion might be depicted as a deliberate act, designed to defraud the state; an expression of disrespect or rejection of existing power relationships; or a final, futile attempt to preserve something of one's smallholdings and

---

[63] *P. Turner* 44 = *P. Sakaon* 44 (331–2).

[64] *P. Oxy.* 3396 (fourth century); *P. Col.* VII.138–40 (307–8, Karanis); *P. Oxy.* 3429 (fourth century); Déléage (1945), 78–9; 119–20; Carrié (1993c), 128–9; 144–5; 149, with important re-interpretations of *P. Oxy.* 3396 at notes 93 and 94; see also *SB* 4422.

[65] *CTh* XI.19.1 (321, Africa); cf. *CTh* V.16.34 = *CJ* XI.68.6 (425, to Valerius, *CRP*).

income. It is presented, alternately, as criminal behavior, a breach of faith, a counsel of desperation.[66] It is also a recurring theme in petitions to government officials from the inhabitants of the villages of Egypt. In these documents, the petitioners customarily describe their own spotless and enthusiastic fulfillment of their liturgies and obligations, before accusing others in their community of shirking their own share or seeking to distribute the collective burden unevenly. We should certainly not lightly dismiss the weight of evidence for tax evasion in the period, and it is not my intention here to deny that small agriculturalists did, in some circumstances, deliberately evade their fiscal responsibilities. Rather, it is to suggest that the vocabulary of tax evasion could, in addition, be enlisted in conflicts that had little, if anything, to do with taxation. Such a strategy was not a novelty of the late Roman period, but the evidence from the period is nevertheless striking for the inventiveness with which the vocabulary is employed. We observe again a subtle appreciation among Egyptian villagers, at least, of what is likely to motivate the state and its representatives to become involved in a dispute that would otherwise not interest it in the slightest. In what follows I briefly outline some patterns evident when communities fragment as a result of fiscal pressure, before exploring some texts where the explicit connection between tax revenues and the conflict in question is somewhat forced.

There can be no doubt that increased fiscal pressure caused the disintegration of some rural communities in the period. Victor of Vita paints a particularly bleak picture of farmers forced by the new tax system to glean the fields and gather wild plants in order to eke out a living in North Africa.[67] Of course, penury was not the only possibility, for peasants had recourse to other options as well, including resistance, turning to powerful neighbors or government officials, and physical flight.[68] In the Egyptian sources, in particular, *anachôrêsis*, flight in the face of fiscal exactions is a strategy attested for peasants throughout antiquity, and both threats and acts of flight can be found in other provinces too.[69] Such an act might be either short-term or long-term, and both are attested as responses to

---

[66] Deliberate, criminal act: e.g. *CTh* XI.24. Disrespect and breach of faith: e.g. Libanius, *Or.* XLVII. Futile counsel of desperation: Salvian, *De Gubernatione Dei*, V.8.38.

[67] Victor of Vita, *Historia persecutionis Africanae Provinciae* III.58.

[68] Resistance: above, 153–4. Powerful figures: *CTh* XI.24.1 (360, Egypt); above, 207–10. Physical flight: above, 210–12.

[69] For Egypt, references are collected by Lewis (1983), 163–5; 183–4, and Goehring (1996), 276 note 49. Also Giliberti (1992), 192; Jaillette (2005), 217; Sirks (2008), 136. MacMullen (1974), 34–5 with note 24, makes brief comments upon the well known second-century inscriptions from North Africa, and evidence from Palestine.

taxation in the late Roman period. In a fourth-century text from Philadelphia, for example, the tax collector observes that the inhabitants had resorted to flight temporarily, in order to evade their fiscal obligations. By contrast, peasants in fifth-century Gaul are described as abandoning their holdings and fleeing to the barbarians or becoming bandits in their efforts to evade the tax collector.[70]

We should also expect that a higher tax burden might compound with other problems such as a loss of productivity or depopulation to create a situation where the inhabitants of a community found themselves unable to pay their taxes. In a petition to the Prefect of Egypt, for example, three members of the village of Theadelphia portray themselves as the last remaining residents of that village and observe that most of their fellow villagers have fled.[71] Those villagers' flight is presented as a response to the decrepit state of their irrigation system and the fact that their land is barren as a consequence. Irrigation had clearly been a problem for this village for some time. In an earlier petition, we witness accusations that the inhabitants of the village of Hermoupolis, which lay closer to the Nile, have failed to maintain the irrigation canals, with the result that the village of Theadelphia has stopped receiving water and is now in an impoverished state. The petitioners request that, in accordance with existing fiscal practices, their tax burden be shared with a wealthier village, in this case, with Hermoupolis.[72]

It is impossible to determine whether the negligence of the residents of Hermoupolis was a result of that village's own parlous socio-economic state or internal upheaval, part of some broader conflict with the village of Theadelphia, or attributable to other factors still. Whatever the reason for the economic hardship experienced by the villagers of Theadelphia, it seems reasonable to posit that it was, at least in part, a factor motivating the decision by some among their number to decamp in search of work elsewhere. But the suspicion remains that the bald presentation of the situation as purely a problem of tax revenues has more to do with the petitioners' attempt to pique the interest of the Prefect than with the realities of a situation that was, no doubt, considerably more complex. At base, a decision precipitated by a combination of physical, environmental and socio-economic factors, and motivated principally by the need to meet

---

[70] W. *Chr.* 382 (359), with commentary of Rea (1994), 267; Salvian, *De Gubernatione Dei* v.5.21–6.26.

[71] To the Prefect: *P. Turner* 44 = *P. Sakaon* 44 (331–2).

[72] *P. Sakaon* 42 (c. 323); Ermatinger (1997), 6. For comparable strategic employment of fiscal concerns in a petition concerning water rights, cf. *P. Wisc* 1.32 (305, Philadelphia).

the subsistence needs of these individuals and their families, is presented as a problem of tax revenues and couched in terms that emphasize the community's collective responsibility for those revenues.

Certainly, the decision by individual members of a rural community to flee physically or to seek the intercession of another in order to evade their fiscal responsibilities had economic effects for the community as a whole. By the principle of collective responsibility, the fugitive's share could be distributed among the remaining members of that collectivity.[73] Additionally, landlords might find themselves out of pocket, for they would still be responsible for the taxes on fields they were not cultivating themselves if their tenants chose to abandon their holdings and move elsewhere.[74] For our current purposes, however, what is of most interest is the effect of this flight, and the accompanying increase in the relative weight of the communal tax burden, upon the structure and ideological integrity of rural communities. Our aristocratic authors are fairly clear on this subject. In the opinion of Libanius, for example, the result was anarchy, as individuals ran rampant in their neighbors' fields with impunity and openly attacked the curial tax collectors. Libanius also describes peasants abandoning their farms, wives, and children and scuttling to the estate of their new military patron, thus breaking up their families and destroying a long-standing tenancy relationship with their landlord.[75]

As we have seen, Libanius' rhetorical purpose is well served by the vocabulary of tax evasion here, and the themes he touches on in this oration are calculated to appeal to his audience. He connects flight, breakdown of community, and tax evasion with the detrimental effects of a military presence in the countryside surrounding the city of Antioch. But we should be careful lest we attribute too much to an unsupportable tax burden, for fiscal pressure was not the only factor that drove peasants to leave their holdings and move elsewhere, and movement was not necessarily a last resort born of desperation. Peasants may be observed marrying and moving from their natal homes, and threatening to decamp if an unpopular bishop is imposed upon them.[76] They might flee because they had stolen from their landlord, or committed some other crime to arouse his wrath.[77] The petition from the inhabitants of Theadelphia to the Prefect of Egypt reveals

---

[73] *P. Oxy.* 1424 (316–18, Dositheou); *CTh* xi.24.1 (360, Egypt).

[74] *P. Cair. Isid.* 127 (310, Karanis); *P. Sakaon* 43 (327, Theadelphia).   [75] *Or.* xlvii.4; 7; 17.

[76] Marriage: Sidonius, *Ep.* v.19; *Testamentum S. Remigii* 66–7; above, 67–9. Unpopular bishop: Augustine, *Ep.* 20*.10; above, 145–7. See Whittaker (1997), 302, with further references. For mobility of labor more generally, see, e.g. Horden and Purcell (2000), 377–91.

[77] Ruricius, *Ep.* ii.20; 51.

that they might also move, either temporarily or permanently, in order to find work. Such a strategy could conflict with the fiscal needs of the state, for they might move to another *origo* or *idia*, and therefore become in the eyes of the tax collector *vagi* or outsiders. But the legal ideals and the physical realities of peasant movement were quite different, and the rural populations of the late Roman world were in fact highly mobile.[78]

Libanius' strategy of deliberately accessing the vocabulary of tax evasion can be observed in petitions from small agriculturalists as well. We should not imagine that these individuals undertook this strategy deliberately to trick agents of the state. On the contrary, it seems that imperial officials were as aware as anybody else of the opportunities that the vocabulary of taxation offered. In a fragmentary early fourth-century document from Karanis, the petitioners assure the *praeses* that they are not simply portraying an issue that touches their own self-interest in fiscal terms, but, rather, that their own interest and the interests of the state run in parallel.[79] This acknowledgment is instructive, for it reveals that access to the state's apparatus of enforcement and legal procedure might be part of a series of negotiations analogous to those we have already observed between the powerful and the less powerful, and couched in terms that explicitly evoked the mutual expectations of a state and its taxpayers.[80] Consequently, we should be sensitive to both the multiplicity of motivations that peasants might have had for seeking to enlist the aid of the state in internecine conflicts, and the deliberateness with which they exploited the vocabulary of tax evasion to that end.

The archive of Aurelius Sakaon, from the village of Theadelphia reveals a variety of petitions to imperial officials, using language which suggests that the matters under dispute revolve around tax evasion. The petition to the Prefect of Egypt mentioned above is explicit in linking flight, tax evasion, and collective responsibility. It is also striking in that Sakaon and his fellow-petitioners claim to have discovered some of their fellow-villagers on the estate of Eulogios and in the Kynopolite nome, and give detailed informa-tion as to the whereabouts of those fugitives.[81] We should certainly expect that, in most circumstances, the location of individuals who had absconded from a community was more or less common knowledge, but often the remaining residents of the community offered up sworn declarations

---

[78] Above, 47–9.   [79] *PNYU* 1a (318–20, Karanis).
[80] Negotiations: above, 158–67. State and its taxpayers: above, 181–6.
[81] *P. Turner* 44 = *P. Sakaon* 44 (331–2).

denying knowledge of the whereabouts of a tax fugitive.[82] In this particular instance, by contrast, both the fugitives and their harborers are named, and the internal affairs of the village have been deliberately exposed to the scrutiny of the state. We have already explored the complex collection of obligations and loyalties within the village community that are likely to have been affected by the decision to submit this petition.[83] By naming Eulogios as well, the petitioners seem to be taking something of a risk: we may imagine that a local landowner would be less than pleased to have attention directed to him in this way. Here too, then, we can surmise that there is more to the story than merely the evasion of taxes and the villagers' wish to be seen to be fulfilling their fiscal obligations.

This petition was no doubt motivated in part by a desire to distribute the village's tax burden more evenly, but it would be overly credulous to assume that this was the sole motivation. By involving the imperial administration in a community's affairs, members of that community opened themselves up to unwelcome public scrutiny as much as they exposed the malfeasance or evasion of their erstwhile neighbors. It is likely, therefore, that this was a calculated decision, motivated by more than the anticipation of economic or fiscal relief. We may surmise that our petitioners envisaged the public apprehension of the individuals they name in their petition to result in some shift in the social architecture of their village community, and that that shift would redound to their own advantage.[84] We may also imagine that they sought to insulate themselves from the unwelcome attentions of a powerful neighbor, or raise the stakes in some kind of disagreement with him. It is therefore reasonable to suggest that recourse to the administrative apparatus of tax collection and the enforcement of fiscal obligations amounted in some circumstances to the enlistment of the personnel of the state in local disputes.

This is not to say that the straits in which the villagers of Theadelphia professed to find themselves were less dire than they claimed. Certainly, the impression that one gains of the fate of this village in the period is of economic and demographic decline. A petition such as this one reveals the fragmentation of the village community when faced with a series of physical, environmental, socio-economic, and fiscal pressures. However, in

---

[82] References are collected by Lewis (1937), 68 with note 5. As Rousseau has observed with reference to anchorite monks, in small face-to-face communities it is likely that in reality the whereabouts of such individuals was known; Rousseau (1999), 151–2.

[83] Above, 103–5.

[84] Calculation: see the discussion of Lewis (2000), 95–6. Cf. Axelby (2007), 37. Naming individuals: Hobson (1993), 204.

other texts from Sakaon's archive, the links between the tax process and the dispute in which he is engaged are not always quite so clear. In a fragmentary papyrus to the *praepositus pagi* denouncing the actions of Heron, Hatres, Pennis, and Aoug, for example, he begins with a series of statements about his ongoing faithful observance of his fiscal burdens with reference to his landholdings around the village of Theadelphia, before accusing his opponents of dispossessing him of a proportion of the aforementioned estate. The fragmentary nature of the papyrus makes definitive analysis difficult, and it is certainly tempting to make the logical connection between Sakaon's continuing capacity to fulfill his fiscal obligations and his possession of the land in question. However, he does not appear to make this connection explicitly. It is therefore possible that the dispute is less about the transmission of taxes to the state than it is about a relatively small-scale property dispute. Sakaon's decision to begin his petition by emphasizing his regular fulfillment of his fiscal obligations may in this context be calculated to galvanize an otherwise reluctant or disinterested government official to become involved in the dispute, and to find in Sakaon's favor in order that the state suffer no interruption to its revenues. Such a strategy is visible also, for example, in the oration of Libanius against the protection from curial tax collectors offered by military men to peasants, where the rhetorician explicitly portrays that protection as leading to a loss of revenue by the state.[85]

A similar example of the enlistment of the apparatus of the state in pursuit of local advantage may be observed in a petition from Aurelius Isidorus to a *praepositus pagi*, which reveals a fierce conflict within the village of Karanis. That conflict is presented as revolving around protection from compulsory liturgies and the effects that this has upon other members of the community.[86] Isidorus protests against his nomination by Heron, Paësius, Horion, and Achillas the village secretary (*grammateus*)[87] to the post of *sitologos*, or tax collector.[88] It is probable that these four are members of the

---

[85] *P. Sakaon* 43 (327). Note also Jouguet (1912), 414–18. Cf. Libanius, *Or.* XLVII. Also above, 9. For blurring of boundaries between economic and moral presentations of tax evasion, cf. Leroy (1992), 322–3.

[86] *P. Cair. Isid.* 68 (309/10, Karanis). Bagnall (1993a), 166, discusses this affair in the context of recourse to litigation by villagers.

[87] The post of village secretary had been abolished in the third century, but *komogrammatei* occur still in fourth-century papyri, and the role was probably filled from within the village, rather than imposed from outside: Bagnall (1993a), 134 with notes 122–3. Further on administrative bureaucracy and registrars in villages: *P. Oxy.* 2665 (305–6); M. *Chr.* 196 (309), with Lallemand (1964), 261 for dating.

[88] The *sitologos* was a tax receiver, responsible in the first instance to the *praepositus pagi*. This office appears in the Egyptian sources alongside a variety of other synonymous or near-synonymous terms, including *dekaprotoi, apodektai, hypodektai,* and *epimeletai*. See, for example, *CJ* X.42.8 (293–305); *P. Cair. Isid.* 9 (309). It appears that *dekaprotoi* were replaced by *sitologoi* and *apodektai* in around 307/8: Thomas (1974), 60–1; 63; 67; also Carrié (1993c), 146.

village's elite, for they are involved in nominations to liturgies. In spite of his protestations of poverty, Isidorus must also be counted among their number, as his almost continuous performance of liturgies over a period of twenty years reveals.[89] He was also an old adversary of these men, having earlier complained of an arson attack by Heron, and finding himself later denounced under oath as responsible for cultivating four *arourae* of wheat which formed part of the same man's estate.[90]

The fact that Isidorus combines an accusation of tax evasion with a complaint about nomination to a post carrying responsibility for ensuring the collection and payment of taxes reveals his decision to portray the current conflict as one over the fulfillment of fiscal obligations. Isidorus' accusation is that these four men had chosen to protect other members of the village from their communal responsibilities, and had in addition apportioned the tax burden unevenly.[91] They had also attempted to avoid culpability for their actions by nominating Isidorus to the post which would be the focus of the attentions of the municipal *exactores* and *compulsores*. Not only was this illegal, it was unjust, for it would ruin Isidorus into the bargain. Isidorus threatens that flight might become his only option if he is compelled to satisfy those officials.[92]

There is a certain rhetorical neatness to the structure of the petition, and a keen awareness also of the value both of couching the dispute in fiscal terms and portraying its actors in stark contrast to one another. We have no way of knowing whether the accusation was in fact justified, but it seems unlikely that tax evasion lies at the heart of his disagreement with these men. It suffices to observe here that the close integration of a complex system of liturgies into the legal system provided a stage upon which the conflicts so central to the competitive, contested environment of the village could be played out. We may therefore conclude that Isidorus' decision to take this case to the *praepositus* is a calculated act in a long-running dispute, one which was designed as much to bring pressure to bear on his adversaries as it was to ensure that he was relieved of the burdensome obligation to act as *sitologos* for the community.

These few vignettes from the villages of Theadelphia and Karanis do not amount to points in a neat, unidirectional narrative of the histories of those

---

[89] *P. Cair. Isid.* 68.4–6. For a discussion of the liturgies Isidorus fulfilled over this period, see Bagnall (1993a), 243.
[90] *P. Cair. Isid.* 65–7 (298–9); 124 (299). See further Bagnall (1993a), 223.
[91] This is the tenor of the accusation with which the extant portion of this petition ends: *P. Cair. Isid.* 68.22–3.
[92] *P. Cair. Isid.* 68.4–6.

communities in the fourth and fifth centuries, far less evidence for their economic or physical decline or robustness in the period. We should not expect the pressures and burdens created by the late Roman tax system to have been the sole factors acting upon the cohesion of a community, nor should we regard a single event to have been definitive of the character of that community. Rather, the incidents noted here illustrate two aspects of relations between peasants and the late Roman state. First, they reveal that the former were well aware of the factors most likely to catch an imperial official's attention and induce him to become involved. Second, they display the multitudinous ways in which peasants might exploit the interests and needs of the Roman state to their own ends and for their own purposes. We may interpret petitions of this sort as documenting the public face of private conflicts, for it is likely that nominations to liturgies, protection from communal obligations, illegal appropriation of lands belonging to another or of the fruits of those lands, as well as accusations of such behavior were tactics that could be employed against an enemy, in combination with physical violence, acts and accusations of witchcraft or sorcery, and gossip.[93]

We may therefore imagine that some, at least, of the petitions to government officials which emphasize the principle of collective responsibility for the community's tax burden reveal peasants enlisting the administrative apparatus of the state in conflicts that are essentially local. These examples are evidence for individuals employing recourse to the Roman administration as one component in a complex, ongoing, multidimensional internal conflict. Further, in such circumstances, accessing judicial proceedings need not have been the final step in the escalation of a conflict, but was rather one among a number of possible weapons that could be wielded concurrently.[94] In each case, the attention of the participants is less upon satisfying the demands of the state than it is upon consolidating their standing in their own community. In such circumstances, the politics of reputation is locally expressed and locally focused, reflecting the relatively limited horizons of the peasantry. But limited horizons are not the same thing as limited ambitions, ignorance of the opportunities for exploiting the demands of the state, or apathy in the face of figures of authority.

Our sources suggest that the tax system of the late Roman world had a profound effect upon socio-economic structures in the period. The legislation reveals a preoccupation with defining the mutual responsibilities of taxpayers, and grouping them into a multitude of fiscal collectivities, both

---

[93] Above, 114–17. Cf. also *P. Cair. Isid.* 69 (310, Karanis).
[94] Local nature of social relations: Wickham (2005b), 524, viewing these from the point of view of aristocrats. Concurrent: contra Hobson (1993), 200.

hierarchically ordered and horizontally articulated. However, the appearance of novelty in the relations that this evidence brings to light must be tempered by enduring continuities in the patterns of interaction around which these group-ings were arrayed. In some circumstances, the tax system brought with it antagonistic relations between small agriculturalists and those charged with collecting taxes from them. In others, by contrast, collusion or mutual incom-prehension is visible. Still others reveal peasants seizing an opportunity to enlist the vocabulary and personnel of the tax system in private, intra-village disputes. It seems reasonable to suggest, therefore, that the directionality of cause and effect between socio-economic structures and the tax system of the period be reversed. Rather than suggesting that it was the new fiscal system of the Tetrarchy that structured social relations in the period, we should acknowledge that the fiscal system adopted and adapted existing social structures. As a consequence, it was, in turn, adopted and adapted by peasants.

Such a conclusion has implications for the way we interpret the responses of peasants and rural communities to change. The evidence from the late Roman world reveals the limitations of broad-brush treatments that empha-size wholesale capitulation, embrace or resistance, and focus principally upon the dynamics of the relationship between the individual or the community on the one hand, and the agent of change on the other. Instead, we should expect a multiplicity of interconnected micro-responses, encompassing accommodation, rejection, and manipulation of new struc-tures, vocabularies, and personnel.[95] We should expect also that those responses were aimed principally at the incorporation, enlistment, or neu-tralization of the agent of change within the localized confines of the community or communities that formed the peasant's social world. We may recall here the petitions of villagers to Simeon the Stylite and place them alongside Salvian's portrait of agriculturalists seeking the protection of their more powerful neighbors. These examples may be compared, in turn, with the conditional and expansive brand of Christianity practiced by the *rustici* of sixth-century Arles and the gifts offered by agriculturalists to members of the imperial bureaucracy as a means of initiating an ongoing and mutually beneficial relationship of reciprocal exchange. In each case we observe a clear-eyed calculation of the benefits and the costs of such a strategy. In each case, the motivations ascribed to these actions by our aristocratic authors appear to have missed the point, for in each case, we may surmise that it was the twin concerns of subsistence and social risk that loomed largest in the decision-making process.

---

[95] Cf. Mood (2005), 219–20; Axelby (2007), 72; Kim (2007), 1010–14, 1019.

Conclusions

The countrysides of the late Roman world contained a multiplicity of communities, each characterized by highly complex, interwoven systems of socio-economic interaction. Those systems involved relationships of reciprocity and mutual support that were transacted vertically with individuals of greater power, wealth, and status, and horizontally with individuals whose socio-economic circumstances were broadly commensurate. The character of a particular community emerged from the combination of horizontal and vertical alliances in specific circumstances, but it is clear that the social dynamics of rural communities in the late Roman world revolved first and foremost around maintaining a balance between the cohesion of the group and the conflicting desires and objectives of the individuals, families, and households of which it was composed.

This book has focused upon that tension, and used it as a tool for explicating the various social matrices that constituted the rural communities of the period. In particular, it has placed the twin phenomena of subsistence and social risk at the center of its analysis. The two are intimately linked: the management of subsistence risk is the principal objective of any peasant household, and characteristically entails among other things involvement in a collection of interactions and relations with other households. Those interactions expand the household's pool of contacts for managing subsistence crisis, but they also increase the likelihood of conflict and disagreement between households. That conflict and disagreement is characteristically managed, negotiated, and defused using a range of strategies, including the mediation by the community of the behavior of its own members through gossip, exchange of goods, services, and expressions of mutual affection, and carefully staged communal activities, as well as recourse to figures of power and representatives of the state by the group or certain of its members.

While detailed evidence for these kinds of interactions within and between rural communities in the period is perilously thin on the ground, our sources do provide a collection of anecdotes and vignettes which can, with caution, be used in the project of recovering the resources available to small agriculturalists, and the survival strategies they employed. In this book, those vignettes have been connected to a series of broader analytical problems and, simultaneously, situated within their unique socio-economic contexts. In the process, an analytical middle ground between the micro-analysis and the grand survey has been carved out. This approach takes advantage of the particular physical, geographical, socio-economic, and political circumstances of the Mediterranean world in the late Roman period in order to construct a picture which recognizes immense diversity, but places that diversity within a structured analytical schema. Further, in concentrating upon the "small politics" of rural communities and their members rather than the objectives of the state or the perspective of aristocratic landowners, this study responds to a burgeoning literature in other scholarly fields on the social world, survival strategies and objectives of the peasantry, and provides an opportunity for dialog between rural studies in the late Roman world and scholarship in other historical and geographical contexts. While the current state of our evidence renders the results pre-sented here suggestive rather than conclusive, it is hoped that they can serve as a step along the way towards a fuller and more complex understanding of the functioning of rural communities, both in the late Roman world and elsewhere.

The particular evidentiary limitations of the period have necessitated the construction of a collection of conceptual models, which have built upon, modified, and posited connections between a variety of theoretical propo-sitions and positions in the scholarly literature. In particular, three propo-sitions have been advanced. The first is that our analysis should properly focus upon explicating the multitude of relations between individuals, their households, families, and communities, rather than upon defining and distinguishing each of these entities analytically from one another. Such an approach also entails acknowledging the mutual implication of the inhabitants of rural communities and the social, economic, political, and cultural structures within which they were enmeshed. The second is that there exists a close, dialectical set of relations between a household's and a community's management of risk, the extent to which individuals embrace and espouse an ideology of reciprocity, and the tools and tactics they use in order to manage their reputations within their communities. As a conse-quence, we must construct an analytical model that acknowledges these connections and seeks to explicate their particular manifestations in specific circumstances. Third, power relations in rural contexts are infinitely diverse, complex, and mutually contradictory. We may analyze the multifarious forms that those relations took in three interconnected ways: relations of dominance and resistance; interactions characterized by negotiation and mutual exploitation; and instances where the acts of one party impact only indirectly or accidentally upon the other. In reconstructing the various social matrices of rural contexts in the late Roman world, we must countenance the coexistence of each of these types of interaction, sometimes even between the same participants.

These theoretically derived models have been tested against the empirical evidence that survives from the late Roman world in pursuit of an analysis which acknowledges the dynamism, flexibility, and adaptability of rural communities in the period. It therefore assumes that in many – though by no means all – situations, those communities, their members and inhabitants were well equipped to adapt to externally generated changes and pressures. In this book, that proposition has been tested with reference to two phenomena. The first is the impact of the new vocabularies of social interaction, power, and authority that accompanied the rise of Christianity, its adherents and officers. The sources reveal peasants, both individually and as communities, accessing, manipulating, and resisting the claims of bishops, holy figures, and the Church as an institution. Equally, however, we may observe some communities experiencing fragmentation or oppression as a result of contact with a particularly ambitious or zealous Christian figure.

The second agent of change in the period is the new tax system of the late Roman empire, which brought with it a greater degree of intervention by the state in the affairs of the municipalities, created new groups and collectivities whose raison d'être was the satisfaction of the fiscal demands of the state, and made small agriculturalists significantly more visible to the state – and, incidentally, to contemporary scholars. In this context, too, we observe some rural communities, at least, resisting, accommodating, manipulating, and evading these new structures and the personnel that went with them. At the same time, others arguably experienced a greater degree of oppression at the hands of the state and its officers, which, together with a variety of other economic and political factors led, ultimately, to their economic decline. Clearly no single narrative can be told of the fates of rural communities in the period, but the model constructed here has been generated with the objective of encompassing this multiplicity of trajectories and tales.

What emerges from this study, then, is immense diversity in the shape, form, and flexibility in the face of pressure exhibited by rural communities in the period. That diversity can be mapped with reference to a small, but diagnostic collection of attributes. The foregoing chapters have focused essentially upon four criteria: the types, characteristics, constituent parts, and relationships between rural communities visible in these landscapes; the extent to which the members and inhabitants of these communities emerge as individuals or groups in our sources and the degree of internal cohesion they display; the form, nature, and character that their various interactions with powerful outsiders took; and their responses to the pressures and changes that accompanied the emergence of new figures of power and the imposition of a new tax system. In constructing and exploring these rural communities, this book has embraced and exploited the anecdotal moments that are dotted throughout our written sources as a means of illuminating not only the expectations of our authors and their audiences, but also the broad contours of the social worlds with which they were interacting, and the uniqueness of the individual circumstances in which they found themselves. Our evidence is patchy and incomplete, and we must be satisfied with a picture that is partial at best. Nevertheless, we observe communities that possessed their own particular characteristics, were subject to specific collections of internal pressures and demands, and responded to those pressures and demands in their own unique ways.

The project of reconstructing the socio-economic contours of the countrysides of late antiquity is, and is likely to remain, a frustrating, imperfect, and incomplete exercise. We are required to pit contexts rich in archaeological and textual sources against others characterized by a dearth of both. The textual evidence that we do possess is immensely varied in genre, purpose, and intended audience, and the suspicion remains that such differences as do exist between our various literary sources are as much the product of variation in the types of texts as in the circumstances they describe. However, these limitations and problems should not discourage us, for the rewards are potentially great, particularly when we place our multifarious contexts explicitly in dialog with one another, and with evidence and theoretical perspectives from other contexts. The object of this book has been to suggest that we must entertain both the uniqueness of specific communities and broad congruences in the social structures and strategies available to the members of those communities. The diversity and contradiction in the evidence for peasant communities in the late Roman world provides an ideal opportunity to undertake such a project.

Bibliography

PRIMARY SOURCES

Acta Pauli et Theclae, in *Acta apostolorum apocrypha* I, ed. R. A. Lipsius, Hildesheim (1959), 235–69.

Agennius Urbicus, in *Corpus Agrimensorum Romanorum = The Writings of the Roman Land Surveyors: Introduction, Text, Translation and Commentary*, ed. and trans. B. Campbell, London (2000), 16–49.

Album ordinis Thamugadensis = A. Chastagnol, *L'Album Municipal de Timgad*, Antiquitas III.22, Bonn (1978). References will be to column and line number of this edition.

Ambrose, *De Officiis*, ed. M. Testard, *CCSL* 15, Paris (2000).

  De Paenitentia = *La Pénitence*, ed. and trans. R. Gryson, *SC* 179, Paris (1971).

  Ep. = *Epistulae*, 3 vols., vol. I (1968), ed. O. Faller; vol. II (1990), ed. M. Zelzer; vol. III (1982), ed. M. Zelzer, *CSEL* 82.1–3.

Ammianus Marcellinus, *Res Gestae*, ed. W. Seyfarth, 2 vols., Teubner, Leipzig (1999).

Apa Mena = *Apa Mena: A Selection of Coptic Texts Relating to St. Menas*, ed., trans. and comm. J. Drescher, Publications de la Société d'archéologie copte: textes et documents 3, Cairo (1946). References to these texts will be by title, then Coptic text, then English text page numbers.

Augustine, *Contra Gaudentium*, in *Scripta Contra Donatistas* vol. 3, ed. M. Petschenig, *CSEL* 53, Vienna (1910).

  Dolbeau = *Vingt-six sermons au peuple d'Afrique*, ed. F. Dolbeau, Paris, (1996).

  Enarr. in Psalm. = *Enarrationes in Psalmos CI–CL*, ed. D. E. Dekkers and I. Fraipont, *CCSL* 40, Turnhout (1961).

  Ep. = *Epistulae*, ed. A. Goldbacher, *CSEL* 34, 57, Vienna (1898, 1911).

  Ep.* = *Epistolae ex duobus codicibus nuper in lucem prolatae*, ed. J. Divjak, *CSEL* 88, Vienna (1981).

Ausonius, *Ep.* = *Epistulae* in his *Works*, 2 vols., ed. and trans. H. G. E. White, Cambridge, MA (1961), vol. II, 3–153.

Basil of Caesarea, *Ep.* = *Epistulae* in his *Opera Omnia*, vol. IV, ed. J.-P. Migne, *PG* 32 (1857), 219–1112.

  Regula a Rufino Latine versa, ed. K. Zelzer, *CSEL* 86, Vienna (1986).

bBava Mesi'a, in *Babylonian Talmud: A Translation and Commentary*, 22 vols., J. Neusner, Peabody, MA (2005).

Besa, *V. Shen.* = *The Life of Shenoute*, intro., ed., and trans. D. N. Bell, Kalamazoo (1983).

Brev. = *Breviarium Alarici sive Lex Romana Visigothorum*, ed. G. Haenel, Leipzig (1849).

Caesarius of Arles, *Serm.* = *Sermones*, vol. II, ed. D. G. Morin, *CCSL* 114, Turnhout (1953).

Cassiodorus, *Variae*, ed. T. Mommsen, *MGH(AA)* 12, Berlin (1894).

Chronicle of Pseudo-Joshua the Stylite, ed. and trans. F. R. Trombley and J. W. Watt, *Translated Texts for Historians*, vol. XXXII, Liverpool, (2000).

CJ = *Codex Justinianus*, *Corpus Iuris Civilis*, vol. II, ed. P. Krueger, Berlin (1954).

Concilia Galliae, a. 314–a. 506, ed. C. Munier, *CCSL* 148, Turnhout (1963).

Constantius, *V. Germani* = Constance de Lyon, *Vie de saint Germain d'Auxerre*, ed., intro. and trans. R. Borius, *SC* 112, Paris (1965).

CTh = *Codex Theodosianus*, ed. T. Mommsen, Berlin (1905).

Dig. = *Digesta Justiniani*, 4 vols., ed. T. Mommsen, P. Krueger, and A. Watson, Philadelphia (1985).

Ed. Diocl. = *Diokletians Preisedikt*, ed. S. Lauffer, Berlin (1971).

Ennodius, *Ep.* = *Epistolae* in his *Opera Omnia*, ed. and comm. G. Hartel, *CSEL* 6, Vienna (1882), 1–260.

Ep. ad Salv. = *Epistola ad Salvium*, in Sulpicius Severus, *Libri Quae Supersunt*, ed. C. Halm, *CSEL* 1, Vienna (1896), 254–6.

Epistula Severi = Severus of Minorca, *Letter on the Conversion of the Jews*, ed. and trans. S. Bradbury, Oxford (1996).

Eugippius, *V. Sev.* = *Vita Severini*, ed. H. Sauppe, *MGH (AA)* 1 *pars posterior*, (1877).

FIRA² = *Fontes Iuris Romani Antejustiniani*, 2nd edn., 3 vols., ed. S. Riccobono, J. Baviera, and V. Arangio-Ruiz, Florence (1968).

Fronto, *Ep. ad M. Caesarum et invicem*, in *Epistulae*, ed. P. J. van den Hout, Leipzig (1988), 1–85.

FV = *Fragmenta quae dicuntur Vaticana*, *FIRA²* II, 464–540.

Gesta Apud Zenophilum, in *S. Optati Milevitani Libri VII*, ed. C. Ziwsa, *CSEL* 26, Turnhout (1893), Appendix, 185–97.

Gregory of Nazianzus, *Orationes*, 2 vols., ed. J.-P. Migne, *PG* 35–6, (1857–1858).

Gregory of Nyssa, *Ep.* = *Lettres*, ed. and trans. P. Maraval, *SC* 363, Paris (1990).
De pauperibus amandis: Oratio duo, ed. A. van Heck, Leiden (1964), 1–37.

Gregory of Tours, *Historia Francorum* = *Gregorii episcopi Turonensis. Libri Historiarum X*, *MGH (Scr. Rer. Mer.)* 1.1, ed. B. Krusch and W. Levison, Berlin (1951).
Liber in Gloria Martyrorum, in *MGH (Scr. Rer. Mer.)* 1.2, ed. B. Krusch, Berlin (1969), 34–111.
Glor. Conf. = *Liber in Gloria Confessorum*, in *MGH (Scr. Rer. Mer.)* 1.2, ed. B. Krusch, Berlin (1969), 294–370.
Virt. Jul. = *Liber de passione et virtutibus S. Juliani*, in *MGH (Scr. Rer. Mer.)* 1.2, ed. B. Krusch, Berlin (1969), 112–34.
Virt. Mart. = *Libri IV De Virtutibus S. Martini*, in *MGH (Scr. Rer. Mer.)* 1.2, ed. W. Arndt and B. Krusch, Berlin (1969), 134–211.

Gregory the Great, *Vita S. Benedicti, ex libro II Dialogorum*, ed. J.-P. Migne, *PL* 66 (1847).

Herodian, *History*, 2 vols., C. R. Whittaker, ed. and trans., Cambridge, MA (1969–1970).

Heroic Deeds of Mar Rabbula, in *Stewards of the Poor: The Man of God, Rabbula, and Hiba in Fifth-Century Edessa*, trans. and intro. R. Doran, Kalamazoo (2006), 65–105. References are to page numbers in Doran's translated text.

Hilary of Arles, *V. Honor.* = Hilaire d'Arles, *Vie de St. Honorat*, ed. and trans. M.-D. Valentin, *SC* 235, Paris (1977).

History of the Patriarchs of the Coptic Church of Alexandria, ed., trans., and ann. B. Evetts, *PO* 1 (1907), 101–214.

Hist. Mon. in Aeg. = *Historia Monachorum in Aegypto*, ed., trans., and comm. A. J. Festugière, Brussels, (1971).

Isidore of Seville, *Etymologiarum sive Originum libri XX*, ed. W. M. Lindsay, Oxford (1911).

Jerome, *Ep.* = *Sancti Eusebii Hieronymi Epistulae*, ed. I. Hilberg, *CSEL* 54–6 Vienna (1996).

  The Letters of St. Jerome, vol. 1, intro. and trans. C. C. Mierow, New York (1963).

  V. Hil. = *Vita Hilarionis*, in *PL* 23, ed. J.-P. Migne (1845), 29–54.

  V. Malchi = *Vita Malchi*, in *PL* 23, ed. J.-P. Migne (1845), 53–60.

John Chrysostom, *Opera Omnia Quae Exstant*, ed. J.-P. Migne, *PG* 58 (1862).

John of Ephesus, *Lives of the Eastern Saints*, ed. and trans. E. W. Brooks, *PO* 17, Paris (1923), 1–307.

Julian, *Ep.* = *Letters*, in *The Works of the Emperor Julian*, vol. ii, ed. and trans. W. C. Wright, Cambridge, MA (1969), 3–235.

  Misop., in *The Works of the Emperor Julian*, vol. 2, W. C. Wright, ed. and trans., Cambridge, MA (1969), 421–511.

Justinian, *Inst.* = *Justinian's Institutes, Translated with an Introduction by Peter Birks and Grant McLeod, with the Latin text of Paul Krueger*, Ithaca, NY (1987).

  Novellae Justiniani, Corpus Iuris Civilis vol. iii, ed. R. Schoell and G. Kroll, Berlin (1968).

Lactantius, *De Mortibus Persecutorum*, ed. and trans. J. L. Creed, Oxford (1984).

Libanius, *Ep.* = *Epistulae*, in his *Opera*, 12 vols., ed. R. Foerster, Teubner, Leipzig (1903–1922). vols. x and xi.

  Or. = *Orationes*, in his *Opera*, 12 vols., ed. R. Foerster, Teubner, Leipzig (1903–1922), vols. i.

Mark the Deacon, *V. Porph.* = *Vie de Porphyre, Évêque de Gaza par Marc le Diacre*, ed., trans. and comm. H. Grégoire and M.-A. Kugener, Paris (1930).

Maximus of Turin, *Serm.* = *Sermones*, ed. A. Mutzenbecher, *CCSL* 23, Turnhout (1962).

Nov. Maj. = *Novellae Majoriani*, ed. P. M. Meyer, *Leges Novellae ad Theodosianum Pertinentes*, Berlin (1905).

Nov. Theod. = *Novellae Theodosiani*, ed. P. M. Meyer, *Leges Novellae ad Theodosianum Pertinentes*, Berlin (1905).

Nov. Val. = *Novellae Valentiniani*, ed. P. M. Meyer, *Leges Novellae ad Theodosianum Pertinentes*, Berlin, (1905).

Optatus, *Contra Don.* = *Sancti Optati Milevitani Libri VII*, ed. and comm. C. Ziwsa, *CSEL* 26, Vienna (1893).

Ordo Salutationis, in A. Chastagnol, *L'Album Municipal de Timgad*, Antiquitas III.22, Bonn (1978), 75–6.

Palladius, *Hist. Laus.* = *Die lateinische Übersetzung der Historia Lausiaca des Palladius: Textausgabe mit Einleitung*, ed. A. Wellhausen, Berlin and New York (2003).

Palladius, *Op. Ag.* = Palladius, *Opus Agriculturae*, ed. R. H. Rodgers, Leipzig (1975).

Pan. Lat. = *In Praise of Later Roman Empires: The Panegyrici Latini*, ed., trans., and comm. C. E. V. Nixon and B. S. Rodgers, Berkeley, Los Angeles and Oxford (1994).

Paradise = *The Paradise or garden of the holy fathers: being histories of the anchorites recluses monks coenobites and ascetic fathers of the deserts of Egypt between* AD 250 *and* AD 400 *circiter compiled by Athanasius Archbishop of Alexandria: Palladius bishop of Helenopolis: Saint Jerome and others*, trans. E. A. W. Budge, London (1907).

Paulinus, *V. Amb.* = *Vita Sancti Ambrosii*, ed. and trans. M. S. Kaniecka, Washington, DC (1928).

Paulinus of Nola, *Carm.* = *Carmina*, ed. G. de Hartel, *CSEL* 30, Vienna (1999).
  Ep. = *Epistulae*, ed. G. de Hartel, *CSEL* 29, Vienna (1999).

Paulinus of Pella, *Euch.* = *Eucharisticus*, in Ausonius, vol. II, ed. and trans. H. G. E. White, Loeb, Cambridge, MA (1961).

pDemai = *The Talmud of the Land of Israel: A Preliminary Translation and Explanation*, vol. III *Demai*, trans. R. S. Sarason, Chicago (2003).

Pliny, *Ep.* = *Epistolae* in his *Letters and Panegyrics*, 2 vols., ed. and trans. B. Radice, Cambridge, MA (1969).

pPe'ah, in *The Talmud of the Land of Israel: a Preliminary Translation and Explanation*, vol. II, *Peah*, trans. R. Brooks, Chicago (1990).

Prudentius, *Peristephanon*, in his *Carmina*, ed. M. P. Cunningham, *CCSL* 126, (1966), 251–389.

Pseudo-Joshua the Stylite, *The Chronicle of Pseudo-Joshua the Stylite*, trans. and comm. F. R. Trombley and J. W. Watt, Liverpool (2001).

Querolus = *Querolus sive Aulularia*, ed. and trans. C. Jacquemard-Le Saos, Paris (1994).

Reg. Ben. = *La Règle de Saint Benoît*, ed. A. de Vogüé and J. Neufville, *SC* 181; 186, Paris (1971–2).

Ruricius, *Ep.* = *Epistolae*, in *CCSL* 64, ed. R. Demeulenaere, Turnhout (1985).

Rutilius Namatianus, *De Red. Suo* = *De Reditu Suo*, in *Minor Latin Poets*, ed. and trans. J. W. Duff and A. Duff, Cambridge, MA (1934).

Sallust, *Works*, ed. and trans. J. C. Rolfe, Cambridge, MA (1960).

Salvian, *De Gubernatione Dei*, ed. C. Halm, *MGH (AA)* I (1877).
  Ep. Tim. ad eccl. = *Timothei ad ecclesiam libri IV*, ed. K. Halm, *MGH (AA)* I (1877), 120–68.

Sidonius Apollinaris, *Carm.* = *Carmina* in his *Poems and Letters*, 2 vols., ed. and trans. W. B. Anderson, Cambridge, MA (1936; 1965), 1.1–327.

Ep. = *Epistolae* in *Poems and Letters*, 2 vols., ed. and trans. W. B. Anderson, Cambridge, MA (1936; 1965), 1.331–483 and 11.

Socrates, *Hist. Eccl.* = Socrate de Constantinople, *Histoire ecclésiastique*, ed. G. C. Hansen, trans. P. Périchon and P. Maraval, comm. P. Maraval, *SC* 477; 493; 505–6, Paris (2004–2007).

Sozomen, *Hist. Eccl.* = Sozomène, *Histoire ecclésiastique*, ed. J. Bidez, trans. A.-J. Festugière, comm. B. Grillet and G. Sabbah, *SC* 306; 418; 495; 516, Paris (1983–2008).

Sulpicius Severus, *Dialog.* = *Dialogi* in his *Libri Quae Supersunt*, ed. C. Halm, *CSEL* 1, Vienna (1896), 152–216.

V. Mart. = *Vita S. Martini* in his *Libri Quae Supersunt*, ed. C. Halm, *CSEL* 1, Vienna (1896), 108–37.

Symmachus, *Ep.* = *Lettres de Symmaque*, 4 vols., ed., trans., and comm. J. P. Callu, Paris (2002–3).

TA = *Tablettes Albertini: Actes privés de l'époque Vandale*, ed. C. Courtois, L. Leschi, C. Perrat, and C. Saumagne, Paris (1952).

Testamentum S. Remigii, in *Defensoris Liber Scintillarum*, ed. D. H. Rochais, *CCSL* 117, Turnhout (1957), 474–87.

Theodoret of Cyrrhus, *Hist. Rel.* = *Histoire des moines de Syrie*, 2 vols., ed. and trans. P. Canivet and A. Leroy-Molinghen, *SC* 234 and 257, Paris (1977 and 1979). *History of the Monks of Syria*, trans. R. M. Price, *CS* 88, Kalamazoo (1985).

V. Dan. Styl. = *Sancti Danielis Stylitae: Vita antiquor*, in *Les Saints Stylites*, ed. H. Delehaye (1923; repub. 1962), Brussels, 1–94.

V. Genovefae, in *Acta Sanctorum* 1, January 3, 137–53.

V. Mar. = Richard, M. (1975), "La vie ancienne de Sainte Marie surnommée Marinos," in *Corona Gratiarum. Miscellanea patristica, historica et liturgica Eligio Dekkers O.S.B. XII Lustra complenti oblata*, I Bruges, (1975), 83–94.

V. Mel. (L) = *V. S. Melania Junioris (Latin)*, *Anal. Boll.* VIII (1889), 19–63.

V. Sim. Styl. (S) = *The Lives of Simeon Stylites*, intro. and trans. R. Doran Kalamazoo (1992), 101–98.

V. Theod. Syc. = *Vie de Théodore de Sykéôn (écrite par Géorgiôs prêtre et higoumène du même monastère)*, ed. and trans. A.-J. Festugière, Brussels (1970).

Vegetius, *Epitoma Rei Militaris*, ed. M. Reeve, Oxford and New York (2004).

Victor of Vita, *Historia Persecutionis Africanae Provinciae* = *Victoris episcopi vitensis Historia persecutionis Africanae provinciae*, ed. M. Petschenig, *CSEL* 7, Vienna (1881).

SECONDARY SOURCES

Abbott, F. F., and Johnson, A. C. (1926), *Municipal Administration in the Roman Empire*, Princeton.

Abu-Lughod, L. (1990), "The romance of resistance: tracing transformations of power through Bedouin women," *American Ethnologist* 17.1, 41–55.

Adams, M. (2006), "Hybridizing habitus and reflexivity: towards an understanding of contemporary identity?" *Sociology* 40.3, 511–28.

Adnès, A. and Canivet, P. (1967), "Guérisons miraculeuses et exorcismes dans l'"Histoire Philothée' de Théodoret de Cyr," *RHR* (1967), 51–82 and 149–79.

Aguilar, J. L. (1984), "Trust and exchange: expressive and instrumental dimensions of reciprocity in a peasant community," *Ethos* 12.1, 3–29.

Akram-Lodhi, A. H. (2007), "Review Essay: Land Reform, Rural Social Relations and the Peasantry," *Journal of Agrarian Change* 7.4, 554–62.

Alcock, S. E. (1993), *Graecia Capta: The Landscapes of Roman Greece*, Cambridge.
 ed. (1997), *The Early Roman Empire in the East*, Oxford.

Alston, R. (1995), *Soldier and Society in Roman Egypt: A Social History*, London and New York.

Andersen, T. B. (1974), "*Patrocinium*: the concept of personal protection and dependence in the Later Roman Empire and Early Middle Ages," unpublished PhD thesis, Fordham University, New York.

Anderson, L. (1997), "Between quiescence and rebellion among the peasantry: integrating the middle ground," *Journal of Theoretical Politics* 9.4, 503–32.

Ando, C. (2008), "Decline, fall, and transformation," *Journal of Late Antiquity* 1.1, 31–60.

Anton, H. H. (1993), "Studien zur sozialen und kirchlichen Führungsschicht Galliens: Germanus von Auxerre, Lupus von Troyes und Trierer Bischöfe des 5. Jahrhunderts," *Jahrbuch für westdeutsche Landesgeschichte* 19, 17–45.

Arcuri, R. (2009), Rustici *e* rusticitas *in Italia meridionale nel VI sec. d.C.: morfologia sociale di un paesaggio rurale tardoantico*, Messina.

Arthur, P. (2004), "From vicus to village: Italian landscapes, AD 400–1000," in Christie, ed. (2004), 103–33.

Atkins, M. and Osborne, R., eds. (2006), *Poverty in the Roman World*, Cambridge and New York.

Aubert, J.-J. (1994), *Business Managers in Ancient Rome: A Social and Economic Study of Institores, 200 BC–AD 250*, Leiden.
 (1995), "Policing the countryside: soldiers and civilians in Egyptian villages in the third and fourth centuries AD," in Le Bohec, ed. (1995), 257–65.

Aune, D. E. (1980), "Magic in early Christianity," *ANRW* 23.2, 1507–57.

Axelby, R. (2007), "'It takes two hands to clap': how Gaddi shepherds in the Indian Himalayas negotiate access to grazing," *Journal of Agrarian Change* 7.1, 35–75.

Bagnall, R. S. (1989), "Official and private violence in Roman Egypt," *BASP* 26, 201–16.
 (1992), "Military officers as landowners in fourth-century Egypt," *Chiron* 22, 47–54.
 (1993a), *Egypt in Late Antiquity*, Princeton.
 (1993b), "Slavery and society in late Roman Egypt," in Halpern and Hobson, eds. (1993), 220–38.
 ed. (2007), *Egypt in the Byzantine World 300–700*, Cambridge and New York.

Bagnall, R. S. and Frier, B. W. (1994), *The Demography of Roman Egypt*, Cambridge and New York.

Bailey, F. G. (1971), "Gifts and poison," in Bailey, ed. (1971), 1–25.

ed. (1971), *Gifts and Poison: The Politics of Reputation*, New York.

Baksh, M., and Johnson, A. (1990), "Insurance policies among the Machiguenga: an ethnographic analysis of risk management in a non-Western society," in Cashdan, ed. (1990), 193–227.

Banaji, J. (1992), "Historical arguments for a 'logic of deployment' in 'precapitalist' agriculture," *Journal of Historical Sociology* 5, 379–91.

(2001), *Agrarian Change in Late Antiquity: Gold, Labour, and Aristocratic Dominance*, Oxford.

(2009), "Aristocracies, peasantries and the framing of the early Middle Ages," *Journal of Agrarian Change* 9.1, 59–91.

Banton, M., ed. (1965), *The Relevance of Models for Social Anthropology*, London.

Barceló, M. and Sigaut, F., eds. (2004), *The Making of Feudal Agricultures?*, Leiden and Boston, MA.

Barker, G. (1989), "The Italian landscape in the first millennium AD: some archaeological approaches," in Randsborg, ed. (1989), 62–73.

(1995), *A Mediterranean Valley: Landscape Archaeology and Annales History in the Biferno Valley*, London.

ed. (1996), *Farming the Desert: The UNESCO Libyan Valleys Archaeological Survey, vol. 1 Synthesis*, Paris.

Barker, G. and Lloyd, J., eds. (1991), *Roman Landscapes: Archaeological Survey in the Mediterranean Region*, London.

Barnes, T. D. (1982), *The New Empire of Diocletian and Constantine*, Cambridge, MA.

Bax, M. (1995), *Medjugorje: Religion, Politics, and Violence in Rural Bosnia*, Amsterdam.

Belayche, N. (2007), "Des lieux pour le 'profane' dans l'empire tardo-antique? Les fêtes entre *konônia* sociale et espaces des rivalités religieuses," *AntTard* 15, 35–46.

Belke, K., Kislinger, E., Külzer, A., and Stassinopoulou, M., eds. (2007), *Byzantina Mediterranea: Festschrift für Johannes Koder zum 65. Geburtstag*, Vienna.

Bender, H. (2001), "Archaeological perspectives on rural settlement in late antiquity in the Rhine and Danube area," in Burns and Eadie, eds. (2001), 185–98.

Bereczkei, T., Birkas, B., and Kerekes, Z. (2007), "Public charity offer as a proximate factor of evolved reputation-building strategy: an experimental analysis of a real-life situation," *Evolution and Human Behavior* 28, 277–84.

Bernstein, H. and Byres, T. J. (2001), "From peasant studies to agrarian change," *Journal of Agrarian Change* 1.1, 1–56.

Besnier, R. and Hopital, R. (1983), "Les communautés rurales dans l'Empire Romain," in *Communautés rurales, vol. 11*, 431–66.

Bielawski, M. and Hombergen, D., eds. (2004), *Il monachesimo tra eredità e aperture*, Rome.

Biele, G., Rieskamp, J., and Czienskowski, U. (2008), "Explaining cooperation in groups: testing models of reciprocity and learning," *Organizational Behavior and Human Decision Processes* 106.2, 89–105.

Bintliff, J. (1991), "The Roman countryside in central Greece: observations and theories from the Boeotia survey (1978–1987)," in Barker and Lloyd, eds. (1991), 122–32.

Blanton, R. E. and Fargher, L. (2008), *Collective Action in the Formation of Pre-Modern States*, New York.

Bliege Bird, R., Bird, D. W., Alden Smith, W., and Kushnick, G. C. (2002), "Risk and reciprocity in Meriam food sharing," *Evolution and Human Behavior* 23.4, 297–321.

Bonneau, D. (1979), "Un règlement de l'usage de l'eau au Ve siècle de notre ère: commentaire de P. Haun. Inv. 318," in Vercoulter, ed. (1979), 3–23.

(1983), "Communauté rurale en Égypte Byzantine?" in *Communautés rurales*, vol. II, 505–22.

Bonney, R. (1975), "A new friend for Symmachus?" *Historia* 24, 357–74.

Boomgaard, P. (1991), "The Javanese village as a Cheshire cat: the Java debate against a European and Latin American background," *Journal of Peasant Studies* 18.2, 288–304.

Boswell, J. E. (1984), "Expositio and oblatio: the abandonment of children and the ancient and medieval family," *AHR* 89, 10–33.

(1988; repub. 1991), *The Kindness of Strangers: The Abandonment of Children in Western Europe from Late Antiquity to the Renaissance*, London.

Bourdieu, P. (1977), *Outline of a Theory of Practice*, Cambridge.

(1990), *The Logic of Practice*, Stanford, CA.

(1992), *An Invitation to Reflexive Sociology*, Chicago.

(2000), *Pascalian Meditations*, trans. R. Nice, Stanford, CA.

Bowden, W., Gutteridge, A., and Machado, C. eds. (2006), *Social and Political Life in Late Antiquity*, Leiden and Boston, MA.

Bowden, W., Lavan, L., and Machado, C., eds. (2004), *Recent Research on the Late Antique Countryside*, Leiden and Boston, MA.

Bowdon, L. (2004), "Redefining kinship: exploring boundaries of relatedness in late Medieval New Romney," *Journal of Family History* 29.4, 407–20.

Bowes, K. (forthcoming), "Rural bishops in late antique Italy: between demography and discourse."

Bowes, K. and Gutteridge, A. (2005), "Rethinking the later Roman landscape," *JRA* 18, 405–18.

Bowman, A. K. (1985), "Landholding in the Hermopolite nome in the fourth century AD," *JRS* 75, 137–63.

Braddick, M. J. and Walter, J. (2001), "Introduction. Grids of power: order, hierarchy and subordination in early modern society," in Braddick and Walter, eds. (2001), 1–42.

eds. (2001), *Negotiating Power in Early Modern Society: Order, Hierarchy, and Subordination in Britain and Ireland*, Cambridge.

Bradley, K. (2003), "Sacrificing the family: Christian martyrs and their kin," *Ancient Narrative* 3, 1–32.

Bradley, K. and Cartledge, P., eds. (2011), *The Cambridge World History of Slavery: The Ancient Mediterranean World*, Cambridge.

Brandes, W. and Haldon, J. (2000), "Tax and transformation: state, cities and their hinterlands in the east Roman world, c. 500–800," in Brogiolo, Gauthier, and Christie, eds. (2000), 141–72.

Braunert, H. (1955), "'Ἰδία: Studien zur Bevölkerungsgeschichte des ptolemäischen und römischen Aegypten," *JJP* 9–10, 211–328.

Breman, J. (1982), "The village on Java and the early-colonial state," *Journal of Peasant Studies* 9.4, 189–240.

Brennan, G., González, L. G., Güth, W., and Levati, M. V. (2008), "Attitudes toward private and collective risk in individual and strategic choice situations," *Journal of Economic Behavior & Organization* 67.1, 253–62.

Brogiolo, G. P., ed. (2003), *Chiese e insediamenti nelle campagne tra V e VI secolo*, Mantua.

Brogiolo, G. P., Gauthier, N., and Christie, N., eds. (2000), *Towns and Their Territories between Late Antiquity and the Early Middle Ages*, Leiden and Boston, MA.

Brown, P. (1971), "The rise and function of the holy man in Late Antiquity," *JRS* 61, 80–101.

(1972), *Religion and Society in the Age of Saint Augustine*, London.

(1981), *The Cult of the Saints*, Chicago.

(1988), *The Body and Society: Men, Women, and Sexual Renunciation in Early Christianity*, New York.

(1992), *Power and Persuasion in Late Antiquity: Towards a Christian Empire*, Madison.

(1998), "The rise and function of the holy man in Late Antiquity, 1971–1997," *JECS* 6.3, 353–76.

(2002), *Poverty and Leadership in the Later Roman Empire*, Hanover, NH.

(2003), *The Rise of Western Christendom: Triumph and Diversity*, AD 200–1000, 2nd edn., Malden.

Brühl, C. (1988), "Problems of the continuity of Roman civitates in Gaul, as illustrated by the interrelation of cathedral and palatium," in Hodges and Hobley, eds. (1988), 43–6.

Bryen, A. Z. (2008a), "Violence, Law, and Society in Roman and Late Antique Egypt," unpublished PhD dissertation, University of Chicago.

(2008b), "Visibility and violence in petitions from Roman Egypt," *GRBS* 48, 181–200.

Bryen, A. Z., and Wypustek, A. (2009), "Gemellus' evil eyes (P. Mich. VI 423–4)," *GRBS* 49, 535–55.

Burns, T. S. and Eadie, J. W., eds. (2001), *Urban Centers and Rural Contexts in Late Antiquity*, East Lansing.

Burton, G. P. (1979), "The *curator rei publicae*: towards a reappraisal," *Chiron* 9, 465–87.

CAH 13 = Cameron, A. and Garnsey, P. D. A., eds. (1998), *The Cambridge Ancient History*, vol. XIII, *The Late Empire*, AD 337–425, Cambridge.

Calbi, A., Donati, A., and Poma, G., eds. (1993), *L'Epigrafia del Villaggio*, Faenza.

Cambi, F. and Fentress, E. (1989), "Villas to castles: first millennium AD demography in the Albegna Valley," in Randsborg, ed. (1989), 74–86.

Campbell, H. and Heyman, J. (2007), "Slantwise: beyond domination and resistance on the Border," *Journal of Contemporary Ethnography* 36.1, 3–30.

Capogrossi Colognesi, L. (1983), "Le communità rurali nell'Italia Romana," in *Communautés rurales, vol. II*, 411–30.

Carlsen, J. (1995), *Vilici and Roman Estate Managers until AD 284*, Rome.

Carlsen, J., Ørsted, P., and Skydsgaard, J. E., eds. (1994), *Landuse in the Roman Empire*, Rome.

Carrié, J.-M. (1976), "Patronage et propriété militaires au IVe s.: Objet rhétorique et objet reel du discours *Sur les patronages* de Libanius," *BCH* 100, 159–76.

(1982), "Le 'colonat du Bas-Empire': un mythe historiographique?" *Opus* 1, 351–71.

(1983), "Un roman des origines: les généalogies du 'colonat du Bas-Empire'," *Opus* 2, 205–51.

(1993a), "L'economia e le finanze," in Momigliano and Schiavone, eds. (1993), 751–87.

(1993b), "Le riforme economiche da Aureliano a Costantino," in Momigliano and Schiavone, eds. (1993), 283–322.

(1993c), "Observations sur la fiscalité du IVe siècle pour servir à l'histoire monétaire," in *L' 'inflazione' nel quarto secolo d.C.: Atti dell'incontro di studio, Roma 23–25 giugno 1988*, Rome, 115–54.

(1994), "Dioclétien et la fiscalité," *AntTard* 2, 33–64.

(1997), "'Colonato del Basso Impero': la resistenza del mito," in Lo Cascio, ed. (1997), 75–150.

Carroll, L. (1999), "Communities and other social actors: rethinking commodities and consumption in global historical archaeology," *International Journal of Historical Archaeology* 3.3, 131–6.

Caseau, B. (2004), "The fate of rural temples in Late Antiquity and the Christianisation of the countryside," in Bowden, Lavan, and Machado, eds. (2004), 105–44.

Cashdan, E., ed. (1990), *Risk and Uncertainty in Tribal and Peasant Economies*, Boulder.

Casiday, A. and Norris, F. W., eds. (2007), *The Cambridge History of Christianity, vol. II, Constantine to c. 600*, Cambridge.

Cecconi, G. A. (1994), *Governo imperiale e élites dirigenti nell'Italia tardoantica: problemi di storia politico-amministrativa (270–476 d.C.)*, Como.

Cérati, A. (1975), *Caractère annonaire et assiette de l'impôt foncier au Bas-Empire*, Paris.

Certeau, M. de (1984), *The Practice of Everyday Life*, Berkeley.

Chaniotis, A. (2002), "The Jews of Aphrodisias: new evidence and old problems," *SCI* 21, 209–42.

Chastagnol, A. (1978), *L'Album municipal de Timgad*, Bonn.

Chastagnol, A., Demougin, S., and Lepelley, C., eds. (1996), *Splendidissima civitas: Études d'histoire romaine en hommage à François Jacques*, Paris.

Chavarría, A. and Lewit, T. (2004), "Archaeological research on the late antique countryside: a bibliographical essay," in Bowden, Lavan and Machado, eds. (2004), 3–51.

Chayanov, A. V. (1966; repub. 1986), *The Theory of Peasant Economy*, trans. C. Lane and R. E. F. Smith, Madison.

Chaytor, M. (1980), "Household and kinship: Ryton in the late 16th and early 17th centuries," *History Workshop* 10, 25–60.

Cheyette, F. L. (2008), "The disappearance of the ancient landscape and the climatic anomaly of the early Middle Ages: a question to be pursued," *Early Medieval Europe* 16.2, 127–65.

Chong, D. (1992), "Reputation and cooperative behavior," *Social Science Information* 31.4, 683–709.

Christie, N. (2000), "Construction and deconstruction: reconstructing the late-Roman townscape," in Slater, ed. (2000), 51–71.

ed. (2004), *Landscapes of Change: Rural Evolutions in Late Antiquity and the Early Middle Ages*, Aldershot and Burlington.

Christol, M., Demougin, S., Duvall, Y., Lepelley C., and Pietri, L., eds. (1992), *Institutions, société et vie politique dans l'empire romain au IVe siècle ap. J. C.*, Rome.

Ciraolo, L. and Seidel, J., eds. (2002), *Magic and Divination in the Ancient World*, Leiden.

Clark. G. (1994), "The Fathers and the children," in Wood, ed. (1994), 1–27.

Clausing, R. (1925; repub. 1965), *The Roman Colonate: The Theories of its Origin*, Rome.

Clement, M. (2008), "The relationship between private transfers and household income with regard to the assumptions of altruism, exchange and risk sharing: an empirical analysis applied to Russia," *Post-Communist Economies* 20.2, 173–87.

Codd, N. (1971), "Reputation and social structure in a Spanish Pyrenean village," in Bailey, ed. (1971), 182–211.

Codou, Y. and Colin, M.-G. (2007), "La christianisation des campagnes (IVe–VIIIe s.)," *Gallia* 64, 57–83.

Colleyn, J.-P. (1983), "Du concept de communauté en anthropologie économique et sociale," in *Communautés rurales, vol. 1*, 23–33.

Communautés rurales = *Les Communautés rurales* (1983), 5 vols., Paris.

Connolly, S. (2010), *Lives behind the Laws: The World of the Codex Hermogenianus*, Bloomington.

Conradt, L. and Roper, T. J. (2009), "Conflicts of interest and the evolution of decision sharing," *Philosophical Transactions of the Royal Society B* 364, 807–19.

Cooper, C. F. (2007a), "Approaching the holy household," *JECS* 15.2, 131–42.

(2007b), *The Fall of the Roman Household*, Cambridge.

Corbo, C. (2006), *Paupertas: La Legislazione Tardoantica (IV–V Sec. d.C.)*, Naples.

Corradini, R., Diesenberger, M., and Reimitz, H., eds. (2003), *The Construction of Communities in the Early Middle Ages: Texts, Resources and Artefacts*, Leiden and Boston, MA.

Cronin, S. (2005), "Resisting the new state: peasants and pastoralists in Iran, 1921–41," *Journal of Peasant Studies* 32.1: 1–47.

Csordas, T. J. (1990), "Embodiment as a paradigm for anthropology," *Ethos* 18, 5–47.

Davis, K. and Fisher, S. (1993), "Power and the female subject," in Fisher and Davis, eds. (1993), 3–22.

de Jong, M. (1996), *In Samuel's Image: Child Oblation in the Early Medieval West*, Leiden.

de Ligt, L. (1990), "Demand, supply, distribution: the Roman peasantry between town and countryside: rural monetization and peasant demand," *MBAH* 9, 24–56.

(1991), "Demand, supply, distribution: the Roman peasantry between town and countryside II: Supply, distribution and a comparative perspective," *MBAH* 10, 37–77.

(1993), *Fairs and Markets in the Roman Empire: Economic and Social Aspects of Periodic Trade in a Pre-Industrial Society*, Amsterdam.

de Ligt, L. and de Neeve, P. W. (1988), "Ancient periodic markets: festivals and fairs," *Athenaeum* 3–4, 391–416.

de Zulueta, F. (1909), "De Patrociniis Vicorum," *Oxford Studies in Social and Legal History* 1, 3–78.

Decker, M. (2009), *Tilling the Hateful Earth: Agricultural Production and Trade in the Late Antique East*, Oxford.

Déléage, A. (1945), *La Capitation du Bas-Empire*, Mâcon.

Delmaire, R. (1989), *Largesses sacrées et res privata: l'Aerarium impérial et son administration du IVe au VIe siècle*, Rome.

(1996a), "Cités et fiscalité au Bas-Empire: à propos du rôle des curiales dans la levée des impôts," in Lepelley, ed. (1996), 59–70.

(1996b), "Quelques aspects de la vie municipale au Bas-Empire à travers les textes patristiques et hagiographiques," in Chastagnol, Demougin, and Lepelley, eds. (1996), 39–48.

Demandt, A. (1984), *Der Fall Roms. Die Auflösung des römischen Reiches im Urteil der Nachwelt*, Munich.

Déroche, V., ed. (2002), *Mélanges Gilbert Dagron* (Association des amis du Centre d'histoire et civilisation de Byzance, Travaux et Mémoires 14), Paris.

Dentzer, J.-M., ed. (1985), *Hauran I: Recherches archéologiques sur la Syrie du sud à L'époque helléristique et romaine*, Paris.

DeWindt, A. R. (1987), "Redefining the peasant community in medieval England: the regional perspective," *Journal of British Studies* 26.2, 163–207.

Díaz, P. C. (2000), "City and territory in Hispania in Late Antiquity," in Brogiolo, Gauthier, and Christie, eds. (2000), 3–35.

Dickie, M. W. (1995), "The Fathers of the Church and the Evil Eye," in Maguire, ed. (1995), 9–34.

Dossey, L. A. (2010), *Peasant and Empire in Christian North Africa*, Berkeley.

Drake, H. A., ed. (2006), *Violence in Late Antiquity: Perceptions and Practices*, Aldershot and Burlington.

Dreyfuss, H. L. and Rabinow, P. (1982), *Michel Foucault: Beyond Structuralism and Hermeneutics*, Chicago.

Drijvers, H. J. W. (1996), "The Man of God of Edessa, Bishop Rabbula, and the urban poor: Church and society in the fifth century," *JECS* 4.2, 235–48.

  (1999), "Rabbula, bishop of Edessa: spiritual authority and secular power," in Drijvers and Watt, eds. (1999), 139–54.

Drijvers, J. W. and Watt, J. W., eds. (1999), *Portraits of Spiritual Authority: Religious Power in Early Christianity, Byzantium and the Christian Orient*, Leiden, Boston, MA, and Cologne.

Drinkwater, J. (1983), *Roman Gaul: The Three Provinces, 58 BC–AD 260*, London.

  (2001), "Women and horses and power and war," in Burns and Eadie, eds. (2001), 135–46.

Drinkwater, J. and Elton, H., eds. (1992), *Fifth-century Gaul: A Crisis of Identity?*, Cambridge.

Du latifundium *au* latifondo = *Du* latifundium *au* latifondo*: Un Héritage de Rome, une création médiévale ou moderne? Actes de la Table ronde internationale du CNRS organisée à l'Université Michel de Montaigne–Bordeaux III les 17–19 décembre 1992*, Paris (1995).

Dunn, A. (1994), "The transition from *polis* to *kastron* in the Balkans (III–IV cc.): general and regional perspectives," *Byzantine and Modern Greek Studies* 18, 60–80.

Dunn, M. (2007), "Asceticism and monasticism, II: Western," in Casiday and Norris, eds. (2007), 669–90.

Durand, A and Leveau, P. (2004), "Farming in Mediterranean France and rural settlement in the late Roman and early medieval periods: the contribution from archaeology and environmental sciences in the last twenty years (1980–2000)," in Barceló and Sigaut, eds. (2004), 177–253.

Durkheim, É. (1933), *Émile Durkheim on the Division of Labor in Society; Being a Translation of His* De la division du travail social, New York.

Durliat, J. (1993), *Les Rentiers de l'impôt: recherches sur les finances municipales dans la "Pars Orientis" au IVe siècle*, Vienna.

Eitrem, S. (1937), "A few remarks on σπονδή, θαλλός and other extra payments in papyri," *SO* 17, 26–48.

Elder-Vass, D. (2007), "Reconciling Archer and Bourdieu in an emergentist theory of action," *Sociological Theory* 25.4, 325–46.

  (2008), "Integrating institutional, relational and embodied structure: an emergentist perspective," *British Journal of Sociology* 59.2, 281–99.

Elliott, A. G. (1987), *Roads to Paradise: Reading the Lives of the Early Saints*, Hanover, NH.

Ellis, L. and F. L. Kidner, eds. (2004), *Travel, Communication and Geography in Late Antiquity*, Aldershot and Burlington.

Emirbayer, M. (1997), "Manifesto for a relational sociology," *American Journal of Sociology* 103.2, 281–317.

Emirbayer, M. and Mische, A. (1998), "What is agency?" *American Journal of Sociology* 103.4, 962–1023.

Emmel, S. (2004), "Shenoute the monk: the early monastic career of Shenoute the archimandrite," in Bielawski and Hombergen, eds. (2004), 151–74.

Erdkamp, P. (1999), "Agriculture, underemployment, and the cost of rural labour in the Roman world," *CQ* 49.2, 556–72.

Ermatinger, J. W. (1997), "The economic death of Theadelphia in the early fourth century AD," *MBAH* 16.1, 1–10.

Evans Grubbs, J. (1989), "Abduction marriage in antiquity: a law of Constantine (*CTh* IX.24.1) and its social context," *JRS* 79, 59–83.

(1995), *Law and Family in Late Antiquity: The Emperor Constantine's Marriage Legislation*, Oxford.

Faure-Boucharlat, É., ed. (2001), *Vivre à la campagne au Moyen Âge: l'habitat rural du Ve au XIIe s. (Bresse, Lyonnais, Dauphiné) d'après les données archéologiques*, Lyon.

Fenster, T. S. and Smail, D. L. eds. (2003) *Fama: The Politics of Talk and Reputation in Medieval Europe*, Ithaca, NY.

Ferraro, E. (2004), "Owing and being in debt: a contribution from the northern Andes of Ecuador," *Social Anthropology* 12.1, 77–94.

Fiema, Z. T. (2001), "Byzantine Petra – a reassessment," in Burns and Eadie, eds. (2001), 111–31.

Fikhman, I. F. (1978), "Les 'patrocinia' dans les papyrus d'Oxyrhynchus," *Actes du XVe congrès international du papyrologie, vol. IV*, Brussels, 186–94.

Finley, M. I. (1976), "Private farm tenancy in Italy before Diocletian," in Finley, ed. (1976), 103–23.

ed. (1976), *Studies in Roman Property*, Cambridge.

Finn, R. D. (2006), *Almsgiving in the Later Roman Empire: Christian Promotion and Practice (313–450)*, Oxford.

Fisher, S. and Davis, K., eds. (1993), *Negotiating at the Margins: The Gendered Discourse of Power and Resistance*, New Brunswick.

Fixot, M. (2000), "La cité et son territoire: l'exemple du Sud-Est de la Gaule," in Brogiolo, Gauthier, and Christie, eds. (2000), 37–61.

Flint, V. (1991), *The Rise of Magic in Early Medieval Europe*, Princeton.

(1999), "The demonisation of magic and sorcery in Late Antiquity: Christian redefinitions of pagan religions," in *Witchcraft and Magic in Europe, vol. II Ancient Greece and Rome*, London, 277–348.

Fontaine, J. (1968), *Sulpice Sévère, Vie de Saint Martin, vol. II Commentaire (jusqu'à Vita 19)*, Paris.

Forbes, H. (1976), "'We have a little of everything': the ecological basis of some agricultural practices in Methana, Trizinia," *Annals of the New York Academy of Sciences* 268, 236–50.

Foss, C. (2000), "Urban and rural housing in Syria: review article," *JRA* 13, 796–800.

Foucault, M. (1978), *The History of Sexuality*, trans. R. Hurley, New York.
(1979), *Discipline and Punish: The Birth of the Prison*, New York.
(1982), "The subject and power," in Dreyfuss and Rabinow, eds. (1982), 208–28.
(1986), "Disciplinary power and subjection," in Lukes, ed. (1986), 229–42. [Originally published in M. Foucault, (1976), *Power/Knowledge: Selected Interviews and Other Writings 1972–1977*, ed. and trans. C. Gordon, New York and Toronto.]
Foxhall, L. (1990), "The dependent tenant: land leasing and labour in Italy and Greece," *JRS* 80, 97–114.
Frakes, R. M. (1993/1994), "Late Roman social justice and the origin of the *defensor civitatis*," *CJ* 89, 337–48.
Frank, G. (1998), "Miracles, monks and monuments: the *Historia monachorum in Aegypto* as pilgrims' tales," in Frankfurter, ed. (1998), 483–505.
Frankfurter, D. (2007), "Christianity and paganism, I: Egypt," in Casiday and Norris, eds. (2007), 173–88.
    ed. (1998), *Pilgrimage and Holy Space in Late Antique Egypt*, Leiden.
Frayn, J. M. (1993), *Markets and Fairs in Roman Italy*, Oxford.
Freter, A. (2004), "Multiscalar model of rural households and communities in Late Classic Copan Maya society," *Ancient Mesoamerica* 15.1, 93–106.
Frézouls, E., ed. (1983), *Crise et redressement dans les provinces européennes de l'Empire (milieu du IIIe – milieu du IVe siècle ap. J.-C.)*, Strasbourg.
Fulford, M. (1996), "Economic hotspots and provincial backwaters: modelling the late Roman economy," in King and Wigg, eds. (1996), 153–77.
Fustel de Coulanges, N. D. (1890), *Les Origines du système féodal: le bénéfice et le patronat pendant l'Époque merovingienne, vol. V of Histoire des institutions politiques de l'ancienne France*, Paris.
Gagos, T. and van Minnen, P. (1994), *Settling a Dispute: Towards a Legal Anthropology of Late Antique Egypt*, Ann Arbor.
Gal, S. (1995), "Review: Language and the 'Arts of Resistance'," *Cultural Anthropology* 10.3, 407–24.
Galbraith, M. (2003), "Gifts and favors: social networks and reciprocal exchange in Poland," *Ethnologia Europaea* 33.1, 73–94.
Gallant, T. W. (1991), *Risk and Survival in Ancient Greece: Reconstructing the Rural Domestic Economy*, Stanford, CA.
Garnsey, P. D. A. (1979), "Where did Italian peasants live?" *PCPhS* n. s. 25, 1–25.
(1980), "Non-slave labour in the Roman world," in Garnsey, ed. (1980), 34–47.
(1988), *Famine and Food Supply in the Graeco-Roman World: Responses to Risk and Crisis*, Cambridge.
(1996), "Prolegomenon to a study of the land in the later Roman Empire," in Strubbe, Tybout, and Versnel, eds. (1996), 135–53.
(2010) "Roman patronage," in McGill, Sogno, and Watts, eds. (2010), 33–54.
Garnsey, P. D. A., ed. (1980), *Non-Slave Labour in the Greco-Roman World*, Cambridge.
Garnsey, P. D. A. and Humfress, C. (2001), *The Evolution of the Late Antique World*, Cambridge.

Garnsey, P. D. A. and Whittaker, C. R. (1998), "Trade, industry and the urban economy," *CAH* 13, 312–37.

eds. (1978), *Imperialism in the Ancient World*, Cambridge.

Garnsey, P. D. A. and Woolf, G. (1989), "Patronage of the rural poor in the Roman world," in Wallace-Hadrill, ed. (1989), 153–70.

Gascou, J. (1985), "Les grands domaines, la cité et l'État en Égypte byzantine," *Travaux et mémoires byzantines* 9, 1–90.

(1997), "Les privilèges du clergé d'après la 'lettre' 104 de S. Basile," *RSR* 71, 189–204.

Gauthiez, B., Zadora-Rio, E., and Galinié, H., eds. (2003), *Village et ville au Moyen Âge: les dynamiques morphologiques*, 2 vols., Tours.

Gellner, E. and Waterbury, J., eds. (1977), *Patrons and Clients in Mediterranean Societies*, London.

Giddens, A. (1976), *New Rules of Sociological Method*, London.

(1984), *The Constitution of Society*, Cambridge.

Giliberti, G. (1992), "Consortium vicanorum," *Ostraka* 1, 177–214.

(1999), *Servi della terra: ricerche per una storia del colonato*, Turin.

Gintis, H. (2003), "Solving the puzzle of prosociality," *Rationality and Society* 15.2, 155–87.

Gioanni, S. (2000), "Moines et évêques en Gaule aux Ve et VIe siècles: la controverse entre Augustin et les moines provençaux," *Médiévales: langue, textes, histoire* 38, 149–61.

Gleason, M. W. (1998), "Visiting and news: gossip and reputation-management in the desert," *JECS* 6.3, 501–21.

Goehring, J. E. (1996), "Withdrawing from the desert: Pachomius and the development of village monasticism in Upper Egypt," *HThR* 89, 267–85.

Goffart, W. (1974), *Caput and Colonate: Towards a History of Late Roman Taxation*, Toronto and Buffalo.

Goldschmidt, W. and Kunkel, E. J. (1971) "The structure of the peasant family," *American Anthropologist* 73, 1058–76.

Goody, J. (1983), *The Development of the Family and Marriage in Europe*, Cambridge.

Gordon, W. M. (1970), *Studies in the Transfer of Property by Traditio*, Aberdeen.

Gouldner, A. W. (1960), "The norm of reciprocity: a preliminary statement," *American Sociological Review* 25.2, 161–78.

Grainger, J. D. (1995), "'Village government' in Roman Syria and Arabia," *Levant* 27, 179–95.

Gramsci, A. (1971), *Selections from the Prison Notebooks of Antonio Gramsci*, ed. and trans. Q. Hoare and G. N. Smith, London.

Grelle, F. (1963), *Stipendium vel tributum: l'imposizione fondiaria nelle dottrine guiriduche del II e III secolo*, Naples.

Grey, C. (2003), "Review: J. Banaji, *Agrarian Change in late Antiquity: gold, labour and aristocratic dominance*," *Economic History Review* 56.2, 379–80.

(2004), "Letters of recommendation and the circulation of rural laborers in the late Roman West," in Ellis and Kidner, eds. (2004), 25–40.

(2005), "Demoniacs, dissent and disempowerment in the late Roman West: some case studies from the hagiographical literature," *JECS* 13.1, 39–69.

(2006) "Salvian, the ideal Christian community and the fate of the poor in fifth-century Gaul," in Atkins and Osborne, eds. (2006), 162–82.

(2007a), "Contextualizing *colonatus*: the *origo* of the late Roman Empire," *JRS* 97, 155–75.

(2007b), "Revisiting the 'problem' of *agri deserti* in the late Roman empire," *JRA* 20, 362–76.

(2008), "Two young lovers: an abduction marriage and its consequences in fifth-century Gaul," *CQ* 58.1, 286–302.

(2011a), "The *ius colonatus* as a model for the settlement of barbarian prisoners-of-war in the late Roman Empire?" in Mathisen and Shanzer, eds. (2011), 147–60.

(2011b), "Slavery in the late Roman world," in Bradley and Cartledge (2011), 482–509.

(forthcoming), "Agriculture and rural life," in Johnson, ed. (forthcoming).

Grey, C. and Parkin, A. (2003), "Controlling the urban mob: the *colonatus perpetuus* of *CTh* 14.18.1," *Phoenix* 57, 284–99.

Grieser, H. (1997), *Sklaverei im spätantiken und frühmittelalterlichen Gallien (5.–7. Jh.): das Zeugnis der christlichen Quellen*, Stuttgart.

Grischow, J. D. (2008), "Rural 'community', chiefs and social capital: the case of southern Ghana," *Journal of Agrarian Change* 8.1, 64–93.

Grossman, P. (1991), "Abû Mînâ," *Copt Encyc* 1, 24–9.

Grossmark, T. (2006), "The inn as a place of violence and danger in rabbinic literature," in Drake, ed. (2006), 57–68.

Groves, J. M. and Chang, K. A. (1999), "Romancing resistance and resisting romance: ethnography and the construction of power in the Filipina domestic worker community in Hong Kong," *Journal of Contemporary Ethnography* 28.3, 235–65.

Guilhiermoz, P. (1902), *Essai sur l'origine de la noblesse en France au moyen âge*, Paris.

Haas, C. (2001), "Alexandria and the Mareotis Region," in Burns and Eadie, eds. (2001), 47–62.

Hachlili, R., ed. (1989), *Ancient Synagogues in Israel, Third–Seventh Century* CE: *Proceedings of Symposium University of Haifa, May 1987*, London.

Hahamovitch, C. and Halpern, R. (2004), "Not a 'sack of potatoes': why labor historians need to take agriculture seriously," *International Labor and Working-Class History* 65, 3–10.

Hahn, I. (1968), "Das bäuerliche Patrocinium in Ost und West," *Klio* 50, 261–76.

Haimes, Y. Y. (2009), "On the complex definition of risk: a systems-based approach," *Risk Analysis: An International Journal* 29.12, 1647–54.

Haldon, J. F. (2007), "'Cappadocia will be given over to ruin and become a desert': environmental evidence for historically-attested events in the 7th–10th centuries," in Belke, Kislinger, Külzer, and Stassinopoulou, eds. (2007), 215–30.

Halpern, B. and Hobson, D. W., eds. (1993), *Law, Politics and Society in the Ancient Mediterranean World*, Sheffield.

Halsall, G. (1992), "The origins of the Reihengräberzivilisation: forty years on," in Drinkwater and Elton, eds. (1992), 196–207.

Halstead, P. (1987) "Traditional and ancient rural economy in Mediterranean Europe: plus ça change?," *JHS* 107, 77–87.

Hamel, G. (1990), *Poverty and Charity in Roman Palestine, First Three Centuries* CE, Berkeley, Los Angeles and Oxford.

Hamerow, H. (2002), *Early Medieval Settlements: The Archaeology of Rural Communities in Northwest Europe, 400–900*, Oxford.

Hanawalt, B. (1986), *The Ties that Bound: Peasant Family Life in Medieval England*, Oxford and New York.

Harding, J. (2005), "Rethinking the great divide: long-term structural history and the temporality of event," *Norwegian Archaeological Review* 38.2, 88–101.

Harmand, L. (1957), *Le Patronat sur les collectivités*, Paris.

Harper, J. K. (2008), "The Greek census inscriptions of Late Antiquity," *JRS* 98, 83–119.

(forthcoming), "Marriage and family in Late Antiquity," in Johnson, ed. (forthcoming).

Harries, J. (1994), *Sidonius Apollinaris and the Fall of Rome, AD 407–485*, Oxford.

(1999), *Law and Empire in Late Antiquity*, Cambridge.

(2001), "Resolving disputes: the frontiers of law in Late Antiquity," in Mathisen, ed. (2001), 68–82.

Harris, O. (1982), "Households and their boundaries," *History Workshop* 13, 143–52.

Heather, P. (1994), "New men for new Constantines? Creating an imperial elite in the eastern Mediterranean," in Magdalino, ed. (1994), 11–33.

(1998), "Senators and senates," *CAH* 13, 184–210.

Heijmans, M. (2006), "Les habitations urbaines en Gaule méridionale durant l'Antiquité tardive," *Gallia* 63, 47–57.

Heppenstall, M. A. (1971), "Reputation, criticism and information in an Austrian village," in Bailey, ed. (1971), 139–66.

Herzfeld, M. (1986), "Closure as cure: tropes in the exploration of bodily and social disorder," *Current Anthropology* 27.2, 107–20.

(2005), "Political optics and the occlusion of intimate knowledge," *American Anthropologist* 107.3, 369–76.

Hezser, C. (2003), "The impact of household slaves on the Jewish family in Roman Palestine," *Journal for the Study of Judaism in the Persian Hellenistic & Roman Period* 34.4, 375–424.

Hilton, R. H. (1975), *The English Peasantry in the Later Middle Age*, Oxford.

Hobson, D. W. (1993), "The impact of law on village life in Roman Egypt," in Halpern and Hobson, eds. (1993), 193–219.

Hodges, R. (1988), *Primitive and Peasant Markets*, Oxford.

Hodges, R. and Hobley, B., eds. (1988), *The Rebirth of Towns in the West AD 700–1050*, London.

Holman, S. R. (2001), *The Hungry Are Dying: Beggars and Bishops in Roman Cappadocia*, Oxford.

Hoogendijk, F. A. J. (1995), "Zwei byzantinische landkäufe," *Tyche* 10, 13–26.

Horden, P. (1993), "Responses to possession and insanity in the earlier Byzantine world," *Social History of Medicine* 6.2, 177–94.

—— (2005), "The earliest hospitals in Byzantium, Western Europe, and Islam," *Journal of Interdisciplinary History* 35.3, 361–89.

Horden, P. and Purcell, N. (2000), *The Corrupting Sea: A Study of Mediterranean History*, Oxford.

Hovelsrud-Broda, G. (2000), "'Sharing', transfers, transactions and the concept of generalized reciprocity," *Senri Ethnological Studies* 53, 193–214.

Howe, L. (1998), "Scrounger, worker, beggarman, cheat: the dynamics of unemployment and the politics of resistance in Belfast," *Journal of the Royal Anthropological Institute* 4.3, 531–50.

Humbert, M. (1983), "Enfants à louer ou à vendre: Augustin et l'autorité parentale (*Ep.* 10* et 24*)," in *Les Lettres de Saint Augustin*, 329–42.

Humfress, C. (2006), "Poverty and Roman law," in Atkins and Osborne, eds. (2006), 183–203.

Hunt, D. (1998), "The church as a public institution," *CAH* 13, 238–76.

Hunt, E. D. (1982), "St Stephen in Minorca. An episode in Jewish–Christian relations in the early 5th century AD," *JThS* 33, 106–23.

Hunter, V. (1990), "Gossip and the politics of reputation in Classical Athens," *Phoenix* 44.4, 299–325.

Hutson, S. (1971), "Social ranking in a French Alpine community," in Bailey, ed. (1971), 41–68.

Jacoby, T. (2008), "The Ottoman state: a distinct form of imperial rule?" *Journal of Peasant Studies* 35.2, 268–91.

Jaillette, P. (1995), "Les atteintes aux biens fonciers: analyse des termes 'invasi' et 'invasor' dans le code théodosien et les novelles postthéodosiennes," in Magnou-Nortier, ed. (1995), 16–75.

—— (2005), "L'Égypte et les dispositions du Code Théodosien sur le patronage des campagnes (XI, 24, 1–6): textes et traduction," *CRIPEL* 25, 197–251.

Johnson, A. C. and West, L. C. (1949), *Byzantine Egypt: Economic Studies*, Princeton.

Johnson, S. ed. (forthcoming), *Oxford Handbook of Late Antiquity*, Oxford.

Johnston, D., Kay, C., Lerche, J., and Oya, C. (2008), "From the new editors," *Journal of Agrarian Change* 8.1, 3–5.

Jones, A. E. (2009), *Social Mobility in Late Antique Gaul: Strategies and Opportunities for the Non-Elite*, Cambridge.

Jones, A. H. M. (1931), "The urbanization of the Ituraean principality," *JRS* 21, 265–75.

—— (1940), *The Greek City from Alexander to Justinian*, Oxford.

—— (1953), "Census records of the later Roman empire," *JRS* 43, 49–64.

—— (1954), "The date and value of the Verona List," *JRS* 44, 21–9 [reprinted in *The Roman Economy*, 263–79].

(1957), "*Capitatio* and *Iugatio*," *JRS* 47, 88–94 [reprinted in *The Roman Economy*, 280–92].

(1959), "Over-taxation and the decline of the Roman Empire," *Antiquity* 33, 39–43 [reprinted in *The Roman Economy*, 82–9].

(1964), *The Later Roman Empire*, 3 vols., Oxford.

(1970), "The caste system in the Later Roman Empire," *Eirene* 8, 79–96 [reprinted in *The Roman Economy*, 396–418].

The Roman Economy = *The Roman Economy: Studies in Ancient Economic and Administrative History*, ed. P. A. Brunt, Oxford (1974).

Jones, A. H. M., Grierson, P., and Crook, J. A. (1957), "The authenticity of the 'Testamentum S. Remigii'," *Revue belge de philologie et d'histoire* 35, 356–73.

Jones, R. F. J., Keay, S. J., Nolla, J. M., and Tarrús, J. (1982), "The late Roman villa of Vilauba and its context: a first report on field-work and excavation in Catalunya, north-east Spain, 1978–81," *AntJ* 62, 245–82.

Jouguet, P. (1912), "Supplément aux Papyrus de Théadelphie," in *Mélanges Cagnat: Recueil des mémoires concernant l'épigraphie et les antiquités romaines dédié par ses anciens élèves du collège de France à M. René Cagnat*, Paris, 407–18.

Kalmin, R. and Schwartz, S., eds. (2003), *Jewish Culture and Society under the Christian Roman Empire*, Leuven.

Kapferer, B. (1997), *The Feast of the Sorcerer: Practices of Consciousness and Power*, Chicago and London.

Kaplan, M. (1992), *Les Hommes et la terre à Byzance du VIe au XIe siècle: propriété et exploitation du sol*, Paris.

(2004), "L'espace et le sacré à Byzance d'après les sources hagiographiques," *Cristianità d'Occidente e cristianità d'Oriente (secoli VI–XI) (Settimane di studio della fondazione Centro italiano di studi sull'alto medioevo, 51)*, 2 vols., Spoleto, 1053–1115.

Kaufmann, F.-M. (1995), *Studien zu Sidonius Apollinaris*, Frankfurt am Main.

Keay, S. (1991), "The Ager Tarraconensis in the late Empire: a model for the economic relationship of town and country in eastern Spain?" in Barker and Lloyd, eds. (1991), 79–87.

Keenan, J. G. (1985), "Village shepherds and social tension in Byzantine Egypt," *YCS* 27, 245–59.

(2007), "Byzantine Egyptian villages," in Bagnall, ed. (2007), 226–43.

Kehoe, D. P. (1988), *The Economics of Agriculture on Roman Imperial Estates in North Africa*, Göttingen.

(2007), *Law and Rural Economy in the Roman Empire*, Ann Arbor.

Kelly, C. M. (1998), "Emperors, government and bureaucracy," *CAH* 13, 138–83.

(2004), *Ruling the Later Roman Empire*, Cambridge, MA.

Kertzer, D. I., Hogan, D. P., and Karweit, N. (1992), "Kinship beyond the household in a nineteenth-century Italian town," *Continuity and Change* 7.1, 103–21.

Kertzer D. P. and Saller, R. P., eds. (1991), *The Family in Italy from Antiquity to the Present*, New Haven.

Kim, S. J. (2007), "Taxes, the local elite, and the rural populace in the Chinju Uprising of 1862," *Journal of Asian Studies* 66.4, 993–1027.

Kimball, M. S. (1988), "Farmers' cooperatives as behavior toward risk," *American Economic Review* 78.1, 224–32.

Kindler, A. (1989), "Donations and taxes in the society of the Jewish villages in Eretz Israel during the 3rd to 6th centuries CE," in Hachlili, ed. (1989), 55–9.

King, A. J., Douglas, C. M. S., Huchard, E., Isaac, N. J. B., and Cowlishaw, G. (2008), "Dominance and affiliation mediate despotism in a social primate," *Current Biology* 18.23, 1833–8.

King, C. E. ed. (1980), *Imperial Revenue, Expenditure and Monetary Policy in the Fourth Century AD*, Oxford.

King, C. E. and Wigg, D. G., eds. (1996), *Coin Finds and Coin Use in the Roman World: The Thirteenth Oxford Symposium on Coinage and Monetary History, 25.–27.3.1993, a NATO Advanced Research Workshop*, Berlin.

Kiss, Z. (1991), "Ampulla," *CoptEncyc* I, 116–17.

Klingshirn, W. E. (1994), *Caesarius of Arles: The Making of a Christian Community in Late Antique Gaul*, Cambridge.

Knight, F. H. (1921), *Risk, Uncertainty and Profit*, Boston, MA.

Kolenkow, A. B. (2002), "Persons of power and their communities," in Ciraolo and Seidel, eds. (2002), 133–44.

Kollock, P. (1999), "The production of trust in online markets," *Advances in Group Processes* 16, 99–123.

Koptev, A. V. (1995), "Époque du rattachement des esclaves ruraux au domaine dans l'Empire romain (Utilisation des documents de droit romain comme source historique)," in Mactoux and Geny, eds. (1995), 103–26.

(2004), "The raptor and the disgraced girl in Sidonius Apollinaris' Epistula V. 19," *Ancient Society* 34, 275–304.

Kraemer, C. J. and Lewis, N. (1937), "A referee's hearing on ownership," *TAPhA* 68, 357–87.

Kramer, B. and Hagendorn, D. (1982), "Zum verhandlungsprotokoll P. Columbia VII 175," *ZPE* 45, 229–41.

Krause, J.-U. (1987), *Spätantike Patronatsformen im Westen des Römischen Reiches*, Munich.

(1991), "Familien und Haushaltsstrukturen im spätantiken Gallien," *Klio* 73.2, 537–62.

Krawiec, R. (2002), *Shenoute and the Women of the White Monastery*, Oxford.

Laiou, A. E. (2005), "The Byzantine village (5th–14th century)," in Lefort, Morrisson, and Sodini, eds. (2005), 31–54.

Lallemand, J. (1964), *L'Administration civile de l'Égypte de l'avènement de Dioclétien à la création du diocèse (284–382)*, Brussels.

Lambert. J. (1953), "Les 'Tablettes Albertini'," *Revue Africaine* 97, 196–225.

Lancel, S. (1983), "L'affaire d'Antoninus de Fussala: pays, choses et gens de la Numidie d'Hippone saisis dans la durée d'une procédure d'enquête épiscopale," in *Les Lettres de Saint Augustin*, 267–85.

Laniado, A. (2002), *Recherches sur les notables municipaux dans l'Empire Protobyzantin*, Paris.

Laslett, P. (1972), *Household and Family in Past Time*, Cambridge.

Latreille, M. and Verdon, M. (2007), "Wives against mothers: women's power and household dynamics in rural Tunisia," *Journal of Family History* 32.1, 66–89.

Lavan, L. and Bowden, W., eds. (2003), *Theory and Practice in Late Antique Archaeology*, Leiden.

Le Bohec, Y., ed. (1995), *La Hiérarchie (Rangordnung) de L'Armée romaine sous le Haut-Empire: actes du congrès de Lyon (15–18 septembre 1994)*, Paris.

Le Roy Ladurie, E. (1978; repr. 1980), *Montaillou: Cathars and Catholics in a French village*, trans B. Bray, Harmondsworth.

Lefort, J., Morrisson, C., and Sodini, J.-P., eds., (2005), *Les Villages dans l'Empire byzantin (IVe–XVe siècle)*, Paris.

Lemert, C. C. and Gillan, G. (1982), *Michel Foucault: Social Theory and Transgression*, New York.

Lepelley, C. (1979 and 1981b), *Les Cités de l'Afrique romaine au Bas-Empire*, 2 vols., Paris.

(1981a), "La carrière municipale dans l'Afrique romaine sous l'Empire tardif," *Ktèma* 6, 333–47.

(1983a), "Liberté, colonat et esclavage d'après la Lettre 24*: la jurisdiction épiscopale 'de liberali causa'," in *Les Lettres de Saint Augustin*, 329–42.

(1983b), "*Quot curiales, tot tyranni*: l'image du décurion oppresseur au Bas-Empire," in Frézouls, ed. (1983), 143–56.

(1989), "Trois documents méconnus sur l'histoire sociale et religieuse de l'Afrique romaine tardive, retrouvés parmi les *spuria* de Sulpice Sévére," *AntAfr* 25, 235–62.

(1996), "Vers la fin du 'privilège de liberté': l'amoindrissement de l'autonomie des cités à l'aube du Bas-Empire," in Chastagnol, Demougin, and Lepelley, eds. (1996), 207–20.

ed. (1996), *La Fin de la cité antique et le début de la cité médiévale de la fin du IIIe siècle à l'avènement de Charlemagne, Actes du colloque tenu à l'Université de Paris X–Nanterre les 1, 2 et 3 avril 1993*, Bari.

(1997), "Quelques témoignages sur l'histoire de l'Afrique romaine épars dans les sermons de Saint Augustin découverts par François Dolbeau," *BCTH* Fasc. B, 24, 203–6.

(1998), "Le patronat épiscopal aux IVe et Ve siècles: continuités et ruptures avec le patronat classique," in Rebillard and Sotinel, eds. (1998) 17–31.

(1999), "Témoignages épigraphiques sur le contrôle des finances municipales par les gouverneurs à partir du règne de Dioclétien," in *Il capitolo delle entrate nelle finanze municipale in Occidente ed in Oriente: Actes de la Xe rencontre franco-italienne sur l'epigraphie du monde romain*, Rome, 235–47.

Leroy, M. (1992), "L'individu et l'impôt: contribution à une sociologie 'cognitive' de l'impôt," *L'Année sociologique* 42, 319–43.

Leschi, L. (1948), "L'album municipal de Timgad et l''Ordo Salutationis' du consulaire Ulpius Mariscianus," *REA* 50, 71–100 with plate 2.

Les Lettres de Saint Augustin = *Les Lettres de Saint Augustin découvertes par Johannes Divjack: Communications présentées au colloque des 20 et 21 Septembre 1982*, Paris (1983).

Lewis, N. (1937), "ΜΕΡΙΣΜΟΣ ΑΝΑΚΑΞωΡΗΚΟΤωΝ: an aspect of the Roman oppression in Egypt," *JEA* 23, 63–75.

(1983), *Life in Egypt under Roman Rule*, Oxford.

(2000), "Brief footnotes on banditry in the papyri," *BASP* 37, 95–6.

Lewit, T. (1991/2004), *Agricultural Production in the Roman Economy* AD *200–400*, London [republished, with a new introductory chapter and updated bibliography, as T. Lewit (2004), *Villas, Farms and the Late Roman Rural Economy (third to fifth centuries* AD*)*].

(2003), "'Vanishing villas': What happened to élite rural habitations in the west in the 5th and 6th centuries A.D.?" *JRA* 16.1, 260–74.

Lieberman, E. S. (2002), "Taxation data as indicators of state–society relations: possibilities and pitfalls in cross-national research," *Studies in Comparative International Development* 36.4, 89–115.

Liebeschuetz, J. H. W. G. (1959), "The finances of Antioch in the fourth century AD," *ByzZ* 52, 344–56.

(1972), *Antioch: City and Administration in the Later Roman Empire*, Oxford.

Ligon, E., Thomas, J. P., and Worrall, T. (2002), "Informal insurance arrangements with limited commitment: theory and evidence from village economies," *Review of Economic Studies* 69.1, 209–44.

Lirb, H. J. (1993), "Partners in agriculture: the pooling of resources in rural *societates* in Roman Italy," in Sancisi-Weerdenburg, van der Spek, Teitler, and Wallinga, eds. (1993), 263–95.

Lo Cascio, E., ed. (1997), *Terre, proprietari e contadini dell'Impero romano. Dall'affitto agrario al colonato tardoantico (Incontro studio di Capri, 16–18 ottobre 1995)*, Rome.

Lo Cascio, E. and Storchi Marino, A., eds. (2001), *Modalità insediative e strutture agrarie nell'Italia meridionale in età romana*, Bari.

Lock, M. (1993), "Cultivating the body: anthropology and epistemologies of bodily practice and knowledge," *Annual Review of Anthropology* 22, 133–55.

Loseby, S. T. (2000), "Urban failures in late-antique Gaul," in Slater, ed. (2000), 72–95.

Lukes, S., ed. (1986), *Power*, New York.

Lupton, D. (1999), *Risk*, London.

Lévi-Strauss, C. (1969), *The Elementary Structures of Kinship*, rev. edn., Boston, MA.

Maas, M. (forthcoming), "Barbarians in late antiquity: problems and approaches," in Johnson, ed. (forthcoming).

MacAdam, H. I. (1983), "Epigraphy and village life in southern Syria during the Roman and early Byzantine periods," *Berytus* 31, 103–15.

MacEachern, S., Archer, D. J. W., and Garvin, R. D., eds. (1989), *Households and Communities: Proceedings of the Twenty-First Annual Conference of the Archaeological Association of the University of Calgary*, Calgary.

Macfarlane, A., with Harrison, S., and Jardine, C. (1977), *Reconstructing Historical Communities*, London and New York.

MacLynn, N. (1995), "Paulinus the impenitent: a study of the *Eucharisticus*," *JECS* 3, 461–86.

MacMullen, R. (1964), "Social mobility and the Theodosian Code," *JRS* 54, 49–53.

(1967), *Soldier and Civilian in the Later Roman Empire*, Cambridge, MA.

(1970), "Market-days in the Roman Empire," *Phoenix* 24, 333–41.

(1974), *Roman Social Relations: 50 BC to AD 284*, New Haven and London.

(1990), "The historical role of the masses in Late Antiquity," in *Changes in the Roman Empire: Essays in the Ordinary*, Princeton, 250–76 and 385–93.

Mactoux, M.-M. and Geny, E., eds. (1995), *Esclavage et dépendance dans l'historiographie soviétique récente*, trans. J. Gaudey, Besançon.

Magdalino, P., ed. (1994), *New Constantines: The Rhythm of Imperial Renewal in Byzantium, 4th–13th Centuries. Papers from the Twenty-sixth Spring Symposium of Byzantine Studies, St Andrews, March 1992*, Aldershot.

Magnou-Nortier, E., ed. (1995), *Aux sources de la gestion publique, vol. II L'invasio des villae ou la villa comme enjeu de pouvoir*, Villeneuve d'Asq.

Maguire, H., ed. (1995), *Byzantine Magic*, Washington, DC.

Malinowski, B. (1922), *Argonauts of the Western Pacific: An Account of Native Enterprise and Adventure in the Archipelagoes of Melanesian New Guinea*, London.

Malone, C. and Stoddart, S., eds. (1985), *Papers in Italian Archaeology IV: The Cambridge Conference, Part IV*, Oxford.

(1994), *Territory, Time and State: The Archaeological Development of the Gubbio Basin*, Cambridge.

Mancassola, N. and Saggioro, F. (2001), "Insediamento rurale e campagne tra Tarda Antichità e Altomedioevo. Territori tra Verona, Brescia e Mantova," *AntTard* 9, 307–30.

Mann, M. (1986), *The Sources of Social Power*, Cambridge.

Marcone, A. (1998), "Late Roman social relations," *CAH* 13, 338–70.

Mathisen, R. W. (1981), "The last year of Saint Germanus of Auxerre," *AB* 99, 151–9.

(1989), *Ecclesiastical Factionalism and Religious Controversy in Fifth-Century Gaul*, Washington, DC.

(1993), "'Nature or nurture?': some perspectives on the Gallic famine of ca AD 470," *The Ancient World* 24.2, 91–105.

(1996), "Crossing the supernatural frontier in Western Late Antiquity," in Mathisen and Sivan, eds. (1996), 309–20.

(forthcoming), "Citizenship," in Johnson, ed. (forthcoming).

Mathisen, R., ed. (2001), *Law, Society, and Authority in Late Antiquity*, Oxford.

Mathisen, R. and Shanzer, D., eds. (2011), *Romans, Barbarians, and the Transformation of the Roman World*, Aldershot and Burlington.

Mathisen, R. and Sivan, H., eds. (1996), *Shifting Frontiers in Late Antiquity*, Brookfield, VT.

Mattingly, D. J. (1989), "Olive cultivation and the Albertini Tablets," *L'Africa Romana* 6, 403–15.

Mattingly, D. J. and Hayes, J. W. (1992), "Nador and fortified farms in North Africa," *JRA* 5, 408–18.

Mauss, M. (1923–4), "Essai sur le don: forme et raison de l'échange dans les sociétés primitives," *Année sociologique* 2nd ser., 30–186.

Mayer, W. (2001), "Patronage, pastoral care and the role of the bishop at Antioch," *Vigiliae Christianae* 55.1, 58–70.

McCormick, M. (2001), *Origins of the European Economy: Communications and Commerce, AD 300–900*, Cambridge and New York.

McGill, S., Sogno, C., and Watts, E., eds. (2010), *From the Tetrarchs to the Theodosians: Later Roman History and Culture, 284–450 CE*, Cambridge and New York.

Mee, C., Gill, D., Forbes, H., and Foxhall, L. (1991), "Rural settlement changes in the Methana Peninsula, Greece," in Barker and Lloyd, eds. (1991), 223–32.

Miele, M. (1996), "La Vita Germani di Costanzo di Lione: Realtà e prospettive storiografiche nella Gallia del quinto secolo," *Memorie, Academia nazionale dei Lincei. Classe di scienze morali, storiche e filologiche* s. 9 vol. 7.2, Rome, 131–242.

Migliore, S. (1994), "Gender, emotion, and physical distress – the Sicilian-Canadian nerves complex," *Culture Medicine and Psychiatry* 18.3, 271–97.

Mirković, M. (1997), *The Later Roman Colonate and Freedom*, TAPhS 87.2, Philadelphia.

Mitterauer, M. (1973), "La continuité des foires et la naissance des villes," *Annales (ESC)* 28, 711–34.

Molm, L. D., Collett, J. L., and Schaefer, D. R. (2007), "Building solidarity through generalized exchange: a theory of reciprocity," *American Journal of Sociology* 113.1, 205–42.

Molm, L. D., Schaefer, D. R., and Collett, J. L. (2007), "The value of reciprocity," *Social Psychology Quarterly* 70.2, 199–217.

Momigliano, A. and Schiavone, A., eds. (1993), *Storia di Roma*, III.1, Turin.

Monnier, H. (1900), "Études de droit byzantin," *Nouvelle Revue historique de droit français et étranger* 24, 37–107; 169–211; 285–337.

Montanari, M. (2003), "La foresta come spazio economico e culturale," in *Uomo e spazio nell'Alto Medioevo*, Spoleto, 301–45.

Mood, M. S. (2005), "Opportunists, predators and rogues: the role of local state relations in shaping Chinese rural development," *Journal of Agrarian Change* 5.2, 217–50.

Morent, E. ed. (1995) *Campagnes médiévales: l'homme et son espace. Études offertes à Robert Fossier*, Paris.

Morrow, P. (1996), "Yup'ik Eskimo agents and American legal agencies: perspectives on compliance and resistance," *Journal of the Royal Anthropological Institute*, n. s. 2.3, 405–23.

Mouterde, R. and Poidebard, A. (1945), *Le Limes de chalcis: organisation de la Steppe en Haute Syrie romaine*, Paris.

Mukhopadhyay, R. (2000), "Village type and family structure: case of Hooghly district of West Bengal," *Journal of the Indian Anthropological Society* 35, 149–63.

Mutch, A., Delbridge, R., and Ventresca, M. (2006), "Situating organizational action: the relational sociology of organizations," *Organization* 13.5, 607–25.

Nachi, M. (2004), "The morality in/of compromise: some theoretical reflections," *Social Science Information* 43.2, 291–305.

Narotzky, S. and Moreno, P. (2002), "Reciprocity's dark side: negative reciprocity, morality and social reproduction," *Anthropological Theory* 2.3, 281–305.

Nathan, G. S. (2000), *The Family in Late Antiquity: The Rise of Christianity and the Endurance of Tradition*, London.

Neri, V. (1998), *I marginali nell'occidente tardo antico: poveri, "infames" e criminali nella nascente società cristiana*, Bari.

Nixon, C. E. V., and Rodgers, B. S. (1994), *In Praise of Later Roman Empires: The Panegyrici Latini*, Berkeley, Los Angeles, and Oxford.

Noethlichs, K. (1981), *Beamtentum und Dienstvergehen: Zur Staatsverwaltung in der Spätantike*, Wiesbaden.

Nörr, D. (1963), "Origo. Studien zur Orts-, Stadt- und Reichszugehörigkeit in der Antike," *RHD* 31, 525–600.

(1965), "Origo," *RE Suppl.* 10, 433–73.

Noy, D. (1993), *Jewish Inscriptions of Western Europe*, 2 vols., Cambridge and New York.

Nutton, V. (1978), "The beneficial ideology," in Garnsey and Whittaker, eds. (1978), 209–21 and 338–43.

O'Donnell, J. J. (1983), "Salvian and Augustine," *Augustinian Studies* 14, 25–34.

Olsen, W. (2009), "Exploring practical horizons of beyond sociology: structure, agency, and strategy among tenants in India," *Asian Journal of Social Science* 37, 366–90.

O'Mahoney, J. (2007), "Constructing habitus: the negotiation of moral encounters at Telekom," *Work, Employment & Society* 21.3, 479–96.

Ørsted, P. with Ladjimi Sebaï, L., Ben Hassan, H., Ben Younes, H., Zoughlami, J., and Bejaowi, F. (1992), "Town and countryside in Roman Tunisia: a preliminary report on the Tunisio-Danish survey project in the Oued R'mel basin in and around ancient Segermes," *JRA* 5, 69–96.

Ortner, S. B. (1995), "Resistance and the problem of ethnographic refusal," *CSSH* 37.1, 173–93.

Palme, B. (2007), "The imperial presence: government and army," in Bagnall, ed. (2007), 244–70.

Papaconstantinou, A. (2002a), "Notes sur les actes de donation d'enfant au monastère Thébain de Saint-Phoibammon," *JJP* 32, 83–105.

(2002b), "Θεια οικονομια: les actes Thébains de donation d'enfants ou la gestion monastique de la pénurie," in Déroche, ed. (2002), 511–26.

Parkin, A. R. (2006), "'You do him no service': an exploration of pagan almsgiving," in Atkins and Osborne, eds. (2006), 60–82.

Parry, J. and Bloch, M. (1989), "Introduction: money and the morality of exchange," in Parry and Bloch, eds. (1989), 1–32.

eds. (1989), *Money and the Morality of Exchange*, Cambridge.

Patlagean, E. (1977), *Pauvreté économique et pauvreté sociale à Byzance 4e–7e siècles*, Paris.

Patterson, J. (1987), "Crisis, what crisis? Rural change and urban development in imperial Apennine Italy," *PBSR* 55, 115–46.

Percival, J. (1992), "The fifth-century villa: new life or death postponed?" in Drinkwater and Elton, eds. (1992), 156–64.

(1997), "Villas and monasteries in late Roman Gaul," *JEH* 48.1, 1–21.

Périn, P. (2004), "The origin of the village in early Medieval Gaul," in Christie, ed. (2004), 255–78.

Petit, P. (1955), *Libanius et la vie municipale d'Antioche au IVe siècle après J.-C.*, Paris.

Pettegrew, D. (2007), "The busy countryside of Late Roman Corinth: interpreting ceramic data produced by regional archaeological surveys," *Hesperia* 76, 743–84.

Pohl, W. (2003), "The construction of communities and the persistence of paradox: an introduction," in Corradini, Diesenberger, and Reimitz, eds. (2003), 1–15.

ed. (1997), *Kingdoms of the Empire: The Integration of Barbarians in Late Antiquity*, Leiden.

Polanyi, K. (1944), *The Great Transformation*, New York.

(1977), *The Livelihood of Man*, New York.

Pollard, N. D. (1998), "The chronology and economic condition of Late Roman Karanis: an archaeological reassessment," *JARCE* 35, 147–62.

Popkin, S. L. (1979), *The Rational Peasant: The Political Economy of Rural Society in Vietnam*, Berkeley.

Potter, T. W. (1995), *Towns in Late Antiquity: Iol Caesarea and its Context*, Sheffield.

Poulter, A. (2004), "Cataclysm on the lower Danube: the destruction of a complex Roman landscape," in Christie, ed. (2004), 223–53.

Price, M. (2003), "Pro-community altruism and social status in a Shuar village," *Human Nature* 14.2, 191–5.

Randsborg, K., ed. (1989), *The Birth of Europe: Archaeology and Social Development in the First Millennium AD*, Rome.

Rapp, C. (2005), *Holy Bishops in Late Antiquity: The Nature of Christian Leadership in an Age of Transition*, Berkeley.

(2007), "Saints and holy men," in Casiday and Norris, eds. (2007), 548–66.

Rapp, R., Ross, E., and Bridenthal, R. (1979), "Examining family history," *Feminist Studies* 5.1, 174–200.

Rathbone, D. W. (1991), *Economic Rationalism and Rural Society in Third-Century AD Egypt: The Heroninos Archive and the Appianus Estate*, Cambridge.

(2008), "Villages and patronage in fourth-century Egypt: *P. Ross. Georg.* 3.8," *BASP* 45, 189–207.

Rea, J. R. (1993), "P. Haun. III 58: Caranis in the fifth century," *ZPE* 99, 89–95.

(1994), "P. Col. VIII 242: Caranis in the fifth century," in Bülow-Jacobsen, eds. (1994), 266–72.

Rebillard, E. and Sotinel, C., eds. (1998), *L'Évêque dans la cité du IVe au Ve siècle, image et autorité*, Rome.

Reed-Danahay, D. (1993), "Talking about resistance: ethnography and theory in rural France," *Anthropological Quarterly* 66.4, 221–9.

Rey-Coquais, J.-P. (1993), "Villages du Liban et de la Syrie Moyenne (de Damas au Coude de l'Oronte) à l'époque impériale romaine," in Calbi, Donati, and Poma, eds. (1993), 137–49.

Reyes-García, V., Godoy, R., Vadez, V., Huanca, T., and Leonard, W. R. (2006), "Personal and group incentives to invest in prosocial behavior: a study in the Bolivian Amazon," *Journal of Anthropological Research* 62, 81–101.

Reynolds, A. (2005), "On farmers, traders and kings: archaeological reflections of social complexity in early medieval north-western Europe," *Early Medieval Europe* 13.1, 97–118.

Reynolds, J. M. and Tannenbaum, R. (1987), *Jews and God-Fearers at Aphrodisias: Greek Inscriptions with Commentary: Texts from the Excavations at Aphrodisias Conducted by Kenan T. Erim*, Cambridge.

Reynolds, S. (1997), *Kingdoms and Communities in Western Europe, 900–1300*, 2nd edn., Oxford.

Rich, J. and Shipley, G., eds. (1993), *War and Society in the Roman World*, London and New York.

Richardson, G. (2003), "What protected peasants best? Markets, risk, efficiency, and medieval English agriculture," *Research in Economic History* 21, 299–356.

(2005), "The prudent village: risk pooling institutions in Medieval English agriculture," *Journal of Economic History* 65.2, 386–413.

Riggs, D. (2001), "The continuity of paganism between the cities and countryside of late Roman Africa," in Burns and Eadie, eds. (2001), 285–300.

(2006), "Christianizing the rural communities of Late Roman Africa: a process of coercion or persuasion?" in Drake, ed. (2006), 297–308.

Ring, R. R. (1979), "Early Medieval peasant households in central Italy," *Journal of Family History* 4.1, 2–25.

Ripoll, G., and Arce, J. (2000), "The transformation and end of Roman villae in the West (fourth–seventh centuries: problems and perspectives)," in Brogiolo, Gauthier, and Christie, eds. (2000), 63–114.

Roda, S. (1981), *Commento storico al Libro IX dell'Epistolario di Q. Aurelio Simmaco*, Pisa.

Rosafio, P. (2002), *Studi sul colonato*, Bari.

Rougé, J. (1975), "À propos des mendiants au IVe siècle: étude de quelques textes," *CH* 20, 339–46.

Rousseau, P. (1999), *Pachomius: The Making of a Community in Fourth-Century Egypt*, 2nd edn., Berkeley, Los Angeles and London.

Rowlandson, J. (1996), *Landowners and Tenants in Roman Egypt: The Social Relations of Agriculture in the Oxyrhynchite Nome*, Oxford.

Rubenson, S. (2007), "Asceticism and monasticism, I: Eastern," in Casiday and Norris, eds. (2007): 637–68.

Ruffini, G. (2008), *Social Networks in Byzantine Egypt*, Cambridge.

Sahlins, M. (1965), "On the sociology of primitive exchange," in Banton, ed. (1965) 139–236.

Ste. Croix, G. E. M. de (1954), "Suffragium: from vote to patronage," *British Journal of Sociology* 5, 33–48.

(1981), *The Class Struggle in the Ancient Greek World: From the Archaic Age to the Arab Conquest*, London.

Saller, R. P. (1982), *Personal Patronage under the Early Empire*, Cambridge.

(1989), "Patronage and friendship in early Imperial Rome: drawing the distinction," in Wallace-Hadrill, ed. (1989), 50–62.

(2002), "Framing the debate over growth in the ancient economy," in Scheidel and von Reden, eds. (2002), 251–69.

Saller, R. P. and Kertzer, D. I., "Historical and anthropological perspectives on Italian family life," in Kertzer and Saller, eds. (1991), 1–20.

Samson, R. (1989), "Rural slavery, inscriptions, archaeology and Marx: a response to Ramsay MacMullen's 'Late Roman slavery'," *Historia* 38, 99–110.

Sancisi-Weerdenburg, H., van der Spek, R. J., Teitler, H. C., and Wallinga, H. T., eds. (1993), *De Agricultura: In Memoriam Pieter William De Neeve (1945–1990)*, Amsterdam

Sanders, G. D. R. (2004), "Problems in interpreting rural and urban settlement in southern Greece, AD 365–700," in Christie, ed. (2004), 163–93.

Sannazaro, M. (2003), "Chiese e comunità cristiane rurali nelle fonti epigraphiche dell'Italia settentionale," in Brogiolo, ed. (2003), 39–55.

Santos-Granero, F. (2007), "Of fear and friendship: Amazonian sociality beyond kinship and affinity," *Journal of the Royal Anthropological Institute* 13.1, 1–18.

Sapin, J. (1998), "À l'est de Gerasa: aménagement rural et réseau de communications," *Syria* 75, 107–36.

Saradi, H. (1994), "On the 'archontike' and 'ekklesiastike dynasteia' and 'prostasia' in Byzantium with particular attention to the legal sources: a study in social history of Byzantium," *Byzantion* 64.1, 69–117 and 64.2, 314–51.

Sarris, P. (2006a), "Continuity and discontinuity in the post-Roman economy," *Journal of Agrarian Change* 6.3, 400–13.

(2006b), *Economy and Society in the Age of Justinian*, Cambridge and New York.

(2009), "Introduction: Aristocrats, peasants and the transformation of rural society, c.400–800," *Journal of Agrarian Change* 9.1, 3–22.

Sartre, M. (1982), "Tribus et clans dans le Hawran antique," *Syria* 59, 77–91.

(1993), "Communautés villageoises et structures sociales d'après l'épigraphie de la Syrie du Sud," in Calbi, Donati, and Poma, eds. (1993), 117–35.

Saumagne, C. (1937), "Du rôle de l'*origo* et du *census* dans la formation du colonat Romain," *Byzantion* 12, 487–581.

Sautel, G. and M. (1959), "Notes sur l'action *quod iussu* et ses destinées post-classiques," in *Droits de l'Antiquité et Sociologie Juridique: Mélanges Henri Levy-Bruhl*, Paris, 257–67.

Schachner, L. A. (2006), "Social life in Late Antiquity: a bibliographic essay," in Bowden, Gutteridge, and Machado, eds. (2006), 41–93.

Scheidel, W. (1995), "The most silent women of Greece and Rome: rural labour and women's life in the ancient world (I)," *G&R* 42, 202–17.

(1996), "The most silent women of Greece and Rome: rural labour and women's life in the ancient world (II)," *G&R* 43, 1–10.

(2001), "Slaves of the soil: review article," *JRA* 13, 727–32.

(2007), "Demography," in Scheidel, Morris, and Saller, eds. (2007), 38–86.

Scheidel, W., Morris, I., and Saller, R. P., eds. (2007), *The Cambridge Economic History of the Greco-Roman World*, Cambridge and New York.

Scheidel, W. and von Reden, S., eds. (2002), *The Ancient Economy*, Edinburgh.

Schilling, D. (2003), "Everyday life and the challenge to history in postwar France: Braudel, Lefebvre, Certeau," *Diacritics* 33.1, 23–40.

Schofield, P. R. (1998), "Peasants and the manor court: gossip and litigation in a Suffolk village at the close of the thirteenth century," *P&P* 159, 3–42.

(2003), *Peasant and Community in Medieval England, 1200–1500: Medieval Culture and Society*, Basingstoke.

Schwartz, S. R. (2003), "Some types of Jewish-Christian interaction in Late Antiquity," in Kalmin and Schwartz, eds. (2003), 197–210.

Scott, J. C. (1985), *Weapons of the Weak: Everyday Forms of Peasant Resistance*, New Haven.

(1986), "Everyday forms of peasant resistance," *Journal of Peasant Studies* 13, 5–35.

(1998), *Seeing like a State: How Certain Schemes to Improve the Human Condition Have Failed*, New Haven.

Scott, S. (2004), "Elites, exhibitionism and the society of the Late Roman villa," in Christie, ed. (2004), 39–65.

Segrè, A. (1947), "The Byzantine colonate," *Traditio* 5, 103–33.

Seston, W. (1946), *Dioclétien et la tétrarchie*, Paris.

Ševčenko, N. (2000), "The hermit as stranger in the desert," in Smythe, ed. (2000), 75–86.

Seymour, S. (2006), "Resistance," *Anthropological Theory* 6.3, 303–21.

Shanin, T. (1982) "Defining peasants: conceptualisations and de-conceptualisations: old and new in a Marxist debate," *Sociological Review* 30, 407–32.

Sharman, J. C. (2007), "Rationalist and constructivist perspectives on reputation," *Political Studies* 55.1, 20–37.

Shaw, B. D. (1981), "Rural markets in North Africa and the political economy of the Roman Empire," *AntAfr* 17, 37–83.

(1982a), "The elders of Christian Africa," in *Mélanges offerts en hommage au Révérend père Étienne Gareau*, Ottawa, 207–26.

(1982b), "Lamasba: an ancient irrigation community," *AntAfr* 18, 61–103.

(1984), "Water and society in the ancient Maghrib: technology, property, and development," *AntAfr* 20, 121–73.

(1991), "The structure of local society in the ancient Maghrib: the elders," *The Maghreb Review* 16.1–2, 18–55.

(2000), "Rebels and outsiders," *CAH* 11, 361–403.

(2008), "After Rome: transformations of the early medieval world," *New Left Review* 51 (May–June), 89–114.

Siegel, D. A. (2009), "Social networks and collective action," *American Journal of Political Science* 53.1, 122–38.

Sijpesteijn, P. J. and Worp, K. A. (1986), "Bittschrift an einen *praepositus pagi* (?)," *Tyche* 1, 189–94.

Silverman, S. (1977), "Patronage as myth," in Gellner and Waterbury, eds. (1977), 7–19.

Sirks, A. J. B. (1982), "Sulpicius Severus' letter to Salvius," *BIDR* 85, 143–70.

(1993a), "Did the late Roman government try to tie people to their profession or status?" *Tyche* 8, 159–75.

(1993b), "Reconsidering the Roman colonate," *ZRG* 123, 331–69.

(1999), "The *Epistula ad Saluium*, appended to a letter of Sulpicius Severus to Paulinus: observations on a recent analysis by C. Lepelley," *Subseciva Groningana* 6, 91–102.

(2001), "The farmer, the landlord and the law in the fifth century," in Mathisen, ed. (2001), 256–71.

(2008), "The colonate in Justinian's reign," *JRS* 98, 120–43.

Slater, T. R., ed. (2000), *Towns in Decline AD 1000–1600*, Aldershot.

Smith, E. A., and R. Boyd. (1990), "Risk and reciprocity: hunter-gatherer socio-ecology and the problem of collective action," in Cashdan, ed. (1990), 167–91.

Smith, J. Z. (1978), "Towards interpreting demonic powers in Hellenistic and Roman Antiquity," *ANRW* II.16.1, 425–39.

Smythe, D. C., ed. (2000), *Strangers to Themselves: The Byzantine Outsider. Papers from the Thirty-Second Spring Symposium of Byzantine Studies, University of Sussex, Brighton, March 1998*, Aldershot and Burlington.

Sobel, E. and Bettles, G. (2000), "Winter hunger, winter myths: subsistence risk and mythology among the Klamath and Modoc," *Journal of Anthropological Archaeology* 19.3, 276–316.

Sodini, J.-P. (2003), "Archaeology and late antique social structures," in Lavan and Bowden, eds. (2003), 25–56.

Sogno, C. (2006), *Q. Aurelius Symmachus: A Political Biography*, Ann Arbor.

Sommerfeld, R. D., Krambeck, H.-J., and Milinski, M. (2008), "Multiple gossip statements and their effect on reputation and trustworthiness," *Proceedings of the Royal Society B* 275, 2529–36.

Sommier, B. (1996), "Les amitiés dans un village d'Andalousie orientale: morale, identités et evolution sociale," *Ethnologie française* 36.3, 477–89.

Souter, A., comp. (1949), *A Glossary of Later Latin to 600 AD*, Oxford.

Spencer-Wood, S. (1989), "Community as household: domestic reform, mid-range theory and the domestication of public space," in MacEachern, Archer, and Garvin, eds. (1989), 113–22.

Stancliffe, C. (1983), *St. Martin and His Hagiographer: History and Miracle in Sulpicius Severus*, Oxford.

Stern, E. M. (1992), "A fourth-century factory for gathering and blowing chunks of glass?," *JRA* 5, 490–4.

Stone, D. L. (2000), "Society and economy in North Africa: review article," *JRA* 13, 721–4.

Stone, D. (2005), *Decision Making in Medieval Agriculture*, Oxford and New York.

Strubbe, J. H. M., Tybout, R. A., and Versnel, H. S., eds. (1996), *ENERGEIA: Studies on Ancient History and Epigraphy Presented to H. W. Pleket*, Amsterdam.

Tate, G. (1992), *Les Campagnes de la Syrie du nord du IIe au VIIe siècle, vol. 1*, Paris.

(1995), "Le *latifundium* en Syrie: mythe ou réalité?" in *Du* latifundium *au* latifondo, 243–52.

(1997), "The Syrian countryside during the Roman era," in Alcock, ed. (1997), 55–71.

(1998), "Expansion d'une société riche et égalitaire: les paysans de Syrie du nord du IIe au VIIe siècle," *Académie des Inscriptions & Belles-Lettres; comptes rendus des séances de l'année 1997, juillet–octobre*, 913–41.

Tchalenko, G. (1953), *Villages antiques de la Syrie du nord: Le Massif du Bélus à l'époque romaine*, 3 vols., Paris.

Teeter, T. M. (2004), "Papyri, archives, and patronage," *Classical Bulletin* 80.1, 27–34.

(1993), "Free-born estate managers in the Graeco-Roman world," in Sancisi-Weerdenburg, van der Spek, Teitler, and Wallinga, eds. (1993), 206–13.

Terrier, J. (2007), "Une archéologie pour aborder la christianisation de l'espace rural: l'exemple de la campagne genevoise," *Gallia* 64, 85–91.

Thomas, J. D. (1974), "The disappearance of the dekaprotoi in Egypt," *BASP* 11, 60–8.

Trombley, F. R. (2004), "Epigraphic data on village culture and social institutions: an interregional comparison (Syria, Phoenice Libanensis and Arabia)," in Bowden, Lavan, and Machado, eds. (2004), 73–101.

Trout, D. (1995), "Christianizing the Nolan countryside: animal sacrifice at the tomb of St. Felix," *JECS* 3, 281–98.

(1996), "Town, countryside and Christianization at Paulinus' Nola," in Mathisen and Sivan, eds. (1996), 175–86.

Tulloch, J. and Lupton, D. (2003), *Risk and Everyday Life*, London.

Van Dam, R. (2007), "Bishops and society," in Casiday and Norris, eds. (2007), 343–66.

van Minnen, P. (1995), "Deserted villages: two late antique town sites in Egypt," *BASP* 32, 41–56.

(1997), "Patronage in fourth-century Egypt: a note on *P. Ross. Georg.* III.8," *JJP* 27, 67–73.

Van Ommeren, M., Sharma, B., Komproe, I., Poudyal, B. N., Sharma, G. K., Cardeña, E., and De Jong, J. T. (2001), "Trauma and loss as determinants of medically unexplained epidemic illness in a Bhutanese refugee camp," *Psychological Medicine* 31.7, 1259–67.

van Ossel, P. (1983) "L'établissement romain de Loën à Lixhe et l'occupation rurale au Bas-Empire dans la Hesbaye Liègeoise," *Helinium* 23, 143–69.

(1992), *Établissements ruraux de l'Antiquité tardive dans le nord de la Gaule*, Paris.

van Ossel, P. and Ouzoulias, P. (2000), "Rural settlement economy in Northern Gaul in the Late Empire: an overview and assessment," *JRA* 13, 133–60.

Vera, D. (1992–3), "Schiavitù rurale e colonato nell'Italia imperiale," *Scienze dell'Antichità: Storia Archeologia Antropologia* 6–7, 292–339.

(1997), "Padroni, contadini, contratti: realia del colonato tardoantico," in Lo Cascio, ed. (1997), 185–224.

(1999), "I silenzi di Palladio e l'Italia: osservazioni sull'ultimo agronomo Romano," *Ant Tard* 7: 283–97.

Vercoulter, J., ed. (1979), *Hommages à Serge Sauneron, vol. II Égypte post-pharaonique*, Cairo.

Verdon, M. (1988), "Virgins and widows: European kinship and early Christianity," *Man* n. s. 23.3, 488–505.

(1998), *Rethinking Households: An Atomistic Perspective on European Living Arrangements*, London and New York.

Veyne, P. (1981), "Les cadeaux des colons à leur propriétaire: la neuvième bucolique et le mausolée d'Igel," *RA* 1981 (2), 245–82.

Villeneuve, F. (1985), "L'économie rurale et la vie des campagnes dans le Hauran antique (Ier siècle avant J.-C. – VIIe siècle ap. J.-C.), une approche," in Dentzer, ed. (1985), 63–136.

Visy, Z. (2001), "Towns, vici and villae: late Roman military society on the frontiers of the province Valeria," in Burns and Eadie, eds. (2001), 163–84.

Voirol, O. (2004), "Reconnaissance et méconnaissance: sur la méconnaissance: théorie de la violence symbolique," *Social Science Information* 43.3, 403–33.

Vuolanto, V. (2003), "Selling a freeborn child: rhetoric and social realities in the Late Roman world," *AncSoc* 33, 169–207.

Wallace-Hadrill, A., ed. (1989), *Patronage in Ancient Society*, London and New York.

Walter, J. (2001), "Public transcripts, popular agency and the politics of subsistence in early modern England," in Braddick and Walter, eds. (2001), 123–48.

Ward, J. O. (1981), "Women, witchcraft, and social patterning in the later Roman lawcodes," *Prudentia* 13, 99–118.

Ward-Perkins, B. (1988), "The towns of northern Italy: rebirth or renewal?" in Hodges and Hobley, eds. (1988), 16–27.

Waterbury, J. (1977), "An attempt to put patrons and clients in their place," in Gellner and Waterbury, eds. (1977), 329–42.

Wedekind, C. and Braithwaite, V. A. (2002), "The long-term benefits of human generosity in indirect reciprocity," *Current Biology* 12.12, 1012–15.

Wegren, S. K. (2004), "Rural adaptation in Russia: who responds and how do we measure it?" *Journal of Agrarian Change* 4.4, 553–78.

Wellman, B., Frank, O., Espinoza, V., Lundquist, S., and Wilson, C. (1991), "Integrating individual, relational and structural analysis," *Social Networks* 13, 223–49.

Whitby, M. (1987), "Maro the Dendrite: an anti-social holy man?" in Whitby, Hardie, and Whitby, eds. (1987), 309–17.

Whitby, M., Hardie, P., and Whitby M., eds. (1987), *Homo Viator: Classical Essays for John Bramble*, Bristol.

Whitehead, N. (1994), "The Roman countryside," in Malone and Stoddart, eds. (1994), 188–203.

Whittaker, C. R. (1978), "Land and labour in North Africa," *Klio* 60, 331–62.

(1980), "Inflation and the economy in the fourth century AD," in King, ed. (1980), 1–22.

(1993), "Landlords and warlords in the later Roman Empire" in Rich and Shipley, eds. (1993), 277–302.

(1994), *Frontiers of the Roman Empire: A Social and Economic Study*, Baltimore and London.

(1997), "Agostino e il colonato," in Lo Cascio, ed. (1997), 295–309.

Whittaker, C. R. and Garnsey, P. D. A. (1998), "Rural life in the later Roman empire," *CAH* 13, 277–311.

Whittlesey, S. M. (1989), "The individual, the community and social organization: issues of evidence and inference justification," in MacEachern, Archer, and Garvin, eds. (1989), 227–34.

Whittow, M. (2007), "Beyond the cultural turn: economic history revived?" *JRA* 20, 697–704.

Wickham, C. R. (1983/1994), "Pastoralism and underdevelopment in the early Middle Ages," in *Land and Power: Studies in Italian and European Social History, 400–1200*, London (1994), 121–54. [Originally published in *Settimane di Studio* **31** (1983), 401–55.]

(1984), "The other transformation: from the ancient world to feudalism," *P&P* 103, 3–36.

(1998), "Gossip and resistance among the medieval peasantry," *P&P* 160, 3–24.

(2005a), "The development of villages in the West, 300–900," in Lefort, Morrisson, and Sodini, eds. (2005), 55–69.

(2005b), *Framing the Early Middle Ages: Europe and the Mediterranean 400–800*, Oxford and New York.

Wirth, G. (1997), "Rome and its Germanic partners in the fourth century," in Pohl, ed. (1997), 13–55.

Wolf, E. (1966), *Peasants*, Englewood Cliffs.

Wood, D., ed. (1994), *The Church and Childhood: Papers Read at the 1993 Summer Meeting and the 1994 Winter Meeting of the Ecclesiastical History Society*, Oxford.

Yanagisako, S. J. and Delaney, C. L. (1995), "Naturalizing power," in Yanagisako and Delaney, eds. (1995), 1–22.

eds. (1995), *Naturalizing Power: Essays in Feminist Cultural Analysis*, New York.

Yeganehlayegh, J. L. G. (1981), "On the relational perspective," *Central Issues in Anthropology* 3.2, 55–69.

Zadora-Rio, E. (1995), "Le village des historiens et le village des archéologues," in E. Morent, ed. (1995), 143–53.

Zelzer, M. (1995), "Der Brief in der Spätantike: Überlegungen zu einem literarischen Genos am Beispiel der Briefsammlung des Sidonius Apollinaris," *Wiener Studien* 108, 541–51.

Zinn, J. O., ed. (2008), *Social Theories of Risk and Uncertainty: An Introduction*, Malden.

Zuckerman, C. (2004), *Du village à l'empire: autour du registre fiscal d'Aphroditô (525/526)*, Paris.

Index

coloni
  in disputes with landlords, 54
  limitations on economic behavior, 203
  limitations on landlords' economic behavior
    vis-à-vis, 202
  manipulate relationship with landlords, 127, 152
  mobility of, 53
  nature of relationship with landlords, 162, 200
  and peasant marriage strategies, 67
  registration and tax system, 7, 192–3, 203
    see also "colonate"; registration in tax rolls;
      tenancy
communal building, 63, 105, 108
communal identity, *see* collective identity
community, communities
  complementarity of conflict and cohesion
    within, 21–2, 149
  compliance with relations of dominance, 151–2
  composition and expectations, 20, 25, 29–31,
    83–4, 111
  definitions, vii, 46–7
  diversity and complementarity of, 28, 47, 56–7
  figures of power disruptive to, 79, 117, 144,
    164, 212
  figures of power incidental to affairs of, 173–4,
    176–7
  internal dynamics determine interactions with
    figures of power, 134–5, 163–4, 166–7
  and multiple figures of power, 145–6
  negotiating with figures of power, 154, 156
  patrons and, 160
  regional, 54–6, 96, 135
  religion as focus for, 55–6
  resistance to figures of power, 154–5
  as risk-management strategy, 62
  village only one form of, 46–7
    see also conflict, conflict settlement; disputes,
      dispute settlement; limited resources;
      reciprocity
community leaders, 94, 95, 96, 135
  see also elders, council of; *seniores*
compliance with relations of dominance, 151–2, 163
  see also power, power relations, power
    networks
compromise, *see* negotiation
conflict, conflict settlement, 39, 112–19
  collective action and, 112–13
  figures of power exacerbate, 65
  grain storage and, 113
  irrigation and, 113–14, 117–18
  motivations, 64, 115–16
  multidimensional, 115
  within communities, 62, 120, 224, 226
  within families, 37–9
    see also disputes, dispute settlement

consortium, 214, 215
contempt, *see* distaste, aristocratic, for peasants
crops, as focus of disputes, 85, 116
  see also grain storage, as source of conflict
cult sites, 55–6
curiales, 123, 124, 140, 147, 209
  as tax collectors, 183–4, 194–5

Daniel the Stylite, 87, 140–1
decisions, decision-making
  by agents of the state, 187
  definitions of, 98–9
  dynamics of group decisions, 99, 103–5, 135
  limitations placed upon, by the state, 202, 203
  motivations ascribed to peasants, 98
  multidimensional, 218–19, 221, 223
  risk management in, 211
    see also agency; rationality of peasant actions
demonic possession
  among members of aristocratic families, 78–9,
    139–40
  controlling responses to, 155–6
  as resistance to figures of power, 87–8, 101–3, 164
disputes, dispute settlement, 65, 213, 222
  between tenants and landlords, 143, 204, 205
  in collective action, 74
  by figures of power, 113, 117–18, 143
  multidimensional, 65, 66–7, 95
  recourse to courts, 204, 223
    see also conflict, conflict settlement; friends,
      friendship
distaste, aristocratic, for peasants, 138, 157, 159,
    160, 162, 172

economic regimes, 16
Edict on Maximum Prices, 53
elders, council of, 93–4
  see also community leaders
enforcement, *see* collective action; decisions,
    decision-making
Epistula ad Salvium, 151
exchange, *see* gift-giving; reciprocity

family, definition, 34–6
  see also household, definition; lifecycle
family life, norms and expectations, 37, 40, 42, 97
field management, 171–2, 193
figures of power, 108, 122–34
  disruptive, 79, 117, 144, 163–4, 212
  incidental to affairs of communities, 173–4, 176–7
  novelty, 137, 147, 154
fiscal system, *see* tax system
friends, friendship, 69–71, 78, 84, 97
  and dispute settlement, 63–4
fundus Thogonoetis, 54, 146

Made in the USA
San Bernardino, CA
16 March 2019